Douglas B. Miller and Loren L. Johns, Editors

BELIEVERS CHURCH BIBLE COMMENTARY

Old Testament
Genesis, by Eugene F. Roop, 1987
Exodus, by Waldemar Janzen, 2000
Leviticus, by Perry B. Yoder, *forthcoming*
Deuteronomy, by Gerald Gerbrandt, 2015
Joshua, by Gordon H. Matties, 2012
Judges, by Terry L. Brensinger, 1999
Ruth, Jonah, Esther, by Eugene F. Roop, 2002
1-2 Samuel, by David Baker, *forthcoming*
1-2 Kings, by Lynn Jost, *forthcoming*
1-2 Chronicles, by August Konkel, 2016
Ezra-Nehemiah, by Steven Schweitzer, *forthcoming*
Job, by Paul Keim, *forthcoming*
Psalms, by James H. Waltner, 2006
Proverbs, by John W. Miller, 2004
Ecclesiastes, by Douglas B. Miller, 2010
Isaiah, by Ivan D. Friesen, 2009
Jeremiah, by Elmer A. Martens, 1986
Lamentations, Song of Songs, by Wilma Ann Bailey and Christina A. Bucher, 2014
Ezekiel, by Millard C. Lind, 1996
Daniel, by Paul M. Lederach, 1994
Hosea, Amos, by Allen R. Guenther, 1998
Joel, Obadiah, Nahum, forthcoming
Micah, Habakkuk, Zephaniah, by Dan Epp-Tiessen and Derek Suderman, *forthcoming*
Haggai, Zechariah, Malachi, by Patricia Shelly, *forthcoming*

New Testament
Matthew, by Richard B. Gardner, 1991
Mark, by Timothy J. Geddert, 2001
Luke, by Mary H. Schertz, *forthcoming*
John, by Willard M. Swartley, 2012
Acts, by Chalmer E. Faw, 1993
Romans, by John E. Toews, 2004
1 Corinthians, by Dan Nighswander, 2017
2 Corinthians, by V. George Shillington, 1998
Galatians, by George R. Brunk III, 2015
Ephesians, by Thomas R. Yoder Neufeld, 2002
Philippians, by Gordon Zerbe, 2016
Colossians, Philemon, by Ernest D. Martin, 1993
1-2 Thessalonians, by Jacob W. Elias, 1995
1-2 Timothy, Titus, by Paul M. Zehr, 2009
Hebrews, by Estella Horning, *forthcoming*
James, by Sheila Klassen-Wiebe, *forthcoming*
1-2 Peter, Jude, by Erland Waltner and J. Daryl Charles, 1999
1, 2, 3 John, by Jay McDermott, 2011
Revelation, by John R. Yeatts, 2003

Old Testament Editors

Elmer A. Martens, Mennonite Brethren Biblical Seminary, Fresno, California
Douglas B. Miller, Tabor College, Hillsboro, Kansas

New Testament Editors

Howard Charles, Anabaptist Mennonite Biblical Seminary, Elkhart, Indiana
Willard M. Swartley, Anabaptist Mennonite Biblical Seminary, Elkhart, Indiana
Gordon Zerbe, Canadian Mennonite University, Winnipeg, Manitoba
Loren L. Johns, Anabaptist Mennonite Biblical Seminary, Elkhart, Indiana

Editorial Council

David W. Baker, Brethren Church
Derek Suderman, Mennonite Church Canada
Christina Bucher, Church of the Brethren
John R. Yeatts, Brethren in Christ Church
Gordon H. Matties (chair), Mennonite Brethren Church
Jo-Ann A. Brant, Mennonite Church USA

 **Believers Church Bible Commentary**

1 Corinthians

Dan Nighswander

HERALD PRESS
Harrisonburg, Virginia

Library of Congress Cataloging-in-Publication Data
Names: Nighswander, Dan, author.
Title: 1 Corinthians / Dan Nighswander.
Other titles: First Corinthians
Description: Harrisonburg : Herald Press, 2017. | Series: Believers church Bible commentary
Identifiers: LCCN 2017019251 | ISBN 9781513802442 (pbk. : alk. paper)
Subjects: LCSH: Bible. Corinthians, 1st--Commentaries.
Classification: LCC BS2675.53 .N54 2017 | DDC 227/.2077--dc23 LC record available at https://lccn.loc.gov/2017019251

Except as otherwise indicated, the text of 1 Corinthians is from the *New Revised Standard Version Bible*, copyright © 1989 by the Division of Christian Education of the National Council of the Churches of Christ in the USA, and used by permission. All rights reserved worldwide. Quotations marked NIV are taken from the *Holy Bible, New International Version*®, NIV®. Copyright © 1973, 1978, 1984, 2011 by Biblica, Inc.™ Used by permission of Zondervan. All rights reserved worldwide. www.zondervan.com The "NIV" and "New International Version" are trademarks registered in the United States Patent and Trademark Office by Biblica, Inc.™ Other versions briefly compared are listed with Abbreviations.

BELIEVERS CHURCH BIBLE COMMENTARY: 1 CORINTHIANS
© 2017 by Herald Press, Harrisonburg, VA 22802. 800-245-7894.
     All rights reserved.
Library of Congress Control Number: 2017019251
International Standard Book Number: 978-1-5138-0244-2
Printed in the United States of America
Cover by Merrill Miller
Interior design by Merrill Miller and Alice Shetler

All rights reserved. This publication may not be reproduced, stored in a retrieval system, or transmitted in whole or in part, in any form, by any means, electronic, mechanical, photocopying, recording, or otherwise without prior permission of the copyright owners.

21 20 19 18 17   10 9 8 7 6 5 4 3 2 1

To Yvonne,

without whose support and encouragement this would not have been possible,

and to our children and grandchildren,

who inspire me to ask questions and to read with imagination.

Abbreviations

*	The Text in Biblical Context
+	The Text in the Life of the Church
//	parallel to
§(§)	section(s)
ABD	*The Anchor Bible Dictionary*. Edited by David Noel Freedman. 6 vols. New York: Doubleday, 1992.
AGJU	Arbeiten zur Geschichte des antiken Judentums und des Urchristentums
AT	author's translation
BCBC	Believers Church Bible Commentary
BCP	Book of Common Prayer
BDAG	Danker, Frederick W., Walter Baur, William F. Arndt, and F. Wilbur Gingrich. *A Greek-English Lexicon of the New Testament and Other Early Christian Literature*. 3rd ed. Chicago: University of Chicago Press, 2000.
BE	*The Brethren Encyclopedia*. 4 vols. Philadelphia: Brethren Encyclopedia, Inc., 1983–84, 2005.
ca.	circa
cf.	*confer*, compare
ch(s).	chapter(s)
d.	died
diss.	dissertation
ed.	edition, editor
e.g.	*exempli gratia*, for example
EN	explanatory notes
esp.	especially
et al.	*et alia*, and others
GAMEO	*Global Anabaptist Mennonite Encyclopedia Online* (http://gameo.org)
Gk.	Greek
ibid.	*ibidem*, in the same place
JBL	*Journal of Biblical Literature*
JSNT	*Journal for the Study of the New Testament*
KJV	King James Version
LXX	Septuagint, the Greek Old Testament
n	note
NABR	New American Bible, Revised Edition
NASB	New American Standard Bible
NET	New English Translation

NETS	*A New English Translation of the Septuagint*. Edited by Albert Pietersma and Benjamin G. Wright. New York: Oxford University Press, 2007. http://ccat.sas.upenn.edu/nets/edition/.
NIV	New International Version (1984 or 2011)
NJB	New Jerusalem Bible
NKJV	New King James Version
NLB	New Living Bible
NovT	*Novum Testamentum*
NovTSup	Supplements to Novum Testamentum
NRSV	New Revised Standard Version
NTS	*New Testament Studies*
par(r).	and the parallel text(s)
REB	Revised English Bible
rev. ed.	revised ed.
RSV	Revised Standard Version
SBL	Society of Biblical Literature
TBC	The Text in Biblical Context
TDNT	*Theological Dictionary of the New Testament*. Edited by Gerhard Kittel and Gerhard Friedrich. Translated by Geoffrey W. Bromiley. 10 vols. Grand Rapids: Eerdmans, 1964–76.
Thomas	Scholars' Translation "The Gospel of Thomas." Translated by Stephen Patterson and Marvin Meyer. In *The Complete Gospels: Annotated Scholars Version*. Edited by Robert J. Miller. Sonoma, CA: Polebridge, 1994.
TLC	The Text in the Life of the Church
v(v).	verse(s)
vol(s).	volume(s)

Contents

Abbreviations..8
Series Foreword 17
Author's Preface 19

Introduction to 1 Corinthians **21**
Corinth..22
Paul..23
Paul and the Corinthians 25
The Christian Assembly in Corinth 27
Paul's Letter 29

GREETINGS AND THANKSGIVING, 1:1-9
The Letter Opening, 1:1-3............................**37**
　　* Call 43
　　* Holy 44
　　+ Holiness/Sanctification 44

Thanksgiving, 1:4-9 ....**46**
　　* Faithfulness of God 50
　　* Waiting for the Apocalypse 50
　　+ Grace 51
　　+ Preaching and Worship 53

THE BODY OF THE LETTER, 1:10–15:58
The Purpose of the Letter, 1:10 ....**59**

Divisions between Believers, 1:11-17..............**63**
　　* Rivalries..69

    * The Ministry of Reconciliation 70
    + Factionalism 70
    + Reconciliation 72

Fundamental Convictions and Values, 1:18–4:21 73
The Gospel of the Crucified Christ, 1:18-25 .74
    * Wisdom 80
    + The Importance of Proclaiming the Gospel 82
    + The Content of the Gospel 83
    + Humility in Proclamation 83
    + Preaching and Worship 84

Values of Shame and Honor in God's Realm, 1:26-31 84
    * Reversed Status 87
    * Shame of the Wise, Strong, and Wealthy 88
    + Image Consciousness 89
    + God's Preference for the "Foolish; . . . Weak; . . . Low
      and Despised" 89
    + Preaching and Worship 91

Spiritual Discernment, 2:1–3:4 91
    * Holy Spirit 96
    + Spiritual Elitism 97
    + Two Kinds of People 99

It's God's Congregation, 3:5-23 100
    * Servant Leadership 107
    * God's Peoplehood 108
    + No Other Foundation 109
    + If We Believe It's God's Church 110
    + Preaching and Worship 113

Paul's Credibility, 4:1-21 114
    * Suffering of Leaders 121
    * Models of Leadership 122
    + Pastors as "Parents" 122
    + "What's in It for Me?" 124
    + Preaching and Worship 125

Summary of Chapters 1–4 127

ISSUES REPORTED FROM CORINTH, 5:1–15:58

Protection of Boundaries against Immorality, 5:1-13 131
- * Incest 139
- * Maintaining Boundaries 140
- + Excommunication 142

Lawsuits and Judgment, 6:1-11 145
- * Dispute Resolution 153
- * Saints Will Judge the World 155
- + Lawsuits between Believers 156
- + Preaching and Worship 157

The Principle of Sexual Purity, 6:12-20 158
- * One Flesh 167
- + Sexuality in Christ 167
- + Preaching and Worship 169

Marriage and Singleness, 7:1-40 170
- * Slavery 185
- * Divorce 186
- + Moral Discernment 188
- + Celibacy 189
- + Same-Sex Marriage 190
- + Preaching and Worship 191

Idol Food and Divisions in the Community, Part 1,
8:1-13 192
- * The Weak 200
- * Idolatry 201
- + Idol Food and Other Idolatries 202
- + The Risks of Knowledge 204
- + Preaching and Worship 206

Subordinating Freedom to Love: A Personal Example,
9:1-27 207
- + Financial Support for Ministers 214
- + Sharing the Gospel 215

Idol Food and Divisions in the Community, Part 2,
10:1–11:1 217
- * Typology: "Examples for Us" 230
- + Imitation of Christ 231

- + Individual Rights 232
- + Preaching and Worship 233

WORSHIP MATTERS, 11:2–14:40
Headship and Decorum, 11:2-16..................239
- * Hair...248
- + Clothing Matters 249
- + Prayer Coverings of Conservative Amish, Brethren, Hutterite, and Mennonite Women....................251

Sensitivity to "the Body" at the Lord's Supper, 11:17-34...252
- * Fellowship Meals in the Bible 261
- * Accounts of the Institution of the Lord's Supper 263
- + Divisions at the Lord's Supper 265
- + Celebrating the Lord's Supper 265
- + Preaching and Worship 268

Manifestations of the Holy Spirit, Part 1, 12:1-31........269
- * Calling Jesus "Lord"....................................278
- * "Body" as a Metaphor of the Faith Community 279
- + "Jesus Is Lord" 280
- + Spiritual Manifestations Today..........................281
- + Body Image Issues 282
- + Preaching and Worship 283

The "More Excellent Way" of Love, 13:1-13..............284
- * Love 294
- + Failure to Love 295
- + Preaching and Worship 297

Manifestations of the Holy Spirit, Part 2, 14:1-40........298
- * Worship in the Bible 307
- * Speaking in Tongues in the First Century 308
- + The Practice of Worship.................................309
- + Speaking in Tongues in the Twentieth and Twenty-First Centuries 313
- + Prophecy in the Twentieth and Twenty-First Centuries...313
- + Intelligible Communication..............................315
- + Silencing Women in the Twenty-First Century...........315
- + Preaching and Worship 316

CHRIST'S RESURRECTION AND OURS, 15:1-58
The "Sure and Certain Hope" of Resurrection, 15:1-58 ...319
- * Postresurrection Appearances of Jesus...................336
- * Resurrection of the Dead 338
- + The Absence of Resurrection Hope among Christians.....340
- + Preaching and Worship 341

THE LETTER CLOSING, 16:1-24
The Letter Closing, 16:1-24........................345
- * The Collection for the Poor...........................352
- + Systematic Giving and Responsible Management of Charitable Gifts 354
- + Part of a Bigger Whole 355
- + Cooperation and Respect between Leaders 356
- + Love the Church......................................357

Outline of 1 Corinthians 359
Essays 363
    Bodies in 1 Corinthians 363
    Church 364
    First Corinthians in the Revised Common Lectionary 365
    Patrons and Clients....................................366
    Scripture Quotations and Echoes in 1 Corinthians 367
    Shame and Honor......................................368
    Spirituality..369
    Vice and Virtue Lists 370
    Who Told Paul What? 371
        What Chloe's People Said 371
        What the Corinthians Wrote......................372
        What the Delegation Reported 374

Map of Greater Corinth 375
Map of the New Testament World 376
Bibliography 377
Selected Resources......................................388
Index of Ancient Sources 390
The Author 401

Series Foreword

The Believers Church Bible Commentary series makes available a new tool for basic Bible study. It is published for all who seek more fully to understand the original message of Scripture and its meaning for today—Sunday school teachers, members of Bible study groups, students, pastors, and others. The series is based on the conviction that God is still speaking to all who will listen, and that the Holy Spirit makes the Word a living and authoritative guide for all who want to know and do God's will.

The desire to help as wide a range of readers as possible has determined the approach of the writers. Since no blocks of biblical text are provided, readers may continue to use the translation with which they are most familiar. The writers of the series use the New Revised Standard Version and the New International Version on a comparative basis. They indicate which text they follow most closely and where they make their own translations. The writers have not worked alone, but in consultation with select counselors, the series' editors, and the Editorial Council.

Every volume illuminates the Scriptures; provides necessary theological, sociological, and ethical meanings; and in general makes "the rough places plain." Critical issues are not avoided, but neither are they moved into the foreground as debates among scholars. Each section offers "Explanatory Notes," followed by focused articles, "The Text in Biblical Context" and "The Text in the Life of the Church." This commentary aids the interpretive process but does not try to supersede the authority of the Word and Spirit as discerned in the gathered church.

The term *believers church* emerged in the mid-twentieth century to define Christian groups with direct or indirect connections to the

Radical Reformation, a distinctive faith expression that arose in Europe during the sixteenth century. These believers were concerned that the church be voluntary and not be aligned with political government. *Believers church* has come to represent an identifiable tradition of beliefs and practices that includes believers (adult) baptism; a voluntary fellowship that practices church discipline, mutual aid, and service; belief in the power of love in all relationships; and a willingness to follow Christ by embracing his cross as a way of life. In recent decades the term has sometimes been applied to church communities informed by Anabaptism, evangelicalism, or pietism, such as Brethren Church, Brethren in Christ, Church of the Brethren, Mennonite Brethren, and Mennonites, as well as similar groups. The writers chosen for the series speak from within this tradition.

Believers church people have always been known for their emphasis on obedience to the simple meaning of Scripture. Because of this, they do not have a long history of deep historical-critical biblical scholarship. This series attempts to be faithful to the Scriptures while also taking archaeology and current biblical studies seriously. Doing this means that at many points the writers will not differ greatly from interpretations that can be found in many other good commentaries. Yet these writers share basic convictions about Christ, the church and its mission, God and history, human nature, the Christian life, and other doctrines. These presuppositions do shape a writer's interpretation of Scripture. Thus this series, like all other commentaries, stands within a specific historical church tradition.

Many in this stream of the church have expressed a need for help in Bible study. This is justification enough to produce the Believers Church Bible Commentary. Nevertheless, the Holy Spirit is not bound to any tradition. May this series be an instrument in breaking down walls between Christians in North America and around the world, bringing new joy in obedience through a fuller understanding of the Word.

—*The Editorial Council*

Author's Preface

Through a lifetime of engagement with the church, I have been occupied with questions about how we can work together and live up to our calling as followers of Jesus. I have found much help in the Scriptures for both personal and corporate growth in faith and faithfulness. One of the richest sources of practical advice is 1 Corinthians, Paul's letter to a cluster of faith communities that have a great deal in common with churches in the twenty-first century. As a pastor, denominational executive, missionary, and teacher, I have found myself turning again and again to this encouraging and challenging letter.

In my doctoral studies at Toronto School of Theology, I had an opportunity to explore some dimensions of 1 Corinthians in depth as I wrote my dissertation on "Paul's Use of Shame as a Sanction in 1 Corinthians." This gave me a chance to find answers to some questions. It also prompted many more questions about the context of the Corinthian believers, about what Paul intended to say to his first readers, and about what that means for the church today. Writing this commentary for the Believers Church Bible Commentary series has given me a framework for engaging these questions over many years.

I wrote the first draft of this commentary on two sabbaticals. The first, granted by Mennonite Church Canada, took advantage of the wonderful library and stimulating community of Anabaptist Mennonite Biblical Seminary in Elkhart, Indiana. The second, granted by Jubilee Mennonite Church, benefited from the cultural and academic resources of Union Biblical Seminary in Pune, India, and the library of the Protestant Institute of Theology in Montpellier, France. I am grateful to all who made these experiences possible, profitable, and immensely enjoyable.

The contribution of published scholars to my understanding of 1 Corinthians is reflected in notes throughout the text. Not formally noted are the influences of many other conversation partners: teachers, students, church members, and fellow believers in Canada, the United States, South Africa (esp. at the Evangelical Seminary of Southern Africa in Pietermaritzburg), and India (esp. at the Union Biblical Seminary in Pune). I thank them all.

Special thanks to several people who helped me to see angles and errors that I missed. Loren Johns, the series editor, and S. David Garber, the copyeditor, improved the writing, corrected errors, and directed me to some important resources. Jon Isaak was the peer reader; Danisa Ndlovu and Tabitha VandenEnden also read and responded to an earlier draft, as did members of the Editorial Council. Each of them identified weaknesses that I have tried to correct. The faults that remain are my own.

My family has endured many years of my preoccupation with 1 Corinthians through my doctoral studies and the writing of this commentary. I thank them for their patience and for distracting me to other important priorities. Above all, the encouragement and support of my wife, Yvonne, has been essential to my well-being and to my determination to persist until this volume is ready to offer to you, the readers.

A group study guide designed for use with this commentary is available as a free download from the Herald Press website.

My prayer is that what I have written will prompt deeper engagement with 1 Corinthians so that the body of Christ will be strengthened and "be united in the same mind and the same purpose" (1:10).

Keep alert, stand firm in your faith, be courageous, be strong.
Let all that you do be done in love.
(1 Cor 16:13-14)

—*Dan Nighswander*
Winnipeg, Manitoba

Introduction to 1 Corinthians

Life in Corinth in 50 CE was hectic. The busyness of a prosperous port, a productive agricultural region, and a manufacturing center drew a multitude of people from many parts of the Roman Empire. With the added attractions of the Isthmian Games, an active artistic community, and the practices of most religions known in the Mediterranean region, the city overflowed with activity, energy, and diversity.

There were a few Christians among its citizens—new Christians. They had been introduced to Jesus by an itinerant missionary, whose name was Paul. Eighteen months after his arrival, Paul moved on, and the believers in Corinth tried to carry on with their newfound faith. They were helped by occasional correspondence with Paul and by other visiting teachers. They were influenced by many other factors: experiences with other religions, social conventions and expectations, personal ambitions, economics, interpersonal relationships—all the stuff of life. Their understanding of Christian faith and their practice of it was flawed in many ways.

Why should we care about this stumbling assortment of Jesus-followers? First, for us who also follow Jesus, these are our people, and we are curious about them. But more urgently, we care because we and they have so much in common. Any Christians who experience division over loyalty to different leaders, any who find it hard to agree on sexual ethics or to live up to them, any who experience conflict between their theological convictions and their social context, any who debate gender roles or worship styles, any who live with spiritually arrogant fellow church members—all these will find common ground with believers in Corinth.

In this commentary we explore one of several letters that Paul, the founder of the Christian community in Corinth, sent to the believers there to sort out their differences, correct their errors, and encourage them in their life together. Throughout the commentary, I will regularly refer to the New Revised Standard Version Bible (NRSV) and New International Version (NIV), sometimes citing others.

However, before we launch into that letter, we need to understand some things about the city, Paul, the Christian assembly, and the letter.

Corinth

Location, location, location. That was Corinth's advantage. Between central Greece and the Peloponnese, a narrow land bridge separates the Gulf of Corinth on the Ionian Sea from the Saronic Gulf in the Aegean Sea. Soldiers, merchants, and others traveling by land had to pass this way. Sailors could substantially reduce travel time and the risk of fierce Mediterranean storms if they could cross the isthmus, only four miles (six and a half kilometers) wide. (Jerome Murphy-O'Connor's [2002] *St. Paul's Corinth* is a good introduction to the literature and archaeology of Roman Corinth. See also the extensive collection of images and the archaeological reports of the American School of Classical Studies at Athens: see "Excavation in Corinth" on the ASCSA website.)

One way to transport goods was to unload a ship in Cenchreae, the Saronic Gulf port, move the goods across the isthmus, and load them onto another ship in Lechaeum, on the Gulf of Corinth—or vice versa. In fact, if the boat was small enough, it could be moved, fully loaded, by way of the *diolkos*, a roadway paved with limestone and grooved to accommodate a wheeled carrier. The *diolkos* had been created sometime around 600 BCE, since the alternative dream of a canal cut through the rock seemed impossible. That dream was revived in the first century; Emperor Nero started construction in 67 CE, but the project could not be completed until 1893.

Because of its strategic location, Corinth was a powerful and prosperous city from the eighth century BCE. In 146 BCE, however, it was destroyed in punishment for its role in a revolt against Rome. A century later, it was refounded on the order of Julius Caesar as a Roman colony, the political capital of the region. New citizens poured in—many of them freedmen and freedwomen, many more slaves. The growing city enjoyed a building boom, with many public buildings and great prosperity. Money flowed from shipping, trade, and related enterprises, from the agricultural produce of the surrounding region, and from manufacturing, especially of the famous Corinthian bronze, from which functional and beautiful products were made (Murphy-O'Connor 2002: 201–18).

Corinth enjoyed the prestige and the financial benefit of being an athletic center. The Isthmian Games, second only to the more famous Olympic Games, were held biennially, and other games were held in between. With a constant flow of people from every part of the known world, Corinth was also a center of religious pluralism. Most prominent was the worship of Aphrodite, goddess of love, beauty, and fertility, whose temple crowned the mountain that looms dramatically over the city, the Acro-Corinth.

Within the city, many temples honored various goddesses and gods. Of particular interest is the temple of Asclepius (Gk. *Asklēpios*), god of healing. It was an extensive facility: besides areas for worship, it accommodated dining and relaxation, much like a modern health spa. Visitors showed their gratitude to Asclepius by leaving clay body parts representing the healing they had experienced; these can still be seen at the museum in Corinth (Witherington: 14–15).

Along with the worship of the classic Greek and Roman divinities, various mystery religions were practiced: the cults of Dionysus and Orpheus, the Eleusinian Mysteries, and others. As in all Roman cities, especially in a city refounded by Julius Caesar himself, the official state religion of the imperial cult in honor of living and dead emperors was a prominent reality in civic life.

Amid all these religious practices and beliefs were a few Jews. They had a synagogue. To this synagogue came a Jew who preached about the resurrected Jesus. His name was Paul.

Paul

Why should we care about Paul? The question may be part of the larger question, why does the Bible matter? But for some people the question is specifically about Paul. Some of the things he wrote—or how people *interpret* what he wrote—make people uncomfortable. This has especially been the case for those who perceive that Paul restricts women's ministry, a restriction they find unacceptable, and for those who reject his restrictive sexual ethics, both heterosexual and homosexual. Some people try to reread Paul to align his writings with their own views. Others simply dismiss him as a less significant voice on theology or ethics. One way to do that is to emphasize the differences between Jesus and Paul and to side with Jesus. However, thoughtful reflection makes it clear that this "solution" is not sufficient. Paul's influence on our understanding of Jesus is inestimable. His letters, the earliest writings in the New Testament, shape how we read the Gospels, the Old Testament, and subsequent church history. Anyone who wants to follow Jesus has to come to terms with Paul.

Everything we know about Paul we learn from two sources. The primary documents are a collection of letters that he wrote. They include a few autobiographical passages and give insight into his ideas, passions, and personality. The secondary sources are the stories and comments written not by Paul but about him. Prominent among these is a collection of stories about Paul written by Luke in the book of Acts. Both primary and secondary sources have limitations. The letters are written for specific occasions and to people whom Paul knew, so they do not include everything he might have wanted to say, and they are not systematic in presenting his "memoirs." Luke had his own agenda in selecting and presenting the stories he tells (see Luke 1:1-4). Part of his agenda seems to have been smoothing over controversies and defending Paul while also convincing those who did not know or believe "the truth concerning the things about [Jesus]" (Luke 1:4) and encouraging those who did believe (Faw: 19–21). Of course, ancient sources never answer the questions we might expect a modern biography to answer about the psychological and sociological factors that shape a person's life.

The first time Luke introduces Paul to his readers, he is called by his Hebrew name, Saul, and he is standing by, approvingly, at the stoning of the first Christian martyr, Stephen (Acts 7:58; 8:1). Since the stoning was instigated by "the synagogue of the Freedmen (as it was called), Cyrenians, Alexandrians, and others of those from Cilicia and Asia" (6:9)—which includes Paul's home city of Tarsus (21:39; 22:3)—we can assume that Paul was affiliated with that synagogue. This may suggest that Paul was a freedman, perhaps even descended from a former slave, though scholarly opinion on the meaning of this synagogue name is divided.

More important to Paul are his Jewish credentials: "circumcised on the eighth day, a member of the people of Israel, of the tribe of Benjamin, a Hebrew born of Hebrews; as to the law, a Pharisee; as to zeal, a persecutor of the church; as to righteousness under the law, blameless" (Phil 3:5-6). Luke adds that he was a Roman citizen from birth (Acts 16:37; 22:27-28; 23:27) and that he had received part of his education in Jerusalem from Gamaliel, one of the great rabbis (22:3).

Something prompted Paul to become zealous in attacking followers of Jesus. From observing the stoning of Stephen (Acts 7:58;

8:1; 22:20) to violent home invasions (8:3) to attacks outside Jerusalem (9:1-2; 22:4-5), his passion for eradicating the sect grew beyond any of his peers (Acts 26:9-12; cf. 1 Cor 15:9; Gal 1:13, 23; Phil 3:6).

Amid this religious fervor against the way of Jesus (Acts 22:4), a dramatic event changed Paul. It is commonly called his "conversion," and it clearly transformed his mind and behavior, but that is not how Paul wrote about it in the letters that we have (Shillington 1998a: 154-63). He says that Christ *appeared* to him (1 Cor 15:8) or simply that he had *seen* Jesus (1 Cor 9:1), who was "revealed" to him (Gal 1:16). In his preaching and face-to-face conversations, Paul may have told the story in much the way that Luke told it (Acts 9:1-20; 22:6-16; 26:12-18), but in his letters he speaks simply of his "calling" to preach to the Gentiles (Gal 1:15-16; cf. Stendahl: 7-23; Peace: 27-29; Segal: 5-7). This encounter with the risen Christ, reinforced by experiences with followers of Jesus (Gal 1:17b-19; Acts 9:10-19; 11:25-26; 13:1-5), was a transformative event for Paul. It caused him to reevaluate his previous life and convictions and provided him a new community and mission (Segal: 3-33, 72-75).

For a pious Pharisee, the idea that Gentiles could become part of God's people without becoming Jews was radically new. But because of his encounter with Christ, Paul devoted the rest of his life to fulfilling his calling to share that "mystery" with Gentiles wherever he had opportunity (Shillington 2011: 164-81), and opportunity eventually took him to Corinth.

Paul and the Corinthians

Luke tells us more about Paul's ministry in Corinth than Paul himself writes. In his correspondence with the believers, there obviously was no need to tell them what they already knew from their own experience.

Sometime in the spring of 50 CE, Paul arrived in Corinth (Acts 18:1-18). There he met Aquila and Priscilla and set up a business partnership with them, using his trade as a tentmaker to earn a livelihood. On the Sabbath, he practiced his real calling: proclaiming Jesus as the Messiah in the Jewish synagogue. Acts reports that Paul consistently spoke in synagogues when he arrived in a new city but was forced out by a hostile response, and so it was in Corinth. His message was met with strong opposition. When it was no longer possible to preach in the synagogue, he either left town or moved into a private home to continue his preaching (Acts 13:14; 14:1; 17:1, 10, 17; 18:4, 19; 19:8). In Corinth he left the synagogue and moved his ministry to the house next door, which was owned by Titius Justus, a Gentile who worshiped in the synagogue but had not converted to Judaism (Acts 18:7). Several people believed and were baptized, and the Christian assembly grew.

Eventually the opposition flared into a public attack that brought Paul before the proconsul, Gallio. From other sources we know he was in office in 50–51 CE or 51–52 (Murphy-O'Connor 2002: 161–69). The case was thrown out, but soon afterward Paul, together with Aquila and Priscilla, moved on to Ephesus. He had been in Corinth for a year and a half (Acts 18:11).

Paul's initial visit to Corinth was the beginning of an extended interaction that included visits, letters, and emissaries going both ways between March 50 CE and May 56 CE. The letter that we know as 1 Corinthians was part of that interaction. Details of the relationship are debated, but as likely as any is the following reconstruction adapted from that of Jerome Murphy-O'Connor (2002: 173–74).

March 50–September 51	• Paul arrives in Corinth and remains for eighteen months (Acts 18:1, 11).
September 52	• Having passed through Ephesus, Jerusalem, Antioch, and Galatia (Acts 18:18-23), Paul arrives in Ephesus (1 Cor 16:8, Acts 19:1), where he stays for two years and three months (Acts 19:8-10).
Summer 53	• Paul writes an admonitory letter (now lost) to Corinth (1 Cor 5:9), probably as the result of information brought by Apollos on his return to Ephesus (1 Cor 16:12).
April 54	• Chloe's staff arrive in Ephesus and seek out Paul, reporting to him some scandalous behavior in the church at Corinth (1 Cor 1:11).
May 54	• Paul sends Timothy to Corinth to check on the well-being of the faith community there (1 Cor 4:17; 16:10-11). • A delegation from Corinth arrives in Ephesus (1 Cor 16:17), bearing a letter to Paul from the assembly (1 Cor 7:1). • Paul writes 1 Corinthians.
June 54	• Timothy returns to Ephesus and informs Paul of the arrival in Corinth of teachers advocating for the full observance of the Law of Moses.
Summer 54	• Paul makes his unplanned second visit to Corinth (2 Cor 2:1-11; 7:6-16; 13:2). • Paul returns to Ephesus via Macedonia (2 Cor 1:23–2:1). • Paul sends Titus to Corinth with the now-lost "Severe Letter" (2 Cor 2:4; 7:8).

September–October 54	• Forced out of Ephesus, Paul begins a new mission in Troas (2 Cor 2:12). • Desperate to find out from Titus how Corinth had reacted to the "Severe Letter," Paul sails to Macedonia (2 Cor 2:13; 7:5; Acts 20:1) before sea traffic ceases for the winter. • With the aid of Timothy, Paul writes 2 Corinthians 1–9.
April 55	• Titus brings 2 Corinthians 1–9 to Corinth.
Summer 55	• Paul, now in Illyricum (Rom 15:19), receives bad news about the situation in Corinth, and in response he writes 2 Corinthians 10–13. • Before the onset of winter, Paul travels south to Corinth.
Winter 55–56	• Paul visits Corinth for the third time (2 Cor 13:1-2), where he spends three months (Acts 20:2-3).
April–May 56	• Paul leaves Corinth for the last time and makes a farewell circuit (Rom 15:31) of the Aegean Sea en route to Jerusalem (Acts 20:3–21:15).

The Christian Assembly in Corinth

In Corinth, as everywhere, the Christians of the first century met in private homes [*Church, p. 364*]. As the believing community grew, Christians assembled in the homes of Stephanas, Crispus, Gaius, and perhaps others (1 Cor 1:14; Rom 16:23). In the absence of other meeting facilities, household units formed the basis for a congregation meeting in their house. Other individuals would attach themselves to one of these household-congregations, or assemblies. Christians did not meet in dedicated church buildings until late in the third century CE (Snyder 1992: 248–49; cf. Gehring).

Meeting in household units and in private homes shaped the early Christian communities. (Reta Halteman Finger and George McClain have written a simulation to give an experience of a house church in Corinth: *Creating a Scene in Corinth: A Simulation*.) The language of family and household is prominent in the New Testament letters, especially in the preferred address, "brothers and sisters." "Household codes," modified from their secular precedents, defined relationships between believers (Eph 5:21–6:9; Col 3:18–4:1; 1 Pet 2:13–3:7). Paul addressed the members as "my children" and called himself their "father" (1 Cor 4:14-15; 1 Thess 2:11) and even their "mother" (Gal 4:19; cf. 1 Thess 2:11). Sometimes he identified himself as a household steward (1 Cor 4:1-2). This vocabulary and concept were present in Judaism long before the early Christians adopted it (Branick: 16–17).

Because Christians met in homes, the leadership of meetings naturally flowed from the roles of household members, including extended family and servants. Adjustments were necessary because some members of the household may not have been believers and because members of other households would join the hosting household. Theological perspective (e.g., Gal 3:28) and leadership abilities gifted by the Holy Spirit (1 Cor 12) also affected leadership roles. Major changes to leadership patterns happened when the places of meeting moved from homes to dedicated buildings.

The Christians who met in the dedicated churches and basilicas showed an understanding of themselves different from that of the Christians meeting in the house churches. Leadership became concentrated in fewer hands, the hands of a special class of holy people. Church activities became stylized ritual. The building rather than the community came to be regarded as the temple of God. Regardless of whether environment determines ideology or ideology determines environment, the link between the two is clear when we examine the shift from the house church to the dedicated church (Branick: 15).

The size of the congregation was limited to the space available. Archaeological evidence shows that spaces to gather in homes were limited. The maximum capacity even in a large house would have been fewer than one hundred persons (Murphy-O'Connor 2002: 178–82). Though several assemblies met in different-sized homes, the total number of Christians in Corinth when Paul wrote was probably fifty, or at most one hundred persons. Their leaders were the heads of the households where they met.

Who were these people? We know the names and something about the status of some of them (Theissen: 94–96).

Chloe was presumably a woman of means and influence, and *her people* traveled, probably for business purposes (1 Cor 1:11).

Crispus or **Sosthenes** (probably two names for one person: see EN [explanatory notes] on 1 Cor 1:1) was a synagogue official and the head of a household, all of whose members became Christians. His conversion to Christianity influenced others. He was a person who traveled, probably for business purposes (1 Cor 1:1, 14; Acts 18:8, 17).

Erastus was a financial official of the city who was probably later chosen as aedile (an official in charge of public works). Consequently, he made a public gift of a section of pavement (Thiselton 2000: 9); he also traveled (Rom 16:23).

Gaius's house served Paul and the entire Christian community (Rom 16:23; 1 Cor 1:14).

Phoebe was a deacon or minister in nearby Cenchreae who provided support to Paul and the congregation. As a patron or benefactor, she also traveled. She was probably wealthy (Rom 16:1-2).

Priscilla (Prisca) and her husband, **Aquila,** hosted a house-congregation and provided support to the apostles; they operated a small business and traveled (Rom 16:3; Acts 18:2, 18, 26; 1 Cor 16:19).

Stephanas was the head of a household who provided services to the Christian community and to Paul and who traveled and served as a representative of the assembly (1 Cor 1:16; 16:15).

Achaicus and **Fortunatus** were companions of Stephanas in their travels and served as official representatives of the assembly (1 Cor 16:17).

Tertius was a scribe (Rom 16:22).

Titius Justus provided lodging for Paul (Acts 18:7).

Jason, Lucius, Quartus, and **Sosipater** were also members of the assembly, though we know nothing more about them (Rom 16:21, 23).

In sum, at least half the members whose names we know were people who owned houses, had the resources to provide services to the Christian community, and had the resources and occasion to travel. Of most of the rest we know too little to infer any social status, but since Paul observed that *not many of you were wise by human standards, not many were powerful, not many were of noble birth* (1 Cor 1:26), it is probable that they were ordinary residents of the city, with many of them probably slaves.

When the assembly gathered, it was for worship, which included prayer, prophecy, speaking in tongues, mutual discipling, singing, and sharing the Lord's Supper. Both women and men participated in these activities (11:4-5—but see the discussion on 14:34-36). Worship happened both in the household assemblies and on occasions when the household groups gathered in one aggregate assembly (Gehring: 173). Sometimes there were baptisms. Sometimes they read letters from Paul (cf. 1 Thess 5:26-27; Col 4:16).

Paul's Letter

First Corinthians is a letter. It is not a narrative, though it contains pieces of narrative. It is not poetry, though it includes sections of poetry. It is not law, though there are some legalistic injunctions and discussions of legal matters in it. It is not a systematic theology or a philosophical essay, though it is deeply infused with theological convictions and shaped by philosophical views. It is better not to call this letter an "epistle," as that now uncommon term suggests something outside of normal correspondence. It is simply a letter.

This fact profoundly shapes our approach to understanding 1 Corinthians. It tells us that this is (1) a unit of communication (2) in written form (3) that was written in specific circumstances (4) as part of an ongoing relationship (5) between two parties.

As many commentators have pointed out, when we read this letter we are "reading somebody else's mail" (Hays 1997: 1). In fact, we are reading only a piece of a larger correspondence and only one side of the conversation. Throughout what follows we will try to imagine what "the other party" was saying and consider how that shapes our understanding of what we read [*What Chloe's People Said*, p. 371; *What the Corinthians Wrote*, p. 372].

Like letters in the twenty-first century, letters in the first century CE followed a standard format (see Elias 1995: 21–23, 348–50; Shillington 1998a: 16–17; Yoder Neufeld: 351–53; Toews 2004: 394–95). They always started with an opening statement that included the name of the sender, the name of the addressee, and a brief greeting. Then there was typically a section of thanksgiving or blessing, often with words of intercession addressed to one or more divinities on behalf of the person receiving the letter. In Paul's letters, the thanksgiving section introduces the main themes to be discussed later and frames them in prayers of thanks, which he says he "always" offers for the community that is receiving the letter (Rom 1:8-15; 2 Cor 1:3-7; Eph 1:3-23; Phil 1:3-11; Col 1:3-14; 1 Thess 1:2-10; 2 Thess 1:3-12; Philem 4-7).

The body of the letter addresses the matter or matters that provide the occasion for writing and is usually the longest section. Finally, it wraps up with a closing that could include formulaic benedictions and final greetings, and sometimes also a reference to the writing process.

Paul followed the standard form of a letter in his day, adapting it to the specific circumstances and his own style within acceptable parameters. Recognizing this, we begin to see a framework for understanding what was being communicated and how. But letter structure alone does not provide adequate clues for understanding the heart of the letter, the body. For that, we must explore the rhetorical style and structure of the letter.

Rhetoric is the use of language to persuade people. Politicians and lawyers, salespeople, preachers, bloggers, and parents use rhetoric when they select, arrange, enunciate, and embody words in order to convince others and affect their beliefs, values, and behaviors.

Paul appears to reject the rhetorical use of language in 1 Corinthians 1–4. He scoffs at *lofty words or wisdom* (2:1) and claims that he would (could?) not use words eloquently (1:17, 20; 2:1, 4). Nevertheless, Paul did write deliberately *and* persuasively, so that even though he appears to reject (other people's) rhetorical skill, he clearly uses rhetorical strategies consciously to the best of his ability with the intention of changing his readers' attitudes and actions as well as their minds. In fact, in the ancient world a common rhetorical tool was renouncing rhetoric and claiming not to be accomplished in using it (D. Martin 1995: 48–49)—much as modern politicians disparage politics and power in their attempts to win office.

We cannot know, of course, how much or what kind of education in the use of rhetoric Paul had received. Ryan Schellenberg (17–56) has argued, against many scholars in recent decades, that Paul did not receive a formal education in rhetoric. Nevertheless, it is possible to evaluate Paul's writings by using the standards set forth in ancient handbooks of rhetoric. We cannot determine what kind of education in rhetorical skills his first readers had, though Paul indicates that many of the Corinthian Christians were impressed by rhetorical skill (1:18-25), but not by his own speech (2:4; 2 Cor 10:10). However, we can safely assume that there was some degree of shared understanding of how one might use language to persuade people to accept particular beliefs, attitudes, and values and then to act in particular ways (D. Martin 1995: 48–55). That is the rhetorical assumption and skill that Paul exercised, or at least tried to exercise, in writing this letter. Although we have a written document, the intention and expectation was that the Corinthians would primarily hear it read aloud in the context of the assembled members, so the tools of oral and public rhetoric would be the effective strategies to employ.

Particular circumstances call for particular kinds of rhetoric. The ancient Greek philosophers divided rhetoric into three types, which Aristotle called forensic, epideictic, and deliberative (*Rhetoric* 1.3.1-6). Forensic rhetoric is the way one would use language in a court setting to accuse or defend a person before judge and jury. Epideictic rhetoric (sometimes called "demonstrative" rhetoric) is used in the marketplace or theater to impress an audience with the speaker's skill. It is the rhetoric of praise and blame, sometimes used to encourage. Deliberative rhetoric is used in places like governing councils to persuade people to make the right decision about some action.

Ancient writers of handbooks on rhetoric, such as Aristotle, Cicero, and Quintilian, analyzed various strategies and taught others how to improve their skill in using language persuasively. Students studied their handbooks and practiced writing arguments, speeches, and letters to develop their persuasive skills. Many others have written rhetorical handbooks since then. Indeed, any text on preaching, salesmanship, public speaking, or the whole field of marketing follows in that tradition.

Scholars have given a great deal of attention to the use of rhetorical conventions in biblical writing (e.g., Watson 1994). Margaret Mitchell is one scholar who has applied this approach to 1 Corinthians. She has demonstrated that throughout the letter as a whole, Paul used the rhetorical tools that were recommended and used in ancient handbooks of rhetoric and in examples of speech and writing for deliberative rhetoric. Mitchell (20–62) identifies four characteristics of deliberative argumentation:

1. The time focus is on the future rather than the past or present; it addresses a course of action to be taken in the future.
2. It appeals to the audience on the basis that it is to their advantage to take the course of action being recommended.
3. It "proves" its point through a series of examples, especially including imitation of historical precedents or of the speaker/writer.
4. It often deals with issues of unity or factionalism.

Mitchell demonstrates that 1 Corinthians has all of these characteristics, as we will observe in the commentary below.

Two conclusions from Mitchell's work are especially important for our reading of 1 Corinthians. First, she has shown convincingly (as others have also argued) that the letter as found in the canonical form is one letter. This answers some earlier studies proposing that the letter might have been compiled from several previous letters or from rearrangements of several parts (see chart in Hurd: 48).

The second conclusion is that the letter is one cohesive argument in support of the thesis statement in 1:10. Thus the entire letter is to be understood as a call to unity for its readers. All commentators agree that the first four chapters address issues of division and disunity, but many read the rest of the letter as addressing a series of issues largely unrelated to each other and marginally, if at all, related to Paul's call to be *united in the same mind and the same purpose* (1:10).

Throughout this commentary, we will read the text with the understanding that it is one extended and multifaceted but cohesive argument against factionalism, and from that perspective it addresses issues that were raised by the Corinthians themselves as part of their ongoing conversation with Paul.

1 Corinthians 1:1-9

Greetings and Thanksgiving

1 Corinthians 1:1-3

The Letter Opening

PREVIEW

First Corinthians is a letter. That observation helps us to know how to read it and what to look for as clues for understanding. This awareness is especially useful in the letter opening, the thanksgiving section, and the closing. In the opening, the first three verses, we expect to see three characteristics of a typical letter—and we do see them. However, what catches our attention is not the conformity to a standard format, but rather the specific content and the nuances found within the format.

These opening sentences express some profound convictions about the nature of the Christian assembly, about believers, and about Paul. Here we read that Paul does not work alone: *our brother Sosthenes* is a cowriter. The sentences address not only the whole Corinthian Christian community but also *all those ... in every place* for whom Jesus Christ is *both their Lord and ours*. Collective and plural forms of words throughout the opening draw attention to the corporate community of faith, as does the blessing from both the Father and the Son of the Holy Trinity.

Prominent in the opening is an understanding of call: Paul is *called* to be an apostle; the believers are *called* to be saints; believers *call* on the name of Jesus.

Finally, Paul says that the believers are *sanctified* and *called to be saints* (NIV, *his holy people*). The behaviors, attitudes, and convictions that we learn about in this letter stretch our understanding of what it means to be sanctified/saints/holy. Already in these opening words we see a signal that these kinds of issues need to be addressed and will be in the rest of the letter.

OUTLINE
The Letter Writers, 1:1
The Letter Readers, 1:2
Greeting, 1:3

EXPLANATORY NOTES

The Letter Writers 1:1

Two people wrote this letter. One inscribed the words, and the other, the one who dictated it, was *Paul, called to be an apostle of Christ Jesus by the will of God*.

We have already been introduced to Paul and his relationship with the Corinthian congregations in the introduction, where we briefly recounted his life story. But when he identifies himself to his readers, he simply writes that he is *called to be an apostle of Christ Jesus by the will of God*. This self-introduction is influenced by his relationship with the readers and the agenda of the letter. The most important identity marker for Paul is that he is an apostle of Jesus Christ and that he was called by the will of God to be so. This title, with slight variations, is how he introduces himself in other letters: Romans, 2 Corinthians, Galatians, Ephesians, Colossians, and *1 and 2 Timothy*, and *Titus*. (Many scholars have questioned whether Paul wrote Ephesians, on which see Yoder Neufeld: 24–28, 341–44, 361–62; and Colossians, on which see E. Martin: 24–25. But it is generally agreed that if not written by Paul, they were written by his followers and are intended to represent his thoughts. In this commentary, these letters are included where comparisons are made to Paul's letters. The authorship of the pastoral epistles of 1 and 2 Timothy and Titus is also disputed, and in this commentary where parallels are quoted, the references to texts from these three will be italicized.)

An apostle is a messenger who has been sent (from Gk. *apostellō*, sent) by another to convey a message. In the New Testament, and especially in the writings of Luke (Luke and Acts), *apostle* was synonymous with "the twelve," who had been called out by Jesus and were sent as his messengers (Luke 6:13 parr.). But Paul included himself among the apostles and defended his right to do so (cf. Gal 1:1).

Two more times in this letter, Paul writes of his apostleship. In 9:1-2 he argues that he is an apostle because he has seen Jesus, and that the Corinthians themselves, presumably because they embraced the Christian faith of which he was the messenger/apostle, are the proof of his apostleship. In 15:8-9 he argues that, although unworthy because of his previous behavior to be called an apostle, even the least of the apostles, he can claim that title because the risen Christ had appeared to him as he had to the rest of the apostles.

Why was it so important to Paul to defend his status as an apostle? Clearly, others were challenging this right (9:1 and the rest of the chapter; see discussion at that point in this commentary) and thus undermining his authority as a leader. As we shall observe below, reestablishing this authority was part of Paul's rhetorical strategy for influencing the faith community. Nevertheless, the claim is not for his sake, as if apostleship were a status to be grasped for personal glory. Paul was not seeking to exercise apostolic authority on his own behalf, but for the one who had called him. Later in the letter (chs. 1–4, 9) it is clear that Paul was faulted for not claiming authority and not acting as was expected of leaders. His response is that his apostleship was not of his own initiative, but God's, and that he represented not his own interests, but the crucified Christ (1:23; 2:2 and throughout). Paul has his vocation, as the members of the Corinthian congregations have theirs (v. 2). God is the author of both vocations.

The specific claim that his call is *by the will of God* may be a hint that his detractors are claiming that his call originated from human sources or even from his own imagination (cf. his defense in Gal 1:1). Alternatively, it may be an attempt to assert the equality, or perhaps the uniqueness, of his call to the calls of other apostles and teachers whose loyalists he challenges in the following paragraphs. Above all, it is an acknowledgment and reminder that Paul is a servant of Christ and steward of God's mysteries (4:1). Therefore he starts the letter with a reminder that he has been *called to be an apostle of Christ Jesus by the will of God*.

. . . and our brother Sosthenes. Although it was rare in the first century to name several persons as cowriters of a letter (Murphy-O'Connor 1993: 562–64), Paul's letters usually do so. His frequent cowriter was Timothy (2 Cor 1:1; Col 1:1), sometimes together with Silvanus/Silas (1 Thess 1:1; 2 Thess 1:1; cf. 2 Cor 1:19), and on one occasion, Tertius (Rom 16:22). Despite Timothy's presence when Paul was writing 1 Corinthians (4:17 implies that Timothy was one of the company who carried this letter to Corinth; cf. 16:10), Sosthenes is the cowriter in this letter. Paul added in his own handwriting a brief greeting at the end of the letter (1 Cor 16:21-22). (See also Gal 6:11-17; Col 4:16-18a; 2 Thess 3:17; Philem 19.)

Little is known about Sosthenes. It is likely, but not certain, that the man named here is the same Sosthenes (previously or alternatively known as Crispus; see Acts 18:8; cf. also Myrou; Fellows) who was a synagogue leader in Corinth and who was beaten by an angry mob in Paul's stead (Acts 18:17). This former leader in the Jewish community—probably a patron rather than a religious functionary (Winter 2001: 296)—had become a Christian and a coworker with Paul and accompanied him to Ephesus. His former status, his suffering public abuse on behalf of Paul, and his subsequent closeness to Paul may have been reasons why Sosthenes would have been held in high regard among the Christians in Corinth. To name him as a cowriter would surely draw a positive connection between these two men.

How Sosthenes contributed to shaping the letter is difficult to determine. He is not named beyond the greeting, and the letter is written primarily in a singular voice (with notable exceptions at 1:18-31 and 2:6-16, if indeed those are meant to refer to specific companions and colleagues rather than a royal "we" or a general comment about "all Christians" or "proper apostles like me"). His influence on the writing may have been minimal. We will therefore take the liberty of speaking of Paul as the author of this letter rather than Paul and Sosthenes.

Perhaps most significant are two facts. First, Paul named his cowriter to signal that he worked with and communicated on behalf of a "team," not as an independent spokesperson. Second, he identified his cowriter (or scribe) as *our brother* (*the brother* in Gk.). Sosthenes's relationship with the assembly is clearly different from Paul's, for Paul identified himself not as a brother but as a father of the community (4:15). Nevertheless, he was "one of the family," and his relationship was to be respected.

Throughout the letter, these themes of collegiality in ministry, respect for fellow workers, and recognition of Christian familial relationships are important.

The Letter Readers 1:2

As noted above, standard letter format in the first century moved from naming the author to naming the addressee(s).

Like all of Paul's letters except for Philemon (and the pastoral epistles), 1 Corinthians is addressed to the whole body of believers, not to an individual, not to the leaders (note the variation in Philippians), and not to one faction or another. When we reach the discussion of the issues in Corinth (1:10 and throughout), we will recognize that this is a deliberate move on Paul's part. Furthermore, the faith community in Corinth is placed into the context of the whole body of Jesus' followers as Paul reminds them that their calling is *together with all those who in every place call on the name of our Lord Jesus Christ, both their Lord and ours* (cf. 2 Cor 1:1). This larger context is important to Paul's argument throughout 1 Corinthians: he draws attention to it elsewhere in the letter (7:17; 11:16; 14:33, 36; 16:1, 19) and frames the letter with a reminder of the larger context at the beginning (1:2) and the end (16:19-20).

The congregations belong to God, Paul reminds his readers (also in 2 Corinthians and Romans). In anticipation of the issues to be addressed in this letter, Paul wishes to remind his readers that the community does not belong to him or to any other leader or teacher. It does not belong to an individual, a faction, or even the whole membership. It is of God and belongs to God (see also on 3:4–4:5 below).

The body that he addresses is in Corinth (see "Corinth" and "The Christian Assembly in Corinth" in the introduction). There was no dedicated building: the believers met in several households. We do not know how they organized themselves, what structures bound the gatherings together, how group decisions were made, or how the leaders of the several gatherings effected cooperation between them.

It is possible that the divisions of loyalty in the assembly (1:10-12 and throughout) to some degree followed the identities of the separate households, though there were clearly divisions within as well as between the households (see 11:18). Yet it was to the whole body of Christians in Corinth that the letter was addressed, not one household. Paul expected the letter to be read in each of the houses or on an occasion when the whole assembly gathered (as suggested in 14:23), and he wanted to bring about changes of understanding, attitude, and behavior both within and between the households.

The specific address to the assembly in Corinth is a reminder that Paul wrote all his letters to a particular audience. He did not write for "the church at large" for all time. Although another letter attributed to Paul suggests that the believers in two cities located near each other should read the letter addressed to the other (Col 4:16; cf. Col 2:1; 4:13, 15), 1 Corinthians contains no hint that anyone other than the first readers would sometime read this.

Because he wrote the letter for a particular occasion to a particular assembly, Paul did not explain all the background to what he wrote. It was not necessary to provide details of which they already knew, except to make a brief identifying reference to a quotation or an issue, as we will note at several points in this commentary. His teaching and advice are contextual. It is quite possible that if he had written to a different context, even on the same matters, he would have written differently. This is one of the interpretive questions that we readers in a much different context of time, place, culture, assumptions, and experience need to discern as we read this letter.

Paul makes two statements about *the church of God that is in Corinth*. He writes that they are *sanctified in Christ Jesus* and that they are *called to be saints* (NIV, *his holy people*). The phrases are parallel, though with nuanced differences. Both phrases locate the initiative for the status of Paul's addressees as *external* to the believers: they are *sanctified* [passive voice] *in Christ Jesus* and *called* [passive voice: the implied subject is God, parallel to the one who has called Paul to be an apostle] *to be saints*.

The common English usage of *saint* to identify a person of exceptional holiness and recognition of such by the institutional church may be distracting to a reader in the twenty-first century. Both *sanctified* (adjective) and *saints* (noun) and the Greek words behind the English translation originally meant "consecrated" or "set apart for special service." The NIV translation, *holy people*, may be preferable, though it too has come to a narrower meaning in English, and the NIV translation of *sanctified* and *holy* leaves no hint of the parallelism that is still suggested by the NRSV's *sanctified* and *saint*. Another solution would be to translate it as *to those who are set aside to be holy in Christ Jesus, called to be holy*.

Finally, in the last phrase Paul brings together (1) the unifying common confession that Jesus Christ is Lord, (2) the unity of all believers, and (3) his own affinity with his readers: the term *ours* includes Paul, his companions in Ephesus (Sosthenes among them), and the believers in Corinth.

Greeting 1:3

The usual greeting in a Greek letter was *chairein*, which comes from the verb meaning "rejoice," but in this context it simply means "greetings." The usual greeting in a Hebrew letter was *shalom*, in this context also meaning "greetings" yet also hinting at rich undertones of meaning: peace, well-being, wholeness, prosperity, harmony. The usual Greek translation of *shalom* was *eirēnē*. Paul's usual greeting brought together a variation on the combined Greek and the Hebrew greetings: grace (*charis*) to you and peace (*eirēnē*) (Rom 1:7; 2 Cor 1:2; Gal 1:3; Eph 1:2; Phil 1:2; Col 1:2; 1 Thess 1:1; 2 Thess 1:2; *Titus 1:4*; Philem 3; *1 and 2 Timothy* have a slight variation: "grace, mercy and peace").

Grace is used 59 times in the Pauline letters (plus 12 times in the pastoral epistles) out of 127 times in the whole Bible. It is a foundational theological emphasis for Paul and has deep personal meaning (Elias 2006: 285–320). The benediction of grace has added significance in this context, as we will discover, for grace is especially what Paul is urging the members of the Corinthian assembly to demonstrate in their relationships with one another. The letter closes with another blessing of grace (16:23).

Peace is not found frequently in 1 Corinthians, but the accomplishment of peace in the faith community is Paul's goal in writing (7:15b; 14:33).

THE TEXT IN BIBLICAL CONTEXT
Call

The Bible frequently talks about people being "called." Besides the quite ordinary expressions of naming or inviting, many of the call references describe a call from God that draws an individual or group out from the ordinary and into a special relationship or circumstance. The prototype of such a call is God's call to Abram and Sarai, recorded in Genesis 12:1-3:

> Now the LORD said to Abram, "Go from your country and your kindred and your father's house to the land that I will show you. I will make of you a great nation, and I will bless you, and make your name great, so that you will be a blessing. I will bless those who bless you, and the one who curses you I will curse; and in you all the families of the earth shall be blessed."

This call entails both a calling "from" and a calling "to." It is a call to individuals that expands into a community experience. It is a blessing whose purpose is to bless others. This is true in many of the call stories in Scripture. Like Abram and Sarai, the prophets and the apostles were called and sent virtually, as it were, in one action.

Key call passages with similar features include these:

Moses (Exod 3:4-10)

Samuel (1 Sam 3)

Isaiah (Isa 6)

Jeremiah (Jer 1)

Amos (Amos 7:14-15)

the first disciples (Matt 4:18-22)

the twelve (Mark 6:7 // Matt 10:1 // Luke 9:1-2)

Paul's own experience of calling, to which he refers in 1 Corinthians 1:1, is reported by Luke in Acts 9, 22, and 26. Paul describes it in his own words in Galatians 1:13-17 (see esp. v. 15). We should understand Paul's call as being of the same kind as the calls of the Abram and Sarai, the prophets, and the twelve. Neither Luke nor Paul speaks of it as a conversion, though it has come to be used by many Christians as the epitome of conversion (see "Paul" in the introduction; cf. Peace: 88–101).

Holy

As it is in 1 Corinthians, *call* in the Bible is often associated closely with *holy* (see Oswalt; A. Kreider). God's call of a people to be holy is reported in Exodus 19:3-6:

> Then Moses went up to God; the LORD called to him from the mountain, saying, "Thus you shall say to the house of Jacob, and tell the Israelites: You have seen what I did to the Egyptians, and how I bore you on eagles' wings and brought you to myself. Now therefore, if you obey my voice and keep my covenant, you shall be my treasured possession out of all the peoples. Indeed, the whole earth is mine, but you shall be for me a priestly kingdom and a holy nation. These are the words that you shall speak to the Israelites."

First Peter echoes this, especially in 1:15, "As he who called you is holy, be holy yourselves in all your conduct," and in 2:9, "You are a chosen race, a royal priesthood, a holy nation, God's own people, in order that you may proclaim the mighty acts of him who called you out of darkness into his marvelous light."

The letter to the Hebrews calls members of the Christian community "holy partners in a heavenly calling" (3:1), and a book in the Apocrypha instructs the community of faith to "implore the Lord's authority that your people, who have been called from the beginning, may be made holy" (2 Esd 2:41).

THE TEXT IN THE LIFE OF THE CHURCH

Holiness/Sanctification

Christians have long debated whether salvation and holiness, or "sanctification," are two steps or one. Various holiness, Pentecostal, and charismatic movements have emphasized the need for a "second work of grace" after an initial conversion or faith commitment, an infusion of the Holy Spirit that makes holy living possible. Others have countered that they are one and the same.

Neither salvation nor holiness is complete without the other. There is a clear ethical dimension to Christian faith, and there is a clear conversion dimension to Christian ethics. One cannot be a follower of Jesus without living toward the perfection of character and behavior that he demonstrated and taught (e.g., Matt 7:21). Hans Denck, a sixteenth-century Anabaptist leader, stated it well: "No one may truly know Christ except one who follows him in life" (Bauman: 113).

There is a sequential relationship between being *sanctified in Christ Jesus* (salvation) and being *saints* (holiness, 1 Cor 1:2): the latter is a response to or outgrowth of the former, and God initiates both. The process is lifelong, never fully achieved, as the rest of the letter amply demonstrates.

The clear implication of Paul's greeting is that all believers are called to be holy, not just specially qualified individuals such as clergy or members of religious orders (Bender and Alderfer).

1 Corinthians 1:4-9
Thanksgiving

PREVIEW

First-century letters typically include a statement of thanksgiving right after the opening. Except for Galatians, Paul's letters include such a statement. This convention is not just a routine formality. The content of this part of the letter serves important functions. Paul uses the thanksgiving to introduce some theological teaching, some ethical exhortation, and some expression of pastoral concern to set a prayerful context for what follows and to introduce the topics to be addressed in the rest of the letter (O'Brien: 12–15, 261–63).

Like an overture in a musical composition, the thanksgiving introduces the themes to be developed later and the circumstances of writing. In this section we thus get our first glimpse of the issues that Paul will address and a hint of the approach that he will take in dealing with them.

In the thanksgiving section of 1 Corinthians, Paul highlights the Corinthian interest in speech and knowledge, gifts with which they have been especially endowed by God. Paul also identifies the ethical and eschatological context that determines the value of these gifts and the community context for exercising them.

OUTLINE

Gratitude to God for Gifts, 1:4-7a
Eschatological and Ethical Values of Gifts, 1:7b-9a
The Community Context of Gifts, 1:9b

EXPLANATORY NOTES
Gratitude to God for Gifts 1:4-7a

Having already blessed his readers with a benediction of grace and peace, Paul now identifies grace as a gift from God. He does so by thanking God for the grace they have received, and further by specifying that the grace is *of God* and *has been given to [them] in Christ Jesus* (v. 4).

Both the NRSV and NIV speak of *spiritual gifts* (cf. 1:7; 12:1) as the evidence of *the grace of God that has been given you in Christ Jesus* (v. 4). However, the Greek word *charisma* means simply *gift* (1:7) and does not distinguish between spiritual and other gifts. In fact, every other place where *charismata* (plural) occurs in 1 Corinthians, both the NRSV and NIV translate it simply as *gifts* (7:7; 12:4, 9, 28, 30, 31). The NKJV and NJB translations rightly do the same in this verse (see EN on 12:1-11).

Paul speaks both specifically and generally about giftedness. In general, he writes that they have been enriched *in every way* (v. 5) and that they are *not lacking in any . . . gift* (v. 7). The specific gifts he names are those of *speech and knowledge of every kind* (v. 5). The NIV translates *with all kinds of speech and with all knowledge*. In fact, the concerns here introduced are not with general speaking and knowledge but with specific types of speaking: rhetorical speech (1:17; 2:1, 4, 13; 4:19-20), speaking in tongues (12:10, 28; 14:2, 9, 19), and prophecy (14:1)—and a particular type of knowledge (8:1, 8, 10).

In the thanksgiving section, however, Paul is only introducing these matters. He will pick up the discussion of gifts in speech and knowledge in the first four chapters, where we will observe that matters of speech (wisdom speech, or rhetoric) and elitist knowledge are of great interest to the Corinthians. He will return to discussion of speech and knowledge in chapters 12–14.

While the Corinthians dwell in thought on the *gifts* that they have been given, Paul draws attention to the *giving and receiving* of the gifts. A competitive spirit about the gifts has divided the Corinthians (ch. 12); Paul would have them unite in humble gratitude to the giver of the gifts. "By means of thanksgiving Paul redirects their confidence from themselves and their own giftedness toward the eternal God, from whom and to whom are all things" (Fee: 43).

Throughout this thanksgiving section, Paul is careful to remind his readers of their dependence on God. He does this by formulating his statements as a prayer of gratitude to God (v. 4). Paul declares that the grace they have received is *of God* (v. 4) and that they *have been enriched in him* (v. 5). It is God who will *strengthen* them (v. 8), God who *is faithful* (v. 9), and God who has *called* them (v. 9). Everything he says about the Corinthians is in the passive voice—the only grammatically active action of the Corinthians is to *wait* (v. 7); everything he says about God is in the active voice. On the one hand, this has the value of encouraging them, for as he says, *God is faithful* (v. 9). On the other hand, it pulls the rug out from under any pretense that the gifts they have, especially those of speech and knowledge, have been earned or are generated by their own efforts or qualifications. He will expand on these themes later in the letter (e.g., 4:7).

Equally remarkable in the first nine verses of this letter are the repeated references to *Christ* (v. 6), *Christ Jesus* (vv. 1, 2, 4), *our/the Lord Jesus Christ* (vv. 2, 3, 7, 8), and *Jesus Christ our Lord* (v. 9)—nine occurrences in nine verses, of which five are in the thanksgiving. "The thanksgiving establishes a shared spirituality which is distinctly Christocentric; in so doing, it establishes the basis upon which the sender and recipients relate through the letter" (Stamps: 455). It is Paul's understanding of Christ that shapes his understanding of the faith community and that motivates and focuses all that he is about to say in this letter.

Eschatological and Ethical Values of Gifts 1:7b-9a

The gifts that God has given, Paul writes, are not an end in themselves. They are an interim grace to be used *as you wait for the revealing of our Lord Jesus Christ* (v. 7). Thus he reminds them that the present level of their spiritual life is not "as good as it gets." The hope that pervades Christianity is that there is a day coming when Jesus Christ will be revealed; the warning is that that day will be a day of judgment. This expectation is named *eschatology*, which means a study of the "end times" (*eschaton* in Gk.). The Corinthians, as we shall see, thought that they were already experiencing the fullness of God's presence and blessing (e.g., 4:8; 15:12). Paul is reminding them that although there is a sense that the kingdom is already here, their experience demonstrates that the kingdom is not yet here in its fullness (Elias 1995: 355-57).

Paul writes that God will *strengthen [the Corinthians] to the end*—implying that they cannot do it on their own strength—*so that [they] may be blameless on the day of our Lord Jesus Christ* (v. 8). In drawing attention to the hope of future perfection, he implies that they are not now blameless—perhaps in these very matters of speech and knowledge—and thus hints at the matters that will be taken up shortly.

The Community Context of Gifts 1:9b

In his greeting, Paul reminds the Corinthians that there is a larger context for their Christian experience, that of the believers *in every place* (v. 2). In the thanksgiving, he reminds them again of this larger context. Three times he states that Jesus Christ is *our* Lord (vv. 7, 8, 9)—not excluding the Corinthians, but not exclusive to them either (see on v. 2).

The metaphor of salvation that Paul uses here is especially relevant to the Corinthian context, yet it is also a rich and apt expression for all Christians' understanding of what God has called them to: *by him you were called into the fellowship* [Gk. *koinōnia*] *of his Son, Jesus Christ our Lord* (v. 9). Anthony Thiselton (2000: 103–5) translates this as *You were called into the communal participation of the sonship of Christ our Lord.* The relationship of *koinōnia* is multidimensional: it is participation in Christ, and it is also participation in the community of those who are in Christ. Paul uses the same word in 10:16 to denote the participation of Christians in the body and blood of Christ in communion. To those who would break fellowship with one another, whom he is about to address, Paul declares that being part of the *church of God* (1:2) means that they have been *called into communal participation of the sonship of Jesus Christ, our [common] Lord.* The word *fellowship* does not mean here what it has so often come to mean in churches—shared meals, social events, and conviviality with people whose company one enjoys—but rather refers to a robust commitment even, if necessary, to the point of death. In other words, "come hell or high water, we're in this together, with Jesus."

Paul introduces several issues in the thanksgiving that will draw more extended discussion in the letter that ensues. The tone of the thanksgiving is a strategic preparation for what follows. Coming to the thanksgiving, as we do, with some awareness of the messy, complicated, and shameful behavior that will be exposed in this letter and the sometimes chiding, even scolding, tone that Paul uses to address the Corinthians, we may be inclined to read or hear these words as ironic, perhaps even sarcastic. However, that would be a misunderstanding of Paul's relationship with the Corinthian assembly (O'Brien: 113–16).

The tone of the thanksgiving, especially if read as if for the first time, without "reading back" what is to follow, is encouraging, affirming, inviting. Paul is sincere in giving thanks for these people and in recognizing their strengths. He has, after all, been the one to call them to faith and to nurture them in faith over an extended period. His passionate concern, evident even in his correction that follows, is here expressed positively. His pastoral heart longs for their well-being and for a warm relationship of shared faith and affection with them. Therefore he draws the contours of divine grace, eschatological hope, and the fellowship of the faith community before he launches into the difficult and risky work that forms the body of the letter.

THE TEXT IN BIBLICAL CONTEXT
Faithfulness of God

A fundamental perspective that Paul brings to his ministry and worldview is that *God is faithful* (v. 9). The adjective form of *faith* is used frequently in the Bible both of God and of the people of God. (On the special case of Paul's use of the "faith of/in Jesus," see Toews 2004: 108–11; Brunk: 305–10.) Although *faith* can refer to a body of belief (e.g., Jude 3) or intellectual conviction (e.g., 1 Cor 2:5), its primary meaning is trust or trustworthiness, that is, an attitude and relationship rather than an idea. Enacted faith is faithfulness.

God's faithfulness to humanity permeates Scripture, as a quick search will amply demonstrate. It is declared, for example, in Deuteronomy 7:9-10: "Know therefore that the LORD your God is God, the faithful God who maintains covenant loyalty with those who love him and keep his commandments, to a thousand generations." However, this does not mean unconditional approval, for the promise continues: ". . . and who repays in their own person those who reject him. He does not delay but repays in their own person those who reject him." Similarly, when God passed before Moses on Mount Sinai, God self-identified as

> The LORD, the LORD, a God merciful and gracious, slow to anger, and abounding in steadfast love and faithfulness, keeping steadfast love for the thousandth generation, forgiving iniquity and transgression and sin, yet by no means clearing the guilty, but visiting the iniquity of the parents upon the children and the children's children, to the third and the fourth generation. (Exod 34:6-7)

Waiting for the Apocalypse

Paul writes that Christians are *wait[ing] for the revealing* [Gk. *apocalypsis*] *of our Lord Jesus Christ* (v. 7). The idea of apocalypse has excited Christians through the centuries, often with enthusiastic and sometimes violent implications. It has further been applied to a genre in secular and religious literature, art, and film that explores the idea of the end of the world, or in the postapocalyptic genre, what happens after the end of the world.

The last book of the Bible is named Revelation (singular, not plural as often incorrectly stated), and sometimes is called "The Apocalypse" because it begins, "The revelation [*apocalypsis*] of Jesus Christ." Its images of war, pestilence, chaos, and destruction, interspersed with scenes of peaceful worship, have dominated popular understanding of the "end times," or eschaton, in Christian-influenced cultures.

Many of Paul's letters also speak of things being revealed. In his letter to the Romans, Paul writes about the wrath of God being revealed in judgment (e.g., 1:17-18; 2:2) and about the revelation of glory (8:18; cf. 1 Pet 4:13) and the revealing of the children of God (Rom 8:19). In his letter to the Galatians, he reports that the gospel was revealed to him (1:11-12), (the truth about) Jesus was revealed (1:16; cf. Eph 3:3), and directions concerning his trip to Jerusalem were revealed (2:2). He writes about ecstatic revelations in 2 Corinthians 12:1, 7. To the Thessalonians he writes about a "lawless one" who will be revealed (2 Thess 2:3-8) and about the repayment, both for good and for evil, that God will bring about "when the Lord Jesus is revealed from heaven with his mighty angels in flaming fire" (2 Thess 1:6-8).

In 1 Corinthians, *revelation* has several dimensions. There is revelation or prophetic word that is identified along with other spiritual manifestations (14:6, 26, 30; cf. Eph 1:17). There is a revelation of building materials as they are tested by fire on *the Day* (1 Cor 3:13). And there is *the revealing of our Lord Jesus Christ* in 1:7.

Throughout the New Testament, there is a dimension of judgment implied by *apocalypsis*, but that is only part of the story. The proper emphasis in 1 Corinthians 1:7 is on *wait[ing]*, not on *revealing*. This places the reader's focus on what is yet to come, on what is still hidden, and is Paul's corrective to those who think that God has already shown everything that is to come.

THE TEXT IN THE LIFE OF THE CHURCH

Grace

The grace of God and the grace of Paul are both evident in this thanksgiving statement. In his greeting, Paul wishes the Corinthians *grace . . . and peace from God our Father and the Lord Jesus Christ* (v. 3).

Immediately he says that grace has already been given, and he expresses thanks *because of the grace of God that has been given you in Christ Jesus* (v. 4). In the rest of the letter, he will chide and criticize them, trying to correct their behavior, their attitudes, and their understanding of spiritual things. Yet he approaches them with respect, affection, and gratitude. His example is a model for all who experience conflict with their fellow believers. The attitude Paul models toward those who oppose him is first of all gratitude for them and their gifts, along with recognition that God has blessed them.

In his book *Life Together*, Dietrich Bonhoeffer described the proper attitude that especially pastors and other church leaders should have toward their congregations:

> If we do not give thanks daily for the Christian fellowship in which we have been placed, even where there is no great experience, no discoverable riches, but much weakness, small faith, and difficulty; if so paltry and petty, so far from what we expected, then we hinder God from letting our fellowship grow accordingly to the measure and riches which are there for us all in Jesus Christ.
>
> This applies in a special way to the complaints often heard from pastors and zealous members about their congregations. [Pastors] should not complain about [their] congregation, certainly never to other people, but also not to God. A congregation has not been entrusted to [the pastor] in order that [she/]he should become its accuser before God and [people]. . . . What may appear weak and trifling to us may be great and glorious to God. . . . The more thankfully we daily receive what is given to us, the more surely and steadily will fellowship increase and grow from day to day as God pleases. (Bonhoeffer: 29–30; quoted in Hays 1997: 20–21)

In a book on responding to difficult behavior by church members provocatively titled *Never Call Them Jerks*, Arthur Paul Boers provides sound understanding and practical advice for practicing grace, especially for pastors and other church leaders. An essential part of the strategy he recommends is to care for oneself, and especially to nourish one's relationship with God. He quotes some advice given by his mentor, Henri Nouwen: "God is the one who loves you deeply. And that's what you have to trust. And keep trusting, keep trusting, keep trusting" (Boers: 132). In other words, to be gracious toward others, one must experience and accept God's grace.

Paul's intention throughout this letter is to instill a gracious respect for each other in members of the Corinthian congregations. He demonstrates this in his own attitude and calls on them to imitate this and other actions and attitudes that he models (4:1; 11:1).

Preaching and Worship

Churches that use the Revised Common Lectionary will hear this passage twice in the three-year cycle. On the first Sunday of Advent in Year B, 1 Corinthians 1:3-9 is assigned to be read together with Isaiah 64:1-9; Psalm 80:1-7, 17-19; and Mark 13:24-37. In that context, the eschatological promise of 1 Corinthians 1:8 is illuminated by the eschatological warning in Mark, and the longing of Isaiah and the psalm are fulfilled in the grace given by *our Lord Jesus Christ*, who is named six times in these seven verses. When one reads this letter's thanksgiving section in the context of the first and second advent hopes, the magnitude of the grace and gifts that Paul recognizes in the Corinthians (and that we might recognize in our faith communities) comes into focus.

The whole of 1 Corinthians 1:1-9 is assigned in the lectionary to be read on the second Sunday after Epiphany in Year A, together with Isaiah 49:1-7; Psalm 40:1-11; and John 1:29-42. Each of these texts recognizes the blessing of God's gifts while also stressing humility in recognizing that they are gifts from God, not of our own doing. Each of the texts, and Isaiah in particular, emphasizes the responsibility that accompanies God's gifts. "[The LORD] says, 'It is too light a thing that you should be my servant [only] to raise up the tribes of Jacob and to restore the survivors of Israel; I will give you as a light to the nations, that my salvation may reach to the end of the earth'" (Isa 49:6).

1 Corinthians 1:10–15:58

The Body of the Letter

1 Corinthians 1:10–15:58

OVERVIEW

As already noted, letters in the first century characteristically began with a greeting and proceeded to a section of thanksgiving. All this was preliminary to the main part of the letter, the body, which conveyed the message of the letter. The letter body itself contained three distinct segments: an opening, middle, and a closing. Paul's letters essentially follow this pattern, with some variations that fall within the standard (White: 153-63). In 1 Corinthians, the opening consists of 1:10-17, and the closing consists of one verse only, 15:58. What lies between these is the middle.

This extended middle is not all one argument. It addresses a series of topics arranged with intentionality and logic that was clear to the writer and perhaps to the first readers, but which we must discover through study of the parts. Our understanding of the relationship between the parts determines our understanding of the purpose of this letter and therefore the meaning that we interpret for both the parts and the whole.

Margaret Mitchell has determined that the body of this letter consists of a deliberative argument (see "Paul's Letter" in the introduction). Mitchell's thesis is that the entire letter of 1 Corinthians is an elaboration of the thesis statement found in 1:10—in other words, that the concern for unity in the faith community is primary and that the specific cases discussed are examples or "proofs" of that one point.

How did Paul decide what issues to address in this letter? We know that the Corinthians themselves set much of the agenda and that information came to Paul from at least three sources. The Corinthian Christian assembly had sent Paul a letter that contained the *matters about which you wrote* (7:1) *[What the Corinthians Wrote, p. 372]*. The official delegation from Corinth that brought the letter to Paul was his second source of information (16:17) *[What the Delegation Reported, p. 374]*. Furthermore, *Chloe's people* brought Paul information about the divisions within the assembly, the unsavory reports of immorality, and the infighting (1:11) *[What Chloe's People Said, p. 371]*.

In the exegesis of specific passages below, we will pay attention to Paul's source or sources of information and how they shaped his response. We will observe that a coherent theme runs through the whole of the letter body: the theme of unity and reconciliation, which is introduced in the thesis statement, 1:10. We will also observe that the issues dealt with have their own integrity as divisive issues and that Paul addresses each with the intention of building up the life of the Christian community.

OUTLINE
The Purpose of the Letter, 1:10
Divisions between Believers, 1:11-17
Fundamental Convictions and Values, 1:18–4:21
Issues Reported from Corinth, 5:1–15:58

1 Corinthians 1:10
The Purpose of the Letter

PREVIEW

This letter has one overarching purpose: to persuade the Christians in Corinth to come together in faith and action and purpose, united by their spiritual connection *in Christ* (1:2, 4 et al.). Paul pleads, exhorts, appeals, urges, and implores them to do so.

The body of the letter begins with a statement that sets out its intention. The rhetorical name for this statement is the thesis statement. In this case, it is not an idea to be argued and defended but rather an outcome that Paul seeks. Some scholars believe that 1:10 is a thesis statement for the first four chapters only, but Margaret Mitchell (198–200) has argued persuasively that it serves as a thesis statement for the entire letter. She shows that it is characteristic of deliberative argument that the thesis statement should lay out a desirable course of action, which in this case is a call for stability and unity among the believers. The thesis statement uses politically loaded terms and, characteristic of Paul's theological anchor, appeals to *our Lord Jesus Christ* as the basis for that course of action. This commentary will work from Mitchell's premise, which will shape our approach to each section of the letter.

EXPLANATORY NOTES

To introduce his argument, Paul writes, *I appeal to you*. The force of his appeal does not carry the weight of a command. As we shall see shortly, some of the Corinthians questioned Paul's authority, so his appeal is grounded not in his apostolic authority but in his convictions about Christ and in the family relationship that Christians have with each other.

The family metaphor is introduced by naming the recipients *brothers and sisters*, an address that Paul uses twenty-one times in this letter. The Greek word *adelphoi* is used for both "brothers" and "siblings," an ambiguity that is also characteristic of earlier English uses of masculine nouns and pronouns. In contemporary English usage, however, the NRSV and now also the NIV are correct in translating it as *brothers and sisters* here and at most places (occasionally substituting *friends* or *my beloved*), because Paul clearly meant to address both male and female members of the assembly. Gordon Fee (53n21), especially arguing from Paul's use of *adelphoi* in Philippians 4:1-3 to address two women, says that "it is therefore not pedantic, but culturally sound and biblically sensitive, for the NIV and other contemporary English versions to render this vocative 'brothers and sisters.'" Thiselton (2000: 114) similarly writes, "It would be more misleading to translate [*adelphoi*] as *brothers* (NJB, NIV [NIV 2011 has *brothers and sisters*]) than as *brothers and sisters* (NRSV, Collins, and Fee)."

The appeal *by* (NRSV) or *in* (NIV) *the name of our Lord Jesus Christ* carries forward the strong Christological focus of the thanksgiving, as noted above. This is not a common formula in Paul's writing (cf. 2 Thess 3:6), but in 1:2 he has defined Christians as *those who in every place call on the name of our Lord Jesus Christ*. In appealing to them now on the basis of that name, he draws attention to the confession they hold in common. This expression is not to be taken as a formula of power or to add weight to Paul's authority over his addressees (contrast 5:4), but as an appeal to what they hold in common as *brothers and sisters*. Now he sets the context not only of the family-like relationship between members, but as all together before the one whom they have confessed to be the Messiah (= Christ) and *our Lord*.

Paul's desire and intention in writing is stated in three ways, the first and last of which are stated positively; the middle one negatively. A literal translation underscores the point: "I urge that you all say the *same* thing, that is, that there be no divisions among you, rather, that you be knit together in the *same* mind and the *same* opinion" (Fee: 54, emphasis added).

Several of the terms used in this verse were commonly used in ancient Greek literature to promote political cohesion and peace. The first of these is *be in agreement* (NRSV), or more literally, *speak the same thing* (KJV; NKJV), which is a term "commonly used in ancient Greek literature to describe the opposite of factionalism" (M. Mitchell: 68; cf. 69-70).

In its various forms (also in 11:18; 12:25; cf. Acts 14:4; 23:7) the Greek word behind *divisions* is frequently used in Greek literature to refer to fragmented communities, often using the metaphor of a body (see 12:12-27; also Rom 12:4-5; Col 1:18; M. Mitchell: 70-74). We will explore the nature of the divisions in the Christian community in Corinth when we look at 1:11.

The third political term, translated as *united*, or somewhat more literally by Fee (54) as *knit together*, is the same word that in Mark 1:19 // Matthew 4:21 refers to the mending or restoring of nets (Fee: 55; Thiselton 2000: 115). In other places where it is used in the same sense, it is translated as follows:

	NRSV	**NIV**	**KJV**	**NASB**	**NLB**
1 Cor 1:10	united	united	joined together	made complete	united
2 Cor 13:11	put things in order	strive for full restoration	be of good comfort	be made complete	grow to maturity
Gal 6:1	restore	restore	restore	restore	help . . . back to the right path
1 Thess 3:10	restore	supply	perfect	complete	fill the gaps
Heb 13:21	make . . . complete	equip	make . . . perfect	equip	equip
1 Pet 5:10	restore	restore	make perfect	perfect (verb)	restore

The word carries connotations of restoring to a previous condition. It also suggests perfection or completion, setting things right. In some ancient medical texts, it was used for resetting dislocated bones, and "it is often used exactly to mean bringing warring factions back together again" (M. Mitchell: 73-74).

A pair of phrases qualifies *how* they should be united: *in the same mind and the same purpose*. The two phrases are synonymous and are often paired together in Greek literature, where they are used to promote concord (M. Mitchell: 76-80). The Greek word *gnōmē* is variously translated here and elsewhere (7:25, 40) as *purpose, thought, judgment,* or *opinion.* Whatever the translation, Paul's point is clear: he calls upon the Corinthians to be in agreement with each other.

It would be wrong to assume from the repeated use of *same* that Paul wanted to achieve uniformity of thought and of action. Rather, he wanted to restore relationships that had been severed through divisions. We should think of the musical term *harmony,* not *unison.* Thus it is appropriate to speak, as Mitchell does, of the "rhetoric of reconciliation." The intention of Paul in this thesis statement serves as the key to understanding the whole of this letter.

The rhetorical and pastoral purpose of this letter is to bring about reconciliation between members of the Christian community in Corinth. Specific examples of division that need to be healed make up the bulk of the letter; but first Paul provides a further "statement of facts" to ensure that the readers of his letter know what he knows about their situation.

1 Corinthians 1:11-17

Divisions between Believers

PREVIEW

"I know what you are doing!" After his forceful statement of his goal for writing this letter and before entering into his arguments, Paul explains his concern by telling his readers what he knows about the factions among them. In deliberative rhetoric, this is called a "statement of facts" (M. Mitchell: 200–202). It is necessary for him to tell them what he knows about their situation and their behavior. He also uses this rhetorical moment to set the agenda for the rest of the letter.

Paul names his sources here and names what he has heard. Using a series of rhetorical questions (what would we do without rhetorical questions?), he shows the foolishness of the basis of their arguments. Finally, in contrast with the criteria on which they were divided, he redefines what is most important for the community's identity: the gospel of Jesus Christ and the power of the cross.

OUTLINE

The Source of Paul's Information, 1:11
Divisions in the Corinthian Assembly, 1:12
Redefining the Center, 1:13-17

EXPLANATORY NOTES

The Source of Paul's Information 1:11

The Corinthians had sent Paul a letter (7:1) in which they named several questions on which they invited Paul to comment *[What the Corinthians Wrote, p. 372]*. They expected the three men entrusted to carry the letter—Stephanas, Fortunatus, and Achaicus (16:17)—to elaborate on the questions and to fill Paul in on other matters happening in the assembly *[What the Delegation Reported, p. 374]*.

Paul intends to answer their questions, but he is going to address them in light of some other information he has about the community—unflattering reports that they might have preferred Paul not hear. Yet he has heard, and that knowledge shapes his response both to what they have asked and to what they have not asked. Therefore it is necessary for him to name his sources and to name the information he has received *[What Chloe's People Said, p. 371]*.

It has been reported to me by Chloe's people, he writes. The Corinthians must have known who Chloe's people were, for Paul feels no need to say more about them. However, this lack of information has stimulated a great deal of speculation.

Chloe was obviously known to the Corinthians and to Paul. She had *people*, presumably slaves or agents (NIV says *household*) who were able to travel between Corinth and Ephesus. The text does not say, as many suppose, that they made the journey frequently; we only know that they reported on this one occasion to Paul. Nevertheless, that Chloe had *people* who traveled suggests that she possessed some wealth and influence.

Some commentators (e.g., Fee [55] and sources he quotes there; followed by Thiselton [2000: 121]) speculate that Chloe's primary location was in Ephesus. But her people were, or perhaps she herself was, integrated enough into the Corinthian assembly to be privy to considerable gossip about what was going on, including what derogatory things people were saying about whom: who was sleeping with whom, who was taking whom to court, that some were consorting with prostitutes, and who was behaving badly in worship, and specifically at the Lord's Supper, an event not open to outside "observers." The depth and nature of their information suggests that they were part of the assembly in Corinth, but their willingness to "give Paul an earful," as Fee (55) puts it, suggests that they were outside the circle of power in the community and probably felt more loyalty to Paul than to other leaders.

It is interesting to speculate whether Chloe, as a woman, was excluded from power (see 14:34-36) or had a different perspective on happenings in the community than what the official delegation carried. Nevertheless, for Paul's reliance on a report from her people to carry the weight of his argument, it was necessary for him to believe that she and her people were credible sources of information and would be recognized as such by the assembly. By naming his independent source, Paul served notice to the congregations that they could not restrict or control the information he received and that he would address the shameful behaviors the members did not want him to know about as well as the more "respectable" issues that they had identified.

Divisions in the Corinthian Assembly 1:12

The specifics of what Paul has heard from Chloe's people will be dealt with in due course. To state the issue most baldly, Paul puts the fundamental issue before them: *There are quarrels among you* (1:11). As we have seen above in the discussion on the thesis statement, 1:10, this in Paul's assessment is the basic and most important issue, the source of all the other matters that he will address and the key behavior that he wants them to change.

The quarrels were plural, as were the *divisions* mentioned in verse 10. Indeed, each of the issues that Paul addresses in this letter (with the possible exception of resurrection, discussed in ch. 15) is a matter of quarreling in Corinth. So we know it was not one matter that divided the community and that there were more than two factions.

Scholars are as divided as the Corinthians were over the nature of the factions in Corinth, and "much of how one views the whole letter is determined by one's approach to this issue" (Fee: 47n23). At the same time, it is also the case that "more often than not the answer which scholars have given to this question has been determined more by what each scholar has brought to 1 Corinthians than by what he has learned from the letter" (Hurd: 107). Thiselton (2000: 123-33) reviews at length the various options that have been put forward.

The focus of this debate is the series of "slogans" found in 1:12, which appears to define as many as four separate factions, or "parties," around which the members of the Corinthian assembly rallied. They are identified as the Paul party, the Apollos party, the Cephas party, and the Christ party. A few commentators have accepted that there were four parties in Corinth (e.g., Conzelmann [34]), but most have suggested that two of the slogans apply to pseudo-parties and have identified one of the slogans as representing the "real" opposition against which Paul (in support of his own party) is writing. All views contradicted by Paul in the letter are therefore attributed to that designated opponent. But which of the slogans represents the real opposition?

Was there a party that "belonged" to Paul? Undoubtedly there were some in the Corinthian assembly whose first loyalty was to him, but nowhere in the letter is there evidence that they were joined together into a "party." Paul does not appeal to nor defend such a party over against other factions. Clearly Paul himself is drawn into the conflicts, and his ministry is one of the issues about which people are disagreeing (e.g., ch. 2; ch. 9, esp. v. 3). Occasionally he defends his authority (e.g., 4:15), but he does not attempt to play his loyalists against others.

Of the four slogans quoted in 1:12, the one with the best case for recognition as a potential "party" is that associated with Apollos. Both Acts and 1 Corinthians report that Apollos had been in Corinth and that he had provided leadership and teaching in the assembly there. Luke describes him as "a Jew named Apollos, a native of Alexandria. He was an eloquent man, well-versed in the scriptures. He had been instructed in the Way of the Lord; and he spoke with burning enthusiasm and taught accurately the things concerning Jesus" (Acts 18:24b-25b). Luke also reports that when Apollos arrived in Ephesus, before he went to Corinth, "he knew only the baptism of John" (v. 25c). That theological gap, however, was corrected by Priscilla and Aquila (v. 26). Shortly thereafter he went on to Corinth—at the same time that Paul arrived in Ephesus (19:1). Some commentators have extrapolated from this information about Apollos that any references to skilled speech must allude to Apollos or that disagreements over baptism may represent a dispute between Apollos and Paul—but this is only speculation.

In 1 Corinthians, Paul mentions Apollos's name seven times, of which six are in the first four chapters (1:12; 3:4, 5, 6, 22; 4:6), where Paul argues that it is inappropriate for people to be aligned with either his own leadership or Apollos's. In the seventh reference, 16:12, Paul says he has urged Apollos to visit Corinth again, but Apollos is determined not to do so.

Paul confronts those who claim allegiance to Apollos in the same way that he confronts those who claim allegiance to himself. He claims a temporal priority for his ministry in 3:6 (see also 3:10 and 4:15), but he dismisses the significance of that by giving credit to God, not to either himself or Apollos (3:7). Paul does not even hint that he and Apollos have theological disagreements between them, nor does he identify what theological disagreements he might have with those who claim allegiance to Apollos.

As for a Cephas party, there is no evidence in 1 Corinthians for this, though Cephas is named in 1:12; 3:22-23, together with Paul, Apollos, and Christ; in 9:5 with *other apostles and the brothers of the Lord*; and similarly in 15:5. Although some have argued otherwise (see Ehrman), it is generally accepted that the Cephas named here is the disciple of Jesus and leader of the Christian movement otherwise known as Peter (John 1:42; cf. Gal 1:18; 2:9, 11, 14). Some commentators (e.g., Barrett; cf. Thiselton [2000: 128-29]) have suggested that any hint of "Judaizing" tendencies is evidence of a Cephas party in Corinth, but this seems to be a case of reading the situation that Paul describes in Galatians 2:11-14 into the Corinthian situation. There is no clear evidence in Acts or in Paul's letters to suggest that Cephas had visited Corinth, though Paul's several references to him suggest that he was known to the Christian community there (Barrett).

Finally, there is the slogan that seems to refer to a "Christ party." Such a faction is not mentioned again. Although several scholars (e.g., Snyder [1992: 36, 43]; cf. Thiselton [2000: 129-33]) have identified this party with various "spiritualist" or "gnostic" attitudes that Paul addresses in the letter, there is no evidence that there was such a party in Corinth. Indeed, Paul asserts that all belong to Christ, regardless of the human leader about which they might (inappropriately) boast (3:21-23).

The rest of this letter does not identify separate parties, and if it were not for the slogans listed in 1:12, we would not project that there were such. "The attempt to identify the parties with the views and practices condemned elsewhere in the epistle, as if the parties represented different positions in a dogmatic controversy, has collapsed under its own weight" (Welborn: 88). The existence of four competing "parties" in Corinth is not borne out in the rest of this letter, and division between those loyal to Paul and those loyal to Apollos was unfounded in Paul's mind (though perhaps still claimed by the members of the assembly in Corinth).

In Galatians and other letters, Paul takes on theological opponents in polemic arguments, but in 1 Corinthians he uses deliberative rhetoric—not to defeat opponents who think differently from him, but to persuade the readers to act differently from how they have been acting. In short, Paul was critical of the Corinthians because they were quarrelsome, not because they disagreed with him.

Redefining the Center 1:13-17

It is startling to read that some of the Corinthian Christians claimed they belong to Christ, implying that the others did not. The claim was apparently startling to Paul as well, for he responds to it with an even more startling question: *Has Christ been divided?* (1:13). The answer must surely be both yes and no: yes, the Corinthians have torn the body of Christ (12:12-27) into fragments; but no, that cannot be so, since Christ is indivisible! In the absurdity of the question, he dismisses the claim.

To press the point home, he adds two further rhetorical questions, which are focused on himself but are equally applicable to other leaders. *Surely Paul was not crucified for you, was he? Or were you baptized in the name of Paul?* (trans. by Thiselton [2000: 109, 137]). The Greek grammatical construction demands a negative answer, as this translation suggests.

Baptism *in the name of* (or *into the name of*) a specific leader was surely not a claim that even the quarreling Christians at Corinth should have made. But being baptized *by* a particular person may well have been claimed as a personal advantage, and that may have come to be expressed as *in the name of* Paul, Apollos, or another leader. As a personal status symbol or mark of allegiance, at least some of the Corinthians apparently claimed that the one who had baptized them was superior to the one who had baptized someone else.

To further undermine the presumed grounds of their divisions, Paul adds that he is glad he had not baptized many of them. The matter, he suggests, is of so little significance that he cannot really remember all whom he had baptized in Corinth. He recalls Crispus and Gaius and as an afterthought adds Stephanas's household and perhaps others. We have noted above that all three whom Paul names are heads of households that hosted assemblies. Crispus was the former patron of the synagogue (Acts 18:8), Gaius hosted the whole assembly in his house (Rom 16:23), and members of Stephanas's household were the first converts in Corinth (1 Cor 16:15). It may be that they in turn baptized others who joined their number, and thus members of three of the key household assemblies could have claimed the "succession" of baptism by Paul. Although he could have claimed these as a significant record of accomplishment and influence, Paul dismisses their significance.

More important than the work of baptizing converts, Paul declares, is the work of preaching the gospel. Was he concerned with correcting an inadequate understanding of baptism? Some scholars have seen evidence of that in this discussion and in the brief reference to baptism on behalf of the dead (15:29). But without stronger evidence, questions about the meaning of baptism are being read into the text where they are not present. While it is clear that (some of) the Corinthians had distorted values related to baptism, it was not their false *theology* that Paul condemned, but that they were focusing on the mechanics of baptism (the status of the person who had baptized each of them), rather than the reality to which their baptism pointed, which is their acceptance of the gospel of the cross of Jesus Christ (cf. Rom 6:3-4).

With the qualification that he preached *not with eloquent wisdom, so that the cross of Christ might not be emptied of its power* (1:17b), Paul introduces the first of his arguments with the Corinthian assembly: the cross of Christ, not human wisdom—however brilliantly articulated—is the central value of Christian faith.

THE TEXT IN BIBLICAL CONTEXT

Rivalries

Competition between leaders—or between the followers of leaders—of God's people is reported throughout the Scriptures. Rivalry between siblings is the theme of one of the earliest stories in the biblical canon, the rivalry between Cain and Abel (Gen 4:1-8). This is a paradigm that shows up in families, including extended families and clan systems as well as nuclear families. There are stories about rivalry between Joseph and his brothers (Gen 37), between Jacob and Esau (Gen 25:27-34; 27; 32–33), and between Moses, Aaron, and Miriam (Num 12), among many examples. When the people of Israel were organized into a kingdom, they rallied around competing kings—first Saul versus David, then David versus Absalom, and so on.

In the New Testament, rivalry between factions defined by loyalty to particular leaders continues. In John's gospel the competitive tension between Peter and the Beloved Disciple (e.g., John 13:23-24; 20:2-9; 21:7, 20-22) reflects the tension between the churches that claimed allegiance to one or the other. A conflict between Paul and his longtime associate Barnabas led them to part company (Acts 15:36-41). Peter and Paul had conflicts over the acceptance of Gentiles as full members of the Christian movement (Gal 2:11-14), apparently even after the matter had been settled in principle at a conference called specifically to deal with it (Acts 15). The apparent conflict between various "parties" in Corinth must be seen in the context of such rivalries.

The Ministry of Reconciliation

In 2 Corinthians, Paul uses the language of reconciliation to describe both what God has done and what God has entrusted to those who follow Christ: "God . . . reconciled us to himself through Christ, and has given us the ministry of reconciliation; that is, in Christ God was reconciling the world to himself, not counting their trespasses against them, and entrusting the message of reconciliation to us" (2 Cor 5:18-19). The language of reconciliation is consistent with Jesus' words about the importance of forgiveness (Matt 18:15-35) and with John's insistence that love for one another is the dominant characteristic of Christian community (John 13:34-35; 1 John 3:10-18).

Being reconciled with God and with fellow believers and promoting reconciliation of people with God and with each other are the essence of God's people.

Reconciliation is the focus of 1 Corinthians—note the title of Margaret Mitchell's study: *Paul and the Rhetoric of Reconciliation*. Indeed, all the Pauline letters have such a focus. Ephesians promotes "making every effort to maintain the unity of the Spirit in the bond of peace" and bases that on the theological affirmation that "there is one body and one Spirit, just as you were called to the one hope of your calling, one Lord, one faith, one baptism, one God and Father of all, who is above all and through all and in all" (Eph 4:3-6; see Yoder Neufeld: 172–75). Similar instructions are found in Romans 14:19. In Philippians 2:2, Paul twice urges his readers to be of the same mind, or of one mind, and follows that with the oft-quoted hymn on "the mind" of "Christ" (vv. 5-11). (Likewise, the pastoral epistles to Timothy and Titus urge the leaders to avoid conflict, competition, and disputes—e.g., *1 Tim 6:3-5*).

THE TEXT IN THE LIFE OF THE CHURCH

Factionalism

Factionalism may be one of the universal characteristics of the Christian church. Perhaps it is heartening to recognize that this was the case from the very beginning.

Major schisms have resulted in the division between the Oriental Orthodox, Eastern Orthodox, Roman Catholic, and Protestant churches. These have been further subdivided into thousands of factions, and their numbers continue to multiply. The conflicts have often been taken to the point where parties excommunicated each other, and sometimes they have been taken to the extreme of killing the opponents individually or en masse.

The Protestant Reformation of the sixteenth century resulted in many of those divisions, and the Anabaptist movement contributed to that. Because of their convictions about the voluntary nature of the church, Anabaptists opposed a state-determined membership and a state-enforced orthodoxy. They also defended individual study of Scripture (made possible by the recently invented printing press and new translations of the Bible into the common languages of the people). This opened the possibility and reality of many competing understandings and loyalties. Enthusiasm for disaffiliating and reaffiliating between groups of believers has continued unabated, especially in the Christian stream known as the believers church. Were Anabaptists and their descendants right in valuing their understanding of right theology above unity? One of the issues that set Anabaptists apart from other churches was the matter of baptism—hence the name, Anabaptists, or rebaptizers, used against them by their detractors. The subsequent history of churches that baptize only adults on their confession of faith (i.e., believers churches) has been further fragmented by disagreements over the mode and forms of baptism. This is particularly ironic in light of Paul's downplaying of the importance of baptism in the face of Corinthian disputes.

From the major schisms to divisions within congregations, the rationale is usually framed as a vital theological issue to which the "right" answer divides true believers from heretics. Behind the stated theological differences, however, are always personality conflicts and power struggles. Status differences, economic competition, and political motivation are hidden behind pious language about restoring the purity of the church, correcting unethical behavior, or correcting false teaching. Those who foster division or who glorify divisions of the past should test their motives carefully. Paul correctly challenged factions in Corinth because of their divisive loyalties to various leaders. Only later did he address the theological and ethical differences among them.

Of course, factionalism is not unique to Christianity. It is found in other faiths, political parties, businesses, families, and sports. It is part of the human condition. The Christian faith is no exception. In every case, there are strong reasons to resist and reduce factionalism—strength, success, and happiness, for example—but the incentive for overcoming factions in the body of Christ is heightened by theological rationale. God's intention for the church, Jesus' prayer for unity (John 17), and Paul's argument with the Corinthians all add to the urgency for Christians to resist the tendency toward factionalism.

Reconciliation

Despite the church's massive failure to obey the Scriptures on reconciliation, there are commendable examples of faithfulness. Christian colleges and seminaries have developed schools of peacemaking as places to research and teach skills of peacemaking in international and local spheres. Mediation services, family counseling services, and other agencies have been started by Christians to promote reconciliation in families, communities, and workplaces. Christian Peacemaker Teams and other organizations have stepped into some of the most conflicted situations in the world. Many publications have explored theoretical and practical dimensions of reconciliation. The resources are available.

It is regrettable that some Christians deny the importance of the work of reconciliation, preferring to focus on right theology rather than the ministry of reconciliation that the Scriptures promote.

1 Corinthians 1:18–4:21

Fundamental Convictions and Values

PREVIEW

The first seventeen verses of this letter are introductory. From 1:18 through the end of chapter 15, Paul tries to move the Corinthians from divisiveness to unity. In doing so he addresses a series of ethical questions, theological errors, pastoral problems, and administrative issues. In 1:18–4:21 he prepares to take on specific issues and give advice for dealing with them. He starts by censuring their improper behavior and thus preparing them to accept his advice, a rhetorical strategy called, in both Greek and English, a "diatribe" (Malherbe: 129-34).

As he launches his case, Paul identifies several fundamental convictions and values that he holds, contrasting them with the values underlying the errors that he wants to correct. In this section Paul upholds certain beliefs:

- The crucified Christ is the heart of the Christian gospel.
- The value that society places on wisdom, power, and prestige is turned on its head in God's realm; the values of shame and honor are reversed.
- Spiritual matters must be spiritually discerned, not measured by nonspiritual criteria.

- The church is called into being by God, and it belongs to God, not to human leaders (servants) nor to the members.
- God's evaluation supersedes human evaluation, both negative and positive, so it is God's approval that should be sought.
- Paul has authority and credibility gained by the integrity of his preaching and life, his role as the spiritual father of the Corinthian congregations, and the deprivation and persecution he has experienced for the sake of the gospel.

These beliefs are not absolutely separated from one another in Paul's discussion of them, and it is difficult to separate them from each other into neat divisions. Bible translations, commentaries, and other studies are generally in agreement that 1:18–4:21 is a unit distinct from what precedes and what follows. They differ widely, however, in the internal divisions they assign to this unit and the function of this section within the whole letter (M. Mitchell: 207). In the discussion that follows, the unit divisions will sometimes overlap, just as Paul's arguments spill into one another, not ending one comment neatly before launching into the next point. Some of the transitions simultaneously conclude one argument and introduce the next, and the themes that repeat throughout give this part of the letter its cohesion and strength.

OUTLINE
The Gospel of the Crucified Christ, 1:18-25
Values of Shame and Honor in God's Realm, 1:26-31
Spiritual Discernment, 2:1–3:4
It's God's Congregation, 3:5-23
Paul's Credibility, 4:1-21

The Gospel of the Crucified Christ

1 Corinthians 1:18-25

EXPLANATORY NOTES
Central to Paul's understanding of the gospel is the crucifixion and resurrection of Christ. He will write at length about the resurrection in chapter 15, but here, at the beginning of this letter, he concentrates on the crucifixion.

In the transitional verses, Paul has identified the purpose for which Christ had sent him to Corinth and all the other places he visited: *For Christ [sent me* (Paul identified himself in 1:1 as *an apostle of Christ Jesus)] . . . to proclaim the gospel, and not with eloquent wisdom, so that the cross of Christ might not be emptied of its power. For the message about the cross is foolishness to those who are perishing, but to us who are being saved it is the power of God* (1:17-18). In 1:23 he names as the summary of his preaching that *we proclaim Christ crucified.* Again in 2:1 he declares, *I decided to know nothing among you except Jesus Christ, and him crucified.* So the *gospel* is summarized in *the cross* (1:17).

Because the written correspondence between Paul and the Corinthians that we have available picks up in the middle of an ongoing conversation (see "Paul and the Corinthians" in the introduction), we do not have an account of what Paul preached when he first arrived in Corinth.

In Acts, Luke reports on two of Paul's sermons, neither of which takes place in Corinth. The first is delivered in a synagogue in Pisidian Antioch. Luke reports that Paul argued here that Jesus is the Messiah who fulfilled some prophetic expectations and by whose death and resurrection forgiveness of sins is available (Acts 13:16-41). The second sermon is delivered to a Gentile audience in Athens. Luke reports that Paul spoke of God as the fulfillment of the Greek religious longing and Jesus as the one appointed to judge the world, as evidenced by his own resurrection (Acts 17:22-31). In addition, Luke provides several summaries, in Paul's voice, of the message he preached. He reminded the elders of the assembly in Ephesus that "I testified to both Jews and Greeks about repentance toward God and faith toward our Lord Jesus" (Acts 20:21). In testifying before King Agrippa about his experience on the road to Damascus, Paul reported:

> [I] declared first to those in Damascus, then in Jerusalem and throughout the countryside of Judea, and also to the Gentiles, that they should repent and turn to God and do deeds consistent with repentance, . . . saying nothing but what the prophets and Moses said would take place: that the Messiah must suffer, and that, by being the first to rise from the dead, he would proclaim light both to our people and to the Gentiles. (Acts 26:20-23)

These secondhand reports (Luke presents himself as a witness only to the sermon in Athens) do not tell us what Paul "typically" preached or what specifically he preached and taught over eighteen months in Corinth.

The brief summaries in 1 Corinthians 1:17-18, 23; and 2:1-2 are the closest we can come to knowing what he had preached when present with them. Beyond this, we can only extrapolate hints from what Paul wrote (in 1 Corinthians) in response to what the Corinthians said or asked . . . in response to what Paul had written . . . in response to issues that had arisen after he left Corinth (see "Paul and the Corinthians" in the introduction) *[What the Corinthians Wrote, p. 372]*. So when this letter was written, we are already several stages removed from Paul's initial preaching.

What was the message that Paul preached? He says it was about *the cross* (1:17, 18). Later he says his proclamation was *a crucified Christ* (following Thiselton 2000: 170–71), *a stumbling block to Jews and foolishness to Gentiles, but to those who are the called, both Jews and Greeks, Christ the power of God and the wisdom of God* (1:23b-24). The Greek word translated as *stumbling block* is *skandalon*. Though it is elsewhere appropriately translated as "stumbling block," and sometimes as a trap or temptation to sin, the meaning here is more accurately caught by "scandal" or "that which gives offense or causes revulsion, that which arouses opposition, an object of anger or disapproval, a stain, fault, etc." (BDAG; cf. Gal 5:11). To Jews, the possibility that Messiah would be defeated and crucified was inconceivable (Segal: 123).

In this passage we see the first of Paul's quotations from the Old Testament *[Scripture Quotations and Echoes, p. 367]*. Verse 19 is a quotation from Isaiah 29:14. To understand the full weight of its relevance for Paul's argument, we must read the larger context of the full quotation and the verse that precedes it in Isaiah:

> The Lord said: Because these people draw near with their mouths and honor me with their lips, while their hearts are far from me, and their worship of me is a human commandment learned by rote; so I will again do amazing things with this people, shocking and amazing. The wisdom of their wise shall perish, and the discernment of the discerning shall be hidden. (Isa 29:13-14)

As we continue through 1 Corinthians, we will repeatedly see that matters of speech ("mouths" and "lips" in Isaiah) are prominent, whether words of rhetoric or words spoken in tongues. Right worship is also an issue in 1 Corinthians (chs. 11–14), especially in the words used (speaking in tongues, prophesying, and praying) and the attitude of the heart in worship (ch. 13). At this early point in his argument, Paul situates the Corinthian values with those that God opposed in Judah at the time when Isaiah wrote. The words and wisdom of which the people of both Judah and Corinth were so proud will be destroyed, and their cherished discernment will disappear (cf. 1 Cor 13:8).

With good reason, Jews demanded signs, and with good reason, Greeks desired wisdom as evidence of a messianic claim (v. 22). What Paul offered was an affront to both *[Shame and Honor, p. 368]*. He offered a narrative of Christ's incarnation, ministry, teaching, and death by an especially cruel execution applied to the most notorious of criminals. *The cross* is a shorthand reference to all of this, with particular focus on the most offensive part of the story, the crucifixion of the one whom Paul proclaimed as *the power of God and the wisdom of God* (v. 24). "The gospel . . . and the proclamation of the cross . . . are shorthand instances of synecdoche *for the whole story of God's purposes which lead up to the cross and follow it*" (Thiselton 2000: 174, emphasis original).

Paul does not identify a particular understanding of how Jesus' crucifixion brings about salvation or atonement. The word *crucified* in both 1:23 and 2:2 is in the grammatical form of a perfect passive participle in Greek, which describes an action that has been completed in the past but has continuing effect in the present. It is not the historical fact of the crucifixion (followed by resurrection and ascension) that Paul has in mind, and certainly not the gory details of the cruel and painful means of his execution. Rather, what he proclaims is the continuing power of the crucifixion to bring about salvation for *those who believe* (1:21).

The cross is the content of Paul's preaching, but the stress of his statement in 1:18 is even more on the preaching than on the content (*contra* Fee: 76). The NRSV and NIV translate verse 18 similarly: *the message about/of the cross*. A better translation, as Thiselton (2000: 153–54) has demonstrated, is *the proclamation of the cross* (cf. v. 21). It is not *information about* the crucifixion of Jesus, and it is not a doctrine that explains the significance of it that Paul has in mind, but the act of proclaiming the cross. The contrast is between the proclamation of the cross in verse 18 and the clever rhetoric or sophisticated speech of eloquent wisdom in verse 17.

Commentators have often focused on the errors that Paul wanted to correct, framing their discussion with an understanding of Paul's "opponents" in Corinth. Undoubtedly there were people in Corinth who defined their beliefs and teaching over against what Paul had taught, and Paul wants to correct what he considers to be their errors. However, the sequence of the interaction is significant. It was Paul who first taught the Christian faith in Corinth (3:6, 10; 4:15). After he left the city, competing ideas were taught and infiltrated the assemblies, and confusion and quarreling ensued. When Chloe's people reported this to Paul, he wrote to recall the Christians to the perspective and understanding that he had preached and taught. Thus the primary focus of his writing is not on the errors of others but on what he wants to uphold here: the fundamental conviction that Christ's crucifixion has the power to bring about salvation (1:17-18).

Against this backdrop, Paul names some of the contradictory ideas that had infiltrated the Christian community. Some, who thought the message of the cross was foolishness, were attracted to a more logical and socially acceptable message of "wisdom"—by which they apparently meant to refer to both the content and the delivery of the message.

Wisdom receives a lot of attention in this section of the letter. Of the twenty-eight times that *wisdom* or *wise* occurs in 1 Corinthians (far more frequently than in any other NT book), all but two fall between 1:17 and 3:20. To what does the term refer? It has been argued by some that the wisdom that impressed the Corinthians was the wisdom of Gnosticism, by others that it was the wisdom of the mystery religions, and by still others that it was the wisdom of Hellenistic Judaism. Surely the argument among scholars as to what "wisdom" is runs parallel to the debate in Corinth itself! As Mitchell (211) says, "The wisdom of the world as defined by Paul in 1 Cor 1:18–4:21 refers not merely to any of these specific religious speculations, though clearly some Corinthians made exclusive claims to some kind of wisdom, but rather to the norms and values of human politics which the Corinthians are mirroring by their factionalism." Paul was not rejecting one school of thought about wisdom, or the rhetorical skill by which wisdom was being argued. He was rather reframing the debate by upholding the crucifixion of Jesus (i.e., *the power of God and the wisdom of God*, 1:24) against which all human constructions of wisdom are found wanting (esp. 1:18-25, but also through 4:21).

The contrast with wisdom would normally be foolishness or folly. *Foolish* and its variants occur ten times in 1 Corinthians, all of them in the first four chapters, with a concentration in 1:18, 20, 21, 23, 25, 27, and the rest at 2:14; 3:18, 19; 4:10. With this meaning it is otherwise found only in Matthew (six times, of which half are in the parable of the wise and foolish virgins—25:2, 3, 8), Ephesians (once, in 5:4), and two times in the pastoral epistles. *Second Timothy 2:23* cautions, "Don't have anything to do with foolish and stupid arguments, because you know they produce quarrels" (NIV). *Titus 3:9* says, "Avoid foolish controversies and genealogies and arguments and quarrels about the law, because these are unprofitable and useless" (NIV).

However, whereas the Corinthians (we may presume) were comparing wisdom and foolishness as measured by human standards of rhetoric and logic, Paul contrasted human foolishness with divine power (1 Cor 1:17, 18) and divine foolishness with human wisdom (1:20, 25). And the foolishness of God is not of the same order as the foolishness or the wisdom of humans, as if they could be placed on a continuum:

God's wisdom...God's foolishness...(gap)...human wisdom...human foolishness

No, the foolishness of God is on a different plane altogether, for God's foolishness is the proclamation of the cross (1:18 and throughout).

One further point must be noted. In 1:18, Paul contrasts *those who are perishing* (NJB, *those who are on the way to ruin*, followed by Thiselton 2000: 154) with *us who are being saved* (NJB, *us who are on the road to salvation*; Thiselton, *us who are on the way to salvation*). Notice both the passive mood and the present participle. The Corinthians were convinced that they had arrived at the goal of salvation through their wisdom (4:8 and implied throughout), but Paul reminds them that salvation is at God's initiative and that it has not yet been completed in them (see above on 1:7-8; also below on 3:5-17 and 15:2).

Paul moves his argument to comment on the Corinthian assembly itself as evidence of the values of God's realm, after which he returns to the matter of preaching, using himself as an example. His sequence has sound rhetorical rationale, but at this point we will comment on what Paul says about his preaching (2:1-5) to consolidate by example what he wrote in principle in 1:17-25.

In essence, Paul reminds the Corinthians (probably unnecessarily, since this seems to be the heart of the scorn some of them have for him: see 2 Cor 10:10) that when he was present in Corinth, he had not used *eloquence or human wisdom* (1 Cor 2:1 NIV) or *wise and persuasive words* (v. 4 NIV) in his preaching. That much they already knew. They also knew, as he here acknowledges, that he had been present among them *in weakness with great fear and trembling* (v. 3 NIV). However, whereas they had subsequently come to see that as a disadvantage and a mark of failure, probably of both ability and character, he was claiming that it was an intentional strategy (v. 2, *I decided*; NIV, *I resolved*) with an important theological rationale: *so that your faith might not rest on human wisdom* (v. 5). On the contrary, his proclamation was done *with a demonstration of the Spirit's power, so that your faith might . . . rest . . . on God's power* (vv. 4-5 NIV).

The *demonstration of the Spirit's power* may have been miracles of healing and dramatic manifestations of the Spirit, but those were the kinds of signs that Paul had said are demanded by Jews and that he denied offering (1:22). The more likely meaning is the divine power of the cross (1:17) to effect salvation (1:18b), even for the least likely candidates, of which the Corinthians themselves were prime examples (1:26-31). This is therefore the only reliable bedrock of their faith (2:5). "What he is rejecting is not preaching, not even persuasive preaching; rather, it is the real danger in all preaching—self-reliance" (Fee: 102).

In this representation of his preaching, Paul echoes the claim of 1:17: *Christ . . . sent me . . . to proclaim the gospel, and not with eloquent wisdom, so that the cross of Christ might not be emptied of its power.* This part of his argument, including 1:26-31, is glowing with that conviction.

THE TEXT IN BIBLICAL CONTEXT
Wisdom

Wisdom gets a lot of attention in 1 Corinthians—in fact more than any other New Testament "book" (see EN above). Most of the discussion is found between 1:17 and 2:13, where the *wisdom of the world* is opposed to the *wisdom of God* (e.g., 1:20-21; 2:6-7). The worldly wisdom, which was apparently highly valued by at least some of the Corinthians, was represented by rhetoric and philosophy. Paul dismissed it. However, he upheld God's wisdom.

God's wisdom could refer to the teachings represented in Jewish wisdom writings. In the Old Testament, these are especially Proverbs, Job, Ecclesiastes, and many of the psalms. In the Apocrypha, they are represented by Sirach (Ecclesiasticus), Wisdom of Solomon, and Baruch. These collections of instruction for living well draw on reason, experience, and observations of how the world works. They sometimes draw from other cultures and traditions, including Egyptian and Greek. And all is placed in the context of divine revelation: "The fear of the LORD is the beginning of wisdom" (Ps 111:10; Job 28:28; Prov 1:7; 9:10; 15:33; Sirach 1:14, 16, 18, 20, 27; 19:20; 21:11; Yoder Neufeld: 362-63).

Delight in God-inspired wisdom is sometimes expressed in poetic form, occasionally to the point that Wisdom is personified as an attractive woman (both the Hebrew and Greek words for wisdom are grammatically feminine): "I loved her and sought her from my youth; I desired to take her for my bride, and became enamored of her beauty" (Wisd of Sol 8:2). Among many others, one example is this:

> Happy are those who find wisdom,
>   and those who get understanding,
> for her income is better than silver,
>   and her revenue better than gold.
> She is more precious than jewels,
>   and nothing you desire can compare with her.
> Long life is in her right hand;
>   in her left hand are riches and honor.
> Her ways are ways of pleasantness,
>   and all her paths are peace.
> She is a tree of life to those who lay hold of her;
>   those who hold her fast are called happy.
>
> (Prov 3:13-18)

New Testament writers frequently take the attributes given to Wisdom in Jewish literature and apply them to Christ. The meditation in John 1:1-18, for example, echoes images from Wisdom of Solomon 7:26-27: "In Jewish theology the 'word' and 'wisdom' of God are synonymous terms" (Charlesworth: 121). The teachings of Jesus reported in the Gospels reflect the language and concerns of Proverbs (ibid.). Likewise, the statement that *the rock was Christ* (1 Cor 10:4) echoes the role attributed to Wisdom in providing water in the wilderness (e.g., Wisd of Sol 11:4).

The close identification of Christ with Wisdom is especially evident in 1 Cor 1:24-30, beginning with *Christ the power of God and the wisdom of God* (v. 24) and culminating with *Christ Jesus, who became for us wisdom from God* (v. 30—against Fee: 80, 91). In 1:24-30, and in fact throughout 1:10–4:21, there are many expressions that echo a poem found in Baruch 3 (Miller: 327). *The mystery of God* (2:1) that is revealed in Jesus echoes the secrets that are revealed by Wisdom (Sir 4:18; 14:21; Wisd of Sol 6:22).

Awareness of the Jewish respect and love for wisdom and the literature that expresses it is essential to understanding Paul's argument that God's wisdom is unlike human wisdom and superior to it.

THE TEXT IN THE LIFE OF THE CHURCH
The Importance of Proclaiming the Gospel
Pastors and church leaders face many demands, expectations coming from themselves, from church members, and from people outside the church. Administration of programs, pastoral care of members, spiritual direction, justice advocacy, conflict resolution, evangelism—the list goes on. One description of pastoral expectations lists "Twenty Pastoral Tasks." What is the right priority among these?

Paul had no hesitation: the most important task for him was proclamation of the gospel. One is reminded of the incident recorded in Acts where the needs of the growing church began to diversify and the demands multiplied.

> The twelve called together the whole community of the disciples and said, "It is not right that we should neglect the word of God in order to wait on tables. Therefore, friends, select from among yourselves seven men of good standing, full of the Spirit and of wisdom, whom we may appoint to this task, while we, for our part, will devote ourselves to prayer and to serving the word." (Acts 6:2-4)

The task of providing for the needs of neglected believers was affirmed, but the priority for the apostles was clearly with prayer and with what Paul called proclamation of *the word of the cross* (1 Cor 1:18 NASB).

Paul's consciousness of his call to be an apostle (1 Cor 1:1; 4:9; 9:1-5) locates his task with that of "the twelve," that is, "prayer and . . . serving the word." He also recognizes, as Luke does in Acts 6, that others are called to the tasks that the apostles are not called to do (1 Cor 12:28-30). He recognizes that the proclamation of the gospel goes beyond preaching. Sharing in the Lord's Supper is also proclamation of *the Lord's death*, which is the same as proclaiming the cross (11:26).

As institutions develop, the energy of the church is often consumed by activity other than proclaiming the gospel. Caring for those who are within the community of faith, passing faith on to our own children, maintaining the assets of our institutions, influencing social and political values and practices and the like—such valuable tasks occupy most of the volunteer time, energy, and budget of the church. Does Paul's commitment above all to proclamation challenge the priorities of Christians and of church leaders in the twenty-first century?

The Content of the Gospel

Since the proclamation of the gospel is the highest priority, it is also important to understand the content of the gospel. In his letters, Paul does not explain what constitutes preaching the cross.

Many people are attracted to a gospel that promises personal blessings. Preachers are tempted to proclaim a gospel that is deemed wise by the standards of the world, with good psychological advice, counsel for strengthening families and improving health, perspective on the political and social issues of the day, and so on. Those who promise health, wealth, success, and happiness draw crowds of people seeking such outcomes.

Paul's detractors were also interested in the trappings of success. They wanted to hear wisdom delivered in attractive oratory. However, Paul says that this is not the Christian gospel. He repeatedly reminds them that the gospel of Jesus Christ is about the cross. It is about what God has already done for us in the incarnation, death, and resurrection of Jesus, not what God can do to help us achieve our personal and corporate goals.

There will always be questions about "the relevance" of the gospel in various contexts. If Paul's example instructs us, the issue that matters is not whether the preaching, worship, and other ministries of the church align with people's demand for *signs* or *wisdom* (1:22), but whether they properly represent the message of the cross. "Effectiveness," "success," and social acceptability are not the right criteria for evaluating the life and witness of the community of faith.

Humility in Proclamation

Paul described his initial preaching in Corinth as being done *in weakness and in fear and in much trembling* (2:3). This not only describes his failure to live up to the Corinthians' standard of skilled rhetoric; it is also the appropriate attitude for one proclaiming a message as important as the gospel. Paul understood the responsibility that his call entailed, and he was awed.

Throughout this letter, beginning in the previous paragraph, 1:26-31, he criticizes those who boast of their spiritual achievements and their wisdom. Repeatedly he writes, *Let the one who boasts, boast in the Lord* (1:31). It is in contrast to their self-confidence and pride that he expresses his own humility about his role in proclaiming the gospel.

Anyone entrusted with the ministry of proclaiming the gospel should do so with an attitude of fear and trembling, for it is a great responsibility.

Preaching and Worship

In the Revised Common Lectionary, this passage (1:18-25) and the following (1:26-31) are assigned to be read five times in the three-year cycle! Each year it is read on the Tuesday of Holy Week. The accompanying texts are Isaiah 49:1-7; Psalm 71:1-14; and John 12:20-36. The connection between this passage and John 12 is the theme of the cross, which *is foolishness to those who are perishing* (1 Cor 1:18), as John 12:34 suggests. The unexpected association of the cross with glory in the gospel passage sets the stage for the inversion of shame and glory in 1 Corinthians. This inversion is also seen in Isaiah 49, especially in verse 7; Psalm 71 is likewise concerned with issues of shame: "In you, O LORD, I take refuge; let me never be put to shame" (v. 1). The theme of God's call also ties 1 Corinthians 1:24, 26 to Isaiah 49:1.

Values of Shame and Honor in God's Realm
1 Corinthians 1:26-31

EXPLANATORY NOTES

Values are reflected in the honor that people grant each other for what they hold to be good and the shame that they impute for what they hold to be bad *[Shame and Honor, p. 368]*. Paul discusses the characteristics and actions that he considers shameful and those that are honorable, and he contrasts his evaluation with that of *the world*, which he understands is influencing the Corinthians (1:27).

In this part of the letter (1:18–4:21), several times Paul speaks explicitly about shame and honor. In 1:27-29 he writes that *God chose what is foolish in the world to shame the wise; God chose what is weak in the world to shame the strong; God chose what is low and despised in the world, things that are not, to reduce to nothing things that are, so that no one might boast in the presence of God*. In 4:10, again in the context of contrasting wisdom and foolishness, weakness and strength, he writes, *You are held in honor, but we in disrepute*.

It is common for minority groups of all kinds to define their honor codes separately from or opposite to those of the majority culture (deSilva: 4–8). Generational shifts take this form: youth define what is honorable and what is shameful among their peers, often in opposition to their parents' values. Gangs do the same over against the majority culture, and so do clubs of various sorts and religious movements and institutions. This is the change that Paul is trying to instill in his readers. However, to change one's value system is a dramatic conversion experience; and anyone who has tried to change the culture (i.e., value system or system of shame and honor) of an institution knows that such changes are difficult to impose on others and difficult to implement consistently even by those who believe that the new values are "right."

Paul was trying to bring about a cultural change in the Corinthian Christians. No doubt this was consistent with what he had first preached, but the tendency to revert to previous values proved strong and was apparently further strengthened by counterteaching upholding values that Paul called *of the world* rather than *of God*. So he emphasized the contrast between those two sets of values and argued, cajoled, and admonished them to embrace the values *of God*.

The values that Paul identifies as being *of the world* are summed up in 1:26-28 as wisdom, power, and status. These are the goals to which the Corinthians aspired, yet he says not many of them had attained such ambitions at the time they came to faith. It is normally assumed that the "call" to which Paul refers is an event in the past, a moment of conversion (cf. 7:18-24), at which point most of the Corinthian Christians were not wise, powerful, or of noble birth, leaving open the possibility that their status has now changed. However, in Greek there is no verb to indicate, as most English translations do, that not many *were* of low status. An equally appropriate translation would be that not many *are* wise, powerful, or of noble birth—and that such a low status continues. The call that they are to consider is not a past event, but a present reality pointing to the future. It is the goal and vision toward which God has called them, a recollection that they are *called to be saints* (1:2). Thus Paul is holding up to them an ideal against which they cannot claim to have achieved preferred status. He does not say that those who were *foolish, weak,* and *low and despised* have now been made wise, strong, and noble; he says that those with high worldly status have been brought low, but not the reverse.

As we have noted above, the recognition that *not many* of the Corinthians were *wise* or *powerful* or *of noble birth* is also a recognition that some of them did fit those categories (see "The Christian Assembly in Corinth" in the introduction; see esp. Theissen). But Paul's interest was not a sociological description of the Corinthian

Christians. He wanted rather to make the theological point that they had been called by God not based on their wealth, power, and status (whether they had it or not) but based on Jesus Christ. Among those who are called, no value is placed on those status markers that carry weight in "the world."

When Paul wrote that *God chose what is foolish in the world to shame the wise; God chose what is weak in the world to shame the strong; God chose what is low and despised in the world, things that are not, to reduce to nothing things that are* (1:27-28), he was not talking about an inversion of status that made foolish, weak, and despised persons superior to their opposites. It was the cross of the crucified Christ that was foolishness, weakness, and despised; and yet that is what holds the highest value in God's realm. If there is anything for Christians to boast about, it is the cross of Christ—which does not even count in terms of wisdom, power, and status. It is *Christ Jesus* who is *wisdom* for Christians—and Paul heaps up further metaphors: besides wisdom, Christ Jesus is also *for us . . . righteousness and sanctification and redemption* (v. 30), all images of salvation (Fee: 90).

Salvation is a gift of grace granted at God's initiative, not a human achievement. Paul's intent here is to elaborate on the understanding of grace (see also on 1:3), which has the dual impact of (1) underscoring the initiative of God rather than of humans (see also on 3:1-7 below) and (2) equalizing the status of all who are *in Christ* (v. 30). Ben Witherington (118) captures the significance of this for the circumstances of this letter.

> An adequate theology of grace undercuts any thought of earning salvation. Salvation in Christ is not a human self-help or self-improvement scheme, but a radical rescue from a form of slavery out of which one cannot earn or buy one's way. Paul must establish this theology of grace at the very outset of his arguments because it is on the basis of that theology that he will undercut all factors that promote factionalism. Grace is not only the great unifier but also the great leveler in the Christian community, which if taken seriously nullifies the importance of all cultural devices used to create social stratification.

No doubt the Corinthians had initially accepted that the crucified Christ was the means and guarantee of their salvation, but subsequently they had returned to the values that prevailed in the surrounding culture. Perhaps because they realized the shame inherent in faith based on so foolish an event as a crucifixion, they sought to make it respectable by cloaking it in wisdom that could compete with the wisdom of other faiths and philosophies (Fee: 71). So they had taken to boasting (which represents, in contrast to shame, not honor but shamelessness) about their accomplishments (1:29; 4:7) and their gifted leaders (3:21), they were *puffed up* (4:7) and *arrogant* (4:18, 19).

THE TEXT IN BIBLICAL CONTEXT
Reversed Status

The reversal of status in God's kingdom, whether in the present or in the eschaton, is a theme that runs through much of the Bible. The Magnificat, Mary's song recorded in Luke 1:46-55, celebrates God's actions: "He has scattered the proud in the thoughts of their hearts. He has brought down the powerful from their thrones, and lifted up the lowly; he has filled the hungry with good things, and sent the rich away empty" (vv. 51-53).

Many biblical stories illustrate the reversal of status because, as God told Samuel when he anointed David as the future king, "The LORD does not see as mortals see; they look on the outward appearance, but the LORD looks on the heart" (1 Sam 16:7). Even the origin of the people of Israel as God's chosen ones is recalled with the recognition that one's ancestor was a wandering Aramean (Deut 26:5-10).

The circumstances of Jesus' birth illustrate God's choice to become human in a setting of humility, powerlessness, and poverty. In his actions, Jesus demonstrated this reversal in his acceptance of the poor and weak, including his choice of table companions (Matt 9:9-13 // Mark 2:15-17 // Luke 5:29-32) and his welcoming the children (Matt 19:13-15 // Mark 10:13-16 // Luke 18:15-17). Many of his parables and other teachings express this inversion—such as the banquet parable (Matt 22:1-10 // Luke 14:16-24), the camel going through the needle's eye (Matt 19:23-26 // Mark 10:23-27 // Luke 18:24-27), the parable of the good Samaritan (Luke 10:30-37), and the Pharisee and the tax collector at prayer (Luke 18:9-14). Even in his prayers Jesus expressed gratitude that God has "hidden these things from the wise and the intelligent and . . . revealed them to infants" (Matt 11:25 // Luke 10:21).

The greatest reversal is the assessment of Jesus' death on the cross. Foolishness and scandal in human evaluation are wisdom and power in God's economy. The experience of the Corinthian Christians—many of them not having been wealthy, powerful, or wellborn—is stated not for its own sake but as an illustration to help them understand that God took the foolishness and weakness of the cross to demonstrate divine wisdom and power.

Shame of the Wise, Strong, and Wealthy

The shame of the triad the wise, strong, and wealthy (vv. 26-28) appears to be a "free quotation" from Jeremiah 9:23-24 (Thiselton 2000: 195):

> Thus says the LORD: Do not let the wise boast in their wisdom, do not let the mighty boast in their might, do not let the wealthy boast in their wealth; but let those who boast boast in this, that they understand and know me, that I am the LORD; I act with steadfast love, justice, and righteousness in the earth, for in these things I delight, says the LORD.

Richard Hays (1997: 34–35) has pointed to a close parallel that exists only in the LXX version of 1 Samuel 2:10. There is an addition that is not found in the Hebrew text and thus not in English translations thereof:

> Let not the clever boast in his cleverness,
>
> And let not the mighty boast in his might,
>
> And let not the wealthy boast in his wealth,
>
> But let him who boasts boast in this:
>
> To understand and know the Lord
>
> And to execute justice and righteousness in the land. (1 Sam 2:10 NETS)

Other examples of shame coming upon the powerful and arrogant are found in the Psalms. Among many such, here are a few examples:

> All my enemies shall be ashamed and struck with terror;
> they shall turn back, and in a moment be put to shame. (6:10)

> Do not let those who wait for you be put to shame;
> let them be ashamed who are wantonly treacherous. (25:3)

> Do not let me be put to shame, O LORD, for I call on you;
> let the wicked be put to shame; let them go dumbfounded to Sheol. (31:17)

> Let them be put to shame and dishonor who seek after my life. . . .
> Let all those who rejoice at my calamity be put to shame and confusion;

let those who exalt themselves against me be clothed with shame
and dishonor. (35:4a, 26)

The Bible gives a lot of attention to matters of shame and honor, and frequently, as in this passage, chastises those who boast and are arrogant *[Shame and Honor, p. 368]*.

THE TEXT IN THE LIFE OF THE CHURCH

Image Consciousness

In first-century Corinth, people placed great value on rhetorical skill. "In our increasingly postliterate age, rhetorical eloquence of a classical sort is no longer highly valued, but self-presentation is. Image has become everything" (Hays 1997: 37).

For many people, image is more important than substance. The advent of social media, which enables people to create the persona (or personas!) by which they want to be known, encourages this. Visual media thrive on transient impressions. Image consultants and advisers are eager to help people construct and maintain the image they choose. This way of experiencing and participating in relationships and life is particularly attractive to some personality types and in some cultures.

The inclination to place a high value on power, wealth, and privilege continues. People who have accumulated these attributes receive honor in churches as they do in other institutions. Christians, like the people around them, attach importance to these measures of success and aspire to them. This adds incentive to maintain the image of success.

Paul's words to the Corinthian believers continue to challenge followers of Jesus to question the values of our cultures and our preoccupation with self-image. Hays (1997: 37) suggests that "whenever we find Christian faith presented in slick, high-tech, high-gloss images, . . . we should ask ourselves immediately whether the gospel that is being proclaimed here is the word of the cross or whether it is some form of human boasting through image manipulation."

God's Preference for the "Foolish; . . . Weak; . . . Low and Despised"

Roman Catholic theologians, influenced by liberation theology, have incorporated the concept of God's "preferential option for the poor" into the church's social teaching. This view has been expanded to include other disadvantaged groups and individuals, so that women, blacks (in the United States and Africa), Dalits, or "outcastes" (in India), and others view themselves as having a preferred relationship with God. There are echoes of ascetic movements throughout the history of Christianity, including mendicant monastic movements that demand a vow of poverty and that value dependency on charity.

In contrast, throughout much of the history of Christianity, people have assumed that God prefers wealthy people: their very wealth is evidence of that. Powerful people and institutions have co-opted God in their favor, and have legitimated that through their reading of Scripture. In recent decades, the "prosperity theology" or "prosperity gospel" movement has declared that God's desire is for all people to prosper in their finances, business, health, and every aspect of life. In other words, if one is not presently *wise by human standards*, or *powerful*, or *of noble birth* (1 Cor 1:26), one should pray to become so and pay a generous tithe in order to obligate God to bring this about.

Any person who is serious about being a disciple and any faithful pastor or teacher must face the Bible's strong teachings on the following:

- generosity toward the poor and weak
- the deceptive power of wealth and power
- the reversal of values in God's reign compared to "the world"
- the cross as the glory of the incarnate God (John 12:23)
- Jesus' relationships and the implication of his parables

Jesus' teaching and example are illustrated by two passages from Matthew's gospel. When talking about children, Jesus warned against doing anything that might harm them: "If any of you put a stumbling block before one of these little ones who believe in me, it would be better for you if a great millstone were fastened around your neck and you were drowned in the depth of the sea" (18:6; cf. v. 10). Matthew also reports how Jesus taught in a parable that in the final judgment people will be condemned or commended on how they have treated "the least of these" when they were hungry, thirsty, a stranger, naked, sick, or in prison (25:40, 45).

Not only personal values and practices are shaped by such teachings. They must also measure the church's corporate practices, priorities, and budgets.

Preaching and Worship

For comments on the use of this passage in the Revised Common Lectionary, see "Preaching and Worship" in TLC on 1:18-25. For more thematic consistency with 1:26-31, in place of the assigned readings one might rather choose to use passages such as 1 Samuel 2:1-10 or Jeremiah 9:23-24; Psalm 25; and Luke 1:45-55.

Spiritual Discernment

1 Corinthians 2:1-3:4

EXPLANATORY NOTES

We have already noticed that 2:1-5 carries forward the discussion of 1:17-25 by offering Paul's preaching as an example of the proclamation of the cross, which does not fit the category of "wisdom" by which the Corinthians wanted to evaluate (negatively) Paul's ministry. He would seem to have proved their negative evaluation; but now he takes a new tack on the matter of wisdom. The gospel, he writes, does not fit the categories of wisdom as defined by philosophy and sought by Greeks (1:22), but it does have a wisdom appropriate to itself and understood by those who are spiritually mature—not including those who are fomenting unrest in Corinth.

In 1:26-31 Paul has challenged the value system of misplaced shame and honor by *human standards* that the Corinthians were reappropriating from *the world*. He brought them down a peg, shaming them on the very points where they had claimed honor. And now he continues to do that.

While acknowledging that his preaching did not measure up to the wisdom standards that the Corinthians were using (2:1-5), Paul claims that he does in fact preach a message of wisdom, but that he shares it only with those who are *mature* (2:6), those who are *spiritual* (2:13), as those who were squabbling among themselves in Corinth were not (3:1-4).

Hays (1997: 39; cf. 40–41) suggests that Paul is writing ironically here, "adopting some of the Corinthians' religious vocabulary in order to beat them at their own game and at [the] same time to show how ridiculous the game is." *Wisdom, secret, mature,* and *spiritual* (2:6-7, 13) should be read, Hays suggests, as if in quotation marks, for Paul is using words that the Corinthians had used to elevate their own spiritual status at Paul's expense. But Paul is not using these words as they did. Rather, he redefines their vocabulary in order to deflate those who were *puffed up* (4:6) and *arrogant* (4:18, 19) and inclined to *boast* (1:29; 4:7).

It cannot be the case that Paul reverses what he has just said and now claims to have depths of spiritual truth that he reveals only to those who have achieved an exalted spiritual state. Yet the attraction of esoteric knowledge is so strong that this passage has been used to further the claim of special knowledge by gnostics in the following century and onward and by spiritual elitists and otherwise insightful commentators ever since (see listing in Fee: 106n227). In fact, Paul was writing to challenge and counteract the Corinthian passion for "wisdom," especially esoteric wisdom accessible only to those who are "spiritual."

The wisdom that Paul proclaims to the *mature* (2:6, in contrast to those who are *infants*, 3:1) is the wisdom he has named in the earlier passage: the crucified Christ. It is a *mystery*, he writes (2:1, 7 NIV [NRSV, *secret*]; 4:1; cf. Rom 16:25-26; Eph 1:9; 3:3-5, 9; 5:32; 6:19; Col 1:26-27; 2:2; 4:3). The Corinthians were familiar with various mystery religions, with rites and beliefs revealed only to the initiates. But Paul names a secret that is publicly proclaimed, a mystery that is transparent to all but those who refuse to believe. Paul's "mystery" is a parody of what the Corinthian Christians had come to hold as valuable, based on the criteria of their cultural context.

As in 1:18-25, Paul contrasts divine wisdom with human wisdom, which here he calls *the wisdom of this age or of the rulers of this age*. We have already observed that Paul uses the terminology of *this world* and *the world to come* to distinguish between those who are "in Christ" and those who are not. Likewise, he uses the terminology of *this age* as a shorthand way of referring to the values and worldview not shaped by Christ (1 Cor 1:20; 2:6, 8; 3:18; cf. Gal 1:4; Eph 1:21; Matt 12:32; Luke 18:30), and *the age to come* refers to the values and worldview shaped by Christ and consistent with the reign of God. In Paul's apocalyptic theology, *the world* and *this age* will continue to exist until *the end, when [Christ] hands over the kingdom to God the Father, after he has destroyed every ruler and every authority and power* (1 Cor 15:24). However, *the world to come* and *the age to come* have already entered space and time with the crucifixion of Jesus and now exist concurrently with *the world* and *this age*.

The Corinthians, Paul writes, are thinking in categories that belong to *this age*, and they have come (back?) under the influence of *the rulers of this age* (2:8). Here *the rulers of this age* are not the cosmic powers of Eph 6:12, but human rulers—perhaps all who are wise, strong, and wellborn, and in particular those who were responsible for crucifying Jesus (Fee: 110; Hays 1997: 44; see full discussion of the options in Thiselton 2000: 233-39). The Corinthians are using human or *unspiritual* categories of the senses and rationality to understand and assess spiritual realities, but that is a futile project doomed to failure (2:9, 14).

Paul writes that God declared the mystery *before the ages for our glory* (v. 7, emphasis added). We will consider *the ages* below, but here we notice that the revelation of the mystery is to bring glory to "us," rather than—as one might perhaps have expected—to bring glory to God. Paul is not here making a point about the contrast between glory that accrues to God and that which is granted to humans. Rather, he is contrasting the glory that God grants to all believers over against the individual glory that some of the Corinthian Christians were claiming for themselves in comparison with other Christians (including Paul) based on their presumed spiritual maturity and wisdom. The inclusive use of the first person plural possessive pronoun is comprehensive of all believers, not exclusively the possession of one party or of those who have achieved a higher level of spiritual maturity. The glory points both to the honor that God gives—even to those who are weak, foolish, and inconsequential (1:26-31)—and to the eschatological glory that awaits those who will be resurrected (15:40-43) together with *the Lord of glory* (2:8).

1 Corinthians 2:9	Isaiah 64:4	Gospel of Thomas 17
	From ages past no one has heard,	Jesus said, "I will give you
What no eye has seen,	[see below]	what no eye has seen,
nor ear heard,	no ear has perceived,	what no ear has heard,
[see above]	no eye has seen	[see above]
nor the human heart conceived,		[see below]
		what no hand has touched,
what God has prepared for those who love him.	any God besides you, who works for those who wait for him.	what has not arisen in the human heart."

Verse 9 includes a quotation apparently from Scripture, but it is not an exact quote from the Old Testament *[Scripture Quotations and Echoes, p. 367]*. The closest parallel seems to be Isaiah 64:4. The non-canonical second-century Gospel of Thomas (17) has a similar saying attributed to Jesus. Origen (third century) said it was a quotation from the Apocalypse of Elijah, but the two known copies of that apocalypse that exist today do not have this phrase, and his claim cannot be confirmed.

The differences between these passages are as noteworthy as their similarities. Though they use similar language in referring to something not identifiable by human senses, Paul is describing an eschatological hope, Isaiah is describing God, and Thomas is describing some kind of gift (probably, in the context of Thomas, some secret knowledge) given by Jesus.

We cannot determine Paul's source for this purported quotation, but Paul does say that the eschatological hope is reserved for those who *love* God. It is not special knowledge of God, but rather love for God, expressed in appropriate behavior (see 1 Cor 13), that determines who is blessed by God and who is cursed (*Let anyone be accursed who has no love for the Lord*, 16:22). The contrast between knowledge and love is restated in 8:1: *Knowledge puffs up, but love builds up.*

The Corinthians valued the rational wisdom expressed in the eloquent rhetorical style that philosophers taught, especially the Sophists (Winter 1997). Therefore Paul goes to some length to assert that God's wisdom is revealed by the Spirit, not by human invention. This is the first extended discussion of the activity of the Spirit, which will be elaborated later in the letter, especially in 12:3-13. Here the focus is on the Spirit of God functioning as the communicator and revealer of God.

Paul argues that just as people know best what is inside their own minds and hearts, so God's Spirit knows the heart and mind of God (2:11). In its laudable attempt to avoid gender-specific language, the NRSV has badly translated this verse. Paul is not discussing how some generic *human spirit* can understand *what is truly human*, but rather that a person's own spirit understands that person's thoughts and intentions better than any other person can. At this point the NIV is a much better translation: *For who knows a person's thoughts except their own spirit within them?*

Because *we* (and here Paul again includes himself, as some of the Corinthians would not; but he also includes all of them) have received these things from God's Spirit, *we* understand its content (v. 12), and *we* express it in words suitable for spiritual matters, not in worldly speech (v. 13).

NRSV translates verse 12b as *the gifts bestowed on us by God*, but the NIV translation is preferable: *what God has freely given us*. Again, the NRSV translates verse 14 as *the gifts of God's Spirit*, and the NIV rightly translates as *the things that come from the Spirit of God* (see EN on 12:1-11).

The distinction between spiritual wisdom and human wisdom is such that those who are spiritual (i.e., those who stand already in the new age as well as the present age) are able to understand both, but those who are not in the new age can understand only human wisdom. To them, spiritual matters are foolishness (v. 14). The expression that Paul uses of them is *psychikos anthrōpos*, meaning people who are part of the natural world or "the person who lives on an entirely human level" (Thiselton 2000: 269). Paul is not speaking, as some of the Corinthian Christians may have spoken, of "less mature" Christians, but of those who are not Christians. They are of *the world* and of *this age*. The alternative to being *psychikos* is being spiritual (*pneumatikos*). And when Paul says that those who are *pneumatikos* are *subject to no one else's scrutiny* (v. 15), he means that they are not subject to the judgment of those who are *psychikos* (cf. 4:3-5; 6:1-6). As he demonstrates amply throughout this letter, those who are unspiritual *are* subject to the scrutiny of those who are spiritual.

The best commentary on *the mind of Christ* (2:16) is the hymn quoted in Philippians 2:5-8.

> Let the same mind be in you that was in Christ Jesus,
> who, though he was in the form of God,
>> did not regard equality with God
>> as something to be exploited,
> but emptied himself,
>> taking the form of a slave,
>> being born in human likeness.
> And being found in human form,
>> he humbled himself
>> and became obedient to the point of death—
>> even death on a cross.

Though we know it only from Paul's quotation in his letter to the believers at Philippi, it is possible that those in Corinth also knew this hymn. In any case, it recalls the point that Paul has been upholding throughout his whole argument: everything is about the cross. Thiselton captures the sense nicely in these words: "All this talk of 'wisdom,' 'secrets,' and 'being spiritual,' he says, amounts to little or nothing—*unless you are open to reappropriate the message of the cross in your innermost being*" (2000: 259, emphasis original).

In yet another—and not yet his final—ironic shaming criticism of the Corinthian Christians (and he is addressing all of them, not one faction or another), Paul tells them that the reason he had not talked with them about secret wisdom nor used elaborate oratory to deliver his message, for which they had criticized him, was that they were not mature enough for it. They were spiritual babies, he writes (3:1)—a putdown in any culture, especially of those who thought themselves *mature* (2:6, giving a parallel censure). The evidence he points to is the jealousy and quarreling that has been reported to him by Chloe's people (1:11), which demonstrates that they are not spiritual (*pneumatikoi*). Yet they are believers, and he cannot properly call them *psychikoi*, so he calls them "fleshly" (*sarkikoi*, 3:3). This does not mean that they were guilty of "sins of the flesh," a common euphemism for sexual misbehavior, but it moves the discussion from an esoteric mental realm of "right thinking" to the pragmatic ethical and physical realm of "right acting." Quite in contrast to their spiritually elitist self-image, their behavior exposes them as driven by "human inclinations." Exposure of this sort is a source of shame, and Paul intentionally uses the leverage of shame to challenge their self-image and try to change their behavior *[Shame and Honor, p. 368]*.

The specific details of their quarreling—their loyalties to Paul or Apollos (or others)—recall the issue that opened this discussion and summarize the evidence (3:3-4). At the same time, it also points forward to the next part of Paul's argument.

THE TEXT IN BIBLICAL CONTEXT

Holy Spirit

The presence and activity of the Holy Spirit permeate 1 Corinthians, as they do the entire New Testament. The manifestations of the Spirit's presence in worship receive concentrated attention in chapters 12 and 14. In chapter 2 the Spirit is introduced as *the Spirit of God* (v. 11), *the Spirit that is from God* (v. 12), and *God's Spirit* (v. 14). It is this Spirit that reveals the wisdom of God (v. 10) and is the antithesis of *human wisdom* (v. 13; cf. v. 4).

The Hebrew and Greek words for *spirit* appear hundreds of times in the Bible. Many of these denote the character or essence of a person or a group. Sometimes forces for good or for evil are identified as spirits. And since the Hebrew and Greek words also mean "breath" or "wind" and in combination may mean many variations on these, it is occasionally unclear what meaning is intended. But often, and clearly when the adjective *holy* is attached, they designate the active presence of God as the Holy Spirit. This happens only twice in the Old Testament (Isa 63:10-11; Ps 51:11; cf. "spirit of the holy gods" in Dan 4:8, 9, 18), but is common in the New Testament. Even without the explicit designation, it is often clear when the reference is to the being that subsequent theological reflection has identified as the "third person of the Trinity."

Whether it was the "Spirit" (NIV) or the "wind/breath" (NRSV) of God that initiated the creation of the cosmos and of humans (Gen 1:2; Job 33:4; Ps 104:30) is not determinable. However, it was clearly the Spirit that came upon people and empowered them for special tasks (e.g., Judg 3:10; 6:34; 11:29; 14:6; 1 Sam 11:6; 1 Kings 18:12). "The pervasive presence of God's Spirit is everywhere assumed in the Old Testament" and is especially prominent in inspiring prophets (Ewert: 25; Num 11:24-30; 1 Sam 10:6, 10; 1 Kings 18:12; Mic 3:8; Hos 9:7; Ezek 2:2).

The gospel writers identify the Holy Spirit's activity in preparation for Jesus' birth (e.g., Matt 1:18, 20) and throughout his life (e.g., Mark 1:10, 12). Luke's gospel and Acts in particular highlight the activity of the Holy Spirit. Even though his gospel is saturated with references to the Spirit, Luke presents the day of Pentecost as a turning point in the Spirit's activity within the community of Jesus' followers (Acts 2:1-4). That activity is expressed above all in the empowering of the Christian movement for its mission (Acts 1:8).

John's gospel portrays Jesus as breathing the Holy Spirit onto his disciples after his resurrection (John 20:22). In anticipation of that event, he had earlier told them that the Spirit would lead them into all truth (16:12-13; cf. 14:17; 15:26) and enable them to do even greater works than he had done (14:12-14).

In Paul's writings, the Holy Spirit is constantly invoked and acknowledged, including about twenty times in 1 Corinthians. Much of what he writes is gathered up in his declaration that "the fruit of the Spirit is love, joy, peace, patience, kindness, generosity, faithfulness, gentleness, and self-control" (Gal 5:22-23).

THE TEXT IN THE LIFE OF THE CHURCH

Spiritual Elitism

There is a great risk in reading this passage superficially; it could lead to spiritual elitism and arrogance. With phrases like *we speak God's wisdom, secret and hidden* (2:7) and *we have the mind of Christ*

(2:16), it is possible to misapply Paul's words to a select group of "insiders" who have spiritual insight and knowledge that is not available to others. If one reads the NRSV translation and understands *gifts bestowed on us by God* (2:12) and *the gifts of God's Spirit* (2:14) to mean prophecy, healing, tongues, and so on, it is easy to claim an extra measure of spiritual giftedness for oneself, though that is the opposite of what Paul was trying to teach (see EN above). Indeed, the claims of special knowledge and special manifestations of the Spirit were the very claims of (some of) the Corinthians that prompted Paul to correct their misperceptions.

Throughout the history of the church, people have made similar claims. Some claim special knowledge through education or intellectual capacity or revelation. Some claim special giftedness through a second (postconversion) blessing of God's Spirit or a unique encounter with God. Some claim that their ethical rigor gives them unusual spiritual authority. The statement that *those who are spiritual . . . are themselves subject to no one else's scrutiny* (2:15) has been used to brush off theological, spiritual, and ethical criticism. From hermits in the deserts of the Middle East in the third century to charismatics and intellectuals of the twenty-first century, this has been a perennial temptation.

The corrective to this misuse of excerpts from Paul's letter is to read more of it. Reading 3:4 reveals that envious and quarrelsome relationships refute any claim to spiritual maturity. Reading 1:18-31 cautions one about claiming special knowledge and wisdom, and chapters 12-14 challenge any claim to superiority of spiritual giftedness. In Philippians 2:5-8, Paul honors humility aligned with *the mind of Christ* rather than arrogance. Finally, recognizing that the wisdom of God is expressed in the crucifixion of Jesus negates any temptation to boast in oneself.

Anabaptists and their descendants uphold *the mind of Christ* as the goal of corporate discernment in decision making.

> The discernment model of decision-making has as a central goal finding God's will for the issue at hand. This model does not ignore good parliamentary procedures, group process, or people, but it emphasizes the importance of finding God's will in relation to the issue in question. The goal of the decision-making process is not to discover the majority opinion but "the mind of Christ." (Lebold)

In this context, *the mind of Christ* is not something that can be possessed as a trophy of spiritual attainment, but rather an ever-present communal goal that followers of Jesus seek together and to which they submit themselves.

Two Kinds of People

Paul writes about two kinds of people: those who are spiritual and those who are not. Spiritual people "get" *the things that come from the Spirit of God* (2:14 NIV), *what God has freely given us* (2:12 NIV), both in the sense that they receive those things and in the sense that they understand them. The unspiritual person *does not accept* and *cannot understand* (2:14 NIV) such things. The things of the Spirit cannot be received intellectually through human wisdom; hence there is limited value in rational apologetics, which is why Paul avoids that approach. (As there are occasional testimonies of people who have opened their minds to spiritual realities through rational argument, that should not be abandoned, but this is not usually the best way to attract people to faith.)

The characteristic of *unspiritual* (2:14) people is that they "live on an entirely human level" (Thiselton 2000: 267-70). This describes vast numbers of people, perhaps especially those in the Global North or in Western societies, who define reality materially and accept only physical or scientifically observable evidence as truth. Many people in Christian churches have this worldview, as did the Corinthians whom Paul addressed. It is incumbent on all believers, not only preachers and teachers, to help people transcend this "entirely human level" as we *speak God's wisdom* (2:7) and testify to the *things God has revealed to us through the Spirit* (2:10).

In a time when many people claim that they are "spiritual but not religious," and when *spirituality* is so widely used that it has no agreed definition, it is important to say that Paul uses *spiritual* to talk about people who are followers of Jesus Christ and who have received the Holy Spirit; those two characteristics are inseparable (12:3). Spiritual people, in Paul's view, are those who *have received not the spirit of the world, but the Spirit that is from God* (2:12). Spirituality is not sensitivity to ephemeral experiences and perspectives. It has content and form in the cross of Jesus taken up by those who would follow him (Matt 10:38; Luke 9:23); it is experienced corporately and ethically (1 Cor 3:3; cf. 12:12-26; 13:1-13) *[Spirituality, p. 369]*.

It is unwarranted to assume that those who are unspiritual by Paul's definition will always remain so. The text does not suggest that the characteristic or status of being spiritual or unspiritual is predestined or fixed. Indeed, Paul's intention is to move those who are unspiritual to become spiritual.

It's God's Congregation
1 Corinthians 3:5-23

EXPLANATORY NOTES

The Corinthian squabbles about loyalty to particular leaders were evidence that they were thinking like people in our present age. They were using human criteria to determine status in the household assemblies of believers. The fundamental mistake they had made was to forget whose body it is. They had begun to fight for honor and privilege as if such qualities belonged to them. Paul's purpose now is to convince them that "it's God's congregation" and that their quarrels are irrelevant and unbecoming in that context.

Against claims of the priority of a favorite leader, Paul argues that no human leader—whether Apollos or himself (3:4, 5, 6, 22; 4:6) or Cephas (3:22; cf. 1:12)—is more than a humble servant. The rhetorical questions and their answer—*What, after all, is Apollos? And what is Paul? Only servants, through whom you came to believe* (3:5 NIV)—are typical strategies of the diatribe (Malherbe: 130).

Paul uses a series of three metaphors to illuminate (1) the understanding that the Christian assembly belongs to God and (2) the proper understanding of leadership and membership in God's congregation. The images are drawn from agriculture (the congregation is God's field), construction (the congregation is God's building), and worship structures (the congregation is God's temple).

The agricultural image of planting and watering (3:6-9) makes several points. The least of these is that Paul's work takes priority, since planting comes before watering. The assertion that those who work in God's field *will each be rewarded according to their own labor* may be intended to imply that Paul deserves a higher wage. At the least, it challenges anyone who might have dismissed his leadership by claiming their own unique and essential role in establishing the assembly.

Stronger than a claim of priority is the claim that Paul and Apollos were equally servants whose work was essential to the establishment of the congregation; without the planting of the seed, there would have been nothing to water; without watering the seed, it would not have germinated and grown. The two leaders—and by extension all other leaders as well—work together for a common purpose. They are all *God's servants, working together*, and Paul will not allow quarrelsome members to drive a wedge between them.

The most important point that Paul wants to make—far more important than rehabilitating his own reputation as a leader or correcting the invented competition between himself and Apollos—is that neither he nor Apollos nor both of them together could cause growth to happen. That power belongs to God alone. The workers who plant and water are nothing, he writes; the only one who matters is God. This means that God is the initiator of the faith community and the source of its power. It further means that Paul and Apollos and the others are servants of God. God not only generates the growth but also owns the field and directs the workers. Paul will shortly make explicit the point that is implicit here: that the master of the servants is the only one with authority to judge, pay, or commend the servants (4:1-5; see also 3:13-15).

In the second image (vv. 9c-15), Paul moves from agriculture to construction. Here Paul identifies himself as a *wise architect/contractor* (v. 10 AT). Note the echo again, as so often in this letter, of wisdom, unfortunately missed by most translations that substitute *skilled* (NRSV, RSV, NET) or *trained* (NJB), but retained in the KJV, NKJV, NASB, NIV.

We will return in a moment to the foundation that Paul had laid. But first, who is the *someone* who is now building upon the foundation (3:10)? Several possibilities present themselves. It was not Apollos (or Cephas), for they were not in Corinth at the time and would not have heard Paul's caution. Besides this, Paul has just said that he and Apollos were equal colleagues—though it would be consistent with the sequence of planting and watering, and indeed with the history of their presence in Corinth, to say that Paul had laid the foundation and Apollos had built upon it. Was he warning unnamed other "builders"—those whom he did not name when he euphemistically named himself and Apollos (4:6), but whom both he and the Corinthians knew to be the real opposition (Thiselton 2000: 349)? Neither of these fits the situation as well as the Corinthians themselves. It was they whose behavior Paul wanted to change. It was not real or imagined itinerant teachers but the ongoing leaders and members of the Christian assembly about whom Paul has heard from Chloe's people and that he addresses throughout this letter. The Corinthians themselves were the *someone else* who continued to build on the foundation (v. 10)—the *each one* who must *build with care* (v. 10 NIV) and the *anyone* and the *each* whose building materials and skill would be tested with fire (vv. 12-13). The metaphor is mixed, since they are both building and builder, but that complexity is not insurmountable in a metaphor.

The foundation upon which Paul had built was Jesus Christ. There is no other—not wisdom, not philosophy, not charismatic leadership. The only foundation is Jesus Christ, and him crucified (2:2; cf. 1:23). From what Paul wrote earlier in 1 Corinthians, we might conclude that the primary meaning he had in mind was that the foundation of Christian teaching is the proclamation of the cross (1:17-18, 23-24; 2:2). Yet later in this same letter, he lifts up the resurrection as the validating event of Christian faith (ch. 15, esp. vv. 12-23). Furthermore, though he rarely does so in other letters, in this one he explicitly quotes teachings of Jesus (7:10; 11:23-25). In short, there is not only one way in which Christ is the foundation. Rather, Paul seems to have in mind the full extent of Jesus' life and continuing work, the fullness of the relationship with Christ that Christians enter through baptism (12:13) and remember through the Lord's Supper (10:16; 11:23-25; see further "No Other Foundation" in TLC below).

If anyone builds on the foundation, Paul writes—and surely the metaphor demands building, because a foundation by itself is useless—then in the eschaton, the last day, the quality of that building will be both revealed for all to see and tested by fire (3:12-13). The builder will experience either reward or loss, depending on the outcome of that test.

There is no warrant for allegorical analysis of the meaning of the several building materials. Nobody builds with gold, silver, or precious stones. Few build with straw or hay. Wood is a common building material, but so also in Paul's day were clay, stone, and brick, which are not mentioned. The only criterion for evaluation, it seems, is whether the material is flammable, not whether it is practical, durable, or beautiful. Clearly, Paul is using apocalyptic imagery, for the use of fire to describe the test of final judgment is common in both the Hebrew Bible and the New Testament (e.g., Mal 3:2; Matt 3:10, 12 parr.; 13:40-42; John 15:6; 2 Thess 1:8).

Paul emphasizes his own role as overall architect or general contractor and the one who built the foundation, and he writes his instructions and cautions to those who continued to build. Nevertheless, in this metaphor, as in the previous one, the primary point he wants to make is that the owner of the building is God. He introduces the metaphor by announcing this: *You are ... God's building* (1 Cor 3:9b). The foundation of the building is Jesus Christ, and the one who will test the workmanship and reward the builders is God.

The third metaphor is also about God's relationship with the congregation: *You* [corporately] *are God's temple. . . . God's temple is holy, and you are that temple* (vv. 16-17). The biggest challenge to correct understanding of this image for English readers is the English grammatical limitation of not distinguishing between the singular and plural of the second person pronoun *you*, an opening for misreading that is avoided in most other languages. So contemporary English readers may be inclined to read this individualistically, as if every individual Christian were a temple in which God's Spirit dwells and whose destruction brings punishment. That point is made in 6:19 but not in chapter 3.

Paul is addressing the collective when he writes that *you are* [Gk. *este*; Fr. *vous êtes*; Ger. *ihr seid*; Sp. *sois*] *God's temple*. The warning against destroying God's temple is not against abuse of the integrity of the human body, valid though that may be. What Paul is addressing is the destruction of the integrity of the spiritual body, the congregation of believers (see 12:12-27), by those who were quarreling over loyalties and status.

The reason why it is forbidden to destroy this temple is because it belongs to God, a point that is driven home three times in two verses by naming that it is *God's temple* and adding that *God's Spirit dwells* there (3:16-17).

The metaphor would have been easily understood by the Corinthian Christians, for Corinth was full of temples dedicated to various divinities (see "Corinth" in the introduction). One needs only to understand that a temple is a space dedicated (*sacred* [NIV] or *holy* [NRSV], meaning "set apart" or "consecrated"; cf. EN on 1:2) to one or more divinities and that such a space is presumed to be under the protection of that god or goddess.

It matters little how much the Corinthians knew of the Jewish temple in Jerusalem. Although the Corinthians must have been quite familiar with a variety of temples, surely it was the Jerusalem temple that must have been in Paul's mind when he wrote these words, for he was a devout Jew and had spent much time in that temple. At the time when Paul was writing to the Corinthians, the temple still stood in Jerusalem. For Paul to declare that the Christian assembly is now God's temple was a radical theological statement. He believed that the gathering of Christians had now supplanted the Jewish temple as the place where God is present, where *God's Spirit dwells* (Segal: 168).

Verses 18-23 recapitulate what has already been written, serving as a summary, lest the main points be lost in the detail. Paul reiterates that (1) human wisdom is different from God's wisdom and does not impart status in the faith community (underscored with supporting quotations from Job 5:13a and Ps 94:11 [slightly modified]); (2) it is futile to boast about human leaders, for all members of the assembly have equal claim on all who have been and are its leaders and teachers; and (3) in any case, the leaders and their teachings all are subordinate to Christ [crucified], and that Christ [and the congregation] belong to God.

What is new in this passage is the personalization of the challenge. Earlier, Paul had asked abstractly and rhetorically, *Where is the wise person? Where is the teacher of the law? Where is the philosopher of this age?* (1:20), but now he personalizes the point: *If any* [singular] *of you* [plural] *think you* [singular] *are wise* . . . (3:18 NIV). To believe oneself wise is deception, Paul declares; and it is *self*-deception, it is not perpetrated by "outsiders" who have come into the assembly to deceive the believers (Fee: 163n445).

The statement that *all things are yours . . . all belong to you, and you belong to Christ, and Christ belongs to God* (3:21-23) would have caught the ears of the Corinthians, for it was a commonplace among Greek and Roman philosophers to assert that "all things" belong to those who are wise (Hays 1997: 60–61). Cicero wrote, "Then, how dignified, how lofty, how consistent is the character of the Wise Man as [the Stoic philosophers] depict it! . . . Rightly will he be said to own all things, who alone knows how to use all things" (*De finibus* 3.22.75 [Yonge]). Seneca elaborates at length the implications of the basic conviction that "the wise man possesses everything" (*De beneficiis*, esp. 7.3–7.4). So the Corinthians would not have been surprised to hear Paul state that all things belong to them. That was in fact the kind of worldly wisdom they accused him of not speaking enough.

Paul moves from the philosophical commonplace to argue first that they should not be quarreling about loyalty to leaders, for all the leaders belong to the whole congregation (in vv. 21 and 22, *yours* and *to you* are plural, not singular), not to mention *the world or life or death or the present or the future* (v. 22). Furthermore, the line of ownership does not end with everything belonging to *the wise* (v. 20). Paul continues, saying that the readers and their leaders belong to Christ and ultimately to God (v. 23). In the face of that realization, the ground of their quarrelsomeness is swept away, and they are left in humbled recognition of their self-deception (v. 18).

The fundamental conviction that the congregation belongs to God is pervasive in 1 Corinthians. In the very first verse, Paul identifies his call to be an apostle as being *by the will of God*. The Corinthians too had been called by God's initiative and at God's will (1:26-31). The letter is filled with statements about God's initiative, actions

1 Corinthians 3:5-23

where God is the explicit subject of the sentence of action or of attribute:

1:9	*God is faithful.*
1:20	*God made foolish the wisdom of the world.*
1:21	*God decided . . . to save those who believe.*
1:27-28	*God chose what is foolish in the world; . . . God chose what is weak in the world; . . . God chose what is low and despised in the world.*
2:7	*God decreed [wisdom] before the ages for our glory.*
2:9	*God has prepared [something] for those who love him.*
2:10	*God has revealed [these things] to us through the Spirit.*
3:6	*God gave the growth.*
3:7	*Only God . . . gives the growth.*
3:17	*God will destroy that person [who destroys God's temple].*
4:9	*God has exhibited us apostles as last of all.*
5:13	*God will judge those outside.*
6:13	*God will destroy both [food] and the [stomach].*
6:14	*God raised the Lord and will also raise us by his power.*
7:15	*God has called you.*
7:17	*God called you.*
8:4	*There is no God but one.*
8:6	*There is one God.*
10:5	*God was not pleased with most of them.*
10:13	*God is faithful.*
11:3	*God is the head of Christ.*
12:6	*God . . . activates all [activities] in everyone.*
12:18	*God arranged the members in the body.*
12:24	*God has so arranged the body.*
12:28	*God has appointed in the church [various gifts].*
14:33	*God is a God not of disorder but of peace.*
15:28	*So that God may be all in all.*
15:38	*God gives it a body as he has chosen.*

In addition to these nominative uses of God as subject of the sentence, there are many references to God in the genitive form, that is, where something is "of God." Paul writes about the will of God (1:1), the congregations of God (1:2; 10:32; 11:16, 22; 15:9), grace and peace from God (1:3, 4; 3:10; 15:10 [two times]), the power of God (1:18, 24; 2:5), the wisdom from/of God (1:21, 24, 30; 2:7), the mystery(ies) of God (2:1; 4:1), the depths of God (2:10), the Spirit from/of God (2:11, 12, 14; 3:16; 6:11, 19; 7:40; 12:3), the gifts from/by God (2:12; 7:7), God's field (3:9), God's building (3:9), God's temple (3:16, 17 [two times]), commendation from God (4:5), Christ belongs to God (3:23), the kingdom of God (4:20; 6:9, 10; 15:50), the commandments of God (7:19), the law of God (9:21), the glory of God (10:31), the image and reflection of God (11:7), the word of God (14:36)—in short, all things come from God (11:12).

These are the explicit references. In addition, there are many implicit references to God as initiator or "owner," including many passive verbal constructions where God is the implied actor, such as 1:5, *in every way you have been enriched*, or where pronouns are used, as in 1:9, *by him you were called into the fellowship of his Son*. In short, the letter is replete with references to God's initiative and acceptance of the fundamental conviction that the congregations, their power, their actions, their members, and their leaders all belong to God. There is therefore no room for boasting about personal achievements (3:18) or *about human leaders* (3:21).

In the subsequent paragraph (4:1-5), Paul applies his understanding of leadership to himself and to Apollos as examples (4:6). They are not objects of allegiance or boasting, for they are simply *servants of Christ and stewards of God's mysteries* (4:1).

Servants (Gk. *hypēretēs*) is a general word for servants or assistants of many kinds. In 3:5, Paul has used another Greek word that is translated as *servant* (Gk. *diakonos* = Eng. *deacon*), and in 3:9, which the NRSV also translates as *servants*, a word better translated as *coworkers* (NIV; Gk. *synergos*, from which we get the English word *synergy*).

Stewards in first-century Roman culture carried considerable authority as managers and overseers of other servants. The word originally referred to the person in charge of a household, and though it was used of persons in charge of other institutions, the household connection was appropriate for Paul's use because the assemblies met in homes (see "The Christian Assembly in Corinth" in the introduction). They frequently carried the full authority of their master in conducting business and were recognized for the responsibilities entrusted to them. Paul calls himself and his fellow workers *stewards of God's mysteries*, because the mysteries are the matters with which they were *entrusted* (NIV). The mysteries, as we have seen in 2:1, 7 (see discussion above) were the message of the gospel.

THE TEXT IN BIBLICAL CONTEXT
Servant Leadership

Two times in this passage, Paul uses *servant* as the designation for his role (3:5, 9). He also uses *servant* and a parallel word, *steward*, in 4:1-2; a steward is a servant or slave who is responsible to manage a lord's property. *Servant* is a common self-designation in Paul's letters (Rom 1:1; 2 Cor 6:4; Gal 1:10; Eph 3:7; Phil 1:1; Col 1:7, 23, 25; 4:7, 12; *1 Tim 4:6; 2 Tim 2:24; Titus 1:1*). It is also used by James (1:1), Peter (2 Pet 1:1), Jude (1:1), and John (Rev 1:1; 15:3; 19:10; 22:9).

Paul's service is to God (sometimes specified as to Christ), not to the congregations. He stresses this when he writes of his accountability, not to any person, but to *the Lord* (4:3-4). *Kyrios* is the Greek word for humans who are lords over servants, and which by extension came to be used as a title for Christ. In this verse, Paul makes use of both the normal and the Christological meanings, affirming that the Lord is his lord.

The synoptic gospels record two sayings of Jesus that also use servant language to speak of discipleship. One of those sayings is reported only by Mark: "[Jesus] sat down, called the twelve, and said to them, 'Whoever wants to be first must be last of all and servant of all'" (Mark 9:35). The context is the disciples' argument about which of them is the greatest. It culminates in Jesus bringing forward children as the ideal of discipleship—not because of their presumed innocence, but because children had low status in that culture, like the humbled status of servants (Matt 18:4). Matthew and Luke retain the story of Jesus upholding children, but omit the parallel statement about servants (Matt 18:1-6 // Luke 9:46-48).

The second synoptic statement on servant leadership is in a longer teaching that includes observations on how "the rulers of the Gentiles" rule. "Those whom they recognize as their rulers lord it over them, and their great ones are tyrants over them" (Mark 10:42 // Matt 20:25-28 // Luke 22:25-27). In contrast to that kind of rule, Jesus says, "It is not so among you; but whoever wishes to become great among you must be your servant, and whoever wishes to be first among you must be slave of all" (Mark 10:43-44).

Although John's gospel does not include this saying, the account of Jesus washing his disciples' feet demonstrates a model of humble service and instructs his disciples to imitate that action on the basis that "servants are not greater than their master" (John 13:1-17).

In each of the Gospels, these statements about servant leadership are remembered in the setting of Jesus heading to Jerusalem and predicting his death. Readers are reminded that Jesus lived according to what he taught. Once again, the cross is the model, not only for disciples, but also for those who would lead disciples.

This view of leadership does not start with the teaching of Jesus. It echoes the Servant Songs of Isaiah (Isa 42:1-4; 49:1-6; 50:4-9; 52:13–53:12). The identity of this servant has been discussed at least since the Ethiopian official asked Philip about it (Acts 8:34). Aside from what Isaiah may have intended, Christians have understood this motif to find its fullest meaning in the life of Jesus (I. Friesen: 451). The gospel writers report that Jesus' understanding of leadership flowed from Isaiah's, and Paul shares that understanding that a leader is a servant.

Servant leadership is rooted in an understanding that the Christian congregations belong to God. This is explored in the following comments.

God's Peoplehood

The testimony of the whole of Scripture is that the establishment of a peoplehood is God's plan for implementing God's will "on earth, as it is in heaven." The call of Abram and Sarai (Gen 12:1-3) is foundational to an intention to "make of you a great [people]" (the common translation, "nation," misleads if readers think of the modern concept of nation-states; cf. Roop: 98). The establishment and repeated restoration of the people of Israel are parts of that plan. The prophet Jeremiah framed God's intention: "Obey my voice, and I will be your God, and you shall be my people" (Jer 7:23). The calling of disciples by Jesus (Matt 4:18-22) and the birthing of the Christian movement at Pentecost (Acts 2:1-10, 44-47) are parts of the plan. Peter writes that God's plan is fulfilled in the body of believers: "You are a chosen race, a royal priesthood, a holy nation, God's own people, in order that you may proclaim the mighty acts of him who called you out of darkness into his marvelous light. Once you were not a people, but now you are God's people" (1 Pet 2:9-10). Paul's repeated insistence that the faith community is the body of Christ makes the same point (1 Cor 12:12-26; Rom 12:4-5; cf. Eph 1:22-23; 5:29-30; Col 1:18, 24).

The idea of peoplehood has shaped the Anabaptist understanding of God's intention for the Christian movement (Bender: 20-22; Redekop: 133-46), and plays a significant part in influencing its ethics (Yoder 1982).

THE TEXT IN THE LIFE OF THE CHURCH
No Other Foundation

The most fundamental presupposition that Paul names (there being no disagreement on prior matters such as the existence of God) is that everything in Christianity is founded on Jesus Christ. At the beginning of the twenty-first century, non-Christians, and even some Christians, question the uniqueness of Jesus Christ for salvation, for understanding God, for moral direction, and for existential meaning. It is crucial to the identity and the vitality of the Christian movement that Christians affirm this confession: Christ is the foundation of our faith and our life.

Although we declare a common conviction that Jesus Christ is the (only) foundation, this affirmation can have many different understandings of its meaning. What is it about Jesus that is the foundation? Some think it is primarily his person, some his teachings, some his miracles, some his crucifixion, some his resurrection, some his future return and judgment, some a combination of these.

For Paul, the crucial matter for Christians to ponder is, "What did Jesus do?" In contrast with the often trite question, "What would Jesus do?" (or simply WWJD), this question has testable historical answers. In other words, this affirmation is not about correctness of doctrine *about* Jesus Christ, but the proclamation (1:17) of his life, death, and resurrection, and especially the scandal of his death (see EN above on 1:18-25). An important argument could be developed about whether the correct emphasis is on what Jesus did (as the more evangelically oriented might wish to frame it) or what God did in and through Jesus (as the more ecumenically oriented might prefer to frame it). Both have validity, and each highlights a truth that must not be lost: mixing or alternating the expressions may give the best theological balance.

First Corinthians 3:11 is a concise and powerful statement of Paul's conviction, but the context of the statement focuses on building on that foundation rather than on the foundation itself. These two dimensions of faith are always present and always somewhat in tension in individual Christians and in the corporate body of believers. On the one hand, the affirmation in creed and worship names and honors the foundational act that God has done in and through Jesus. Some Christians dwell on this and minimize the necessity of a human response of holy living, service, and witness. On the other hand, the missional mandate motivates us to build on that foundation. Some Christians dwell on this and neglect to give attention to God's prior action. Both poles are wrong.

If We Believe It's God's Church

The point that Paul is making in this section is profoundly important for believers in the twenty-first century to hear and absorb. From the local congregation to the global Christian movement, the church does not belong to its members or its leaders: it belongs to God. As we recognize this simple truth, it affects our life together in profound ways. On the one hand, it removes human claims of ownership or control. On the other hand, it confronts anyone who dismisses the importance of the church. As an institution created by and belonging to God, it cannot be scorned by any who love and serve God.

To take up the second point first, there is a spirit abroad that rejects the church's importance and relevance even for Christian life. The rapidly growing number of people in the Global North who claim to be "spiritual but not religious" is the result of many factors, including these:

- the privatization of religious experience
- the human-centered and individual-centered worldview that assumes that spirituality—and ultimately, God—is at the service of whatever I am seeking, which may be entirely different from what someone else is seeking
- the customization of faith by a smorgasbord approach of picking whatever pieces are attractive from any faith (and making up whatever is needed to fill the gaps)
- reaction to the many and grave faults of Christian institutions and their leaders

The church in general as well as in its local expressions is indeed flawed and is easily scorned. Lines from an oft-omitted verse of Samuel John Stone's 1866 hymn "The Church's One Foundation" say it honestly:

> Though with a scornful wonder
> Men see her sore oppressed,
> By schisms rent asunder,
> By heresies distressed . . .

If that is our primary perspective, it will come as a surprise to read Paul's ringing affirmation that "Christ *loved the church* and gave himself up for her, in order to make her holy by cleansing her with the washing of water by the word, so as to present the church to himself in splendor, without a spot or wrinkle or anything of the kind—yes, so that she may be holy and without blemish" (Eph 5:25b-27, emphasis added). The stanza of "The Church's One Foundation" quoted above concludes with a word of hope:

> Yet saints their watch are keeping,
> Their cry goes up, "How long?"
> And soon the night of weeping
> Shall be the morn of song!

The whole hymn, based as it is on 1 Corinthians 3:11, is an affirmation that the church belongs to God and is loved by God.

The other error that many make is to begin to think and act as though they own the church. The way people talk about congregations and denominations, agencies, or programs often sounds as if they are owned by the participants: "Not in *my* church we won't." "Our church . . . their church . . ." "What have they done to my church?" A pastor who was feeling threatened on congregational leadership issues said, "Why should I let others tell me what to do? I started this church. If they don't like the way I run it, they can start their own."

Competition between pastors, competition between factions wanting to control particular decisions, and rivalry between denominations and agencies is often framed by competition for market share and donor support. If it's God's church, such divisions are irrelevant distractions at best and sins against God at worst.

If it's God's church, people do not determine its goals or strategies. Discernment replaces decision making. The question is not "What do we want to do?" but "What does God want to do?" It is not the same thing (see Lebold). Believing that all members have a perspective and gifts to contribute to the discernment of God's will (see below on ch. 12) does not lead to the conclusion that all members have an equal vote in decisions.

Church structures reflect the prevailing secular ideals for administration at the time they were founded. Orthodox and Roman Catholic structures are shaped by the administration of the Roman Empire, with hierarchies of officials. Lutheran and Reformed churches have structures that reflect the shifting political landscape of the sixteenth century. The Anglican/Episcopal church reflects British monarchy (modified over the centuries as the monarchy has changed). Anabaptist and other free churches are structured democratically, reflecting that political pattern that emerged during the Protestant Reformation. Newer independent and charismatic churches echo the "business model" of entrepreneurial initiative, and this is often lauded in other churches and church agencies. Indigenous churches in Africa and Asia are structured like the villages and extended families from which they emerge. Yet Jesus' words describing the leadership of "the rulers of the Gentiles" and saying, "It will not be so among you" (Matt 20:25-27) should be a strong caution against applying secular leadership assumptions and strategies in God's church, as many books and seminars urge.

So how is a church structured when it belongs to God? How does it discern God's will? How does it organize itself to do God's will?

Richard Hays (1997: 76) points out that "the church . . . is not a democracy. Christian leaders are accountable to another authority. What is required is faithfulness to God, with or without the support of popular opinion in the church. It is all too easy for the members of a congregation to fall into the habit of thinking of the pastor as *their* employee."

What is the effect on God's church of generations of pastors who see themselves as accountable to the church board or membership meeting? What is the effect of generations of accountability to a bishop or other hierarch, or to a synod? In what ways are the role and message of pastors influenced by the employee mentality on the part of pastors and the employer mentality on the part of congregations? Was Paul right in refusing to be financially dependent upon the congregations he founded (see 1 Cor 9)—and was their dismay over this a consequence of their resultant loss of control?

What difference would it make to pastoral calls, reviews, or evaluations if it were understood that the pastor is more fundamentally accountable to the Lord than to the church? Perhaps such processes are irrelevant if we believe, as Paul says, that *it is a very small thing that I should be judged by you or by any human court. I do not even judge myself* (4:3). This does not mean that pastors are not accountable, for *it is required of stewards that they be found trustworthy* (4:2). How do a pastor and a congregation assess the "trustworthiness" of God's servant?

If we understand the church to belong to God, then those who participate and who lead have a higher sense of responsibility and calling than if we think the church belongs to its members or to the denomination. There is also a freedom to change, to follow God into new initiatives, or to accept the closure of a congregation or a ministry program. Since we do not determine its destiny and progress, there is always a sense of mystery and adventure as we seek to understand and participate in what God is doing.

In a conflicted situation, there is a great risk of identifying one faction's views with God's will and using such language to shut down other voices, sometimes in the name of maintaining unity. Throughout 1 Corinthians we see this happening in the Corinthian congregations. We also see that Paul avoided taking sides on many issues. Despite his passion for the congregations he had planted (3:6) and founded (3:10), he was convinced that the church belongs to God.

Preaching and Worship

First Corinthians 3:5-23 and the following paragraph in 4:1-55 are rich in themes that could be developed in reflecting or preaching. These include:

- declaring, honoring, worshiping Jesus as the foundation of our understanding of and access to God, the grounding of our faith and our life
- proclaiming the life, teaching, crucifixion, and resurrection of Jesus as all essential to our faith
- honoring the corporate body of Christ as God's intended structure that is illuminated by the metaphors of temple and field
- honoring those who have built well on the foundation
- naming and confessing failures to build on the foundation, as well as choices of bad building materials (e.g., bad theology, culture confused with faith, inappropriate strategies, distorted priorities)
- confession of fractiousness and our claims to ownership of the congregation, which in fact belongs to God

- warnings against destruction of God's temple—yet with wise discernment of what that means lest we use this to silence honest disagreement or prophetic voices
- recognizing the great variety of ways that God's building has been built up—the ecumenical context, the global context, and the variety of gifts, expressions, strategies, and worship styles

The Revised Common Lectionary assigns 1 Corinthians 3:1-9, 10-11, 16-23; and 4:1-5 to be read respectively on the sixth, seventh, and eighth Sundays after Epiphany in Year A. The omission of 3:12-15 is probably intentional because it is a difficult paragraph. But preachers should read and preach on this passage of judgment as well.

Paul's Credibility
1 Corinthians 4:1-21

EXPLANATORY NOTES

Chapter 4 has an awkward tone, as if this were a difficult part of the letter for Paul to write. He alternates between cajoling, arguing, threatening, teasing, and instructing—all with the goal of asserting himself as one whom the Corinthians should heed as they work out what it means to be a Christian community. Some modern readers are put off by this goal or by Paul's execution of it, thinking that it is unseemly for him to write so confrontationally (e.g., v. 21) and to promote himself as one to be imitated (v. 16; cf. 11:1; see Thiselton's [2000: 371-73] response to Elizabeth Castelli [97-115]). But his defense seems warranted in the context where some believers had chosen to imitate other leaders with values and a worldview antithetical to the Christian gospel and where some members were denigrating Paul's skill and credibility as a leader.

We must remember that the church at Corinth was a church with no established Christian tradition, no members who had been believers longer than about three years at the most, no written gospels, and no authoritative Torah to regulate behavior. They were being forced to invent the Christian life as they went, and they were obviously having some trouble doing so. Under these circumstances, a living, visible example of how to "walk" in the ways of the gospel was indispensable (Hays 1997: 74).

We should not think of Paul as attempting to gain or exercise authoritarian power over the community, but rather should recognize that he was trying to reestablish his credibility—not as an end in itself, but in order that the Corinthians would pay attention as he called them back to the vision for being God's people.

From Paul's comments it is evident that he is responding to questions, probably even challenges, from the Corinthians regarding his credibility as their leader. He dismisses their judgment (v. 3), which can only mean that he is aware they have judged him and found him wanting. They question his credibility as a leader; he questions their qualifications as judges. Many commentators believe that the whole purpose of these first four chapters (some say even of the whole letter) is to refute his accusers and (re)establish his authority over the congregations (e.g., Schütz: 187-203; Plank). But we have noticed other important issues that also have been addressed, and we will see that while Paul is concerned in chapter 4 with admonishing the congregations (v. 14), he assumes the right to do so without regard for their qualms about his authority and skill in leadership.

The first paragraph of chapter 4 is transitional. We have already discussed it (see on 3:5-23, EN, and "Servant Leadership" in TBC) as Paul's application to leaders, including himself, of the principle that "it's God's church." In chapter 3 he identifies himself as one of *God's servants* (3:9), and at the beginning of chapter 4 he writes that he and Apollos *are servants of Christ and stewards of God's mysteries* (4:1).

As a steward, Paul acknowledged that he was accountable to his lord/the Lord, but he denied any accountability to those who were passing judgment on him. Likewise, he dismissed self-evaluation, even though his own conscience was clear (cf. 2 Cor 1:12; Phil 3:6). Krister Stendahl (78-96) has demonstrated that Paul did not struggle with the kind of "introspective conscience" that Martin Luther experienced and through which Paul has been read in Europe and North America since the sixteenth century. Yet Paul did recognize the possibility of self-deception and subordinated his self-assessment to that of the Lord (1 Cor 4:4).

Stewards are accountable to their master, not to the judgments and criticism, whether petty or substantial, of *any human court* (4:3), by which Paul means the court of public opinion rather than a court of law, though he will address that subject in chapter 6. Paul recognizes the onus of accountability, but his accountability is to the Lord rather than to humans, and the time of reckoning will be the final judgment, at which all will be revealed, and not in the present transitional age when *we see in a mirror, dimly* (13:12). The idea of judging has been introduced in 2:14-15 and will be picked up again in 9:3. Like the assembly and its leaders—and indeed everything—judgment belongs to God (see also Matt 7:1-5).

In summary, Paul's understanding of ministry as servanthood and stewardship shapes his defense of his credibility with the Corinthian congregations.

The Corinthians had an inadequate understanding of eschatology (see EN on 1:7). Once again, Paul reins them in: the eschaton is not yet, and they must not get ahead of the program by judging prematurely what must wait for the final day (2:5).

As part of his argument, Paul quotes a saying that is difficult to attribute and puzzling to many readers: *Nothing beyond what is written* (4:6). He writes that he wants the readers to learn through the example of himself and Apollos what the saying means. His goal is clear enough: *so that none of you will be puffed up in favor of one against another*. So we know that he continues to address the problem of arrogance and competitiveness that has divided the assembly. But how is he trying to convince them in this statement?

Scholars are not agreed on the meaning of *all this* that Paul writes he has applied to Apollos and himself (2:6). How much of what precedes is to be included? He first mentioned Apollos and himself in 1:12, and there he also referred to Cephas and Christ. The narrower focus on only Paul and Apollos begins at 3:5, introduced by verse 4. We might therefore consider that *all this* refers to 3:5–4:5, especially the depiction of the two leaders as equals who mutually respect each other's work and who subordinate any personal considerations to their shared task of serving the Lord and proclaiming the gospel.

What is written is Scripture. Thiselton (2000: 352–56) identifies seven possible meanings for *what is written*, of which the most plausible are either "all Scripture" or more narrowly the several verses of Scripture that Paul has quoted or alluded to in the letter to this point. These include Isaiah 29:14, about God's rejection and destruction of human wisdom (1 Cor 1:19), and Jeremiah 9:23-24, which says that people should not boast in their wisdom but in the Lord (1 Cor 1:31). The source of the quotation at 2:9 is disputed, but the meaning is that God has initiated what could not be conceived by human wisdom. A quotation from Isaiah 40:13 underscores human limitations before God (1 Cor 2:16). Paul refers to Job 5:12-13 and Psalm 94:11, again to make the point that human wisdom is futile in God's evaluation (1 Cor 3:19-20). In summary, his quotations show that *what is written*, in this context, is the inadequacy of human wisdom, which is the very point that Paul has made by the example of

Apollos and himself and that he states explicitly yet again at the end of 4:6.

Some scholars think that the reference to the Corinthians being *in favor of one against another* (4:6) refers specifically to their inclination to prefer Apollos over Paul (Fee: 179-85). But it need not be limited to that one understanding. It seems more likely that Paul meant it generally, using Apollos and himself as examples but meaning that the Corinthians should not get puffed up about *any* leader, since their boasting should be in Christ (1:31).

Once again, Paul pursues his criticism of the Corinthians' propensity for boasting and arrogance. He introduced his concern about this first in 1:26-31, challenging their right to boast about their own accomplishments or indeed anything other than *the Lord*. Here in 4:7 he presses further, reminding them that everything they have or have accomplished has been given to them as a gift for which they can claim no personal credit. In 3:21 he dismissed their grounds for boasting about specific leaders, including himself. Boasting is further criticized in the rest of the letter (5:6; 9:15-16; 13:3-4; 15:31). Being *puffed up* (4:6) or *arrogant* (vv. 18, 19; using the same word in Greek) is synonymous with boasting, as can be seen in the parallel usage both here and in 13:4. The contrast between puffing up and building up is shown in 8:1. Paul accuses the Corinthians of being arrogant in 4:18-19 and again in 5:2. Boasting and arrogance are unseemly behaviors: Aristotle had written, "To speak at great length about oneself and to make all kinds of professions, . . . this is a sign of boastfulness" (*Rhetoric* 2.6.11 [Freese]). They are also theological errors because they arrogate to humans the credit that belongs to God.

Earlier, Paul had written that *God chose what is foolish in the world to shame the wise; God chose what is weak in the world to shame the strong; God chose what is low and despised in the world, things that are not, to reduce to nothing things that are* (1:27-28). Now he takes up that theme, using his personal situation to bring shame upon those Corinthians who were boastful of their achievements and status in depictions that can only be understood as ironic. They claim to have become rich, powerful (*kings*), wise, strong, and honorable (4:8-10). In this claim they were probably following the example of Cynic and Stoic philosophers who called themselves kings, rich, and wise (Hays 1997: 70-71).

On the other hand, by his own admission and apparently by their accusation, Paul was, *last of all*, a spectacle, a fool, weak, disreputable, *hungry and thirsty, . . . poorly clothed and beaten and homeless, and . . . weary from the work* (4:9-12); they also criticized him for supporting himself through physical labor (with *hands*, 4:12; ch. 9). In sum, he had become *like the rubbish of the world, the dregs of all things* (vv. 8-13; cf. similar "catalogs of afflictions" in 2 Cor 4:8-12; 6:4-10; 11:23-30; 12:10; Rom 8:35-36; Thiselton 2000: 365-68). The portrayal was shaped by the practice of Roman generals in triumphal parades where triumphant troops were followed in procession by their defeated foes, bound and humiliated, on their way to execution only after being exhibited in their shame before crowds of gloating citizens. Despite all this humiliation or shame heaped upon him, Paul can still claim that, like Jesus, *when reviled, we bless; when persecuted, we endure; when slandered, we speak kindly* (vv. 12b-13a).

At this point the power of Paul's writing is such that "many commentators on this section blush for the Corinthians' shame in hearing this argument!" (M. Mitchell: 221n189). His accusation is that they had adopted the values of philosophies that were contrary to Christian values and were modeling themselves after Cynic and Stoic philosophers rather than after Paul and Apollos. Abraham Malherbe (141-43) lists examples of Cynic and Stoic philosophers reciting the hardships they had encountered and commending themselves because of adversity they had faced, but the examples he cites speak of self-discipline in the face of physical hardship and not of the humiliation that Paul is describing (cf. Witherington: 388-89).

After this bitter passage, the tone becomes conciliatory. As he draws this preliminary discussion (1:18-4:21) to a close, Paul forthrightly explains his reason for writing what he has written. Although he has clearly shaped his words to shame the Corinthians, he writes that this is not his purpose—or at least not his ultimate purpose. He has written in this way rather to admonish them. The difference is that shame is a competitive advantage to be held *[Shame and Honor, p. 368]*, while admonition intends to bring about change in behavior in order to restore honor. To put it another way, the Corinthians were acting shamelessly in their boasting. Paul wanted to instill a sense of shame in order that they would change their behavior and thus be unashamed. It is for this purpose that he has previously employed a reproachful tone in questions (e.g., *Do you not know?* [3:16]) and a censorious tone in his statements about his readers (e.g., on their *human wisdom* [1:25; 2:5, 13], *You think you are wise in this age* [3:18], and *It is a very small thing that I should be judged by you* [4:3]).

As he often draws on family language to soften harsh words—especially *brothers and sisters* (see EN on 1:10)—so he does here. He addresses them as *beloved children* (4:14; he also speaks of Timothy as *my beloved and faithful child in the Lord*, v. 17) and speaks of himself as their *father* (v. 15), whose discipline can come from *a rod of discipline* (4:21 NIV; or *a stick*, NRSV) or *in love and with a gentle spirit* (v. 21 NIV). This fatherly responsibility for disciplining children is an image that prepares the way for the corrections to be offered in the rest of the letter while also representing the sharp reproof of 1:18–4:21. It reflects the Jewish understanding of a father's responsibility best stated in Proverbs 3:11-12; 13:24; 19:18; 22:15; 23:13-14. Responsibility for teaching and disciplining children could be delegated to a "custodian" or teacher, but the father retained responsibility for their upbringing.

The injunction to imitate Paul (v. 16) is offensive to some people today and probably also offended some Corinthians who did not see him as an example worthy of imitation. Clearly, the instruction to emulate his behavior shows that right behavior and not only right thinking was important to Paul (Fee: 199–200, 203). He repeats the instruction in 11:1, identifying also the example that he follows: *Be imitators of me, as I am of Christ.* In other letters he only rarely uses the language of imitation (Eph 5:1; 1 Thess 1:6; 2:14), and in none of those cases is it an instruction that others should follow him. In the circumstances in Corinth, however, he deemed it appropriate to uphold himself, in the role of their spiritual father, as a model for their behavior. Since their Christian faith was relatively new and they did not have access to the written Gospels or instructions, the modeling of a more mature Christian was essential guidance. Indeed, the Corinthians themselves had demonstrated their need for role models by attaching themselves to philosophers and other teachers. Paul was recalling them from imitation of people who belong to the world (e.g., 3:19) and *this age* (1:20; 2:6, 8; 3:18) and instead offering himself and his experiences, as just recalled, as the example for them to follow. Yet he did not thereby mean that they must live in every way as he did (e.g., 7:7). What he was pleading with them to imitate was his humble subordination to the gospel of the crucified Christ.

The value of mentors and role models and the importance of parents as models of behavior were known in ancient times. Some four centuries before Paul, a letter appeared that was (probably falsely) attributed to an Athenian philosopher, Isocrates (436–338 BCE), which included such instructions.

> If you will but recall your father's principles, you will have from your own house a noble illustration of what I am telling you. . . . I have produced a sample of the nature of Hipponicus, after whom you should

pattern your life as after an ensample, regarding his conduct as your law, and striving to imitate and emulate your father's virtues, for it were a shame . . . for children not to imitate the noble among their ancestors. (quoted in Malherbe: 125-26)

It is unusual to refer to the sending of an envoy (4:17) or to travel plans (v. 19) this early in a letter (Paul returns to these matters in the more normal sequence of writing in 16:5-11). But for rhetorical reasons, it is important that Paul alter the usual pattern. He wanted to be sure that they would receive Timothy as his envoy with the authority to speak on Paul's behalf *to remind you of my ways in Christ Jesus* (v. 17) and to clarify both what has been written to this point in the letter and what will be forthcoming as Paul begins to address specific questions. Furthermore, both Timothy's presence as his proxy—indeed, the very model of a *beloved and faithful child in the Lord*, as Paul wishes the Corinthians to be—and Paul's own later presence would expose their actions and in particular their response to his admonition. (Does his promise to send Timothy as his envoy echo Jesus' parable of the tenants [Matt 21:33-46 // Mark 12:1-12 // Luke 20:9-19], which is often read as an allegory of God's sending of Jesus?)

Finally, Paul throws a personal challenge to those who are skeptical of his qualifications. After Timothy reports back, Paul will come in person and see for himself whether they are "full of hot air" or whether they have spiritual substance. In the contrast between talk and power (1 Cor 4:19-20), Paul returns to a theme introduced in 2:4-5. When he first mentioned it, he was defending his ministry. Now he is taking the offensive and challenging theirs. Just as their dismissal of him was based on their criteria for successful ministry, so his challenge is based on his criteria, which in turn stand on an understanding of the nature of *the kingdom of God* (3:20). He concludes the challenge with a warning: if the report from Timothy is unsatisfactory, he will come to them *with a stick* (or *rod of discipline*, NIV); but if they conform to his instructions, he will come *with love in a spirit of gentleness* (4:21).

Paul's credentials for teaching and leading the community, and specifically for disciplining and instructing the Corinthians on the matters that will follow, are these:

1. He is God's servant, not the assembly's servant (4:1-5).
2. The humiliation and abuse that he has suffered are consonant with God's values and intention (vv. 9-13).

3. He is the spiritual father of the Christian community in Corinth, even of those who have embraced Christian faith through the preaching of others (v. 15).
4. Although distance now limits his power (though he is accused in 2 Cor 10:10 of being more powerful in writing than in person), he will soon be coming to them and will demonstrate again the power with which he has preached among them (1 Cor 4:18-19; cf. 2:4).

THE TEXT IN BIBLICAL CONTEXT
Suffering of Leaders

This is not the only time that Paul wrote about the suffering he experienced as a missionary and apostle. There are several such "catalogs of afflictions," accounts of humiliation and abuse that he had suffered (see 2 Cor 4:8-12; 6:4-10; 11:23-30; 12:10; Rom 8:35-36; also Plank; Thiselton 2000: 365-68).

Yet Paul's experience is not unique. The book of Acts describes the suffering of Peter and other early leaders (5:17-42; 12:1-5), including those who suffered at the hands of Paul and his associates (7:58–8:3; 9:1-2; 22:19-20)! Extrabiblical accounts report on the suffering and martyrdom of almost all the original apostles, and such experiences continue to the present day (see van Braght).

Jesus also experienced abuse, especially in the hours preceding his death (e.g., Mark 14:43–15:37).

Suffering in leadership is not limited to the New Testament experiences. James advised his readers, "As an example of suffering and patience, beloved, take the prophets who spoke in the name of the Lord" (James 5:10). He specifically mentioned Job as one such example (v. 11). The suffering servant passages in Isaiah (Isa 42:1-4; 49:1-6; 50:4-9; 52:13–53:12) are read by Christians as applying to Jesus, and they aptly do, though they were written with other leaders in mind (I. Friesen: 451). Jeremiah is sometimes called the suffering prophet because of all the opposition and ridicule he experienced (Martens: 18-19), and Hosea is portrayed as a suffering servant (Guenther: 50-52).

Leadership in God's realm is not demonstrated by wealth, power, or honor, as the Corinthians imagined. Leaders can expect to suffer. Paul's experience of being mistreated in his leadership role was not unique (see "'What's in It for Me?'" in TLC below).

Models of Leadership

Paul's challenge to those who undervalued his leadership was based on his perspective that their expectations of leadership were inappropriately shaped by philosophers, particularly by Cynic and Stoic philosophers who called themselves kings, rich, or wise (Hays 1997: 70-71). His own views were also shaped by his theological presuppositions and his experiences, as well as his gifts. We have seen in 1 Corinthians 3-4 that Paul uses a variety of metaphors to describe his role(s)—farmer, wise architect, servant, and steward—and he uses others elsewhere.

Within his own Jewish tradition, Paul had many different models from which to draw. Among the varieties of leadership exercised in the Old Testament are those of prophets, priests, and kings. Recent studies of leadership models in the Bible have demonstrated a much greater variety of terms that are used. For example, David Bennett has created a complex taxonomy of "biblical images for leaders and followers" that draws primarily from the metaphors that Jesus used in talking with and about his disciples. Paul Minear identified ninety-six "images of the church in the New Testament" and sixteen images of leadership that relate to those models. Donald Messer lists some "contemporary images of Christian ministry" in addition to naming biblical and traditional images (cf. "Servant Leadership" in TBC for 3:5-23).

Another leadership image, the shepherd, is used often in the Old Testament (e.g., 2 Sam 5:2; Jer 23:1-4; Zech 11:1-17) and in the New Testament (e.g., John 10:1-16; Acts 20:28; 1 Pet 5:1-4). Jesus contrasts the commitment of a shepherd who owns the sheep with that of a hired hand who does not care for the sheep and readily abandons them when there is a threat (John 10).

There is no single or even dominant model of leadership in the Bible, and there is no biblical text that gives a definition or prescription for leadership. To understand a biblical view of leadership, it is necessary to use many images, each illuminating some aspect but not the whole of God's intention for the relationship between leaders and followers.

THE TEXT IN THE LIFE OF THE CHURCH

Pastors as "Parents"

Most pastors, missionaries, and other leaders share Paul's heart of love for the church (1 Cor 4:14-21). Sadly, there are exceptions to this. All church leaders can identify with the frustration Paul expresses in this passage and elsewhere throughout this letter despite his love. But for the most part, his longing for his beloved "children" to experience the fullest possible measure of God's grace, to love each other as he loved each of them, and yes, to love and respect him in return—such longing surely echoes in the hearts of those who serve God's people.

The use of familial language here and throughout the letter best represents Paul's attachment to his readers (see EN above). In 1 Corinthians, more than any other letter (twenty-two times), he uses sibling language to address his readers. This is one of only two places in any of his letters where he uses *father* to name his relationship with them. The other is in 1 Thessalonians 2:10-11, where he uses the simile "like a father" to express "how pure, upright, and blameless our conduct was toward you believers" (though in the previous verse he addresses his readers as "brothers and sisters"). He also speaks of Timothy as being "like a son" and "my own dear child" (Phil 2:22; see Zerbe: 177-78; 1 Cor 4:17) and Onesimus as "my child, . . . whose father I have become" (Philem 10).

Some readers who have experienced or witnessed toxic family systems or the absence of positive family systems find it difficult to understand or accept this language. In some circles it has become impossible to honor paternal or fatherly care because "paternalism" carries only negative connotations. But those who have experienced the love and compassion of a caring father or who have been such a father immediately understand Paul's intention.

In "Models of Leadership" (TBC above), we noted the variety of ways of talking about leadership in the Bible. Much of that language is based on relational concepts rather than on task or role. In some contemporary writing about pastoral ministry, images are proposed to illuminate some aspect of the relationship between pastor and congregation as an alternative or to broaden the understanding for both congregation and pastor. Some of these metaphors are coach, counselor, spiritual director, facilitator, midwife, and clown (Messer explores these and more). The exclusive use of "father" language, as in Roman Catholic circles, to designate or address priests adds to the difficulty for some to accept women as pastors and spiritual leaders. It is important to use a variety of metaphors to be faithful to the Scriptures and to communicate with people who have many different personal and cultural experiences. To hear Paul's voice accurately, it is valuable to hear a positive, loving, hopeful, and encouraging tone in his "parental" word at the end of chapter 4.

"What's in It for Me?"

In a course on leadership for leaders of nonprofit organizations, the professor pressed the class members to ask themselves, "What's in it for me?" Several Christian ministry leaders in the class cringed, having been trained to think of their work as service to others, not to ourselves. Yet there is value in honestly naming the rewards we get from our work, whether paid or volunteer. That could include a salary, the satisfaction of making a difference in people's lives, or the fulfillment of a promise. If in honesty we must admit to seeking less honorable rewards—perhaps control over others, or inflating our status—that too should be named and appropriate measures taken.

It is important to recognize how easy it is to deceive oneself about one's motives; it is much easier to see them in others. Sometimes people convince themselves that their concern is for others' well-being when they are really driven by a desire for power or control. While we should always be alert to self-deception and should seek the assessment of others to help identify it, there is an equal risk of attributing inappropriate motives to others as a way of avoiding their counsel and critique. Both of these risks occur in our experiences of family and intimate relationships. They are also present in the church. Some readers have been suspicious of Paul's motives in correcting the Corinthians, but it is more faithful to the text and more profitable for our spiritual growth to assume the integrity of his words (cf. Thiselton 2006: 78–79).

So how would Paul have answered the question, "What's in it for me?" In 1 Corinthians 9 he will give part of his answer in these words: *I do it all for the sake of the gospel, so that I may share in its blessings* (9:23). In short, if he fails he will be *disqualified* (v. 27) from gaining the *imperishable* [*wreath*] (v. 25). The hope of his own salvation and the gratification of sharing that with others is the only reward he needs or will accept, since he has refused financial support from the Corinthians for his ministry (see EN on 9:3-14) *[Patrons and Clients, p. 366]*.

Here in chapter 4, his answer is, "What's in it for me is abuse, humiliation, and suffering." Is that evidence of an unhealthy mind or low self-esteem? What do we say about Paul's experience or, for that matter, about Jesus' experience, or the other examples identified in "Suffering of Leaders" (TBC above)? What about the Scriptures that anticipate suffering as the normal experience of Christians: "We also boast in our sufferings, knowing that suffering produces endurance, and endurance produces character, and character produces hope, and hope does not disappoint us, because God's love has been poured into our hearts through the Holy Spirit that has been given to us" (Rom 5:3-5).

Many people in Western society are motivated by self-gratification and personal success, and they want it delivered soon. That includes many people in Christian churches. The attitude of many is close to that of the Corinthians who said, *Already [we] have all [we] want! Already [we] have become rich! Quite apart from [others we] have become kings [or children of the King]!* (1 Cor 4:8). While this may not be the experience of Christians in the developing world, it is what many of them aspire to.

Because fulfillment and recognition are highly valued, many Christians, when they do not experience the financial rewards or the respect or gratitude that they seek, abandon their work. Sometimes they even abandon Christ and the church in disappointment and bitterness. It is easy to understand that people whose labor and passion are unappreciated by their fellow believers lose hope and courage to carry on.

As disciples of Jesus, it is fitting for us to think carefully about what we expect and what we value as our reward for following him. As volunteers or as salaried workers in the church, whether ordained or not, an additional layer of assessment is needed: Why do we do what we do? Are we motivated by power, status, and financial rewards? Would we continue to work as servants and stewards *without* the rewards we value? Or should we adjust our expectations of reward to something more in keeping with the countercultural values that Paul espoused for his ministry?

Much has been written about "wounded healers" that informs and encourages both pastors and congregations in coming to terms with the suffering of leaders and the question, "What's in it for me?" The classic and still excellent treatment of this is Henri Nouwen's *The Wounded Healer: Ministry in Contemporary Society*.

Preaching and Worship

Churches that strictly use the Revised Common Lectionary will not get a chance to hear 1 Corinthians 4:6-21 because it is not included in the assigned readings. A preacher in such a setting will want to find opportunities to use the riches of this text for congregational instruction. The consideration of "What's in it for me?" is urgent in many churches, and Paul's teaching is a good antidote to the false gospel of wealth and personal success. Verse 20 is helpful as a text from which to reflect on the importance of deeds instead of words.

(*Power* here does not mean "might" or "coercion," but action or solid efficacy [Thiselton 2006: 80].) Of course, the contrast between Paul's experience and the claims of the Corinthians can be used to illustrate the point of 1:26-31 when preaching on that passage.

Summary of Chapters 1–4

These first four chapters of 1 Corinthians have established a basis from which Paul can address the specific issues in the life of the Christian assemblies in Corinth. After the formalities of opening a letter (formalities written so that they already carry significant substance for the Corinthians), Paul states his thesis (1:10) and explains what he has heard from Chloe's people that gave rise to his concern for the community's fractiousness. Then he sets forth some fundamental values and convictions, the basis from which he will address the issues that have been presented by Chloe's people, by the letter he has received, and by the carriers of the letter. These convictions and values include the following:

1. The heart of the gospel is the pronouncement of the crucified Christ.
2. God's values of shame and honor reject the world's definitions of what is honored and what is shameful.
3. Spiritual discernment is different from the wisdom of this age and governs the Christian community.
4. The Christian community and its leaders (indeed the whole world) belong to God.
5. Paul's authority and credibility are based not on worldly or this-age criteria, but on his consistent representation, in his preaching and in his life, of the crucified Christ.

Throughout these first four chapters, Paul always has in mind the fundamental issue that he is concerned to address: the factionalism of the faith community. He understands that the factions have been stirred up by people who have lost sight of the unifying and impelling values and convictions that he has preached. They were emulating non-Christian philosophers and seeking personal status by denigrating Paul's qualifications for leadership. Their understanding of leadership was distorted and their understanding of the gospel was diluted. Before addressing the concrete matters over which they were divided, Paul needed to correct their attitudes and establish his qualifications to instruct them. That is what he has addressed in these first four chapters.

With all this preparation in place, Paul is now ready to address a series of specific issues. These issues occupy the remainder of the letter body.

1 Corinthians 5:1–15:58

Issues Reported from Corinth

1 Corinthians 5:1-13
Protection of Boundaries against Immorality

PREVIEW

Before Paul can advise the factions how to unite, he must clarify what membership in the community is. Chapters 5 and 6 address issues of community boundaries. With three separate "case studies," these chapters attempt to clarify who is "inside" and who is "outside" the body of believers. The first issue (5:1-13) concerns sexual morality, as does the third (6:12-20). Between these discussions, there is a section on the morality of litigation (6:1-11).

How did Paul know that these situations had developed in Corinth? Presumably they emerged after he had left. There is no hint that the faith community or its leaders reported these to Paul. Indeed, as we shall see, they seemed to find no moral ambiguity about any of these. The only probable source for these scandalous allegations is Chloe's people. Without request or permission, these messengers reported "the dirt" to Paul, who replied with passion and censure. Is it significant that the people who report the unflattering news from Corinth are identified by their association with a woman, that they were servants, and that they may have been from Ephesus and not from Corinth (see EN on 1:11)? Perhaps any one factor or a combination of these factors gave them the courage to be outspoken about issues that the recognized Corinthian leaders would rather not have told Paul.

OUTLINE

The Scandal, 5:1-2
The Prescribed Resolution, 5:3-5
The Principle behind the Prescription, 5:6-8
The Implication of This Case for Understanding Community
   Boundaries, 5:9-13

EXPLANATORY NOTES

The Scandal 5:1-2

Paul begins by bluntly confronting the readers with the story he has heard: *It is actually reported that there is sexual immorality among you, . . . for a man is living with his father's wife.* With these words, Paul conveys his horror about what he has heard (Fee: 218). The situation is so shameful, according to Paul, that it should not even be talked about. Following immediately after the charge that *some of you, thinking that I am not coming to you, have become arrogant* (4:18) and a warning that when he comes it may be *with a stick* (4:21), this concrete proof of misbehavior in their midst is intended to burst the bubble of their presumed maturity and honor (4:8).

The Greek word that is here translated *sexual immorality* is *porneia*. In secular Greek it meant prostitution, and was sometimes censured but often condoned. In Hellenistic Judaism, however, its use was generalized to include all sexual activity outside marriage. Sometimes it was used in the Greek translation of the Old Testament (Septuagint, LXX) to render the Hebrew word for "harlotry" in a metaphorical sense to refer to idolatry, and sometimes in reference to marriage within forbidden degrees of relationships (e.g., marriage to a close relative: see Lev 18:6-18; 20:11-12). Sometimes it meant unlawful conduct in general, but most often it referred to some kind of sexual impropriety (*TDNT* 6:579-95).

The exact nature of the *porneia* addressed in this passage is defined: the man *is living with* (lit. *has*) his father's wife. Clearly this was his stepmother, not his own mother. Beyond that, we are curious about many facets of the relationship but will never know. It seems impossible that she was still married to the father, but was she divorced from him or a widow? Were the man and his stepmother married or cohabiting without marriage? The list of questions goes on. Both Paul and the Corinthians knew the answers to these, and it was not necessary for Paul to clarify the situation. It was not any of these nuances that was offensive, but the simple fact of the sexual union between a man and his stepmother, a relationship that we would call incest or marriage within forbidden degrees of relationship.

Although Paul wrote that such behavior *is not found even among pagans*, there were well-known examples where this had happened. In particular cases and in general, however, such relationships were condemned. Among the Romans, Cicero (*"In Defense of Cluentius"* 5.12-6.16 [66 BCE]), Gaius (*Institutes* 1.63 [ca. 60 CE]), and others reacted to infamous situations of such relationships and stated explicitly that they were forbidden (Yarborough: 90n3). Aristotle (*Rhetoric* 2.6.4) and Musonius Rufus (Lecture 12) had declared such relationships to be shameful. In Judaism too, such a relationship was forbidden, though not unknown (Gen 35:22; 49:3-4; Testament of Reuben). Jewish tradition viewed *porneia* as "the Gentile sin" (Jubilees 25:1). The fact that this particular form of *porneia* was forbidden even among Gentiles (some translations say *pagans* [NRSV, NIV]; others say *Gentiles* [KJV, NKJV, NET, NJB]; cf. EN on 12:2) increased its offensiveness to Paul as a Christian Jew and, incidentally, confirms that Paul viewed the Corinthian Christians as ex-Gentiles.

The woman involved gets no attention from Paul. This is surprising in a cultural context that limited women's sexual activity but not, for the most part, men's. In chapter 7 of this letter, Paul holds women and men equally accountable for their sexual activity, but here he pronounces judgment only on the man (cf. 6:12-20). Perhaps Paul understood that this situation was not her choice and she was therefore not at fault. Most readers assume, however, that the woman was not a believer and hence not bound to the discipline of the assembly (v. 12). Although the man was clearly a member of the assembly, Paul does not even address him directly. The letter is addressed to the faith community, not to individual members.

It is to the assembly, therefore, that Paul addresses his strongest criticism. *And you* [emphatic] *are arrogant! Should you not rather have mourned, so that he who has done this would have been removed from among you?* (v. 2; cf. v. 6). Paul has already criticized the boasting and arrogance of the Corinthian believers in 1:29, 31; 3:21; 4:6, 7, 18, and 19. In 4:18-19 he threatened to "call the bluff" of the shameless boasters when he comes to Corinth. Now he is starting the process by confronting them in the letter.

Again we have many questions for which there are no answers in the text. Was Paul critical of the *act* of boasting or the *content* of their boast? Was the community proud *because* of the member's behavior or *despite* it? How could they have justified this situation, much less boasted about it?

One explanation that has been suggested is that the offensive situation was justified by the man and the community on the principle that when the man converted to Christianity, he became a new person, and all former relationships (i.e., as a stepson) were dissolved, so he now felt free to marry this "unrelated" woman (Daube: 223-27). Although rabbis debated such possibilities (and in the end rejected the argument that a man would be free in such a situation), it seems unlikely that the Corinthians would have known or cared about the rabbinic debate, so this solution is unsatisfactory.

Another suggestion is that the concept of freedom, perhaps similar to the view that gnostics held in the second century, would have provided justification for this act (Schmithals: 237, referring to Irenaeus, *Against Heresies* 1.6.3). But although Paul confronts the argument of freedom in 6:12-20, he does not mention it here.

These two and other attempts to explain the man's behavior focus on the rationale that he might have used to defend his actions. None of the proposals has proved fully satisfactory. Instead of seeking a theological or legal *rationale* that the man might have used to justify his decision to take his father's wife, several scholars have looked for possible *motives* for his action.

In Roman times, marriage was contracted primarily for procreation and material benefit rather than sexual attraction. It is quite possible, therefore, that upon the death of his father, a man would be motivated to take his father's widow as his wife in order to keep the estate intact, including the dowry that the stepmother had brought to the marriage (Chow: 132-40; Clarke: 80-85). Such a motive would presumably have been felt more strongly by a wealthy person than a poor person without dowry or estate. Furthermore, it would have been more likely that a wealthy person, rather than a poor one, could flaunt the legal proscription of such relationships successfully. Both Chow and Clarke argue, therefore, that the guilty man was probably a wealthy patron on whose wealth the assembly depended and in whose membership in their community the Christians took pride *[Patrons and Clients, p. 366]*.

Whatever the reasons and assumptions behind this situation, Paul clearly was affronted by both the behavior of the man involved and the arrogant tolerance—perhaps even shameless, gloating satisfaction—of the rest of the believers. He ordered immediate corrective action.

The Prescribed Resolution 5:3-5

What the believers should have done immediately, Paul suggests, was to mourn and remove the offender from the assembly (v. 2b).

Since they have not done so earlier, he insists that they do it now. Emphatically distancing himself from their inaction (*for my part* [v. 3 NIV], in contrast to *and you* [v. 2]), he describes the public action that must be taken to repudiate this immoral member. The guilty man must be removed from the realm of God, the community of faith, and banished to the realm of Satan, the world.

The rite of exclusion that he prescribes sounds simple. In a public gathering, with Paul too being present *in spirit*, they are to *hand this man over to Satan* (vv. 4-5 NIV). This cryptic instruction invites many questions, both as to procedure and as to its intent.

An important feature of Paul's instruction is the public setting for the rite. In addition to insisting that the whole congregation should assemble for it, three times Paul draws attention to his own presence *in spirit* with them. Furthermore, he reminds them that *our Lord Jesus* is present (twice in v. 4).

Jerome Murphy-O'Connor (1977) and several others have argued that *in the name of the Lord Jesus* modifies *the man who has done such a thing*, indicating that the man's defense was that his behavior was done in Jesus' name (cf. v. 4 NRSV footnote). Another grammatical possibility is that the assembly should take place *in the name of our Lord Jesus*, as in the NIV 1984, JB, and NEB translations. It seems to make better sense, however, to understand the phrase as modifying *I have already pronounced judgment*, as in the NIV, RSV, NRSV, GNB, and NABR. Fee (228), who had earlier adopted this last reading, argues that "the best answer lies with seeing the phrase basically as modifying the entire sentence."

Exposure to "the public eye" (whether real or imagined) is essential to the experience of shame, and shame was the sanction that Paul wanted to apply to this situation. Thus it was important that Jesus, Paul, and the whole Christian assembly should witness this disciplinary action.

Several people have tried to show that Paul really expected the assembly to turn the guilty man over to Roman authorities (*Satan*) for punishment, probably execution. However, there is no hint in the text or in Paul's usual way of dealing with sin that would support such an extreme measure (cf. Brenneman: 113). Without recourse to the courts or other sanctions (see 6:1-11), only shame could be brought to bear on the man and, by association, on the arrogant believers who approved or tolerated his actions *[Shame and Honor, p. 368]*.

The purpose of handing the man *over to Satan for the destruction of the flesh* was *so that his spirit may be saved in the day of the Lord* (v. 5; cf. Brenneman: 198-200 et passim). Both the destruction of the flesh and the salvation of the spirit have attracted much discussion. Did Paul believe that exclusion from the assembly would cause the man literally to shrivel up and die, or at least suffer severe pain? We have dismissed the possibility that the civic authorities would execute the man for this offense, but did Paul anticipate possible suicide in reaction to the intense shame of a public excommunication? And how would any of these possibilities lead to the salvation of the man's spirit?

When he uses the word *flesh* (Gk. *sarx*), Paul does not usually mean "body." His attitude toward the human body is positive, or at least morally neutral. Indeed, as we shall see in chapter 15, Paul does not think of death as a destruction of the flesh or body while the spirit lives on; instead, he anticipates a resurrection of the body. Paul characteristically uses *flesh* in contrast to *spirit*, but not as a way of dividing a person into two parts (much less the alleged three-part division of body, soul, and spirit). *Flesh*, as Paul uses the word, refers to the whole person outside of Christ (see 3:1-3 and corresponding EN; see also Brenneman: 86–92). It has an ethical or theological meaning, rather than a physical or material sense. Thus Paul here is anticipating the destruction of the "fleshliness" (*sinful nature*, NIV 1984) of the man, not of his body (cf. Snyder 1992: 61–62, 257). If indeed the unethical flesh were destroyed and the offender turned to Christ, then the Spirit-filled person would be saved on the day of the Lord, as Paul and the Scriptures teach.

What is true of the individual member is also true of the corporate community. In the Greek text, no possessive pronoun is attached to either *flesh* or *spirit* in verse 5; translators have inserted *his* spirit as an interpretive gloss (Shillington 1998b: 34). Turning the guilty man over to Satan will destroy fleshliness and open the possibility of saving the spirit, but the text does not specify that it is the guilty man's *fleshliness* that will be destroyed nor that it is his *spirit* that will be saved. Since Paul's concern seems to be more for the faith community than for the individual member, it is entirely possible that he is thinking that the removal of a "fleshly" person from the assembly will destroy the community's fleshliness and save it as a spiritual corporate body *in the day of the Lord* (v. 5). Just as the destruction of the individual sinner's fleshliness leads to salvation of that person's spirit, so too in the corporate setting of the assembly must fleshliness be removed for the spirit to thrive (cf. Shillington 1998b: 31–32). This echoes the atonement ritual of the scapegoat described in Leviticus 16, whose "central purpose . . . [is] to rid the community of its evil contamination" (49).

Paul points this out to his readers as the principle behind his prescription.

The Principle behind the Prescription 5:6-8

Paul uses imagery from the Feast of Unleavened Bread to make his point about removing impurities from the congregations. This ancient festival was so closely associated with the Passover festival that the two names became virtually interchangeable, and eventually they became fully integrated (Luke 22:1). In preparation for the festival, Jewish families assiduously tried to remove every vestige of leavening agents from their homes in memory of the unleavened bread that their ancestors ate during their escape from Egypt (Exod 12:14-20; Lev 23:4-8; cf. Mishnah Pesach 1:1; *ABD* 6:755–65). In Jewish literature, leaven represents evil (e.g., Mark 8:15; Jesus' parable comparing the kingdom of God to leaven, Matt 13:33 // Luke 13:20-21, is a rare exception to this). Likewise, Paul urges the Corinthian believers to remove every hint of *malice and wickedness* from the congregations (1 Cor 5:8). Though Christ now replaces the Jewish Passover lamb, the followers of Jesus have inherited the principles behind the Jewish practice. Like yeast, the sin of the offending member will contaminate other members, Paul argues, much as we might appeal to the common saying that "one bad apple spoils a whole barrel" (cf. 15:33; Gal 5:9).

Since he has already hinted at his concern for the public reputation of the Christian community (1:26-29), and since he has named both the public knowledge and the public condemnation of this specific situation of sexual immorality (5:1), it seems that Paul was also concerned about restoring the reputation of the believers. Shame adheres to one's associates. It is characteristic of shame that if a person behaves shamefully, that person's family, race, class, profession, business associates, neighbors, and faith community are also implicated in the shame *[Shame and Honor, p. 368]*. Thus the exclusion of the man who has brought shame upon himself and the assembly will restore the community's reputation. Paul applies this principle of separation from offending persons not only to this situation but also to every similar situation.

The Implication of This Case for Understanding Community Boundaries 5:9-13

The general lesson that Paul draws from this particular case is that there is a clear and defined boundary around the believing community. *Anyone who bears the name of brother or sister* (5:11) is inside those boundaries; everyone else is outside. The boundary is characterized in this passage by the moral character of the people on either side of it. This does not imply that one crosses the boundary by achieving or failing to achieve certain moral standards. It does claim, however, that certain character standards are expected of insiders that are not expected (though of course they may also be present) of outsiders.

Paul alludes to an earlier letter that he had written to the Corinthians (v. 9; cf. "Paul and the Corinthians" in the introduction). Now he feels it necessary to correct an apparent misunderstanding of that letter. *I wrote to you in my letter not to associate with . . . immoral persons* (v. 9), he reminded them. But they had misunderstood that earlier letter to say that he meant immoral persons outside the assembly. This application, of course, would have been literally impossible *since you would then need to go out of the world* (v. 10). The greater problem, however, was not that they were avoiding immoral outsiders, but that they were not avoiding immoral insiders. By applying Paul's earlier instructions only to those outside the faith community, the Christians in Corinth had excused insiders of immoral conduct, such as the man who was living with his father's wife. That misunderstanding Paul now corrects: *But now I am writing to you not to associate with anyone who bears the name of brother or sister who is . . . immoral* (v. 11).

Underlying this clarification is a principle that applies both to the present case and to the one that will follow: even Paul has no authority to judge in the present the moral behavior of persons who are outside the community of believers. *God will* (the verb is future) look after them (5:13a), and *the saints* will participate in that eschatological judgment (6:2; see EN below). Within the community, however, Paul has the authority to judge; in fact, he has an obligation to do so. So do all Christians. Therefore Paul repeats his earlier command: *Drive out the wicked person from among you* (5:13b).

Do not even eat with such a one, Paul instructs (5:11b). What exactly he meant by that has been debated. Was it that all shared meals, including family eating, should be avoided? Or did he mean only the fellowship meal that accompanied worship (cf. 11:17-34), or perhaps only the symbolic meal of the Lord's Supper (11:23-26)? Since there is no qualification of the ban, and since the intention is to create great distance between the assembly and *such a one*, it seems most likely that Paul intended to exclude such a person from any community fellowship meal. We will look again at the importance of fellowship meals as boundary markers when we consider 11:27-32 (cf. Jamir: 167).

Finally, we must note the kinds of immorality that Paul lists in this paragraph. In fact, there are two lists. The first includes *the [sexually] immoral* [Gk. *pornois*], . . . *the greedy and robbers, or idolaters* (v. 10). The second includes these four categories and adds two more: a *reviler*, a *drunkard* (v. 11). These two lists (and a similar one in 6:9-10) fit a pattern of ethical teaching that was common in the New Testament world: listing vices to be avoided or, on the other hand, virtues to be pursued *[Vice and Virtue Lists, p. 370]*. While not intended to be complete, the lists do specify kinds of behavior not acceptable for Christians.

In summary, this part of Paul's argument for the unity of the Christian community focuses on the community's boundaries. Not every person is included. The distinctions between those who are inside and those who are outside, he argues, must be clearly maintained. Within the community, moral purity is expected; those who refuse to conform are to be removed from the corporate body.

THE TEXT IN BIBLICAL CONTEXT

Incest

Four passages in the Torah define which relatives are prohibited from sexual relations. They are Leviticus 18:7-18; 20:11-21; and Deuteronomy 22:30; 27:20, 22, 23. The lists are not equally comprehensive, but one cannot infer that a relationship not mentioned is considered acceptable. For example, none of the three prohibits father-daughter relations, but it is universally understood that such were prohibited in the Israelite culture. All four lists include "your father's wife" as a prohibited relationship. In Leviticus, the chapter texts go on to identify incest as being practiced by "the nations I am casting out before you" (18:24; 20:23).

The Bible is frank about violations of these prohibitions when they did occur. Abraham, accused of falsely calling Sarah his sister instead of his wife, replied, "Besides, she is indeed my sister, the daughter of my father but not the daughter of my mother; and she became my wife" (Gen 20:12), which is explicitly forbidden in Leviticus 18:9 and Deuteronomy 27:22. Lot's daughters conspired to get impregnated by their father (Gen 19:30-38). A simple report that "Reuben [son of Jacob] went and lay with Bilhah his father's concubine" (Gen 35:22) is subsequently identified as the cause of his downfall: "You shall no longer excel because you went up onto your father's bed; then you defiled it—you went up onto my couch!" (Gen 49:4). King David's son Amnon raped his half sister Tamar. She resisted, saying, "Such a thing is not done in Israel," though she also assured him that their father would give permission for Amnon to marry her if he were asked (2 Sam 13). Later, Tamar's brother, Absalom, demonstrated his rebellion against King David by having sexual relations with his father's concubines in "a tent . . . upon the roof . . . in the sight of all Israel" (2 Sam 16:21-22). Ezekiel reports God's condemnation of Jerusalem because "in you they uncover their fathers' nakedness. . . . One commits abomination with his neighbor's wife; another lewdly defiles his daughter-in-law; another in you defiles his sister, his father's daughter" (Ezek 22:10-11).

Though such incidents are reported, they are not condoned and are explicitly prohibited in the Levitical Holiness Code and in Deuteronomy.

Maintaining Boundaries

Concern for defining boundaries—for distinguishing between those who are inside and those who are outside of the people of God—is demonstrated throughout the Bible. Maintaining the boundaries by excluding ("cutting off") those who violate community standards is often attested. On the other hand, those boundaries were permeable. There is a pervasive tradition of accepting into the boundaries people from the outside, such as Ruth, the Moabite woman who was the great-grandmother of King David (Ruth 4:13-17; Matt 1:5-6), and Rahab the prostitute (Josh 2, 6). Similarly, insiders could become outsiders when guilty of wrongdoing (e.g., Achan in Josh 7).

Examples of boundary maintenance by exclusion can be found in Exodus 12:15, 19; Leviticus 17:4, 9; and Numbers 19:20. The first of these is especially interesting as a parallel to 1 Corinthians 5 because it commands expulsion of a person who has eaten leavened bread during the Feast of Unleavened Bread, the very festival to which Paul also alludes in his comments on purity in the community.

A particularly severe example of expulsion is described in Ezra 10. After the return from Babylonian exile, Ezra was distressed about the intermarriage of Jewish men with non-Jewish women. He summoned all the men of the tribes of Judah and Benjamin to Jerusalem with the warning that if any failed to come, "all their property should be forfeited, and they themselves banned from the congregation of the exiles" (10:8). After the matter was addressed and enforcement procedures were established, all those foreign wives and their children were "sent . . . away," and the holiness of the faithful was reestablished (10:44).

In the New Testament are several passages closely connected with the exclusion formula in 1 Corinthians 5:5. Closest in language is the reference found in 1 Timothy 1:20 to "Hymenaeus and Alexander, whom I have turned over to Satan, so that they may learn not to blaspheme." Despite the similarity of the expression "turned over to Satan," there are important differences between these two actions. The author of 1 Timothy appears to have acted independently, whereas Paul instructed the Corinthians to act corporately with his presence *in spirit*. More important is the fact that 1 Timothy says nothing about the destruction of the flesh or the salvation of the spirit. Instead, there is a much more modest purpose: "so that they may learn not to blaspheme." Nevertheless, the goal of restoration does seem to be implied in 1 Timothy 1:20 and is explicitly stated in 1 Corinthians 5:5.

This hope of restoration through a process that might go so far as to include temporary exclusion from the community is discussed also in Matthew 18:15-17. Though the language of handing over to Satan is not used in that passage, the result of exclusion, "Let such a one be to you as a Gentile and a tax collector," is equivalent to casting one into the realm of Satan, outside the realm of God (see Gardner: 284-86).

A further parallel might be noted in 2 Thessalonians: "Take note of those who do not obey what we say in this letter; have nothing to do with them, so that they may be ashamed. Do not regard them as enemies, but warn them as believers" (2 Thess 3:14-15). Although there is no dramatic expulsion formula or rite, this does seem to approach the spirit of 1 Corinthians 5 in several ways. First, it is addressed to believers, not to outsiders. Second, there is a complete prohibition against social relations. And finally, the intention is the same: to use shame as a sanction to bring about behavioral changes.

The instructions in 2 Thessalonians 3:14 are much like similar instructions in Galatians 6:1; James 5:19-20; and 1 John 5:16, all of which recommend attempting to restore an offender or "wanderer" and imply or explicitly state that this should be done "in a spirit of gentleness" (Gal 6:1).

Such a spirit of gentleness and an example of restoration as the final result of exclusion is shown in 2 Corinthians 2:5-11. Many scholars have suggested that the person referred to here is the very man whose case is addressed in 1 Corinthians 5 (e.g., Kruse:

129–39). Even if it is not the same person, the counsel to "forgive and console" an offender whose repentance is demonstrated by "excessive sorrow" clearly applies to a situation similar to that found in this passage.

In summary, Paul's insistence on clearly defined boundaries around the community of faith and the expulsion of anyone who refuses to live up to the (moral) standards expected of insiders represents a concern that is found throughout the Bible and in nonbiblical Jewish literature as well, such as the Dead Sea Scrolls (e.g., Community Rule, 1QS 5.25–6.1).

THE TEXT IN THE LIFE OF THE CHURCH
Excommunication

The practice of excluding from the church those who fail to live up to its standards has continued in various forms since the first century. Sometimes expulsion and the threat of expulsion were applied to enforce doctrinal conformity, as in the aftermath of many of the early councils of the church, when disagreeing parties excommunicated (i.e., denied communion to) each other. Often the consignment *over to Satan for the destruction of the flesh* of people considered heretics was carried out literally and immediately by various horrible methods of torture and execution.

Excommunication was also threatened and sometimes carried out for other reasons. When the church became powerful and exercised its power in cooperation with the state, excommunication was one of the strongest tools available to the church to enforce compliance and conformity. Because there was only one church and all citizens were part of it, excommunication by the church was tantamount to being expelled from one's family and community and placed outside the protection of the state.

During the upheavals of the Reformation, all parties excommunicated their opponents, and most added persecution and execution to spiritual exclusion. Anabaptists (for the most part) were the only Christians who did not resort to physical violence to exclude those who disagreed with them; nevertheless, they did freely and sometimes zealously excommunicate each other. Some Anabaptist groups, notably the Amish and some groups in the Netherlands, also practiced a form of exclusion called "the ban" as an application of Paul's instructions *not to eat with such a one* to all meals, not only the Lord's Supper. There were vigorous disagreements (and mutual excommunications) over whether the ban included all familial and spousal contact as well as social and spiritual relationships (see articles on "Ban," "Church Discipline," and "Excommunication" in *GAMEO*; also *BE* 1:386-89; cf. Brenneman: 22-31).

With graphic detail, Patrick Friesen's story *The Shunning* describes the personal and familial disruption caused by excommunication and the ban in a Mennonite community in rural southern Manitoba in the early part of the twentieth century. Although it is a fictionalized account, it accurately expresses the pain that has been associated with this practice and that has contributed to a growing distaste for it.

In recent years, the threat of excommunication and banning has become less potent and is rarely practiced in most churches. One reason for this is that people are less dependent on any one community for social and spiritual connections. One who is excommunicated from a congregation can easily switch allegiance to another congregation or denomination where the standards are different. One who is banned from social relationships by one community can usually find acceptance in another community. Few people accept the exclusive power of the church to grant or withhold salvation. In addition, an evangelical Christian theology that prioritizes a personal relationship with God minimizes the relevance of church membership to personal salvation. As V. George Shillington (1998b: 30-31) puts it, "An excommunicated member of a modern (or postmodern) church, less dependent on community status for living in an industrial society than a member in a Pauline community would be for an agrarian society, might not be so inclined to consider the institutional church of Euro-America a way to be saved at the end-time."

Paul Hiebert's introduction to Christian studies of the concepts of bounded sets and centered sets has been welcomed by some who are uncomfortable with the older emphasis on focusing on and enforcing the boundaries of church membership. Whereas bounded sets have rigid boundaries that define who is in and who is out, centered sets are defined by one's relationship with the center, especially whether one is moving toward or away from the group's center (Hiebert). While some Christians have welcomed this shift in paradigms, a substantial movement in the opposite direction emphasizes reinforcing boundaries and enforcing them by "disfellowshiping" dissenters.

Postmodern Christians who are reticent to exclude people and who distrust authority structures and institutions are uncomfortable with Paul's language of expulsion and condemnation. So were the Corinthian Christians. But postmodern Christians also recognize the value of personal and communal boundaries. So the ambivalence in thinking and in practice continues.

Jesus' vision of the grand inclusive table of the kingdom need not be taken as instruction to remove all boundaries from Christian communities. Jesus made a great point of the inclusive invitation to all, but he also insisted that choices be made. There is good reason to have community boundaries. They help to shape identity and a sense of belonging (E. Kreider 1997: 130).

Paul will pick up the discussion of boundary maintenance again when he addresses the (mis)practice of the Lord's Supper in 1 Corinthians 11:17-34.

1 Corinthians 6:1-11
Lawsuits and Judgment

PREVIEW

Paul next addresses an issue that frequently arises between people: One person has a grievance against another. How can it be resolved? Who will arbitrate between the disputing parties?

There are many connections between chapters 5, 6, and 7 in 1 Corinthians. The language of judgment that occurs in 5:12-13 continues in 6:1-6. In 5:12, Paul declares that members of the assembly should judge *those who are inside*. In 6:1-6, he criticizes them for inviting outsiders to judge between believers. In 6:12-20, the presenting issue, as in 5:1-5 and in 7:1-9, 36-38, is sexual morality; and the theological argument of chapter 6 applies also to the issues in chapters 5 and 7. In 6:9-11 there is a list of vices that includes and extends the lists found in 5:10, 11 *[Vice and Virtue Lists, p. 370]*. Paul believes that the Corinthians had not learned the significance and implications of their identity as Christians. In the issues addressed in the previous chapter and here, they were not distinguishing between being inside or outside the community of faith (M. Mitchell: 231).

Some scholars have argued that the matter brought before an external court (1 Cor 6) had to do with the "incestuous" relationship discussed in chapter 5 (Richardson), but that connection does not fit the text. The connection between these matters is not sexual ethics but rather the shame of the community and its failure to attend properly to community boundaries.

As in chapter 5, Paul here addresses especially the congregations (vv. 1-6). Unlike in chapter 5, here he also addresses the people involved (vv. 7-8). In both discussions he concludes with a general comment on behaviors that disqualify persons from membership in the community of believers or from inheriting the kingdom of God.

OUTLINE

Shame on the Assembly, 6:1-6
Shame on the Litigants, 6:7-8
Boundary Markers of God's Kingdom, 6:9-11

EXPLANATORY NOTES

Shame on the Assembly 6:1-6

How dare you? Paul writes (AT). Normal English word order obscures the horror that Paul expresses in response to what he has heard, but in Greek the first word is *How dare you?* At least one person (perhaps several at different times, since he addresses *anyone* [AT], not a particular person) has taken a fellow believer to court. Once again Paul is responding to information that he has received from Chloe's people that is critical of persons with power and status. Because the Corinthians know what he is talking about, it is not necessary for him to provide details about the case or cases. For later readers, this generates frustration because we do not know the circumstances.

Most commentators understand that the subject of litigation is a financial dispute, since *ordinary matters* (vv. 3, 4) are normally cases involving money and property and verses 7-8 specifically mention fraud (NIV, *cheat*). Beyond that we can only speculate about the possible content or circumstances of the case. The NIV translation of verse 3, *the things of this life*, may unfortunately suggest that Christians are to be concerned about transcendent or spiritual matters and not about temporal matters *of this life*. The point of the argument is that Christians *should* in fact judge *ordinary matters* of life, not refer them to secular authorities.

But who would have been instigating litigation? In Corinth, the courts, especially those that attended to civil matters (a "small claims court," Thiselton 2000: 428) were strongly biased in favor of persons with money, power, and status. The cost of pursuing litigation was high, and only the wealthy used the courts to pursue their interests (Chow: 76-80, 127-30; A. Mitchell: 572-81). It was forbidden for social inferiors (children, freedmen, private citizens, and persons of low rank) to take their superiors (parents, patrons, magistrates, or persons of high rank) to court (Winter 1994: 107-8). The reputation of courts and of judges may have contributed to Paul's designation of them as *unrighteous* (NRSV) or *ungodly* (NIV) in 6:1, and quite possibly was also why they were *despised* (AT) and why their *way of life is scorned in the church* (v. 4 NIV). *Those who have no standing* (6:4 NRSV) is a weak translation of a word usually translated more strongly (see Rom 14:3, 10; 1 Cor 1:28; 16:11; 2 Cor 10:10; Gal 4:14; 1 Thess 5:20).

Because of the costs and other barriers of access to the courts, we can be sure that the persons initiating the lawsuits were among the *wise, powerful,* and wellborn (cf. 1:26) members of the assembly. We can also be sure that the persons being sued for fraud were among the lower-class members.

As always, Paul is concerned for the needs of the weaker members of the body, and that concern itself would have motivated him to address this matter. But another important issue is at stake: the reputation of the community when members resort to litigation against one another. As they did in other matters (see 11:17-34 and corresponding EN), the wealthy were humiliating those who were poorer and of lower status. It was therefore a matter of members shaming other members. Paul responded by shaming those who were so brash as to humiliate their fellow believers: *I say this to your shame,* he writes (6:5) *[Shame and Honor, p. 368].*

The rationale that Paul advances for his criticism is based on his eschatological convictions. Christians, *the saints* (see on 1:2), are destined to judge the world (6:2) and even angels (v. 3—the exact meaning of this is uncertain, but clearly it points to an exalted role for believers in the final judgment; see Thiselton 2000: 430–31). How is it then that they are unable to judge *trivial cases* (v. 2) like financial squabbles between brothers in the family of faith (vv. 5-6)? The NRSV (as also the NIV) usually translates the Greek word *adelphoi* as "brothers and sisters." Here the translation *believers* diminishes the sense that the dispute is "within the family." Since the social circumstances would have determined that men were disputants in this matter, and to avoid a very awkward construction, it seems appropriate here to translate the word as "brother," following NIV (cf. Hays 1997: 95). The relationship is *brother . . . against brother . . . before unbelievers.*

Paul cuts to the quick with his sarcastic challenge: *Can it be that there is no one among you wise enough to decide . . .* ? (v. 5). Wisdom was the particular claim of the Corinthians (1:20-31; 2:6-16). How shameful then that their actions demonstrate their lack of the wherewithal to apply their wisdom to the settling of disputes among themselves! Their recourse to "outsiders" creates the embarrassing situation of "washing the family's dirty laundry in front of strangers," but it brings by far the most shame on those persons who otherwise claimed a more than normal amount of wisdom—among whom were probably those initiating the lawsuit(s), since they were most likely those who had the social status and financial means to do so.

Although he appeals to a theological rationale, Paul pursues his argument through a series of rhetorical questions. *How dare you?* he asks. *Do you not know? Are you incompetent? Do you not know? Do you appoint? Can it be? Why not rather? Do you not know?*

The characteristic question of a diatribe, *Do you not know?* occurs ten times in 1 Corinthians (otherwise in Paul's letters only in Rom 6:3, 16; 7:1; 11:2). Three of those are in 6:1-11 (vv. 2, 3, 9), three more in the second half of chapter 6 (vv. 15, 16, 19), and the others at 3:16; 5:6; 9:13, 24. Some of these refer to general information (9:13, 24) or even proverbs (5:6), but all those in chapter 6 refer to fundamental understandings of Christian faith, in particular to eschatology (6:2, 3, 9) and to the ethical significance of the body (6:15, 16, 19; cf. 3:16). Often in the letters to the Thessalonians (1 Thess 1:5; 2:1-2, 5, 11; 3:3-4; 4:2; 5:2; 2 Thess 2:6; 3:7) and occasionally elsewhere, Paul reminds his readers of what they already know by writing "You yourselves know" or "You know that . . ." But in 1 Corinthians he consistently uses the negative *Do you not know?* indicating that they were acting as if they did not know what they should have known.

We notice that Paul is not attempting here to establish an alternative court system to serve Christians, as Jews had been granted by the Romans (Thiselton 2000: 425). He does not address any of the questions that such an institution would need to consider, such as the appointment of judges, testimony, standards of proof, or punishments. Paul has in mind simple mediation between disputing members of the family of faith in the context of household assemblies with lots of face-to-face contact.

Shame on the Litigants 6:7-8

Although his strongest criticism is directed to the congregations as a whole, in this case Paul also has some strong criticism of the person(s) who initiated litigation. If indeed they were persons of status, and probably therefore leaders who had taken fellow members (*brothers*) before the *unrighteous* judges, then the criticism in 6:7-8 is in fact directed to the same people as mentioned in verses 1-6.

After suggesting that the assembly should institute an alternative dispute-resolution system to deal with *trivial cases* of conflict, he now says even that would be a concession, a "lesser evil" rather than a good way to handle such situations. *The very fact that you have lawsuits among you means you have been completely defeated already* (v. 7 NIV). The NRSV translation, *already a defeat*, is not strong enough; it is a humiliation, a complete and utter defeat, a moral failure to have lawsuits between members of the assembly. To demand one's rights is unseemly for those whose model is the cross (1:18-31) and who have *the mind of Christ* (2:16), as Paul will demonstrate with his own example in 9:19-23 and generally argue in 8:1–11:1.

The preference for suffering rather than suing was expressed by various ancient philosophers. Musonius Rufus mused, "Will the philosopher prosecute anyone for personal injury?" (Lutz, 78.10). He argued that there is nothing shameful about suffering a personal injury, but that it is shameful to initiate an injury or insult against another (cf. Lecture 3, "That women too should study philosophy"; 40.30). "The sensible man would not go to law nor bring indictments, since he would not even consider that he had been insulted. Besides, to be annoyed or racked about such things would be petty. Rather he will easily and silently bear what has happened, since this befits one whose purpose is to be noble-minded" (Lecture 10 78.7-11). Socrates is reported by Plato (*Gorgias* [Jowett]) to have said repeatedly that "to do injustice is a greater [evil], and to suffer injustice a lesser evil." The "wise" people in Corinth did not need to wait for Paul's word: other philosophers had made the same point. They were not living up to their own claims, much less the standards that Paul proclaimed.

Fee (265-66) thinks that 1 Corinthians 6:7 addresses the plaintiff in the lawsuit and verse 8 addresses the accused. This may have been the case, and certainly Paul would have been critical of anyone who *wronged and defrauded*, especially a fellow member of the assembly. But if we understand that the lawsuit had been launched by a person of status and financial advantage, knowing that the courts favored such and were reputed to be corrupt, it is even more likely that he was accusing the plaintiff of using the courts to *wrong and defraud* the accused. The plaintiff, who should have been willing to suffer a minor wrong or to seek remediation through the intervention of fellow believers, was rather guilty of inflicting a greater wrong on the accused.

Paul was intense in his scorn of the people involved in this court case. He was critical of those who would cheat and mistreat fellow believers, critical of those who would use the unjust court system against others in the family of faith, and critical of the assembly that tolerated such behavior.

Boundary Markers of God's Kingdom 6:9-11

In the final paragraph of this discussion (vv. 9-11), Paul summarizes the theological implications of the case he has just made: people who are unrighteous will be excluded from God's reign in the age to come. Christians have been transformed by God's action through Jesus Christ and the Holy Spirit, and they must no longer live by the values and practices of the unrighteous. As illustrations of unrighteous behavior, the lists that Paul has already used in 5:10-11 are repeated and expanded, thereby tying these two cases together as specific examples under one overarching ethical concern.

This paragraph opens with the sarcastic rhetorical question, *Do you not know that wrongdoers will not inherit the kingdom of God?* The same Greek root word is translated as the verb *wrong* (NRSV) or *cheat* (NIV) in verse 8, *unrighteous* (NRSV) or *ungodly* (NIV) in verse 1, and *be wronged* in verse 7.

Paul further underscores their willful ignorance with a warning: *Stop deceiving yourselves!* (AT). The verb is in the present imperative, meaning that they should stop the behavior that is already happening (Fee: 267n237).

In both statements he continues his attempt to deflate the Corinthians' puffed-up arrogance about their sophisticated wisdom. On these basic spiritual matters, they are ignorant and self-deceived (see above 6:2-3, *Do you not know?*). In their quarreling (1:11) they have lost sight of their identity in Christ, and in fighting over *ordinary matters* (6:3) they have lost sight of eternal values.

Paul lists ten vices that exclude people from inheriting the kingdom of God. In 5:10 he had identified four. In 5:11 he restated those and added two more, identifying them as practices that disqualify persons from continuing membership in the assembly. In 6:9-10 he repeats the earlier list and adds another four.

Paul is not presenting these as a comprehensive list of unrighteous behavior. In Romans 1:29-32 he lists twenty-one vices for which people "deserve to die"—and even that is not comprehensive. Each of the items listed here was a genuine issue in the Corinthian Christian community, and Paul intentionally chose to name these specific behaviors as disqualifications from membership in God's kingdom [*Vice and Virtue Lists, p. 370*].

Most of the items listed name behavior that he has criticized or will criticize in this letter. Five of them deal with sins of greed and grasping: theft, greed, drunkenness, reviling, and swindling. Four

1 Corinthians 6:1-11

items deal with sexual sins: fornication, adultery, "male prostitution," and "sodomy" (see chart below). One item—idolatry—stands alone in this list, unless it hints of prostitution as a practice of idolatry (6:12-20, esp. 15: cf. EN below).

Although eight of these items reflect major issues addressed in this letter, the two that do not have generated the most discussion among scholars and in the church in recent years. They are the two that refer to homosexual acts. In Greek they are *malakoi* and *arsenokoitai*. Uncertainty about the meaning of the two words is represented by the many different translations, some of which are listed below.

	malakoi	*arsenokoitai*
ASV	effeminate	abusers of themselves with mankind
KJV	effeminate	abusers of themselves with mankind
NAB	boy prostitutes	practicing homosexuals
NAS	effeminate	homosexuals
NET	passive homosexual partners	practicing homosexuals
NIV 1984	male prostitutes	homosexual offenders
NIV	men who have sex with men	
NJB	the self-indulgent	sodomites
NKVJ	homosexuals	sodomites
NRSV	male prostitutes	sodomites
REB	sexual perverts	
RSV	sexual perverts	
Thiselton 2000	perverts [or those involved in pederastic practices]	men who practice sexual relations with men
Barrett	catamites	sodomites
Collins	perverts	homosexuals

Both words are rare in Greek literature, despite the frequency of homosexual practice in Hellenistic (Greek) society. In the New Testament, both words occur only one other time. *Malakoi* is found in Matthew 11:8 and its parallel passage, Luke 7:25, where it is rightly translated as "soft." In nonbiblical writings it usually means "soft," or by metaphorical extension, "effeminate." Rarely does it mean "males who submit to sodomy" (BDAG). Paired with *arseno-koitai*, and set in the context of the ethical significance of actions included in this list of vices, it is clear that in this case it carries a sexual meaning. The interpretive issue is whether all such relationships are included in the condemnation or only those involving prostitution or pederasty (Scroggs: 29-65, 85-122). Although it may be possible to make the case for the more limited definition in other passages, here there is no inherent reason to think that it means anything more or less than males who submit to sodomy. The NRSV and NIV 1984 translation, *male prostitutes*, which reflects Scroggs's argument, is "too narrow a reading," and the REB translation *sexual pervert* (covering both *malakoi* and *arsenokoitai*—presumably this would apply also to the NIV's rendering, *men who have sex with men*) is "too broad" (BDAG).

Arsenokoitai occurs only here and in *1 Timothy 1:10*. It may have been a word that Paul himself (or the author of *1 Timothy*) coined to name the practice of males (Gk. *arsēn*) having sexual relations (Gk. *koitē* = coitus) with males. There is little debate about its meaning, though Scroggs attempts to limit its application to men who have sex with young boys (in an exploitative or prostituted relationship), pairing it with his interpretation of *malakoi* (29-65, 85-122; Brownson: 273-75).

Despite the varied translations, it is clear that both words refer to aspects of homosexual activity (see Winter 2001: 110-20). The global church, and perhaps especially in North America and Europe at the beginning of the third millennium, has a special calling to discern God's will for persons who are attracted to others of the same sex. The inclusion of these two words in the list of vices does not answer the questions that are being asked in the twenty-first century (Brownson: 275).

Thiselton describes the purpose of the list of vices in this way:

> *He is not describing the qualifications required for an entrance examination; he is comparing habituated actions, which by definition can find no place in God's reign for the welfare of all, with those qualities in accordance with which Christian believers need to be transformed if they belong authentically to God's new creation in Christ.* (2000: 439, emphasis original)

The culmination of his argument is in 1 Corinthians 6:11: *But you were washed, you were sanctified, you were justified in the name of the Lord Jesus Christ and in the Spirit of our God.* The three verbs are not sequential experiences but are three ways of describing the one spiritual reality and experience of salvation, "the one fundamental transformation that has occurred for those who now belong to Christ," which is represented by (not effected by) baptism (being "washed"; Hays 1997: 98).

Significant here is the incipient idea of the Trinity, a theological concept that was defined in postbiblical times and elaborated in the creeds of the church on the basis of Scriptures such as this one, where Jesus Christ, the Spirit, and God are named in one breath as collectively the initiator of the washing, sanctification, and justification of believers.

Much has been made of the contrast between former behaviors and the transformation that occurs through the experience of being washed, sanctified, and justified. The possibility of change is fundamental to the gospel. Yet some people apply this proclamation almost exclusively to homosexual activity and same-sex attraction—though Paul does not address the latter. Any application of the above must be applied equally to all the actions listed: fornication, idolatry, adultery, thievery, greed, drunkenness, reviling, and robbery. Indeed, it seems that the more important categories are those mentioned repeatedly: fornication, or [hetero]sexual immorality (Gk. *porneia*), is named four times (5:9, 10, 11; 6:9); greed, robbery, and idolatry three times each (5:10, 11; 6:9); and reviling and drunkenness twice (5:11; 6:10). Thievery, adultery ([hetero]sexual immorality), *malakoi*, and *arsenokoitai* are each listed only once. Although Paul is adamant in insisting that the Corinthians had truly been washed, sanctified, and justified, it was still necessary to remind his readers that these behaviors are inappropriate for those who are in Christ.

Paul restates the theological conviction that he has stated repeatedly, and he ties it inseparably to its moral implications. God, through Jesus Christ and the Holy Spirit, has acted in the lives of those who believe, and that has made them new persons, with new minds, new values, new attitudes, new behaviors, and new relationships. Sadly, the Corinthians, who sought so hard to achieve status and acceptance in the world, did not realize that status and acceptance in God's kingdom had already been granted them freely by God's own actions.

THE TEXT IN BIBLICAL CONTEXT

Dispute Resolution

The first point Paul makes is that *to have lawsuits at all with one another is already a defeat for you. Why not rather be wronged? Why not rather be defrauded?* (6:7). This is not a parallel to Jesus' teaching to "come to terms quickly with your accuser" (Matt 5:25). That is advice to a person being sued: they should negotiate a timely resolution outside the courts. Paul's instruction goes beyond that to address those *initiating* a lawsuit. It is in keeping with Jesus' instructions to those who are wronged and who might consider launching a legal defense or vigilante retribution.

> You have heard that it was said, "An eye for an eye and a tooth for a tooth." But I say to you, Do not resist an evildoer. But if anyone strikes you on the right cheek, turn the other also; and if anyone wants to sue you and take your coat, give your cloak as well; and if anyone forces you to go one mile, go also the second mile. Give to everyone who begs from you, and do not refuse anyone who wants to borrow from you. (Matt 5:38-42)

In both cases the lesson is that it is better to suffer wrong than to fight back. Yet it is significant that Jesus' words imagine a situation where one is imposed upon by "an evildoer," whereas the Corinthian situation is a conflict between fellow believers, or "brothers."

On the one occasion when Jesus was asked to arbitrate between brothers over the settling of an estate, he refused, saying, "Friend, who set me to be a judge or arbitrator over you?" (Luke 12:13-14). He used the occasion to teach against being preoccupied with material possessions and neglecting the things of God, using the parable of the rich fool (12:15-21). Perhaps Paul was thinking similarly.

The second issue is how to deal with conflict within the faith family when it is not possible or appropriate to walk away and *suffer injustice* (1 Cor 6:7 NJB). In that case, Paul says, it should be dealt with by wise members of the assembly. *When any of you has a grievance against another, . . . [take] it before the saints* (v. 1). He does not, however, give any direction as to how that should be done. For those, we turn to Jesus' teaching in Matthew 18:15-17.

Jesus addresses a situation where "another member of the church sins against you" (Matt 18:15 NRSV, NIV 1984; NIV 2011 follows other manuscript evidence in omitting "against you")—surely the equivalent to having *a grievance against another*. He instructs that such a matter should, if possible, be dealt with directly between the parties involved. If that is not successful, one or two others should be brought in; and if they are not able to sort out the matter, it should be brought before the whole congregation. Jesus identifies a high level of authority for the Christian community in discerning such matters: "Whatever you bind on earth will be bound in heaven, and whatever you loose on earth will be loosed in heaven" (Matt 18:8; see Gardner: 281–82, 284–86; Kuepfer: 33–41).

The community of the Dead Sea Scrolls had a similar instruction on confronting disagreements with others in the community.

> They shall rebuke one another in truth, humility, and charity. Let no man address his companion with anger, or ill-temper, or obduracy, or with envy prompted by the spirit of wickedness. Let him not hate him [because of his uncircumcised] heart, but let him rebuke him on the very same day lest he incur guilt because of him. And furthermore, let no man accuse his companion before the Congregation without having admonished him in the presence of witnesses. (Community Rule, 1QS 5.25–6.1)

Saints Will Judge the World

The saints will judge the world, Paul writes. *Do you not know that we are to judge angels?* (1 Cor 6:2-3). In contrast with the instructions, just a few verses previously, to not judge outsiders (5:12), here he anticipates that such judgment will be theirs at a future time. The fault he had criticized earlier was a matter of timing: *Do not pronounce judgment before the time, before the Lord comes, who will bring to light the things now hidden in darkness and will disclose the purposes of the heart* (4:5). Possibly the Corinthians themselves claimed that *the saints will judge the world*, along with other glories already achieved (cf. 4:8; cf. also Thiselton 2000: 425). This would add further irony to Paul's point that such a claim is belied by their inability to deal with current issues. Certainly they had the timing wrong, as the promised judgment is in the eschaton, while their judgment issues are in the present.

Saints judging angels is an innovation here, but the idea that "holy ones" will participate in judging the world is common in Jewish apocalyptic literature. The Book of the Watchers, the first known Jewish apocalypse, begins, "The Holy One will come forth from his dwelling. . . . Behold, he comes with myriads of his holy ones [= angels] to execute judgment on all" (1 Enoch 1:3, 9). The deuterocanonical Wisdom of Solomon promises that "the souls of the righteous . . . will govern nations and rule over peoples, and the Lord will reign over them forever" (3:1, 8). The voice that instructed John to write to the churches said, "To everyone who conquers and continues to do my works to the end, I will give authority over the nations; to rule them with an iron rod, as when clay pots are shattered—even as I also received authority from my Father" (Rev 2:26-28; cf. 3:21; 20:4).

The Gospels report that Jesus made similar promises to his followers. "When the Son of Man is seated on the throne of his glory, you who have followed me will also sit on twelve thrones, judging the twelve tribes of Israel" (Matt 19:28). And again, "You are those who have stood by me in my trials; and I confer on you, just as my Father has conferred on me, a kingdom, so that you may eat and drink at my table in my kingdom, and you will sit on thrones judging the twelve tribes of Israel" (Luke 22:28-30).

The anticipated role in judgment is an application of the promise that "if we have been united with him in a death like his, we will certainly be united with him in a resurrection like his" (Rom 6:5). Resurrection "like his" includes participation in his eschatological judgment.

THE TEXT IN THE LIFE OF THE CHURCH
Lawsuits between Believers

Christians individually and in groups have a sorry history of taking each other to court for the kinds of matters that Paul condemns. Common among these are disputes over business disagreements, inheritance, and family issues. Disputes about ownership and control of church property also happen, especially when fellow believers part ways.

Some situations experienced in life are not represented in this text. Matters covered by criminal law are not addressed. The principle of not taking fellow believers to court has been used to avoid legal responsibility for everything from unlawful dismissal and unfair employment practices to physical and sexual abuse. Churches and church-based processes are often inadequate for dealing with these, while secular society's expectations are increasingly sophisticated. Failure to deal adequately with such abuse and evidence of attempts to cover up illegal behavior eventually cause shame and other serious repercussions.

Another circumstance outside the consideration of this passage is that of a lawsuit between a believer and a nonbeliever. For either litigation or mediation to be successful, both parties must recognize the legitimacy of the process and the judge. When one party does not submit to the wisdom of believers, it usually will not work to bring that party before the church. A believer should not feel guilty about using the secular legal system in the process of conducting business or pursuing redress when wronged by unbelievers. And a believer who is sued by an unbeliever or who is charged under the criminal law should respond within the framework of the secular legal system.

Even in such circumstances, Christians should consider their witness of faith in their actions (see the thoughtful advice by Richard Church in *First Be Reconciled: Challenging Christians in the Courts*). First, one's actions in business and in all relationships with others should be conducted with honesty, integrity, and fairness, not grasping for personal gain or doing harm to others. Second, whenever possible, one should pursue the less litigious processes of mediation and arbitration, in which resolution is negotiated rather than imposed, with the intention of achieving satisfaction for all parties.

Followers of Jesus have been at the forefront of developing mediation services and other alternative strategies for dispute resolution as approaches toward better outcomes for all parties. In many jurisdictions, such alternatives have been welcomed by the justice systems. They have been effective in cases of family and community conflict and in industrial and even international conflicts. The literature on restorative justice and the resources related to it are growing rapidly.

Followers of Jesus have been deeply involved in improving the justice system in many countries, promoting fairer trials, improving prison conditions, and advocating for the elimination of the death penalty. It is a stain on the church's witness when those who claim the identity of Christian call for harsh penalties, punitive rather than restorative justice, and even for the death sentence in particularly scandalous cases.

Preaching and Worship

The Revised Common Lectionary does not include the reading of 1 Corinthians 6:1-10, perhaps because few Christians can imagine applying it to "the way things are" in the twenty-first century. Nevertheless, there are important lessons here, including the matter of alternative conflict resolution strategies instead of taking one another to court. It would be profitable to preach the message that Christians have been *washed, . . . sanctified, . . . and justified* and should put aside the vices listed and any others that were part of their previous life—and not apply the text only to people who experience same-sex attraction, as some preachers do.

1 Corinthians 6:12-20
The Principle of Sexual Purity

PREVIEW

The relationship between Christian faith and sexual ethics was confusing for the Christians in Corinth. In addition to the incest addressed in 1 Corinthians 5, and in contradiction of some people insisting on celibacy (ch. 7), some men were visiting prostitutes. News of this development gives Paul an opportunity to do some teaching on general principles of sexual ethics for followers of Jesus.

A transitional phrase (*It is actually reported*, 5:1) introduces a series of topics that extends through two chapters. Another transitional phrase (*Now concerning the matters about which you wrote*, 7:1) starts the next section. The three issues in chapters 5 and 6 demonstrate the failure of the Corinthians to live out the implications of the gospel. In responding to their failures, Paul locates their life in relation to what God in Christ has already done and, simultaneously, in relation to what God will do in the eschaton.

The paragraph in 6:9-11, discussed above, is a transition from the preceding paragraph that also introduces the next argument. Since four of the items listed as vices are clearly sexual activities, and the fifth, idolatry, may imply literal or metaphoric prostitution, the connection to the issue addressed in verses 12-20 is strong.

Paul continues to deal with matters that were reported by Chloe's people (5:1) *[What Chloe's People Said, p. 371]*. There is no hint that the matter of consorting with prostitutes was identified in the letter from the assembly [*What the Corinthians Wrote, p. 372*] or by the three men who carried the letter [*What the Delegation Reported, p. 374*]. But the subject is entirely consistent with the kinds of issues that Chloe's people reported (1:11): the shameful practices, the fractured relationships, and the "dirt" on the assembly in Corinth.

Once again we see that the Corinthians were separating faith from ethics, spirit from body, and spiritual identity from social interaction. And once again we see that Paul scorns their lack of spiritual wisdom in contrast with their self-image as being wise. Once again he lays the theological groundwork of eschatological hope and God's initiative or "ownership." And once again he builds an argument that addresses both a specific issue in Corinth and general principles to guide the behavior of Christians—in this case, their sexual activities.

OUTLINE

Corinthian Slogans and Christian Critiques, 6:12-14
Why It Is Wrong to Consort with Prostitutes, 6:15-17
General Principles for Sexual Ethics, 6:18-20

EXPLANATORY NOTES

Corinthian Slogans and Christian Critiques 6:12-14

First Corinthians is one side of a conversation, and we do not hear the other side (see "Paul's Letter" in the introduction). To understand the conversation, at some points we must reconstruct what the other side was saying. Occasionally we are helped in this because Paul tells us what he has heard from or about the Corinthians, either from their letter or from one of his oral sources, such as Chloe's people (1:11), Stephanas, Fortunatus, or Achaicus (16:17).

In this passage we find the first two instances of a series of statements that Paul quotes from the Corinthians. Many scholars believe that in 1 Corinthians 6:12, 13; 7:1; 8:1, 4, 5-6, 8; 10:23; and 11:3, we can legitimately see quotations, either from the Corinthians' letter to Paul or of slogans that he has heard that they use (Hurd: 67-68). There may be additional passages where Paul quoted the Corinthians or common sayings. Translations often put these in quotation marks, but because the earliest Greek manuscripts did not include punctuation, such designations are not in the original texts and are inserted as a matter of interpretation. The best clue is when Paul writes something that does not fit with his argument and then immediately contradicts or corrects it.

I have the right to do anything (6:12 NIV) or *I am free to do anything* (REB) is clearly a claim that the Corinthians have made. Here the NRSV translation, *All things are lawful for me*, is unfortunate because it suggests that the issue is one of legalities, as if morality were defined by (civil or criminal) law, which neither Paul nor the Corinthians were suggesting. The saying is quoted twice in verse 12 and, with a slight variation, twice in 10:23. In this repeated quotation we see the essence of the Corinthian attitude toward ethics: personal rights and freedoms determine the limitations on behavior, and personal satisfaction ("the pursuit of happiness," as in the U.S. Declaration of Independence) is the proper motivation for behavioral choices. It is consistent with their claim to having already attained what they want, already being *kings* (4:8) and having wisdom (4:10). In fact, this is exactly what Stoic and Cynic philosophers and many Corinthians in the privileged class might claim as their ethic of personal freedom (Winter 2001: 81–82).

Each of the four times this slogan is quoted, it is followed by a mitigating statement or a balancing corrective. Although everything may be permitted, as the Corinthians claim, Paul counters by reminding them that *not all things are beneficial* (6:12; 10:23). *Beneficial* is also a value in Stoic and Cynic thought, so it counters one philosophical slogan with another, rather like contrasting a popular saying with another. A modern example of this is that "Out of sight out of mind" contradicts "Absence makes the heart grow fonder." Paul's first response is thus an appeal to personal benefit, not to the greater good of the community or any such transcendent value.

The second response, *I will not be dominated by anything* (6:12), again counters their argument with a similar argument, for the determination to be free applies not only to freedom from moral constraint but also to freedom from passion or compulsion. Thiselton (2000: 461) translates verse 12b as *"Liberty to do anything": but I will not let anything take liberties with me.* Those who indulge their passions to demonstrate their freedom risk being dominated by, used by, or even addicted to those very passions or the persons with whom they indulge. Finally, Paul points out that *not all things build up* (10:23), reminding them that there are values more important than personal freedom. These include community good and perhaps even personal growth, much as one might say, "No pain, no gain." In the present context, the emphasis is on maximizing personal advantage, thus Paul builds on the rationale that the Corinthians use, but inverts the conclusion drawn. There is still, however, awareness of the community impact of individual actions. *"Part of the grammar of* union with Christ is to share Christ's concern for the well-being of the other, and to let go of his or her own freedoms in order to liberate the other" (Thiselton 2000: 462, emphasis original).

Besides the influence of Stoic and Cynic philosophers, it is possible that the Corinthians were influenced by Paul's preaching about freedom from the regulations of Jewish Torah laws. Although we do not know what he had taught in Corinth, we do know from Paul's letters (esp. Galatians) and from Luke's reports in Acts on his teaching in other places that Paul adamantly insisted Gentile Christians did not need to be circumcised or bound by kosher food laws and other Jewish regulations. It is possible that the Corinthians took this teaching of Paul and exaggerated it, or at least that they took from it permission to adopt the ethics of the Stoic and Cynic philosophers.

The second Corinthian slogan that Paul quotes is *Food is meant for the stomach and the stomach for food, and God will destroy both one and the other*. There is some scholarly disagreement about this quotation: some think that only the first half is the quotation and the second half is Paul's rebuttal (NRSV). Others think the entire statement came from the Corinthians (NRSV margin). A third and more likely possibility is that Paul has put together two Corinthian sayings. Since Paul's argument is based on his conviction that the body has spiritual significance and will be resurrected by God (6:14; cf. ch. 15), it would be contradictory for him to say that God will destroy both food and stomach. Such a statement in fact supports the Corinthian attitude: it is all temporary and passing away, so it does not matter what we do with the body.

The Corinthians were interested in food and their freedom to eat what they wanted, as we will see in chapters 8 and 10 (see esp. 10:23-30) and in 11:17-22, 33-34. Because gluttonous consumption of food and drink was often associated with sexual promiscuity at banquets and festivals (Winter 2001: 82–84, 280–82), the application of the same principle to sexual practices is obvious (6:13).

Paul challenges both premises. First, he declares that *the body is not meant for fornication, but for the Lord* (v. 13). If you misunderstand its purpose, you misunderstand how to use it. And second, he adds, *God raised the Lord and will also raise us by his power* (v. 14). God will not destroy the body but will raise it just as God raised Jesus. The full discussion of this point will be made in chapter 15, but here Paul briefly refers to it, as if he assumes his readers understand something of the doctrine of resurrection and that they can draw out the implications of the resurrection for the sexual use of the body.

Why It Is Wrong to Consort with Prostitutes 6:15-17

To this point Paul has not stated what kind of sexual immorality he is challenging, but now it becomes clear. Chloe's people have told Paul that some of the Christian men (how many is not Paul's concern) in Corinth were consorting with prostitutes. It can be assumed that it was a socially accepted sexual practice in Corinth to visit prostitutes, though probably not more so than in other cities with similar populations, industries, and economies. Although Paul's original teaching may have challenged that behavior, at least some of the men, apparently defending themselves with the arguments identified in 6:12-13, were continuing in that practice.

Do you not know? Paul rails again (v. 15; see EN on 6:2-3). Continuing in diatribe fashion to berate their lack of the wisdom that they claim, he sets out three fundamental understandings that they should have known about bodies:

1. Christians' bodies are members of Christ.
2. Sexual relations create one body out of two.
3. The Christian's body is a temple of the Holy Spirit.

The first thing they should have known is that as Christians their identity—physical as well as spiritual—belongs to Christ: *Do you not know that your bodies are members of Christ?* (v. 15). The implication is that a member of Christ should not be made a member (sexual pun intended) of a prostitute. *God forbid* (ASV, KJV). *Out of the question!* (NJB). *Certainly not!* (NKJV).

The second thing they should have known is the understanding of the nature of sexuality expressed in the Hebrew Scriptures: *Do you not know that whoever is united to a prostitute becomes one body with her?* (v. 16). The phrase draws on the fundamental understanding of sexual union expressed in Genesis 2:24—"A man leaves his father and his mother and clings to his wife, and they become one flesh"—a verse also quoted by Jesus (Matt 19:5-6 // Mark 10:7-8). The expression "one flesh" points to the fullness of kinship ties represented in marriage, not limited to but certainly including sexual relationships (Brownson: 87).

There is no suggestion in Genesis or in any later quotation of Genesis 2:24, including the present passage, that all sexual union is bad. Indeed, the "one flesh" of husband and wife is honored, celebrated, and even commanded in Scripture (see EN on ch. 7). But there is also no room in the biblical understanding of sexuality for "casual" sex. Sexual relations with a prostitute (or, by extension, any casual "hookup") are "a parody and distortion of a true one-flesh union, and [are] thus to be avoided" (Brownson: 101).

Sexual intercourse itself—regardless of the context, the relationship, or the intentions of the participants—binds two people together into a union of "one body," but only the full kinship union of marriage creates God's intention of "one flesh." Paul elaborates the implication of this by explaining that the unity of becoming one flesh with a prostitute is incompatible with the prior identity of a Christian being one spirit with the Lord. You just can't be one with Christ and one with a prostitute!

Many cultures consider adultery to be an offense against one's spouse. In some cultures, it is an offense against the spouse's father or other relatives. In many cultures, premarital sexual relations are considered acceptable because there is no prior commitment of fidelity to one person, but once the marriage commitment is made, or even a preliminary exclusive commitment of betrothal established, sexual activity outside that relationship is considered a violation.

Paul does not follow this logic. There is no hint whether the men who are visiting prostitutes are married or single; the distinction was probably not made in Corinthian culture. Paul's argument is rather based on the priority of a commitment to Christ (becoming *one spirit with him*, v. 17), which excludes union (of *one body*) with anyone other than a spouse (who is also *in the Lord*, 7:39).

All of Paul's arguments apply to men (and presumably, if such were the situation, also to women) who have sexual relationships outside marriage, whether with prostitutes or other illicit partners. In the case of Corinthian men consorting with prostitutes, another dimension is significant. Some, perhaps many, of the prostitutes in Corinth were associated with pagan deities. Though the assumption that some temples featured "sacred" prostitutes has been dismissed by many (e.g., Budin [esp. 261–65]), sexual promiscuity involving prostitutes was associated with some pagan rituals, and especially meals (Winter 2001: 82–85; cf. Witherington: 12–13, esp. n34; also Rosser). If the Corinthian men were visiting such prostitutes, the sexual immorality was compounded by spiritual immorality. Forming a one-flesh union with a prostitute affiliated with a pagan deity is idolatry because it adulterates the Christian's union with Christ. In chapter 10, Paul again links sexual immorality and idolatry (10:7-8). He warns the Corinthians to *flee from idolatry* (10:14 NIV), just as here he warns them to *flee from sexual immorality* (6:18 NIV).

General Principles for Sexual Ethics 6:18-20

Paul bluntly states the general principle of sexual purity: *Shun fornication!* (v. 18), or *Flee from sexual immorality!* (NIV). That includes consorting with prostitutes and all forms of sexual impropriety (Gk. *porneia* and related terms, 5:1 [two times], 9, 10, 11; 6:9, 13b, 18 [two times]; *prostitute*, 6:15, 16, from the same root). It echoes the warning in Proverbs 6:25-33 and the example of Joseph fleeing the seductive wife of his employer, Potiphar (Gen 39:7-10). The injunction is clear.

The second half of the verse, however, is not clear. What did Paul mean when he wrote that *every sin that a person commits is outside the body* (v. 18)? And why is fornication unique in being *a sin against the body itself*? Commentators have suggested that this should be taken lightly (Witherington: 169), or they have tried to explain it in a variety of ways. The NIV attempts to smooth the language by inserting *other*, which is not in the Greek, to distinguish between *all other sins* and sinning *sexually*, but that still doesn't explain why Paul would have disregarded all the other ways that people abuse and sin against their bodies.

Jerome Murphy-O'Connor has proposed it was the Corinthians, not Paul, who held that *every sin a person commits is outside of the body*, and that Paul counters by saying *but the immoral person sins against his own body* (NET; other commentators have followed his suggestion; cf. Murphy-O'Connor [1978: 391–96]; cf. Hays [1997: 105]; Fee [289–90] notes it as a possibility, though he is not convinced). We have suggested that quotations from the Corinthians are identified primarily by the juxtaposition of a statement and its immediate rebuttal, which this represents. Furthermore, it is consistent with Corinthian theology and inconsistent with Paul's theology to claim that sins are *outside the body* and therefore irrelevant to one's spiritual condition. The response, *Whoever sins sexually, sins against their own body* (v. 18 NIV; not NRSV, *the body itself*), belies the claim in general, and it specifically addresses the issue of sexual immorality, which is Paul's immediate concern. This is the most satisfactory understanding at present for this otherwise awkward statement.

The third *Do you not know* in this section is a theological affirmation that the human *body is a temple of the Holy Spirit* (v. 19). Significantly, Paul uses the present tense of the verb to indicate that even for those who deny it (those Corinthians against whom he is arguing) or for those who abuse it (those who unite their bodies with the bodies of prostitutes), the fact is that their bodies *are* temples of the Holy Spirit. It is not a matter of purifying the body in order that the Holy Spirit might dwell there, but of living out the implications of the conviction that the Holy Spirit dwells there already. As Fee (292) notes, the Corinthians claimed to be spiritual, but "they thought the presence of the Spirit meant a negation of the body; Paul argues the exact opposite: The presence of the Spirit in their present bodily existence is God's affirmation of the body." As always, Paul also reminds his readers that the Holy Spirit comes to them as a gift from God, not on the basis of having been deserved or achieved by human effort.

This is the second time in this letter that Paul uses the image of a temple in which God's Spirit dwells—a metaphor that has even greater impact if the prostitution named in this passage is indeed associated with pagan deities and practices (see above on vv. 15-17). Here the image is applied to the individual bodies of believers. In 3:16-17 the subject is the plural *you*: it is the corporate body of believers, the assembly, which is the temple. Later in this letter (ch. 12), Paul will elaborate on the metaphor of the body as a way of understanding the relationships between individual members.

Paul is not only talking about individual sexual purity here. His insistence that a member of the body of Christ must not become one flesh with a prostitute grows out of an understanding of both dimensions of God's temple. The individual's relationship with Christ is defiled, but so also is the relationship with other members of the body, fellow members of Christ *[Bodies in 1 Corinthians, p. 363]*.

Paul's affirmation that *you are not your own* (v. 19), which is part of the *Do you not know* statement and effectively a summary of the whole argument, was the very antithesis of the Corinthian worldview. The claim to be free from any constraints (v. 12), the claim that God will destroy both body and food (v. 13), and the claim that what one does with one's body does not matter (v. 18) were all built on the assumption of individual rights, personal autonomy, and freedom. But as Hays (1997: 107) puts it, the Corinthians' "argument focuses on the rights and freedoms of the individual, Paul's focuses on the devotion and service owed to God." To paraphrase Paul in verse 19, "Surely you Christians should know that you are not your own and independent, you belong to God; God's Spirit lives in you, and your body as well as your soul is a member of Christ." This conviction is a complete reversal of the Corinthian (and the postmodern) worldview.

In his final comment on this issue, Paul summarizes the argument. The theological affirmation is *You were bought with a price*; the ethical implication is *Therefore glorify God in your body* (v. 20).

The language of purchase is usually understood to reflect the slavery practices common in the first century. Earlier commentaries spoke of the purchase as a purchase of freedom from slavery. More recent studies, however, have argued that the purchase represents the metaphor of a transfer of ownership, not a release from slavery (D. Martin 1990: 63). The focus here is not on who sold the slave, nor on the price paid, but only on who made the purchase. Speculation on the mechanics of atonement is not warranted (Thiselton 2000: 477). The point is that Christians have been purchased as slaves of Christ. Since the status of a slave is derived from the owner (D. Martin 1990: 1-49), to be Christ's slave is a high honor.

Honor is indeed on Paul's mind here. The word that is consistently translated here as *price* is most often translated as *honor* or some equivalent. In a few cases in Acts, and in reference to the money paid to Judas for betraying Jesus (Matt 27:6, 9), *price* is appropriate, but otherwise throughout the New Testament it is always translated as *honor*, except here and in the parallel statement in 1 Corinthians 7:23. English may not have an adequate equivalent to use here, but readers should notice that whereas *price* and *glory* do not otherwise occur together, *honor* and *glory* are frequently paired, from Romans 2:7 to Revelation 21:26. Paul is drawing his readers' attention to the relationship between the honor that Jesus has paid for them and the glory that they owe in return. In a culture that pays careful attention to the continuum between honor/glory and shame, honor is indeed a value beyond price [*Shame and Honor, p. 368*].

Paul's assertion that Christians should glorify God in their bodies was a strong challenge to those in Corinth who argued that what one does with one's body has no spiritual significance. Furthermore, his exhortation directed at men was a surprising challenge. In societies that value honor and avoid shame, the common assumption is that women's sexuality has moral significance and men's sexuality does not. That it continued to be difficult to accept is demonstrated by the many, though late, manuscripts that added *and in your spirit, which are God's* (v. 20, see KJV). But that negates Paul's point, which was that the physical bodies of believers—both men and women—are temples of God, temples where God should be honored. That honor must not be compromised by sexual union with prostitutes, especially those who practice their sexuality in honor of other deities.

THE TEXT IN BIBLICAL CONTEXT
One Flesh
Paul's argument about sexual ethics is based in part on the concept that sexual relations bind two people into one unit. This applies, according to Paul, not only in the committed relationship of marriage, but even in casual sexual unions, so that *whoever is united to a prostitute becomes one body with her.... For it is said, "The two shall be one flesh"* (v. 16). The quotation is from Genesis 2:24: "Therefore a man leaves his father and his mother and clings to his wife, and they become one flesh."

Although this statement is found early in the Old Testament, it is never again picked up in the Hebrew Bible as a defining statement about marriage. But when Jesus was asked about divorce (Matt 19:5 // Mark 10:6-8), he quoted this text as the definitive statement of God's intention in marriage. Jesus said that the one-flesh union disallows anyone from breaking it by divorce: "So they are no longer two, but one flesh. Therefore, what God has joined together, let no one separate" (Matt 19:6). In this case, the application points to the strength of the union created by sexual intercourse in marriage. It is not to be taken lightly.

In 1 Corinthians 6, the application is quite different, but the point is still that sexual intercourse is not to be taken lightly. Even in an encounter that both parties understand to be transient, a bond is formed. The Greek word translated as *is united* often means "glued," and Paul seems to be suggesting that, like an instant superglue, sexual union forms a bond that is meaningful and difficult—perhaps impossible—to dissolve. His use of language otherwise used for marital sexual union demonstrates that he does not see a qualitative difference between marital and nonmarital sex. There is no other place in the Bible that proposes this understanding.

The letter to the Ephesians (see above) picks up this quotation again, applying it to marriage and simultaneously using it as an analogy that helps people to understand the relationship between Christ and the church (5:31-33).

THE TEXT IN THE LIFE OF THE CHURCH
Sexuality in Christ
The slogans that Paul rejected sound familiar in twenty-first-century Western culture. "Our bodies are made for sex" and "Sexual activity is essential for a healthy and satisfying life." "Anything is okay

between consenting adults" and "What they do is nobody else's business." As Canadian prime minister Pierre Trudeau famously said (in a 1967 debate on decriminalization of homosexuality), "There's no place for the state in the bedrooms of the nation."

People of faith who deplore the hyper-sexualization of culture sometimes give the impression that sex is problematic, "dirty," and sinful and needs to be suppressed.

One lesson we can bring forward from Paul's teaching is that our physical bodies are good. They are *members of Christ* (v. 15), *temple[s] of the Holy Spirit* (v. 19). He does not accept the dualistic partitioning of physical and spiritual, of body and soul. When Paul contrasts flesh and spirit (3:1-3), he does not mean physical bodies. He does not dismiss the body as an impediment to the moral or spiritual life, and unlike the Corinthians, he does not dismiss the moral significance of the body because *God will destroy* it (v. 13; see EN).

Paul's argument is that *you are not your own. . . . Therefore glorify God in your body* (vv. 19-20). How is our self-understanding, our self-image, and our behavior affected if we believe that our sexual body belongs to God? That sexual behavior is not a private matter, but something in which God takes an interest? That sexual misbehavior, including abuse and infidelity, is not only an offense against people, but also an offense against God? That good sexual expression glorifies God?

Glorifying God in our bodies is not just about restricting inappropriate behavior. It is also about practicing appropriate behavior. More, it is about having right understandings and attitudes. In the lead chapter of *Sexuality: God's Gift*, Anne Krabill Hershberger and Willard Krabill suggest the following seven "foundation stones" (19) for a healthy acceptance and enjoyment of this gift:

1. A proper theology of the body accepts the physical, mental, and spiritual dimensions as parts of who we are and recognizes them as a gift from God.
2. A proper sexual theology based on the Bible's "affirmation of gender differences [is] a blessing from God when we allow love to permeate our relationships, and a sense that each individual is valuable as a sexual person" (22).
3. Respect for males and females honors both as equal and valued.
4. Integration of sex and life recognizes that we are always sexual beings and that sexuality is expressed not only in sex but in all aspects of relationships.

5. The sexuality of all people is affirmed, including those who are celibate, disabled, and seniors.
6. Sound sex education from parents, the faith community, and schools helps children understand the impact of their sexual decisions and instills a realistic and positive body image.
7. Celebration of sex practices the great commandment: "Love the Lord your God with all your heart, and with all your soul, and with all your mind" and "Love your neighbor as yourself" (Matt 22:37, 39).

Preaching and Worship

This passage is assigned by the Revised Common Lectionary to be read on the second Sunday after Epiphany in Year B. The assigned psalm for the day is Psalm 139:1-6, 13-18, which is a useful reminder that "I am fearfully and wonderfully made. Wonderful are your works; that I know very well" (v. 14). Together these passages suggest a sermon on sexuality affirming that the human body, including its sexual dimensions, is "wonderful" and *is a temple of the Holy Spirit within you, which you have from God,* and is intended to be used to *glorify God* (1 Cor 6:19-20). That this passage objects to consorting with prostitutes is also applicable to casual sexual encounters, use of pornography, and other nonmarital sexual actions. All these are important matters for Christians to address, as well as the issues of marital sexual expression that are discussed in the next chapter.

1 Corinthians 7:1-40

Marriage and Singleness

PREVIEW

Marriage for Christians in first-century Corinth was complicated. It was complicated for husband and wife, who in some cases did not share a commitment to follow Jesus and whose sexual relationship was convoluted by uncertainty around the mores of the Christian assembly. It was further confused by the influences of other philosophies, the practices of other religions, and debates within the Christian community about celibacy and singleness, which may have been prompted by Paul's example and earlier teaching. So it is not surprising that they turned to Paul with some questions.

Now, for the first time in this letter, Paul turns to the letter he has received from the Corinthians and begins to respond to their questions. *Now concerning the matters about which you wrote*, he begins (7:1). We have observed that the letter we have is only one side of the correspondence, and thus our understanding of the Corinthian side of the conversation can only be reconstructed by speculation based on what Paul wrote (see "Paul's Letter" in the introduction). Yet our understanding of Paul's counsel depends to a large extent upon our reconstruction of the letter that he had received from them.

The one unambiguous reference to their letter is in 7:1. Many scholars believe that later topics introduced by the phrase *Now concerning . . .* (Gk. *peri de*; 7:1, 25; 8:1; 12:1; 16:1, 12) were also raised in their letter *[What the Corinthians Wrote, p. 372]*. Although the expression can simply mean "on the next topic," the further common characteristic of all the passages introduced in this way is the tone and method of argument. Here we do not find the heated defensiveness of chapters 1-4 or the thundering denouncements of chapters 5-6 and 11:17-34. (In 11:1-16 is an exception that will be discussed below.)

When Paul responds to the questions raised by the letter he has received, he argues with less passion and more logic. He provides fewer details about what they have said, presumably because all the readers of his letter were aware of the letter that they had sent, and a brief reference like *Now concerning virgins* (7:25) would suffice to let them know what he was taking up. In contrast, when he was responding to oral reports, they did not know what he knew, so he provides them (and incidentally also us) with more contextual information. In chapter 7 and most of the remainder of the letter body, we have fewer cues and more variety of interpretation of what the situation in Corinth really was.

It is interesting that Paul chose to delay his response to the letter until this far into his writing. Though he responds seriously and at length to their questions, it is clear that he wanted to set the agenda. He weaves his responses to the letter and to the oral reports into the fabric of a comprehensive whole shaped by his analysis of the underlying problem: the factionalism of the faith community (1:10). So before dealing with specific and public ethical and theological issues, he insists on addressing the matters of broken relationships within the assembly and the strained relationship between the assembly and himself. He needed to reestablish the foundational concepts—such as the proclamation of the crucified Christ, the as-yet-unfulfilled eschatological hope, the initiative of God, and the redefined familial relationships of the community of faith—before he would address their questions.

Perhaps he wanted to signal that the "dirty laundry" aired by the (probably less prominent) servants of Chloe were more urgent than the (presumably) more socially acceptable and rational disagreements and questions raised by the letter and its carriers. Certainly his refusal to succumb to the congregation's agenda demonstrates that we cannot assume he answered their questions in sequence as they were asked, and it even raises the possibility that he was selective and did not respond to all the issues they had named (*contra* Hurd).

Two matters from the Corinthian letter are introduced by *Now concerning . . .* in chapter 7. The first is presented by a statement quoted from their letter: *It is well for a man not to touch a woman* (v. 1). The second is a question or a statement from them *concerning virgins*

(v. 25). What Paul has to say about these matters is often misunderstood and has led to some unfortunate misapplications. Because issues of sexuality, marriage, divorce, and gender relations are both important and complex, we especially need to pay careful attention to Paul's writing on these affairs. To do that, we also need to understand what was happening in Corinth that elicited Paul's counsel as offered. Finally, Paul locates the discussion on marriage in the context of sexual immorality (*porneia*) as one of the contributing factors to his larger concern, the factionalism of the community (1:10). Tolerance of an inappropriate sexual relationship violates community boundaries (5:1-13), consorting with prostitutes violates the unity of the body of Christ (6:12-20), and conflicts in marital relations (ch. 7) disrupt the household of faith.

OUTLINE

To the Married: Enjoy Sexual Union, 7:1-7
To the Formerly Married: Be Celibate or Marry, 7:8-9
To the Married: Do Not Initiate Divorce, 7:10-16
To the Engaged: Marriage Is Good, but Not the Highest Good, 7:17-38
To the Widows: Summary, 7:39-40

EXPLANATORY NOTES

To the Married: Enjoy Sexual Union 7:1-7

Now concerning the matters about which you wrote, Paul begins (v. 1). By this we know that the subject matter is not one that he has initiated. He does not set out to describe and define a comprehensive understanding of gender relationships, sexuality, or marriage, but confines himself to what is relevant to *the matters* that the Corinthians had presented.

The first thing to clarify in reading Paul's response is that he is talking about sex. The word translated *touch* (v. 1) can mean a variety of touches, but here it specifically means sexual intercourse, as the NIV translates it: *to have sexual relations with a woman* (a notable improvement from the NIV 1984 translation, *to marry*). The instruction that every man should *have his own wife* and every woman should *have her own husband* (v. 2) does not mean that everyone should get married; Paul advises otherwise later in this chapter. The expression "to have someone" was and is a common euphemism for sexual relations (cf. 5:1), and Paul is saying that married men should be having sex with their wives and married women should be having sex with their husbands.

Why is it necessary for Paul to instruct married couples to have sexual relations? Because there were people in Corinth who believed that *it is well for a man not to touch a woman* and were pressuring married couples to forego sexual intimacy. Many readers, wrongly crediting this statement as Paul's own view, have concluded that Paul was a misogynist, opposed to sex, and out of touch with human sexual desires. But as the NRSV and NIV rightly punctuate verse 1, it was some Corinthians who held this view, and they applied it to married people. They also had raised a question about single people, but that is not addressed until verse 25.

This negative attitude of some Christians in Corinth toward sexuality could have been shaped by various influences. Common in popular religion was an association between sexual abstinence and spirituality. Indeed, some of the philosophers, including some Cynics and Stoics who appear to have been favored by the Corinthians, argued that being unmarried was an advantage in the pursuit of wisdom. And despite the value that Judaism placed on marriage and procreation, some Jewish groups promoted sexual abstinence (notably the Essenes and the Therapeutae). As we shall see later in this chapter, Paul himself was celibate and promoted celibacy; so in writing to him, the Corinthians would have been justified in expecting that he would support their ascetic views. Many later Christians enthusiastically promoted the value of celibacy and practiced it in desert cells and monastic houses.

This ascetic tendency seems quite at odds with the sexual immorality that the Corinthians apparently defended and against which Paul wrote in chapter 5 (note esp. vv. 1, 9, 10, 11) and in 6:12-20 (also 6:9). Some scholars have suggested that there were two polarities of thought and practice in Corinth: the libertines (represented in chs. 5 and 6) and the ascetics (represented in ch. 7). But the unique circumstances of the man who was *living with his father's wife* (5:1-5) are not related to the topics addressed in chapter 7. And consorting with prostitutes (6:12-20—the same word, *porneia*, is used in 6:13, 18; and in 7:2) was perhaps prompted by futile attempts to live by the ascetic standard of not "touching" one's spouse. So perhaps the tension was not between ascetics and libertines, but between the ascetic standards and the reality of sexual impulses.

The Corinthian slogan *It is good for a man not to have sexual relations with a woman* (NIV) is worded from the male perspective. Consistent with the usual practice in the first-century world, women's perspectives, especially in marital and sexual matters, were not addressed. It must have been shocking, therefore, for the congregations in

Corinth to read Paul's reply in which he repeatedly addresses men and women equally:

> *Each man should have sexual relations with his own wife,*
>> *and*
>
> *each woman with her own husband* (v. 2 NIV).
>
> *The husband should fulfill his marital duty to his wife,*
>> *and likewise*
>
> *the wife to her husband* (v. 3 NIV).
>
> *The wife does not have authority over her own body but yields it to her husband.*
>> *In the same way,*
>
> *the husband does not have authority over his own body but yields it to his wife* (v. 4 NIV).
>
> *Do not deprive each other except by <u>mutual</u> consent and for a time, so that you may devote yourselves to prayer* (v. 5 NIV, emphasis added).

This balancing of instructions to women and men continues in verses 10-13 (divorce), 14 (making one's spouse holy), 16 (saving one's spouse), 28 (freedom to marry), and 32-34 (anxiety).

These strong statements of mutuality in marriage (cf. Eph 5:21), especially in marital sex, mitigate the cultural assumptions so common throughout human history of a "double standard" in sexual ethics that assumes male dominance in sexual relations, the priority of the man's sexual desires, and greater constraints on female than on male sexual activity. We have already seen that Paul challenges these assumptions by ascribing shame to the behavior of the man who "has" his father's wife (5:1-13) and by denying Christian men the right to have sex with prostitutes (6:12-20). Throughout chapter 7, he repeatedly goes beyond the Corinthians' assumptions and addresses men and women equally on sexual and marital matters.

The assumption in Roman culture (and in a great many other cultures throughout time) would not have questioned Paul's statement that *the wife does not have authority over her own body, but the husband does* (v. 4a). But nothing in the culture would have prepared them for the second half of his statement: *likewise the husband does not have authority over his own body, but the wife does* (v. 4b). Combined with the assertion in the previous paragraph that a man's body is a member of Christ (6:15), a temple of the Holy Spirit (6:18), and not his own (6:19), this is a significant constraint on the presumption that a man may satisfy his sexual urges however and whenever he wishes (cf. 6:12-13).

Readers often assume that the *concession* that Paul offers (v. 6) is permission to resume sexual relations after a period of abstinence for the sake of prayer. In fact, the concession is that by mutual agreement some couples might determine to give priority to prayer and abstain from sexual relations (v. 5). He does not command this, but he permits it.

Paul's general principle is that married couples should enjoy sexual union. To the Corinthians he concedes that there may be occasions for sexual abstinence, but not, as they argued, for perpetual celibacy within marriage. Although he has chosen to remain single and celibate and endorses that choice for others, he, unlike the Corinthians, is not willing to impose that requirement on others. Paul is realistic about the power of sexual desire and about its destructive as well as positive potential.

To the Formerly Married: Be Celibate or Marry 7:8-9

Having addressed married couples, Paul turns next to *the unmarried and the widows*. The word that is translated *unmarried* (Gk. *agamois*; *a* = not, *gamois* = married) is properly understood to mean "formerly married," and specifically in juxtaposition to *widows*, it is understood to mean *widowers* (v. 8; see Fee: 318–19; cf. v. 11, where it refers specifically to divorced women, and v. 34, which distinguishes *unmarried* from *virgins*).

Paul identifies with their marital status; although currently unmarried, he may have been married formerly (Murphy-O'Connor 1996: 62–65). As he identifies with them, he recommends that they choose the same option of celibacy that he has chosen. There is no word in Greek for the second *unmarried* in English translations of verse 8; the text literally says, *It is better if they remain [so], as also I [do]*. He will shortly explain his reasons for this.

But Paul is not doctrinaire about this, nor does he insist, as apparently some Corinthians did, that widows and widowers *must* remain unmarried. Again, the ethical priority of confining sexual relations to one's spouse takes precedence, and Paul says that if the desire for sex is strong, then the unmarried should marry.

The NRSV and NIV have added *with passion* in verse 9 as an interpretive comment on the Greek text, which is simply *to burn*. Without that clarification, some readers have wrongly understood that the burning refers to the fires of hell. Some have understood Paul to be grudgingly conceding that marriage is a lesser evil than unbridled passion, but an evil nevertheless. It is important to remember that the view Paul was correcting here is not one that celebrated the goodness of marriage and marital sex, but one that denied it: some Corinthians would have said that it is better to burn than to marry, but Paul reversed their ethical priorities.

To the Married: Do Not Initiate Divorce 7:10-16

Some of the Corinthians, perhaps experiencing the challenge of maintaining celibacy within marriage that was being promoted in the assembly, may have determined that divorce was a preferable alternative. Paul first addresses women who might have wanted to divorce (the modern distinction between separation and divorce was unknown), which might suggest that it was primarily women who considered and perhaps had already taken this step. One might even speculate that they did so to escape pressure from a husband (perhaps not a believer) who was not willing to forego sexual relations.

This Paul does not condone, because there is a commandment from the Lord that believers not initiate divorce. Paul underscores the fact that this command is from the Lord because he wants to distinguish between what Jesus taught and what he himself is teaching: in verse 12 he specifies that he is speaking, not the Lord; likewise in verses 25 and 40. It is rare for Paul to appeal explicitly to Jesus' teachings (the other cases are 9:14 and 1 Thess 4:15-17). The teaching to which he alludes here is found in the Gospels at Mark 10:2-12; Matthew 5:31-32; 19:3-12; and Luke 16:18—though only the Markan version specifies the possibility of a woman initiating divorce. According to these accounts, Jesus spoke against divorce and remarriage by defining the subsequent marriage as adulterous. In light of the current discussion with the Corinthians, Paul interprets this as a command not to divorce, but concedes the possibility that some would divorce.

Divorce could have been a way to become single in order to remain celibate, as Paul recommended. Some members of the assembly apparently pressured people to do so. But being cognizant of the realities of sexual temptation, Paul recognized that it could also lead to marrying another. (Perhaps some women, wanting to marry a man with less ascetic principles, were seeking divorce not because they sought freedom from sexual obligation, but freedom from a husband who wanted to abstain from sex.)

Although he first addresses women on this matter, Paul continues his practice of treating women and men equally by adding, *The husband should not divorce his wife* (1 Cor 7:11c).

Paul's instruction here is to the one initiating divorce, not to the one who is abandoned at the spouse's initiative. Presumably the advice he has already given to the unmarried and widows (vv. 8-9) addresses the one who is abandoned.

Paul now addresses *the rest* (v. 12). He has already addressed the unmarried and widows (v. 8) and the married (v. 10). Shortly he will address virgins (v. 25) and write *about* (though not *to*) those who are engaged (v. 36). With such a comprehensive list of addressees, *the rest* seems not to be another classification of marital status, but another class of married person who may be considering divorce, specifically those men and women (again, treating both sexes equally) who are Christians married to unbelievers (vv. 12-16).

Paul's advice here is quite contrary to the harsh injunction to separate from unbelievers in 2 Corinthians 6:14–7:1. That passage is difficult to understand in its context (see Shillington 1998a: 153-58, 278-81). Here we need only note that the latter passage represents the opposite view to the current passage. It is probable that at least some of the Corinthians held to the harsher view.

Paul advises that when believing women and men are married to unbelieving spouses who are willing to remain married, the believer should not initiate divorce. If the unbeliever initiates divorce (v. 15), the situation would be the same as that of the abandoned spouse, who is like the unmarried person in verses 8-9. In any of those situations, Paul advises remaining single and celibate, but if that is not a viable option, then they are free to marry.

It is to peace that God has called you, Paul writes (v. 15c). This applies no less to family situations than to relationships in the household of faith, relationships in business, or relationships between nations. As he had advised the Corinthians in their business dealings to accept wrongs from others but not to do wrong to others (6:7), so now in marital issues he instructs that they should not initiate divorce, but if the unbelieving partner chooses to separate, they should *let it be so* (v. 15a). This, he believes, will make for peace, and in Roman society it was peace or concord, not love or happiness, that was the goal of marriage (Witherington: 170). In writing this letter, Paul's intent was the achievement of peace not only within the family but also and especially in the assembly, which would have been deeply affected in the event of a marital breakup, and in which apparently there was already dispute about marital ethics.

Paul's rationale for remaining together is unusual. In another context in this same letter, Paul warns that *bad company ruins good morals* (15:33), much like the common saying that "one bad apple spoils the whole barrel." This is the basis of the separation counsel in 2 Corinthians 6:14–7:1 and of the yeast imagery. Earlier in this letter, Paul quotes the common saying that *a little yeast leavens the whole batch of dough* (5:6). There he associates yeast with sin, drawing on the Passover practice of carefully removing all yeast from the house to prepare for the Feast of Unleavened Bread. But yeast can also have positive associations. Though Jesus sometimes used yeast as a negative image (Matt 16:6, 11-12 // Luke 12:1 // Mark 8:15), he let yeast be positive in the parable of the woman who leavened all the bread with a small amount of yeast (Matt 13:33 // Luke 13:21).

Paul does not use the metaphor of yeast in this passage, but he does reverse the usual anxiety about the contagiousness of sin to declare that holiness is also contagious. The unbelieving spouse is *made holy* (v. 14) and may even be saved (v. 16) by association with and the influence of the believing spouse (see Blomberg). Furthermore, children of that union are also holy (v. 14c).

In this paragraph, which speaks to a situation that Jesus had not addressed, Paul carefully points out that this advice is his own extrapolation from Jesus' teaching (v. 12). Undoubtedly that gives it lower status than a commandment (v. 10), but Paul claims that it is informed by the Spirit of God and is thus valid counsel for the Christian community (vv. 25, 40). Both in extrapolating from the teachings of Jesus to find counsel in new situations not addressed directly by Jesus and in being careful to qualify that counsel as being his own, Paul provides a model for discerning the application of Jesus' teachings to the situations where followers of Jesus must make ethical decisions.

To the Engaged: Marriage Is Good, but Not the Highest Good 7:17-38

Three times in this section Paul states the underlying principle that he uses to address each marital status and the questions about which the Corinthians had written to him:

> Let each of you lead the life that the Lord has assigned, to which God called you. (v. 17)
>
> Let each of you remain in the condition in which you were called. (v. 20)
>
> In whatever condition you were called, brothers and sisters, there remain with God. (v. 24)

Between these statements he presents illustrations, the first having to do with circumcision (vv. 18-19), and the second with slavery (vv. 21-23; cf. 12:13). Their use here is primarily to prepare readers for applying the thrice-stated principle to marriage in the following paragraph.

The selection of these three social status indicators—ethnicity (circumcision), class (slavery), and sex (marital status)—as criteria that are irrelevant between Christians is not accidental. Paul also lists these three in Galatians 3:27-28: "As many of you as were baptized into Christ have clothed yourselves with Christ. There is no longer Jew or Greek [circumcision], there is no longer slave or free [slavery], there is no longer male and female" (cf. 1 Cor 12:13).

Both circumcision and uncircumcision are *nothing* for Christians, Paul writes (1 Cor 7:19; cf. Gal 5:6; 6:15). The Corinthian assembly apparently included both Jews and Gentiles, and unlike in Galatia, this does not seem to have been a source of conflict. We do not know whether any of the Gentiles who became Christians sought circumcision or whether any Jews who became Christians sought to *remove the marks of circumcision*, as some Jews did in order better to fit into the Gentile culture (v. 18; cf. 1 Macc 1:15). Nevertheless, Paul uses this example to illustrate his point that circumcision, and the ethnic identity that it represents, is not worth fretting about for Christians.

His point seems to be weakened by a contradictory comment. While claiming that circumcision is nothing, he adds, *But obeying the commandments of God is everything* (v. 19b). Yet circumcision is a commandment of God (Gen 17:9-14)! In other letters, Paul deals with circumcision in more detail as a synecdoche (a part that stands for the whole) for the whole of the Torah law, and though he is adamant that Gentiles are not obligated to become Jews in order to become Christians—and thus Gentile men need not be circumcised to become members of the Christian community—Paul still insists, as he does here, that other ethical commands need to be obeyed by Gentile and Jewish Christians alike. Fee (345) suggests a reasonable resolution for this dilemma, that circumcision in this letter (unlike in Galatians) is primarily a sociological issue in that it determines "Jew or Gentile" in an ethnic sense, rather than a theological or ethical issue.

The second illustration is parallel to the first. Paul writes that the social status defined by slavery or freedom is irrelevant for Christians. Echoing the reversal of status that he has described in 1 Corinthians 1:27-28 and repeating what he has written in 6:20a, he says that slaves who are Christians have been freed by the Lord, *bought with a price*, while those who were free have become slaves of Christ (7:22-23a). In any case, he advises, *Do not be concerned about it* (v. 21b).

The difficult line in this argument is the second half of verse 21. The NRSV says, *Even if you can gain your freedom, make use of your present condition now more than ever*. A footnote gives an alternative reading: *Avail yourself of the opportunity*. The marginal reading is to be preferred here, or the NIV's *Although if you can gain your freedom, do so* (also KJV, NASB, NET, NKJV, REB, RSV—but not NJB). Paul's point is not that everyone *must* remain in their current status (a reading that has been used to support the continuance of slavery and many other forms of oppression), but that social status of slavery or freedom is not determinative in God's realm.

With these two examples and the repetition of his basic instruction, Paul has made the point that in all matters of status the Corinthian Christians should accept their circumstances and not invest excessive energy in trying to change them. This counsel (not a command) is offered for a particular time: the underlying reason for this will be explained shortly. But first he applies the principle to the topic he is addressing: marriage.

The discussion about circumcision and slavery provided the background for Paul to address the next issue from the Corinthian letter. Once again, because the readers knew what they had written to Paul, it was not necessary for him to explain the issue, so he simply names the topic: *concerning virgins* (v. 25).

Exactly who the virgins are or what the Corinthians had asked Paul—or perhaps stated rather than asked—we cannot know. From his response, it appears that they are young women engaged to be married, and the question placed before Paul has to do with applying the Corinthian slogan in their situation: *It is good for a man not to have sexual relations with a woman* (v. 1 NIV). One wonders how many people there were in this situation in the Corinthian assembly, and whether the Corinthians had identified this issue as a singular case or for any such case. Paul's response is general and applicable to as many as may presently or in the future be in that circumstance.

Once again Paul applies his Spirit-inspired wisdom to a question on which Jesus had not left a commandment and on which there was no scriptural guidance. His advice applies the same principle that he has previously applied to circumcision and slavery: *I think that it is good for a man to remain as he is. Are you pledged to a woman? Do not seek to be released. Are you free from such a commitment? Do not look for a wife* (vv. 26b-27 NIV). Although the topic title is *concerning virgins* (feminine), the principle is addressed to men. Yet he continues, as throughout this chapter, to address equally the men and the women in each marital status. The category *pledged to a woman* probably refers, especially in view of the present context, to persons engaged to be married, not those who are already married (NRSV and most translations say *wife*; the Greek word can mean either).

And once again Paul's counsel, though clear about his own preference for singleness and celibacy, is stated less categorically than what we can reconstruct of the Corinthian argument. So he assures those who are considering marriage, *If you marry, you do not sin, and if a virgin marries, she does not sin* (v. 28a).

The reasons for recommending singleness are not universal but rather specific to the immediate circumstances as Paul perceived them. He believed that it was expedient *because of the present crisis* (v. 26a NIV; NRSV's *impending* is possible, but *present* is grammatically preferable). He explains further that *those who marry will experience distress in this life, and I would spare you that* (v. 28). In this he was not meaning to state a general observation about marriage, either realistic or cynical, and from it we cannot presume any reference to his own experience of marriage. The distress and the impending crisis has to do with his understanding of the nearness of the apocalyptic eschaton: *I mean, brothers and sisters, the appointed time has grown short* (v. 29a), *for the present form of this world is passing away* (v. 31b).

Commenting further on this anticipation of the imminent end of this age, Paul says,

> *From now on those who have wives should live as if they do not; those who mourn, as if they did not; those who are happy, as if they were not; those who buy something, as if it were not theirs to keep; those who use the things of the world, as if not engrossed in them. For this world in its present form is passing away* (vv. 29b-31 NIV).

In 7:1-7 he has instructed against married people living celibately, and having just granted that those who want to marry should do so with a clear conscience, he is not now reversing that. Paul was a craftsperson who was dependent on people buying his products (see ch. 9); we presume that he did not mean people should stop buying and selling. We should not understand that he is advising an end to or a reversal of all emotion, but rather that every experience of life should be shaped by eschatological anticipation, including not just marriage and marital sexual relations. This is not a Stoic argument for detachment from the concerns and activities of life for the sake of character development, nor is it a Corinthian spiritual ascetic repudiation of all things material, but rather a reprioritization of all things in the light of the impending end of the present age.

Paul carried a heavy burden of anxiety for the Christian communities that he had established. As he wrote in a later letter, "Besides other things, I am under daily pressure because of my anxiety for all the churches" (2 Cor 11:28). Because of his experience, he gave advice that he believed would reduce the anxiety of believers. Recognizing that whether married or unmarried, Christian men and women alike are *anxious about the affairs of the Lord*, he also understood that those who are married have additional anxieties *about the affairs of this world* and about pleasing their spouse (1 Cor 7:32-34), and he hoped to spare them the multiplication of anxiety. This concern echoes verse 28, though the focus here may be less on impending eschatological stresses and more on the ongoing concerns of daily family life. In his several reasons for advising against marriage, Paul never provides or endorses reasons for refraining from sexual relations within marriage beyond temporary abstinence for prayer (7:5). He insists that those who marry should be sexually active (vv. 2-7); it is the comprehensive commitment of marriage that gives him hesitation.

Once again he repeats his flexibility. While he has good reasons for advising singleness—*to promote good order* [cf. better translations: *to promote decorum* (AT); *that you may live in a right way* (NIV); *for that which is seemly* (ASV); *for the sake of propriety* (NABR); *to be beyond criticism* (REB); or *for what is proper* (NKJ)] *and unhindered devotion to the Lord* (v. 35b)—this advice is not a command or restraint for those who decide to marry.

This chapter begins by addressing the assembly, speaking to its treatment of marital sexual relations, and countering its restrictive standards. The first four paragraphs (7:1-16) are voiced primarily in the third person; the discussion is about what *they* should be expected to do (except in v. 5). Verse 16 is the transitional point where the people affected are directly addressed. Verses 17-35 are addressed to *you*. In 7:36-40, Paul reverts to addressing the assembly and talking not *to* but *about* those who wish to marry. As in the beginning of the chapter, he is here speaking to the community's views on marriage and sex, not to those who are making the decisions.

There is ambiguity about the meaning of *his passions are strong* (v. 36). Some earlier versions of NIV translated the Greek word *hyperakmos* as *she is getting along in years*, and it continues as an alternate translation in the footnote. Both are possible. It literally means *beyond a high point*. The prefix *hyper-* can add a temporal sense (past) or an intensified sense (above) to the root *akmos* (cf. Eng.: *acme*), meaning "prime" or "peak." Since women usually married when they were young and men when they were older, *past one's prime for marrying* could more naturally apply to a woman. Most translations assume that if the meaning is *beyond the boiling point* (AT), it must refer to the man, but grammatically it could mean either the man or the woman. The most likely meaning is that strong sexual passion in either or both parties is legitimate motivation to marry (cf. v. 9).

To engaged men, whom some would urge not to consummate their marriage, Paul says that it is *no sin* to *marry* if one's *sexual passions are strong*, and *if anyone thinks he is acting shamefully* (AT; cf. EN on 13:5; [Shame and Honor, p. 368]) *toward his fiancée* by not consummating the marriage contract, then *let him marry as he wishes* (7:36). On the other hand, Paul applauds those who are able to live celibately and who freely choose to do so. His advice here is the same as what he has offered in verses 8-9 to those who were formerly married. Addressing the community, Paul says there must be no external compulsion (*being under no necessity*, v. 37) to refrain from marriage or from enjoying marital sex. It is to the assembly, not the young man or his fiancée, that Paul says, *Let them marry* (v. 36c).

The complexity of understanding exactly who the *virgins* are in this discussion is increased by Paul's address to only the men in this paragraph. Were the social conventions such that the woman had no say in the matter? That seems to contradict the following paragraph (vv. 39-40), where a widow is assumed to have control over whom she marries. Surely if a man breaks his engagement and decides not to marry, the woman is free to marry another, just as any virgin or widow or divorced woman is. As for the engaged man, since most marriages were arranged (Witherington: 170), did he have any freedom to make his own decision?

Presumably if Paul had thought of it, he also would have written in this paragraph that the same applies to women. Yet it is possible that a specific situation in Corinth had been reported to Paul, either in the letter or by its carriers, in which some members of the assembly were pressuring a young man not to marry his fiancée. Verse 38 summarizes Paul's advice for the whole chapter: either action is morally appropriate, but one is more expedient.

To the Widows: Summary 7:39-40

In the closing verses of this chapter, Paul returns to the topic of widows remarrying. He adds no new information or argument beyond what he has already stated in verses 8-9, so there must have been some rhetorical reason for naming them again. We might speculate, though it is impossible to verify, that the letter from the Corinthians featured a question or comment about widows, so Paul chose to return to that issue to wrap up his discussion of marital issues. Perhaps it was especially on widows that the assembly had tried to impose restrictions or even a particular case involving a widow that they had placed before him in their letter. While Paul declares his personal preference to be in line with those who avoided marriage, he balances that with a strong declaration of freedom for the widow to *marry anyone she chooses, only in the Lord*, and not to be bound to her previous husband after his death (v. 39).

Although he had addressed men in the previous paragraph, here he addresses only women; these two paragraphs contrast with his usual pattern of carefully addressing women and men equally. It is likely that there would have been more widows in the congregations than widowers (and probably more than engaged couples), given the demographics of Corinth. In any case, this brief comment, appearing immediately after his discussion of engaged couples, serves to demonstrate that Paul applies his advice equally to younger and older members, women and men, whether single, married, divorced, or widowed.

His final comment addresses his authority to speak to these matters. It is possible that people in Corinth, as today, questioned Paul's credibility as an unmarried man in addressing matters of marriage and sex. He claims as his qualification not only his own experience, but also the Spirit of God. That he says *I think that I too have the Spirit of God* (v. 40) may suggest that others have made that claim for themselves.

Throughout this chapter Paul is careful to do the following:

1. He affirms what he can of what the Corinthians believe and value.
2. He allows great flexibility for those whose conscience calls or permits them to balance their sexual desires and their commitment to Christ differently than his own commitment—provided it is within the parameters of marriage and of membership in the body of Christ.
3. He distinguishes between his own counsel and that of the Lord.
4. He places the onus for moral discernment on the individuals involved, by mutual discernment, considering always the

priority of their commitment to Christ and the effect on their fellow believers.

At no point does Paul refer to the bearing of children or the presence of children in his discussion of marriage, with the brief exception of mentioning that children are *made holy* through a believing parent (v. 14). It may be that the people who were choosing to remain single or celibate within marriage were among the wealthy members of the assembly, since the poor could not afford not to have children to look after them in their old age (Witherington: 177n31). In any event, it is clear that Paul does not understand sexual union only or primarily in relation to procreation, and he does not explicitly name children as part of the complexity of divided loyalties or even as a concern in light of the *present crisis* (v. 26).

THE TEXT IN BIBLICAL CONTEXT

Slavery

In his discussion about marriage, Paul makes a brief statement about slavery—but not the typical ball-and-chain metaphor that some use. His point is rather that a change in faith commitment does not demand a change in marital status, just as it does not demand a reversal of circumcision or escape from slavery.

This brief comment, which minimizes the significance of slavery and assumes its practice, has been used in the argument that the Bible condones or promotes the institution of slavery (see review of arguments on both sides in Swartley 1983: 31–66). In fact, the practice of slavery in the Roman Empire was pervasive, and Christians lived with that reality (D. Martin 1990: 317–18). But seeds of change were already sown in the way Christian slaves and masters related to each other (Zerbe: 55–57).

The presence of both slaves and free people as equal participants in the assembly is assumed in Galatians 3:28; 1 Corinthians 12:13; and Colossians 3:11. The letter to Philemon, carried by a runaway slave whom Paul sent back to his master, gives instructions to receive the slave as a "beloved brother" (v. 16) and a strong suggestion that he be freed and returned to Paul as an assistant, even as it assumes the continued validity of the master-slave relationship. Paul instructs slaves to respect and serve their masters, which would be predictable in the context. But sometimes he also instructs masters to treat their slaves kindly (Eph 6:5-9; Col 3:22–4:1; cf. *1 Tim 6:1-6; Titus 2:9-10;* 1 Pet 2:18-20). Furthermore, slave traders are included in a list of "the lawless and disobedient, . . . the godless and sinful, . . . the unholy and profane" (*1 Tim 1:9-10*).

One of Paul's preferred ways of identifying himself was "slave of Jesus Christ" (e.g., Rom 1:1, footnote; cf. EN and "Servant Leadership" in TBC on 1 Cor 3:5-23, above). He also claims to have voluntarily become a *slave to all* (1 Cor 9:19) and says elsewhere that "with my mind I am a slave to the law of God, but with my flesh I am a slave to the law of sin" (Rom 7:25). For one who was a freedman (a former slave or, presumably in Paul's case, the son of a former slave: Acts 6:9; 7:58–8:1; cf. "Paul" in the introduction), these are dramatic statements.

The Gospels do not report that Jesus said anything directly weighing the issue of slavery in society, though he did recognize the practice in several parables (Matt 13:24-30; 18:23-35; 21:33-44; 22:2-10; 25:14-30; Luke 17:7-10; 20:9-16) and other teachings (e.g., Matt 10:24-25; 24:45-51).

The Old Testament reflects a culture that assumed slavery. It is first mentioned in Noah's curse on his grandson Canaan (Gen 9:24-27). Abraham, Isaac, and Jacob had slaves (e.g., Gen 24:35; 30:43). The Scriptures include laws to protect slaves, though masters could beat them, even to death—provided they did not die immediately (Exod 21:20-21; but cf. vv. 26-27). These laws were nuanced, depending on whether the slave was male or female, Hebrew or "alien," and in general they were more protective of the slaves than were surrounding cultures. The slavery laws of the Old Testament, however, were not active in the New Testament era, when such practices were regulated by Roman law and customs.

Divorce

The gospels of Mark and Mathew report a conversation between Jesus and some Pharisees about appropriate grounds for divorce (Mark 10:2-12; Matt 19:3-12). The Pharisees initiated the conversation with a question that reflected a lively debate between rabbis about divorce based on a reading of Deuteronomy 24:1-4. The passage forbids a man from remarrying a woman whom he once divorced if she has subsequently married another man and then been divorced or widowed by her new husband. In setting up the ruling, the text poses a hypothetical case where "a man marries a woman who becomes displeasing to him because he finds something indecent about her" (Deut 24:1 NIV; Heb.: "something naked"; LXX: "something shameful"), and he divorces her. Some rabbis understood the phrase to apply only if the wife were discovered to have been sexually unfaithful. Others understood it to apply to anything a man might find displeasing, including burning dinner.

When Jesus was asked which view he took, he answered with the narrower reading: the passage only considers divorce in the case of adultery. Furthermore, he pointed out that God's original intention was for fidelity and unity in marriage (Mark 10:6-8; Matt 19:4-6; quoting Gen 2:24), and it was only "because of your hardness of heart" that the Mosaic law allowed divorce (Mark 10:5 // Matt 19:8) The right question to ask is not "When does God allow divorce?" but rather "What is God's ideal for marriage?" (Geddert: 230-32, 240-41).

A parallel statement is found in the Sermon on the Mount, where Matthew reports that Jesus recognized the legal provision for divorce but declared that remarriage after divorce is adultery for both parties—unless adultery has taken place before the divorce (Matt 5:31-32; 19:9). Just before saying this, Jesus affirmed the legal prohibition against adultery and strengthened it to include lustful looking at a nonspouse (Matt 5:27-30). Luke's gospel also reports Jesus' statement that marriage after divorce is adultery for both parties (Luke 16:18).

David Instone-Brewer has argued that in addition to the provision for divorce in the case of adultery, there was another provision in the Torah for divorce in the case of neglect: "If he takes another wife to himself, he shall not diminish the food, clothing, or marital rights of the first wife. And if he does not do these three things for her, she shall go out without debt, without payment of money" (Exod 21:10-11). This provision was not being debated in Jesus' time, as far as we know, and his questioners did not ask him to comment on it, so there is no record of Jesus speaking to this situation (Instone-Brewer 2006: passim; cf. Instone-Brewer 2007).

Jesus' criticism of those who take marital vows lightly is like that of Malachi 2:13-16, which declares that God hates divorce, marital faithlessness, and violence. But Jesus' final comment, given only to his disciples, seems to recognize that the instruction in Deuteronomy acknowledges the reality of marriage: some people will divorce. When his disciples reacted that nobody should marry if divorce is not an option, Jesus said, "Not everyone can accept this teaching, but only those to whom it is given. . . . Let anyone accept this who can" (Matt 19:10-12).

Other than what the Gospels report, the only place where divorce is discussed in the New Testament is in 1 Corinthians 7. The view of some of the Corinthian Christians seems to have allowed, encouraged, or demanded divorce for Christians who were married to unbelievers. Though it is not stated, they might have found support from Ezra 9–10, where the Israelite men were forced to "send away" the non-Jewish women they had married during the exile, together with their children. Paul, however, dismisses this and argues that the believer should not initiate divorce. Instead of the believer being defiled by the relationship, the unbeliever is made holy, and so are their children (1 Cor 7:12-16). The Gospels do not report that Jesus addressed the circumstances that the Corinthians faced. Paul's instructions rely on his own Spirit-inspired, trustworthy judgment (vv. 12, 25, 40).

Otherwise, Paul's comments cohere with Jesus' rejection of initiating divorce. But Paul too recognizes that there will be circumstances where a person is abandoned by his or her spouse, perhaps because of the person's Christian values and practices. In that case, Paul says the one who is abandoned is *not bound*, a provision that echoes Exodus 21:10-11 and the recognition of Jesus that some concessions are necessary "because your hearts were hard" (Mark 10:5 NIV; Matt 19:8 NIV).

THE TEXT IN THE LIFE OF THE CHURCH
Moral Discernment

The matters addressed in this chapter were undoubtedly difficult for the Corinthian believers. They are complicated matters because they deal with sexuality and relationships, aspects of life that elicit strong emotions. All the members of the Corinthian assembly had their own sexual longings and experiences, their frustrations with marriage or with singleness, and many other personal influences that shaped their convictions. And apparently there were at least some who wanted to impose their own convictions on others.

Christian churches that face issues like this in the twenty-first century can learn from Paul's example how to do moral discernment with such highly emotional matters.

First, notice Paul's tone. His words are measured, reasoned, and respectful (1 Cor 7:6, 35). He recognized the value of various perspectives and honored everyone's experience and convictions. He recognized that people are not all the same (v. 7). Paul attributed positive motives to all, assumed they could make appropriate decisions for themselves (vv. 36-37), and held hope for positive outcomes (v. 16).

Second, however he came by it, Paul took seriously what *the Lord* said (v. 10). He also recognized that the current questions went beyond what the Lord had said. Paul was honest in distinguishing between his own convictions, based on his experience and what the Holy Spirit was saying to him, and what had come from Jesus and the Scriptures (v. 25).

Third, Paul demonstrated extraordinary sensitivity to people whose situation is different from his own. He did not impose answers, nor did he withdraw from the responsibility to share in corporate discernment of moral dilemmas. Although he was comfortable with his circumstances as an unmarried man and could happily recommend that to others (vv. 7-8), he was able to imagine and honor the experiences of married men, of women, of widows and widowers, of those engaged to be married, and of those contemplating or having experienced divorce. Paul acknowledged that he could not impose his experiences on others, as so many are tempted to do. Yet he did not shrink from saying something to them, as so many others are tempted to do. He remained engaged in the discernment that others needed to do for themselves, and provided perspective and encouragement.

Corporate moral discernment is essential to the life of the church, and it is often poorly done. It would be profitable for faith communities to explore this chapter as a case study in moral discernment. It will not do, of course, for one person to give a lecture on how Paul applied biblical principles to new questions. Paul's example should be explored, and it should also be applied. The discerning community (congregation, small group, synod, or other configuration) should grapple with an issue relevant to its life, asking, what does the Lord say? What do we, who *think that* [we] *too have the Spirit of God* (v. 40), say? What are the convictions that shape us, such as eschatological expectation (vv. 26, 31), the importance of maintaining peace (v. 15), the value of learning from experiences and examples (vv. 7, 8), the weighing of lesser evils (vv. 9, 36), and the distinguishing between concessions and commands (vv. 6, 10, 15, 35)? How can we discover the mind of Christ?

Celibacy

In the years after the New Testament was written, many Christians adopted the view of some Corinthians that sex is bad and that celibacy and virginity are better than marriage. The apocryphal Acts of Paul and Thecla, for example, describes the miraculous interventions of God to protect the virginity and the life of a young woman, Thecla, who committed to live celibately because of Paul's preaching. Other stories of virgin martyrs (always women) were widely circulated and lauded. Early church fathers, such as Tertullian, Jerome, Augustine, and Ambrose, endorsed celibacy, often with strongly misogynistic language (Colón and Field: 173–76).

Since the fourth century, the Roman Catholic Church has mandated that clergy and members of religious orders take vows of celibacy. Orthodox churches allow or require clergy serving in congregations to be married, but monks, bishops, and higher officials are required to be celibate.

In the Protestant Reformation, compulsory (and often abused) clergy celibacy was one of the practices that were denounced and discarded. Martin Luther rejected his monastic vow of celibacy and married Katharina von Bora, a former nun. Likewise, Michael and Margaretha Sattler left their respective religious orders, married, and became leaders in the Anabaptist movement (Bossert, Bender, and Snyder).

For Protestants and lay Catholics, there are few models and resources to help embrace a call to celibacy. Evangelical Christianity in North America has loudly embraced "family values" that honor marriage and dishonor singleness. While insisting that unmarried heterosexuals and all nonheterosexuals abstain from sexual intercourse, the attitude toward celibacy has generally been perplexity, suspicion, and hostility.

In the Western world, sexual activity is assumed to be a human right and essential to well-being, and those who are celibate are pitied and scorned. At the same time, sexual impropriety by non-celibates and even by "celibate" clergy destroys lives and brings disrepute on the church. The case that "celibacy must be reinvented in today's church" (Colón and Field) is strong. If Christians

> would learn to think about their choices between marriage and singleness within the framework of the church's mission to carry the gospel to the world, . . . our conversation in the church about these matters would begin to pose a serious challenge to Western culture's frantic idolatry of sexual gratification as a primary end of human existence. (Hays 1997: 133; cf. Nash and Conrad articles in Hershberger: 107–15, 211–29)

Same-Sex Marriage

Although Paul mentions same-sex relations in his writings (see on 1 Cor 6:9-11, above; cf. Rom 1:26-27), there is no evidence that he contemplated the possibility of same-sex marriage. For the church in the twenty-first century, this is a possibility that must be considered.

Some have suggested that Paul's counsel to the Corinthians about focusing sexual energy in a heterosexual marriage might also point the way toward faithfulness for those whose attraction is to persons of the same sex (e.g., Schlabach; Brownson [141–45]). Paul's assertion—*If they are not practicing self-control, they should marry. For it is better to marry than to be aflame with passion* (v. 9)—is argued to be true for all people. Promiscuity is wrong and harms not only the individuals who participate in it but also the social order. God has instituted the covenant of marriage to provide a framework of fidelity for intimate relationships, including sexual union. Denying the possibility of a sanctioned commitment of permanence and faithfulness condemns people *to be aflame with passion* and often to sexual promiscuity.

Of course, Paul's commendation of celibacy would also apply to those who are attracted to people of the same sex. But we have seen that Paul, unlike the Corinthians whom he opposed, did not demand that all people refrain from sexual intimacy.

Preaching and Worship

Preachers would serve their congregations and the Scripture well by using 1 Corinthians 7 to do the following:

1. Address the value of the single and celibate life
2. Affirm respectful and equal sexual intimacy in marriage
3. Address the complex issues of divorce
4. Speak about the challenges of marriage (*the married [person] is anxious about . . . how to please [their spouse]*, vv. 33-34)
5. Correct prevalent value systems, reminding believers that serving God is more important than one's circumstances and more important than "family values"

In churches that adhere strictly to the Revised Common Lectionary, this chapter is never read, except for verses 29-31, which do not deal with these important issues.

1 Corinthians 8:1-13

Idol Food and Divisions in the Community, Part 1

PREVIEW

Abruptly, Paul changes topics between chapter 7 and chapter 8. The shift is introduced by the expression *Now concerning . . .* We have discussed this transitional phrase above (preview for ch. 7): it is probably a reference to the letter that Paul received from the Corinthians. Paul assumes that the Corinthians know the background and the issue that he takes up here, which is the moral appropriateness of Christians eating food that has been offered to idols.

Regulations around food consumption are important matters of faith and culture. They control *what* one eats, including kosher (Jewish) or halal (Muslim) regulations, vegetarianism, and culturally defined understandings of what is fit or unfit to eat (e.g., mice, dogs, horses, intestines), and *how* (with hands, and if so, which hand; with what utensils; with what etiquette). There are also regulations that define *with whom* one eats (social status and caste, kinship relationships, gender separation, purity) that may bar people from eating with certain other people, at least at particular times or in particular circumstances. Regulations also define *where* eating is appropriate (in private, public, sacred spaces) and *when* (periods of fasting, feasting, seasonal prohibitions or requirements).

Questions about the ethics of food consumption were important to the early Christians. When people embraced Christianity, they entered into new relationships and a new culture. When the

1 Corinthians 8:1-13

Christian leaders met in Jerusalem to determine which, if any, of the regulations from the Hebrew Scriptures were binding on Gentile Christians, three of the four items named had to do with eating, and the first of those was "to abstain from food sacrificed to idols" (Acts 15:29 NIV).

As always, we wish we had a copy of the letter that Paul received so we could understand what the Corinthians were asking of him. In the absence of their letter, we can only guess at the weight of seriousness they placed on these matters and the nature of the questions, or perhaps statements, they put forward. What we do have is Paul's letter, and from it we can determine that Paul treated this topic extensively and carefully. For him, the matter of food offered to idols and the related issues raised and illustrated by that specific question were important. He devotes three chapters—from 8:1 to 11:1—to this set of issues.

The general outline of Paul's arguments is this:

8:1-13	The basis of ethical decision making: Paul rejects knowledge (theology) in favor of love (relationships) as the basis for ethical behavior.
9:1-27	Experiential arguments: Paul is an example of sensitivity to fellow Christians in the exercise of his freedoms.
10:1-14	Scriptural arguments: Biblical precedents are related to idolatry.
10:15-22	Theological arguments: Communion declares our loyalty to Christ and to the body of believers.
10:23-11:1	Paul gives advice on the presenting and underlying issues.

The concerns addressed in chapters 8-10 continue in the following chapters as well. Chapter 11 takes up two issues, headship and decorum in worship (vv. 2-16) and sensitivity to others in the Lord's Supper (vv. 17-34). Chapters 12-14 consider manifestations of the Spirit in worship. The arguments that Paul presents on each of these issues parallel the arguments that he presents on idol food (Thiselton 2000: 607).

The first half of chapter 8, verses 1-6, engages a series of statements that appear to have been quoted from the Corinthians themselves, most likely excerpts from the letter they sent (7:1). In the second half, 8:7-13, Paul introduces his own agenda, pushing beyond the questions they had raised and setting forth a broader moral principle that encompasses the more focused question that they had identified.

By adding quotation marks, the NRSV identifies the following statements as originating with the Corinthians, probably in each case quoting common sayings:

All of us possess knowledge (v. 1).

No idol in the world really exists, and *There is no God but one* (v. 4).

Food will not bring us close to God (v. 8).

There is a broad consensus among scholars that the quotations in verses 1 and 4 are from the Corinthians. There is less agreement about verse 8 (see below). Some scholars believe that verses 5-6 are also (entirely or in part) quoted from the Corinthian letter (Hurd: 67-68). While quotations from their letter appear elsewhere throughout Paul's letter (see on 6:12, 13; 7:1; 10:23; 11:2), this is the greatest concentration of such references. The sign that these sayings come from the Corinthians and not from Paul is that in each case, as we shall see, Paul responds to the saying with a rebuttal.

OUTLINE

Love for the Family of Faith, Not Knowledge, Is the Basis for Ethical Discernment, 8:1-6
Applying the Principle to the Issue of Eating Idol Food, 8:7-13

EXPLANATORY NOTES

Love for the Family of Faith, Not Knowledge, Is the Basis for Ethical Discernment 8:1-6

The presenting issue that Paul turns to in 8:1 is *food sacrificed to idols.* The Greek word is simply *what is offered to idols.* In most of the religions practiced in Corinth, it was common to offer food, most often meat, to the gods in their temples. After the offering or dedication to the god, the worshipers—or their guests—who had brought meat then ate the meat. On festive occasions, when many animals were sacrificed in honor of a god or gods, some of the meat was sold in the marketplace. Some have suggested that this was about the only time that meat was available in the markets (Murphy-O'Connor 2002: 161). If available at all, meat was expensive, and those who were wealthy and socially well connected had more frequent and greater access to meat both from the market and in the temple. Though such persons did not constitute a large portion of the Corinthian assembly (some, but *not many*, Paul writes in 1:26), Corinth was a prospering commercial center, and it is likely that some of the congregational members were benefiting from the economic growth. Undoubtedly these members wanted to take full advantage of the perceived advantages of their newly acquired wealth. Eating in the temples was a benefit of their acquired social status and essential to their continuing financial success (Witherington: 186).

Luke reports that at a crucial meeting in Jerusalem, the apostles identified four of the Jewish purity laws that applied to Gentile believers (Acts 15). The first of these was that they should "abstain from what has been sacrificed to idols" (Acts 15:20, 29; 21:25). (The other prohibitions were "blood, . . . what is strangled, and . . . fornication," v. 29.) Although there is no evidence that these formed a prominent role in Paul's preaching, we presume that he did convey the intent of that instruction to the congregations he established after that conference. That could provide a partial explanation of why some members of the Corinthian assembly avoided eating food offered to idols. Others, apparently those who wrote the letter to which Paul was responding, took this injunction lightly, for reasons that we will see below. This disagreement was presented to Paul for arbitration, with the letter writers assuming that Paul would side with them.

Before Paul addresses the issue directly, he must deal with the underlying attitude and assumption that *all of us possess knowledge* (1 Cor 8:1).

Since Paul immediately refutes this statement, we know that it came from the Corinthians, who probably stated it in their letter to him. It is difficult to know where they intended to place the stress of their statement. Is it an inclusive claim that *all* of us have knowledge, contradicting the exclusive attitude that only *some* of us do? Is it an in-group claim that all of *us* have knowledge, against *others* (i.e., *you* or *them*) who do not have it? Probably both claims are implied: someone within the Christian community is arguing that everyone in their group, whether the whole assembly or a faction within it, has knowledge.

Knowledge was highly valued in the Corinthian community. In the introductory thanksgiving, Paul named knowledge as one of the gifts that the Corinthians had and for which he gave thanks: *in every way you have been enriched in him, in speech and knowledge of every kind* (1:5). Chapter 8 is the first extended discussion of knowledge (vv. 1

[twice], 2, 7, 10, 11). It also occurs in 12:8; 13:2, 8; 14:6; and 15:34. Proportionately, 1 Corinthians uses *knowledge* more frequently than any other New Testament book except 2 Peter.

Sometime after the writing of 1 Corinthians, a religious worldview evolved that was called Gnosticism because of the emphasis it placed on knowledge (Gk. *gnōsis*). When Paul wrote, this had not fully developed, but we can see in this discussion a hint of what later emerged in its full form. Knowledge possessed by "us" was the basis for behavioral choices and spiritual values, the grounding of ethics and theology.

Paul's ethics, however, were not built on knowledge, but rather on relationships. *Knowledge puffs up*, he writes dismissively, *but love builds up* (8:1). Being *puffed up* (sometimes translated *proud* or *arrogant*) has already received attention several times in this letter (4:6, 18-19; 5:2; see EN) *[Shame and Honor, p. 368]*. In 13:2, Paul sets knowledge and love against each other, and in 13:4 he again says that love is *not puffed up* (NET, for the same Greek word as in 8:1). This may have been a particular temptation in Corinth. Outside of 1 Corinthians, this word is used only one other time in the New Testament (Col 2:18). The claimed gift of knowledge is in the one who possesses it, so knowledge is self-inflating. But love can only be interpersonal, so it builds up the community substantively and lastingly.

Paul dismisses knowledge as an appropriate basis for ethics as well as the Corinthians' claim to it. The very fact that they claim knowledge, he writes, demonstrates that they do not have it, because they have not rightly discerned the place and role of knowledge in ethical discernment (v. 2).

In moving the focus from head (knowledge) to heart (love), Paul writes that love leads to knowledge, but he adds another twist to his logic. Whereas we might expect him to say "Anyone who loves God knows God" as an application of the adage "To know one is to love one," Paul writes, *Anyone who loves God is known by him* (8:3, emphasis added). Thus he dismisses their claim to *possess* knowledge, reserving that right for God. In Galatians 4:9 he makes a similar inversion, writing, "You have come to know God, or rather to be known by God" (cf. 1 Cor 13:12). In both cases he reminds his readers of the fundamental theological conviction that it is God who takes the initiative toward a relationship with humankind.

Although he rejects their claim to knowledge, Paul addresses it. He quotes two specific claims from their letter: *No idol in the world really exists* and *There is no God but one* (v. 4). Paul agrees with both claims, but he reframes them not as statements of fact but as statements of faith. He acknowledges that some people believe there are other gods or lords, though he dismisses that claim by calling them *so-called gods* (v. 5). But as his own faith statement he affirms that *for us* [i.e., for himself and for the Corinthian believers, as for all Christians] *there is*

> *one God, the Father,*
> *from whom are all things and for whom we exist,*
> *and one Lord, Jesus Christ,*
> *through whom are all things and through whom we exist.* (v. 6)

This affirmation, stated with rhetorical flourish and parallelism, is a quotation from a Christian hymn or confession, no doubt one that Paul has taught to the Corinthians. On this he agrees with those who have written to him. What they do not agree on is the application of this conviction. The people who have written to him inferred from it that it does not matter what you eat. But Paul argues that this theological affirmation does not give one liberty to ignore what others see in one's behavior.

Applying the Principle to the Issue of Eating Idol Food 8:7-13

On yet one more point Paul disagrees with the Corinthians who wrote to him. They claimed, *All of us possess knowledge*; he replies, *Not everyone* (v. 7). Either their circle of *us* did not include everyone in the assembly or their sensitivity to some of the members was inadequate. Paul points out that there are some in the congregations who do not *possess* this particular piece of *knowledge*, and he insists that their concerns must be considered when discerning the ethics of eating.

After reminding his readers that some people believe in multiple gods or idols (v. 5), Paul points out that some members of the assembly are overly affected by the cultural context in which they live. They are *accustomed to idols* (v. 7), either from the lingering effects of their previous belief systems or from their Christian rejection of those systems. Knowing that certain food has been offered to an idol, they continue to think of it as *food offered to an idol*. In their sweeping inclusiveness of *all of us* (v. 1), the "strong" members of the congregations have excluded those who are not at the same place in their thoughts or spiritual maturity.

As Gerd Theissen (145–74) has pointed out and others have elaborated, it is quite likely that the ethical implications of eating idol food were affected by social and economic considerations. In Corinth, feasts were frequently held in many temples. Wealthy people held festivities in such places—weddings, birthdays, parties, and business dinners. To be successful in business or in social circles, one had to attend and to host such events. The temples were dedicated to deities or idols, and the food served there was dedicated or offered to the deity in its honor. Poorer members of the community and of the assembly were not included in these festivities. Their diets rarely included meat, which they associated with temple worship. Furthermore, besides their limited experience with eating meat and other food in the temples, the poor had less access to education (knowledge) and were probably more inclined to ascribe spiritual—not only culinary—attributes to such food (see Witherington: 191–95; also Murphy-O'Connor 2002: esp. 161–67; and many others).

Food will not bring us close to God, the Corinthians wrote (v. 8). English translations suggest that food does not enhance our relationship with God. The Greek wording is less positive, perhaps even implying a threat. It hints that standing close to God may be punitive rather than a reward. Thiselton (2000: 645–47) and several others translate it as *Food will not bring us to God's judgment*. If this is what the Corinthians wrote, then they were arguing that it is ethically important for Christians to eat food offered to idols to prove they do not believe that the idols have any power (Murphy-O'Connor 1979).

Either the Corinthians (NRSV footnote) or Paul (NRSV main text) added *We are no worse off if we do not eat, and no better off if we do* (cf. Thiselton 2000: 647–48). It seems more likely that these were Paul's words, since they contradict the argument that it is morally better to demonstrate one's freedom by eating in the temples. The statement that neither eating nor not eating is morally preferable is consistent with what he wrote in other letters (Rom 14:17, 20; Gal 2:11-13). Paul agrees with, and even expands, their argument that what one eats is not an ethical issue. It just does not matter.

And yet Paul thinks that what one eats *does* have ethical significance—not because the food itself is morally good or bad, but because of the social meaning attached to the food and the effect that eating or not eating has on relationships. Love is more important than knowledge, he argues, and although he agrees that *food will not bring us close to God* (or to God's judgment), he instructs that the Corinthians' freedom should be subordinated to the needs of their fellow believers, especially those who do not *possess knowledge* and who are sensitive to the idolatrous practices of their context—those whom, perhaps quoting the Corinthians themselves, Paul calls *the weak* (v. 9).

Weak is used five times in this paragraph and six other times in this letter, and *weakness* occurs twice (2:3; 15:43). In every case the weak are accorded special consideration and honor. In 1:27, Paul writes, *God chose what is weak in the world to shame the strong*. In 4:10, in his sarcastic dismissal of his detractors, he identifies himself with the weak: *We are weak, but you are strong*. The claim is elaborated in 9:22: *To the weak I became weak, so that I might win the weak*. He does not make a parallel claim for those who are not weak. The last use of *weak*, in 11:30, is different in that it refers to those who are physically weak and ill. With this exception, we should understand *the weak* in Corinth to be those who are both economically and religiously insecure, and *the strong* as those who are secure in faith, in finances, and in their social status (Thiselton 2000: 611).

In Paul's concern that *the weak* will be adversely affected by the actions of others, we see more clearly what the issue was for the Corinthians. Those who argued for liberty believed that there was nothing wrong in *eating in the temple of an idol* (v. 10). At this point in the discussion, the issue was food served in the temples of other gods, not food for sale in the marketplace (contrast 10:25). Those who wrote to Paul were arguing for their right to eat in such a temple, but Paul was concerned that those who were less secure in their faith would understand that right as permission also to worship the idol to whom the temple and the food were dedicated.

The word translated as *encouraged* (NRSV) or *emboldened* (NIV) is a term of building, with the same root as is translated in 8:1 as *builds up*. A better translation in verse 10 would be *built up* (Fee: 386). The implication seems to be that the "strong" Corinthians wanted to build up the knowledge of the "weak" so they too could, with a free conscience, eat in such temples (426–27). But Paul says that instead of building up, they are only inflating or puffing up (v. 1), and that their intended building up would actually lead to destruction (v. 11).

If "weak" Christians who were attentive to the culture of idol worship saw fellow believers entering a temple to eat, they might be tempted to ignore their conscience and slip back into idol worship. In that case, their faith would be destroyed and Christ's death on their behalf would be rendered useless. The *stumbling block* (v. 9) is not simply an offense, but also a means whereby a person may be caused to fall into immorality and abandon his or her commitment to follow Christ.

The great error of those whom Paul is addressing is their lack of consideration for some members of the spiritual family, their *brothers and sisters* (vv. 11-13 AT). Most translations avoid the repetition, but in Greek it thrice calls for care of *brothers and sisters*, thus highlighting the familial relationship. The circle they have defined as "us" is too small. They have overlooked that Christ died for all believers, not only for themselves and like-minded people (v. 11). In dismissing *the weak*, those with *knowledge* are also dismissing Christ and his death (v. 12).

For his part, Paul declares his willingness to forego actions that would be morally permissible to avoid causing a moral lapse in one of the *weaker* members of the faith community (v. 13). The next chapter elaborates his personal practice of this principle.

THE TEXT IN BIBLICAL CONTEXT

The Weak

We have noted that this letter speaks of *the weak* more often than any other part of the New Testament and that the Bible reveals God's particular affection for the poor and weak (see "God's Preference for the 'Foolish; . . . Weak; . . . Low and Despised'" in TLC on 1:26-31).

The weak whom Paul defends in this passage are not those who are powerless, but those who have a weak conscience. In his letter to the Romans, Paul also wrote about such people. There he described them as "weak in faith," mentioning that some who are weak "eat only vegetables" (14:1-2). It was not the weakness of their stomachs that determined their diet; it was their conscience that did not permit the eating of meat. Undoubtedly it was a situation much like what arose in Corinth. Paul's advice to the Romans was the same: "Those who eat must not despise those who abstain, and those who abstain must not pass judgment on those who eat; for God has welcomed them" (v. 3). One difference between 1 Corinthians 8 and Romans 14 is that in writing to the Corinthians, Paul addresses *the strong*, whereas he does not in Romans. *The weak* are those who are most fragile in their faith. They are the ones most concerned to put protective boundaries around their own and others' behavior. Richard Hays (1997: 145) wisely notes that sometimes

> it is argued that [certain behaviors] might cause offense to more scrupulous church members [and] we are obligated to avoid such behaviors for the sake of the "weaker brother's conscience." The effect of

such reasoning is to hold the entire Christian community hostage to the standards of the most narrow-minded and legalistic members of the church. Clearly this is not what Paul intended.

It is important to distinguish between having a weak conscience and manipulating the members of the community of faith.

Idolatry

Monotheism, the exclusive worship and service of Yahweh, is the heart of biblical faith. It is constantly reaffirmed by praying the Shema, still recited in daily and occasional Jewish prayer services: "Hear, O Israel: The LORD our God, the LORD is one" (Deut 6:4 NIV). The first two of the Ten Commandments forbid having other gods and making idols (Exod 20:3-4).

The cultures that surrounded Israel throughout the biblical period worshiped many gods and goddesses, and it was a constant temptation for the people of Israel to join them. This happened for many reasons, including impatience with Yahweh (Exod 32), materialism (Deut 31:20), and the hope, for example, that appeasement of Baal would produce success in agriculture: after all, it worked for the Canaanites. Intermarriage with those who worshiped other gods led many Israelites, even King Solomon (1 Kings 11:1-6), to do the same and was therefore strongly opposed (Deut 7:1-4; cf. Ezra 9:14–10:19; Neh 13:23-27).

The prophets railed against the people of Israel and its leaders for their worship of other gods and for making representations of them. Isaiah scoffed at anyone who would cut down a tree, burn some of it as fuel, and "the rest of it he makes into a god, his idol, bows down to it and worships it; he prays to it and says, 'Save me, for you are my god!'" (Isa 44:17).

Typical of the warnings of the Old Testament is this example:

> Take care not to make a covenant with the inhabitants of the land to which you are going, or it will become a snare among you. You shall tear down their altars, break their pillars, and cut down their sacred poles (for you shall worship no other god, because the LORD, whose name is Jealous, is a jealous God). You shall not make a covenant with the inhabitants of the land, for when they prostitute themselves to their gods and sacrifice to their gods, someone among them will invite you, and you will eat of the sacrifice. (Exod 34:12-15)

This warning links idolatry, prostitution, and eating food sacrificed to idols, which also are linked together in 1 Corinthians.

In another letter, Paul describes idolatry as what happened when people "exchanged the glory of the immortal God for images resembling a mortal human being or birds or four-footed animals or reptiles" (Rom 1:23). The result, he says, is that God gave them up to their chosen idolatrous life, a life turned in on self and disconnected from God's love, a life that eventually would become untenable and end in destruction. By violating their true selves in relation to God, they gave themselves over to every sort of immorality—sexual, interpersonal, familial, commercial, and political. The result, he says, is that God abandoned those who abandoned God.

> God gave them up to a debased mind and to things that should not be done. They were filled with every kind of wickedness, evil, covetousness, malice. Full of envy, murder, strife, deceit, craftiness, they are gossips, slanderers, God-haters, insolent, haughty, boastful, inventors of evil, rebellious toward parents, foolish, faithless, heartless, ruthless. (Rom 1:28-31)

This is a typical example of how biblical and postbiblical writers describe the results of idolatry. The deuterocanonical book of Wisdom of Solomon, for example, says that "the worship of idols not to be named is the beginning and cause and end of every evil" (14:27) and lists numerous examples.

> For whether they kill children in their initiations, or celebrate secret mysteries, or hold frenzied revels with strange customs, they no longer keep either their lives or their marriages pure, but they either treacherously kill one another, or grieve one another by adultery, and all is a raging riot of blood and murder, theft and deceit, corruption, faithlessness, tumult, perjury, confusion over what is good, forgetfulness of favors, defiling of souls, sexual perversion, disorder in marriages, adultery, and debauchery. (Wisd of Sol 14:23-26)

THE TEXT IN THE LIFE OF THE CHURCH
Idol Food and Other Idolatries

Most Christians in North America and Europe do not encounter the situation Paul deals with in chapters 8 and 10. But Christians in other parts of the world face situations much like what the Corinthians faced. As people migrate and the distance between cultures shrinks, such circumstances are more likely to increase even where they have not been issues. Some associate idols with demons. Even if strong Christians know that there is one God, those who have had firsthand experience with demons know their power continues to be real.

In Pune, India, Sunanda (name changed) and her sisters have become Christians, but the other members of her family follow other religions. When she visits her aunts and uncles, they offer her food that has been dedicated to various gods. She refuses to eat, and they get angry. Others in her congregation work in large companies where refusal to accept food offered to idols in celebration of a boss's promotion might harm their own advancement or jeopardize their position. In such circumstances, some people choose to accept it out of courtesy, knowing that the gods are not real and have no power. Sometimes they will take the food and discard it when they have a chance. Sometimes they refuse, and that refusal may be graciously accepted or result in great personal cost.

In Pietermaritzburg, South Africa, Jabulani (name changed), a Christian and a theology student, goes home for the funeral of an uncle. There is a feast, and a steer is slaughtered. Some of the meat is given to the ancestors to appease them, and the rest is served to the guests. Although he has been freed from the burden of fear that many Zulus (and other African peoples) have for their ancestors, Jabulani is concerned about the witness he gives to his traditionalist and perhaps nominally Christian relatives if he eats the meat or if he doesn't eat it. Some of his friends say, "If eating is worship, then don't do it; if it's not worship, it's just food." What is the best Christian action in such circumstances?

In cultures where food does not have associations with other gods, the same principles may apply to other symbols. These require careful discernment by Christians to avoid diluting loyalty to God, whom we know through Jesus Christ. The idols that compete for attention and service are legion. For example, idols of materialism are a great threat to Christian faith. Pope Francis, like many others, has identified it as "the new idolatry of money."

> One cause of [the economy of exclusion] is found in our relationship with money, since we calmly accept its dominion over ourselves and our societies. The current financial crisis can make us overlook the fact that it originated in a profound human crisis: the denial of the primacy of the human person! We have created new idols. The worship of the ancient golden calf (cf. Ex 32:1-35) has returned in a new and ruthless guise in the idolatry of money and the dictatorship of an impersonal economy lacking a truly human purpose. The worldwide crisis affecting finance and the economy lays bare their imbalances and, above all, their lack of real concern for human beings; man is reduced to one of his needs alone: consumption.
>
> While the earnings of a minority are growing exponentially, so too is the gap separating the majority from the prosperity enjoyed by

those happy few. This imbalance is the result of ideologies which defend the absolute autonomy of the marketplace and financial speculation. Consequently, they reject the right of states, charged with vigilance for the common good, to exercise any form of control. A new tyranny is thus born, invisible and often virtual, which unilaterally and relentlessly imposes its own laws and rules. Debt and the accumulation of interest also make it difficult for countries to realize the potential of their own economies and keep citizens from enjoying their real purchasing power. To all this we can add widespread corruption and self-serving tax evasion, which have taken on worldwide dimensions. The thirst for power and possessions knows no limits. In this system, which tends to devour everything which stands in the way of increased profits, whatever is fragile, like the environment, is defenseless before the interests of a deified market, which become the only rule. (Francis I, *Evangelii Gaudium*, §§55–56)

Some Christians think there is nothing wrong with eating "food" that has been sacrificed to the idols of money and the economy or marketplace. Others have a conscience against certain investments, or accumulating unnecessary possessions, or selling products that harm the environment and people. Paul's advice to the Corinthians can also be applied to such decisions: love for brothers and sisters, especially the weak, trumps knowledge and rights in ethical living.

The Risks of Knowledge

Knowledge, in the sense of information and ready access to it, has rapidly multiplied through the twentieth and into the twenty-first century. As in ancient Corinth, knowledge continues to be highly esteemed, yet it is easily taken for granted. And there are risks associated with this valued gift.

It is easy to claim that *all of us have knowledge*, or at least ready access to knowledge. But there are limits to this perceived abundance of knowledge. It is limited by access to information technology and by burgeoning strategies to control information through suppression and distortion. As the abundance of information grows, so also does the importance of wisdom and discernment to know what is true, important, and valuable. Paul wrote to the congregation in Philippi, "Finally, beloved, whatever is true, whatever is honorable, whatever is just, whatever is pure, whatever is pleasing, whatever is commendable, if there is any excellence and if there is anything worthy of praise, think about these things" (Phil 4:8). Much of the information available in the information age is a distraction from this goal.

Within the faith community, the multiplication of information on every front demands careful discernment. As the consensus of Christendom comes to its end, new understandings emerge of the world, faith, Scriptures, ethics—indeed, of everything. And a new consensus has *not* emerged, even among Christians. Various factions of Christ's body claim that "all of us know" because they communicate constantly with like-minded people. Those who hold opposing views do the same.

For this reason, a good measure of humility about what we "know" is both honest and fitting. In reaction to the dogmatism of fanaticism and fundamentalism in Christianity as well as other religions and ideologies, the value of doubt and the danger of certainty is recognized by many people (e.g., Berger and Zijderveld; Enns).

When faith is defined as having the right ideas or assenting to correct creeds or theological statements, it is head knowledge only. Many people, both Christians and non-Christians, think that believing the right things defines a Christian. They speak of "believers in Jesus," not of "followers of Jesus." But when the Bible says "Believe," it rarely means "have the right ideas." Rather, it means "have faith in" or "be faithful to." When a person tells another, "I believe in you" or "I have faith I you," it does not mean the person thinks the other exists; it means "I have confidence in you; I trust in you." It is a statement about a relationship, not an idea. It comes from the heart, not the head. That is why Paul argues that the Christian life is not built on knowledge, but rather on relationships. *Knowledge puffs up*, Paul writes dismissively, *but love builds up* (1 Cor 8:1).

"For Paul, community is primary and what is good for community should guide conduct. For the Corinthians that Paul is addressing, the individual or one's social clique is primary, and personal fulfillment is primary" (Witherington: 197). Paul is challenging the ethic that elevates "the right to choose" or any other rights-based ethic above consideration for others (cf. "Individual Rights" in TLC on 10:1–11:1).

Finally, there is a risk in locating Christian identity in knowledge as a set of doctrines or ideas. If belief is only intellectual, then the corollary is that what happens in the rest of the person has no bearing on one's relationship with God. Those who "know" believe that what one eats (8:1-13) or what sexual relations one has (6:12-20) are immaterial to Christian faith and commitments. They argue the same about how one handles money and possessions, how one treats employees or relates to neighbors, whether one participates in the military or owns slaves. But Paul argues that all these parts of life are relevant to faith, that what people do with their bodies and their relationships and every aspect of life is part and parcel of what is going on in their relationship with God.

Preaching and Worship

This chapter is assigned for reading in the Revised Common Lectionary (Year B, fourth Sunday after Epiphany). Although many related Scripture passages connect with the themes of food offered to idols, none of these is assigned for reading on that Sunday. The preacher will want to supplement the assigned readings with texts listed in "Idolatry" (in TBC above).

1 Corinthians 9:1-27
Subordinating Freedom to Love: A Personal Example

PREVIEW

Consistency between "what you preach" and "what you practice" is essential for personal integrity and for persuasive communication. Paul moves from argument to testimony as he offers himself as an example to illustrate his argument and to demonstrate his ideal.

The general outline for chapters 8–10 was set out in the preview to chapter 8, above. In chapter 8, Paul identifies both the presenting issue of eating food offered to idols and the underlying issue of love as the basis for determining whether behavior is ethical. In the present chapter, he shares his own experience as an example of sensitivity to fellow Christians in the exercise of his rights. In the next chapter he will present scriptural and theological arguments before returning to the starting point and giving his advice on the presenting and underlying issues.

After expressing his concern that love should trump freedom in determining ethical behavior, Paul concludes chapter 8 with the claim that *if food is a cause of their falling, I will never eat meat, so that I may not cause one of them to fall* (v. 13). This is the starting point for what follows. First, he reasserts his claim to be an apostle and describes some of the rights that apostles can rightly expect. But Paul has forfeited those rights for the sake of more important goals:

that he might save some people and share in the blessings of the gospel (9:22-23).

OUTLINE
Paul's Claim to Be an Apostle, 9:1-2
The Rights of an Apostle, 9:3-14
Why Paul Has Forfeited His "Rights," 9:15-27

EXPLANATORY NOTES
Paul's Claim to Be an Apostle 9:1-2
Paul's assertion that he is an apostle was introduced in the first words of this letter: *Paul, called to be an apostle of Christ Jesus by the will of God* (1:1). In this letter he writes about *us apostles* several times, both explicitly (e.g., 4:9; 15:9) and implicitly (e.g., 3:5-9). In the opening verses of chapter 9 he again asserts his claim that he is an apostle, based on two lines of reasoning. The first is that he has *seen Jesus our Lord* (9:1), a ground of apostleship that he also raises in chapter 15. The second point is that the Corinthian believers themselves are the fruit of his apostolic activity. In a later letter to the same community, Paul writes similarly, "Surely we do not need, as some do, letters of recommendation to you or from you, do we? You yourselves are our letter, written on our hearts, to be known and read by all" (2 Cor 3:1b-2).

Both of these grounds are stated as rhetorical questions in which the Greek grammatical form invites and assumes that the reader will answer yes. This is nowhere near the intensity and comprehensiveness of the defense of his apostleship that Paul mounts in 2 Corinthians 10–13 and Galatians. Here he assumes that his readers will acknowledge the facts as he states them. He does not intend to convince them but to remind them that he has a status and role that entitles him to certain privileges. But it is not to claim those privileges that he so writes, but rather to point out that he has forfeited those rights for the greater good of the faith community and the greater success of the proclamation of the gospel. The point of chapter 9 is that Paul offers himself as an example of one who has subordinated his own freedom for the sake of his love for others and for the gospel, a personal illustration of the principle he has set forth in chapter 8.

The Rights of an Apostle 9:3-14
In this chapter, Paul advances his argument primarily through rhetorical questions. There are nineteen questions in chapter 9.

Seventeen of those are in verses 1-14. Two of the questions (vv. 13 and 24) ask, *Do you not know?* This is a characteristic expression used in Greek diatribes to shame the readers into acknowledging that they should have known this to be true (cf. 3:16; 5:6; 6:2, 3, 9, 15, 16, 19). The rest are expressed in constructions that in Greek are emphatic and imply that the reader must agree with Paul. The questions are not open-ended: Paul intends them to serve his argument by eliciting agreement with him.

The first part of Paul's defense (v. 3) is to claim the rights that are his on the basis of *human authority* (v. 8). Having reminded his readers that he is an apostle, Paul proceeds to name two rights that apostles assume. The right to *food and drink* (v. 4) is in the first place the right to earn their living by preaching, a right that Paul expands upon in verses 6-14. It also reminds us that the larger context of this argument is the question about eating food that has been offered to idols. The right to be accompanied by a wife who is a believer (v. 5) is not developed into a full argument, but it reminds us of the discussion on marriage rights in chapter 7 and may hint at some criticism of Paul's choice to remain single and celibate (see 7:7).

Of all the Pauline writings, 1 Corinthians has the most to say about "rights," and these are concentrated in chapter 9. Here Paul is using a term and a concept that the Corinthians themselves valued, as we have already seen in 8:9, where Paul cautions them against using their *rights* (NIV), *freedom* (NIV 1984), or *liberty* (NRSV) at the expense of the weaker members of the community. Now he offers himself as an example of one who chooses not to exercise his rights (9:18).

What options were available for financial support of a missionary in the first century CE? They were the same as the options available to philosophers and itinerant teachers (Hock: 52-59):

1. Many teachers charged fees for their teaching.
2. Many others accepted the patronage of a wealthy person in exchange for teaching in the household and enhancing the status of their benefactor *[Patrons and Clients, p. 366]*.
3. Cynic philosophers eked out a livelihood by begging in the streets.
4. The fourth possibility, though chosen by few philosophers and teachers, was to work at a trade to earn a living while teaching and proclaiming their views without charge or obligation.

Paul chose this fourth option (cf. 1 Thess 2:9; 2 Thess 3:7-12). While he accepted with gratitude some donations of support (2 Cor 11:7-9), especially from believers in Philippi (Phil 4:10-20, on which see Zerbe: 250–59), he did so only when he was ministering in another area, and not from the community where he was currently preaching. This practice of self-support was clearly controversial. It even led some believers to question his legitimacy as an apostle or a teacher; they were perhaps embarrassed that their leader worked with his hands at a menial task and was not able to live off the earnings of his teaching. This was an issue in Corinth, as we see especially in 2 Corinthians 11:7-9, and was apparently emerging as an issue when Paul wrote 1 Corinthians. Paul's insistence on supporting himself by a trade, to the point of exhaustion (4:12), was one of the factors that caused some of the Corinthians to question his suitability as a leader and teacher.

To substantiate the claim that he is entitled to financial support, Paul first names three analogies from ordinary experience. Soldiers, farmworkers, and shepherds are entitled to be paid for their work, he states, and so also should those who preach the gospel. Elsewhere in his writings, Paul uses soldiers (Phil 2:25; Philem 2; cf. *2 Tim 2:3*), farmworkers (1 Cor 3:6-8), and shepherds (Eph 4:11, usually translated as "pastors") as metaphors for Christian leaders. But here he seems to have in mind only the literal meaning that people who serve in any form of human labor are entitled to earn their food by their work.

To the arguments from rights he adds the authority of a Scripture reference, the law instructing that an ox should be free to eat from the grain that it is threshing (1 Cor 9:9). The quotation is from Deuteronomy 25:4, where it appears in a series of laws that grant rights to the poor and needy, including the right to glean from fields and vineyards and olive trees, and the right of a widow to be impregnated by her husband's brother in order to bear a son in the name of the dead man. In that context, the instruction has both a literal and a representative application, the intention of which is to provide for the needs of the poor and disadvantaged. Paul extends the application to include those who do spiritual work, whom he says must not be deprived of the material things they need for survival. The NIV translation—*Surely he says this for us, doesn't he?*—is better than the NRSV's *Does he not speak entirely for our sake?* (v. 10). Paul is not dismissing the application of the text in its original context but rather is expanding it allegorically to the question he is discussing (Longenecker 1999: 109–10).

The instructions in Deuteronomy 25 apply to oxen and to people who are in need. There are also specific instructions that govern how *those who are employed in the temple service get their food from the temple, and those who serve at the altar share in what is sacrificed on the altar* (1 Cor 9:13; cf. Deut 18:1-8; Lev 21:1-16). Paul says that Jesus applied those instructions to those who preach the gospel (1 Cor 9:14). Here he uses an indirect quote. Although Paul had not known Jesus directly, he had been instructed in some of the stories about Jesus, and apparently one of those included a saying like that which Luke (an associate of Paul: Col 4:14; Philem 24; *2 Tim 4:11*) recorded, in which Jesus instructed his disciples, upon sending them on a preaching mission, to "remain in the same house, eating and drinking whatever they provide, for the laborer deserves to be paid" (Luke 10:7; cf. Matt 10:10; also *1 Tim 5:18*, which likewise brings together both the Deuteronomic law and the Jesus saying).

Why Paul Has Forfeited His "Rights" 9:15-27

To this point in his argument, Paul has been making the case that he has the right, supported by law and precedent, Scripture, and the teaching of Jesus, to receive financial support for preaching the gospel (see on 1:17; 15:1). He has stated that he does not take advantage of the rights that are his (9:12). He takes up this point in the rest of this chapter. It is both the specific point he wants to make about his financial support and the general point he wants to make in the larger argument that personal rights should be voluntarily subordinated to love for the weaker members of the family of faith.

Why does Paul not accept his entitled financial support? He answers in terms of his commission to preach the gospel. He has received this commission as an obligation, not of his own choosing, and he thinks it not right to accept payment for doing what he is obligated to do. "What's in it for me?" he asks (see "'What's in It for Me?,'" TLC on 4:1-21), and he answers his own question: *Just this: that in my proclamation I may make the gospel free of charge, so as not to make full use of my rights in the gospel* (v. 18).

Although he starts to name his financial independence as grounds for boasting, he quickly dismisses this as *no ground for boasting* (v. 15). Elsewhere in this letter, Paul has spoken against boasting. In 1:29 he says that *no one might boast in the presence of God*, and then declares that the only ground of boasting is *in the Lord* (1:31). He also disparages boasting in 3:21; 4:7; 5:6; and 13:3, 4. In 15:31 he allows himself to boast but only of the Corinthians themselves and only *a boast that I make in Christ Jesus our Lord.* Since he is so consistently opposed to boasting, why here does he almost slip into that language? Most likely some of the Corinthians had spoken of his boastfulness about his self-support, and as he does so often, Paul quotes their phrase and immediately rejects and corrects it. *Ground for boasting* in 9:15 should probably be in quotation marks.

The bottom line in Paul's decision to support himself rather than accept support from others is that he considers it a more effective way of proclaiming the gospel. *For though I am free with respect to all, I have made myself a slave to all,* he writes, and then emphasizes his purpose: *so that I might win more of them* (v. 19).

He names some of the kinds of people whom he has chosen to become like in order to win them. *To the Jews I became as a Jew, in order to win Jews* (v. 20). Paul was himself a Jew by birth and by commitment. As he wrote to the Philippians, he was "circumcised on the eighth day, a member of the people of Israel, of the tribe of Benjamin, a Hebrew born of Hebrews; as to the law, a Pharisee; as to zeal, a persecutor of the church; as to righteousness under the law, blameless" (Phil 3:5-6). Why does he write that he *became as a Jew* (1 Cor 9:20, emphasis added)? In Philippians he goes on to write that "these I have come to regard as loss because of Christ" (3:7). He seems to be saying something similar here: that he no longer finds his identity in a Jewish way of life, but to create openings for preaching the gospel effectively among Jews, he voluntarily takes on, or retains, the identity that he shares with them.

Perhaps more significant than including in this list (indeed, starting the list with) the assertion that he *became as a Jew* is the omission of the fact that he also became as a Gentile! Since he follows immediately with a parallel statement about being *under the law,* and since most of the Christians in Corinth were Gentiles, it would seem appropriate for him to include that statement.

To those under the law I became as one under the law (though I myself am not under the law) so that I might win those under the law, he writes (1 Cor 9:20). And he balances that with its opposite: *To those outside the law I became as one outside the law (though I am not free from God's law but am under Christ's law) so that I might win those outside the law* (v. 21).

To the weak I became weak, so that I might win the weak (v. 22). Here, finally, Paul gets to the point that he is addressing throughout this section of the letter: sensitivity of *the strong* (1:27) toward *the weak* on matters of conscience. The matter of exercising one's right to eat any food, including food offered to idols, must be understood in the context of his overriding passion for winning people.

In short, Paul writes, *I have become all things to all people, that I might by all means save some* (v. 22). Yet he has omitted naming two significant categories of people. Of the four categories that he mentions, the middle two are balancing opposites: *those under the law* and *those outside the law*. Surely his readers in Corinth would have expected him to do the same with the other two examples, but he writes of becoming as a Jew without adding that he also became as a Gentile, and he writes of becoming weak without adding that he became strong. In observing which sides he felt compelled to address, we can deduce from which sides the wind was blowing. Paul was clearly being accused not of being "too Gentile," but of being "too Jewish"; not of being "too strong," but of being "too weak." His defense was the argument that he had indeed chosen to identify with the Jews and with the weak not of necessity but intentionally, for evangelistically strategic reasons.

Paul's final argument (vv. 24-27) appeals to the Corinthians' awareness of the self-discipline of athletes, who subordinate their entitled human freedoms to the goal of winning in their competition. He could be confident that they would understand this analogy because the Isthmian Games were an important part of the Corinthian life and culture. (Unfortunately, Greco-Roman competitions such as the Isthmian Games included only individual and not team sports; otherwise Paul could have used that image to illustrate another important point about the nature of the faith community and the submission of members to each other and to higher goals; cf. Hays 1997: 158.)

The *perishable wreath* that athletes at the Isthmian Games competed for was made of pine branches (Thiselton 2006: 146) or withered celery (Murphy-O'Connor 2002: 17, 101). The wreath for which Paul was competing was of course metaphorical, but still more real and more permanent than celery.

His final comment in this paragraph may lead to a misunderstanding. When Paul writes that *I punish my body and enslave it, so that after proclaiming to others I myself should not be disqualified*, he is not disparaging the human body, as if self-abuse and self-denial were desirable or even necessary for faithful Christian life. For Paul, "the body is not the enemy of the spiritual life; rather, it is the *instrument* of that life" (Hays 1997: 156). His comment must be understood in the context of the athletic metaphor, that self-discipline for the sake of a higher goal is good for Christians as it is for competitors in sports. In the context of the presenting question of chapters 8–10, disciplining one's own body not to eat foods that might cause weak believers to stumble in their faith is necessary for the well-being of the body of Christ.

THE TEXT IN THE LIFE OF THE CHURCH
Financial Support for Ministers

It is rare to find people who are critical of their pastor, as the Corinthians apparently were, for *not* accepting (more) financial support. It is easy to find examples of preachers who use their position to their own benefit. They abound in the public imagination and are far too common in reality. On the other hand, many faithful pastors have labored and do labor without complaint despite inadequate and begrudging support. Their families, however, may resent it, even to the point of destroying their relationship with God and with the people of God. Paul's concern that married persons are *anxious about the affairs of the world, how to please [their spouse], and [their] interests are divided* (7:33-34) applies to pastors whose salaries are inadequate for their family's legitimate needs.

Pastoral support should consider the pastor's financial need and provide encouragement to the pastor (and the pastor's family) to minister joyfully and freely. Objective resources like denominational salary guidelines or predetermined mathematical formulas that take into account the local cost of living and average income have been useful in freeing pastors and congregations from awkward and divisive salary negotiations.

Paul argues well that those who serve the body have a right to financial support. But financial support, whether from the congregation or the diocese, also shapes ministry and controls what pastors can say or do without jeopardizing their financial security and that of their family. That is why Paul refused to be paid by the people to whom he currently ministered. His example is a challenge to all ministers to consider the impact of the salary. "Anyone whose vocation is to proclaim the gospel should stop and ask from time to time, 'Who is footing the bill for me to do this, and what implications does that have for the content of my ministry?'" (Hays 1997: 157). Although the model of professional ministry is built on the rights of pastors described in 9:4-14, some serious consideration should be given to imitating Paul's example of self-support, perhaps especially when financial resources for maintaining or starting churches are limited. Voluntarily giving up one's rights, including the right to an adequate salary, is entirely different from having one's rights taken away by others.

For those, like Paul, who minister without salary, foregoing even the comforts that others take for granted, what is the reward for their labors? Only that they are doing what they know themselves to be compelled to do. Indeed, that should be the only motivation for ministry, whether salaried or not. God calls, commissions (9:17), and even obligates (v. 16) particular people to proclaim the gospel. Nobody should be a pastor *of [their] own will* (v. 17). See also "Individual Rights" in TLC on 10:1–11:1.

Sharing the Gospel

Nothing was more important to Paul than sharing the gospel with others. He was willing to *endure anything rather than put an obstacle in the way of the gospel of Christ* (v. 12), and to *do it all for the sake of the gospel, so that he might share in its blessings* (v. 23) because an obligation was laid on him, and *woe to me if I do not proclaim the gospel!* (v. 16). The Greek word for *gospel* means "good news," and the word for sharing the gospel is *euangelizō*, which has been adopted into English as *evangelize.*

Not all early Christians were as invested in evangelism as Paul was. If they had been, he would not have had to write as he did. But Paul offered himself as a model and wanted others to share his zeal. Enthusiasm for sharing the gospel drove many to work toward the "great commission" of Jesus, whose last words recorded by Matthew were an instruction to "go . . . and make disciples of all nations, baptizing them in the name of the Father and of the Son and of the Holy Spirit, and teaching them to obey everything that I have commanded you" (Matt 28:19-20).

Christian faith spread rapidly, despite early resistance and persecution. After it became the official state religion of Armenia (304 CE), the Roman Empire (380), and Ethiopia (330), the spread of Christianity was intertwined with political ambition. When European nations and enterprises began to colonize other parts of the world, they took Christian faith with them. This often contributed to the oppression and exploitation of Indigenous peoples, but Christian missionaries also worked against the abuses of colonialism and empowered people toward spiritual and political freedom, dignity, health, and prosperity (Woodberry).

At the beginning of the Reformation in Europe, the need for evangelism was not obvious. Everybody was a Christian because all infants were baptized into the state church of their region, whether Catholic, Lutheran, or Reformed. Anabaptists believed that church membership should be voluntary, not imposed, and that baptism should follow an informed adult decision to follow Jesus. They refused to respect the monopoly of the state churches and felt compelled to share the gospel with their neighbors. Many of them were compelled by persecution to move to new areas, and some chose to travel for the purpose of mission. Wherever they went, they established communities of believers who lived out their discipleship, including the great commission. In August 1527, a gathering of Anabaptist leaders meeting in Augsburg, Germany, established some points of theological agreement and commissioned several missionaries. It was the first mission conference, and it became known as the Martyrs' Synod because so many attendees were later persecuted to death (Hege and Bender).

Many factors affect the fluctuating passion of Christians for sharing the gospel, including cultural influences, materialism, evolving theological trends, and embarrassment over past mistakes. In the post-Christendom and postmodern ethos of Western culture, the appropriateness of proclaiming the gospel has been called into question. At the same time, new ways of understanding what God is doing in the world have produced new enthusiasm for sharing the good news with as much passion as Paul demonstrated. Vital to the emerging visions and strategies is the humility and sensitivity that Paul showed in his willingness to give up his own rights and privileges for the sake of the gospel.

1 Corinthians 10:1–11:1
Idol Food and Divisions in the Community, Part 2

PREVIEW
Switching from personal example to scriptural example, Paul continues to answer the Corinthians' question(s) about eating meat dedicated to idols in pagan temples. His first response has been to urge sensitivity to *the weak* (8:1-13), using his own experience as a model (9:1-27). He concludes that point by saying it is wrong to participate in meals that would offend some members of the faith community: *If food is a cause of their falling, I will never eat meat, so that I may not cause one of them to fall* (8:13).

Now he argues that eating meat in the temples is wrong because of the association with idols. He does this with a biblical argument, then a theological argument. It's an interesting sequence: first experience (informed by biblical analogies), then the biblical argument, then the theological argument. Finally comes the ethical conclusion: he instructs the Corinthians on what they should do about eating food offered to idols.

OUTLINE
Biblical Arguments, 10:1-14
Theological Arguments, 10:15-22
What to Do, 10:23–11:1

EXPLANATORY NOTES

Biblical Arguments 10:1-14

As he does so often in this letter, Paul introduces the argument with a rhetorical flourish typical of the diatribe: *I do not want you to be unaware, brothers and sisters* (10:1). It is a reminder that, despite their claim to superior wisdom, they had overlooked an obvious and important point.

The impact Paul wants to have on his readers connects to his underlying concern: to restore unity within the faith community (1:10). So he first reminds them of the apparent unity of the spiritual ancestors, the Israelites whom God delivered from slavery in Egypt (Exod 13–15), and of the unity or continuity between those Israelites and the present community of faith in Corinth.

The Corinthian readers may have been surprised that Paul would write to them of the Hebrew people as *our ancestors*. Most of the Christians in Corinth were Gentiles, not Jews. Nevertheless, Paul has no qualms about identifying them as spiritual—if not biological—descendants of the Hebrews and as incorporated into the people of God ("grafted in," as he would later write to the Romans in 11:17-24 (cf. 1 Cor 12:2, *You used to be Gentiles* [AT]). Paul takes for granted the continuity between the Old Testament people of God and the New Testament people of God, and we should presume that it was part of his initial teaching in Corinth and elsewhere.

Paul first lists some of the experiences that all the Hebrews had in common

> *Our ancestors were all under the cloud, and*
>
> *all passed through the sea, and*
>
> *all were baptized into Moses in the cloud and in the sea, and*
>
> *all ate the same spiritual food, and*
>
> *all drank the same spiritual drink. For they drank from the spiritual rock that followed them,*
>
> *and the rock was Christ.* (1 Cor 10:1-4)

The repetition of *all* serves at least two purposes. It shows an image of unity among the Israelite ancestors in the time of the exodus. It also reflects the unity that Paul is calling for in Corinth: the shared experiences, the shared baptism, and the shared *spiritual food* and *spiritual drink* of the ancestors are clearly a reminder that Christians in Corinth also share common experiences, baptism, and communion.

The stories to which Paul refers are easily recognized. The *cloud* is the pillar of cloud that went before the Israelites to represent God's presence (e.g., Exod 13:21-22). The story of the Israelites passing safely *through the sea* while the pursuing Egyptian army drowned is well known (Exod 14:19-31). The *spiritual food* was material food: the manna and the quails that God provided for nourishment in the wilderness (Exod 16; Num 11), which was provided spiritually, that is, by God. And the *spiritual drink* was water provided by divine intervention from a rock (Exod 17:1-6).

The two elaborative comments that Paul adds to the historical references are less obvious. The first of these is the phrase *baptized into Moses in the cloud and in the sea*. This is explained by many commentators as a shorthand way of saying that the Israelites were "baptized in [the name of] Moses" (e.g., Thiselton 2000: 725). There is otherwise no suggestion that the presence of the cloud was called a baptism, and the crossing of the sea was on dry ground (Exod 14:22). Rabbinic tradition dating from as early as the first century CE already associated the exodus event with baptism and on that basis required Jewish converts to be baptized (Longenecker 1999: 102). It would overstretch an already-strained metaphor to draw conclusions about the mode of baptism or the appropriate age of baptism from this. Paul's point is not that the Israelites experienced "protosacraments" of baptism and Lord's Supper, but that they, like the Christians in Corinth, had all experienced benefits from God, benefits they subsequently ignored in favor of pursuing idols.

More difficult is the statement *For they drank from the spiritual rock that followed them, and the rock was Christ* (v. 4). Many have puzzled over the identity of the spiritual rock. How could the rock follow the Israelites? And what does this have to do with Christ? In first-century Jewish thought, the wisdom of God was personified and credited, among other things, with providing for the Israelites in their wilderness wanderings (Thiselton 2000: 728-29; cf. "Wisdom" in TBC for 1:18-25; see also 2:1-5). The deuterocanonical book of Wisdom of Solomon (written in the first or second century BCE) includes this passage:

> A holy people and blameless race wisdom delivered from a nation of oppressors.... She gave to holy people the reward of their labors; she guided them along a marvelous way, and became a shelter to them by day, and a starry flame through the night. She brought them over the Red Sea, and led them through deep waters; but she drowned their enemies, and cast them up from the depth of the sea.... When they were thirsty, they called upon you, and water was given them out of flinty rock, and from hard stone a remedy for their thirst. (10:15–11:4)

"Clearly ... Paul was attributing to *Christ* the role previously attributed to divine *Wisdom*" (Dunn 1998: 270; see 267-93; cf. Prov 8). In this letter, where wisdom is such an important issue, Paul has already identified the preexistent (before Jesus) Christ as *the power of God and the wisdom of God* (1:24), who *became for us wisdom from God* (1:30). So the metaphor was not so much created by Paul as co-opted and adapted by him when he substituted Christ for Wisdom (*contra* Fee: 80, 91, 495-96).

The experiences that all the ancestors shared provided spiritual and material blessing. *Nevertheless,* Paul writes, *God was not pleased with most of them, and they were struck down in the wilderness* (v. 5). The NIV translation, *their bodies were scattered in the wilderness,* is closer to the force of the Greek than the NRSV's *they were struck down* (cf. NJB, *their corpses were scattered over the desert*).

Paul names four actions of *some of* the ancestors that add up to *most of them* (but not *all,* as in the previous paragraph), with the result that *they were struck down*:

- idolatry (Exod 32:3-6): impatience led to sacrifices offered to a golden calf, in whose honor they *sat down to eat and drink, and rose up to revel*; notice that Paul highlights their eating rather than their sacrificing

- sexual immorality (Num 25:1-9): sexual relations with Moabite women led to sacrificing to the Baal of Peor

- putting Christ to the test (Num 21:4-9): because of their grumbling (Ps 78:18 adds "demanding the food they craved"), God sent serpents among the people; we should understand that Paul was again, as in 1 Cor 9:4, referring to the preexistent Christ in anticipation of the Corinthian situation

- complaining numerous times (esp. reported in Exod 15-17; Num 14-17)

The reference to the story of the golden calf (1 Cor 10:7; Exod 32:6 is quoted explicitly) is especially appropriate to the situation in Corinth because of the association between the feast of food offered to idols and the sexual *revelry* (NIV) that followed. "Peripatetic brothel keepers supplied prostitutes for grand occasions and they may have done so for the 'after dinners' entertainment for those attending the banquets" (Winter 2001: 281). In verse 8, the relationship is repeated, though in reverse order, as the illicit sexual relations led to idolatry. Indeed, "sexual immorality and idol food are also *always* linked in the NT" (Witherington: 221, emphasis original). Elsewhere in the New Testament (cf. Acts 15:29; Rev 2:14, 20) and in other Jewish writings, "idol food" is accompanied by sexual immorality" (Fee: 503). Recall that Paul has already addressed the issue of sexual activity, probably in the context of idolatry, when he wrote about consorting with prostitutes in 6:12-20.

Paul frames this list with the assertion that the experiences of the ancestors serve as examples to his readers. In introducing the series of warnings, he writes, *Now these things occurred as examples for us, so that we might not desire evil as they did* (v. 6). At the end of the list he repeats, *These things happened to them to serve as an example, and they were written down to instruct us* (10:11). It would be wrong to understand that the Israelites suffered in order to instruct future generations. Their suffering was the consequence of their action. That is the lesson for future generations, including but not only Paul's time.

The expression *setting our hearts on evil things* (NIV) or coming to *desire evil* (NRSV) in 10:6 translates a Greek word otherwise translated in a variety of ways, including "covet" (Exod 20:17; Rom 7:7), "lust" (Matt 5:28), or "crave" (Num 11:34). In Numbers 11, the Israelites craved meat: "The rabble among them had a strong craving; and the Israelites also wept again, and said, 'If only we had meat to eat!'" (v. 4; cf. vv. 13, 34). God responded to the demand by providing an abundance of quails, but that resulted in a plague that led to the death of many (vv. 31-34). Since some of the Corinthians also craved meat that was available only, or at least primarily, at temple feasts, the parallel is close and the warning is clear.

How does the experience of their spiritual ancestors speak to the Corinthians? The Greek word that is translated *examples* in both the NIV and NRSV is *typos*, from which come the English words *type* and *typology*. *Example* is a good translation, but a fuller sense of the meaning would be *paradigm* or perhaps *formative model* (Thiselton 2000: 732). "In Paul's view . . . the function of biblical texts (at the risk of simplistic generalization) is that of spiritual and ethical *formation*, which may also entail *transformation*" (731, emphasis original). Paul's intention in reviewing this history of the ancestors is to shape the behavior of the readers.

The warning to the Corinthians is now brought home with a statement that begins with *hōste* in Greek, which should be translated more strongly than *so* (10:12 NIV, NRSV)—perhaps by *so then* or *therefore*, as it is in 5:8. From the portrayal of their self-confidence in Paul's depiction of them in chapter 1, we know that many Corinthians see themselves as those who *are standing* (10:12). This is especially applicable to the "strong" members, who were confident that they could eat food in temples that had been dedicated to an idol (see on 8:1-13). To this topic Paul now returns, and his transition is a warning: *Watch out that you do not fall* (10:12).

Verse 13 is directed to both the "strong" and the "weak" members of the assembly. To those who are anxious about the *temptations* (NIV) or *testing* (NRSV) that they face, it reassures of God's faithfulness and capacity to strengthen their resistance. But to those who are arrogant, who *think* they *are standing*, it serves as a warning. They cannot plead a special exemption, as if their temptations were irresistible or unique. The temptations are in fact common human testing that can and must be resisted. Foremost among these, as the next verse highlights, is the temptation to worship idols—which is the concern of chapters 8-10. "The Corinthians then are to endure and prevail over the temptation to go to idol feasts" (Witherington: 224).

God's faithfulness has been identified in 1:9 in relation to the promise that *he will also strengthen you to the end, so that you may be blameless on the day of our Lord Jesus Christ* (1:8). As here, the statement declares the possibility of resisting temptation and tests, but only because of God's reliable empowerment.

For both the strong and the weak, the promise of God's faithfulness does not remove personal responsibility for dealing with temptation or testing. The examples of the Israelites demonstrate that people advantaged in faith and in divine blessing can and do sin, and that they suffer the consequences.

Theological Arguments 10:15-22

Paul has argued from the Scriptures that idol worship is dangerous. In doing so, he has already prepared his readers to think of the Lord's Supper in relation to idolatry. The Israelites, he wrote, *all ate the same spiritual food, and all drank the same spiritual drink* (10:3-4). Now he elaborates that precedent into a theological argument against idolatry based on eating the bread and drinking the cup of the Lord's Supper.

The argument that he advances here is parallel to the one he used in 6:12-20 against consorting with prostitutes. In both cases, he argues that a prior commitment to Christ precludes participation in parallel acts that represent a competing commitment. As he had argued that one cannot be joined with Christ's body and also join with the body of a prostitute, so now he argues that one *cannot partake of the table of the Lord and the table of demons* (10:21).

In verse 15, Paul sets up his readers to follow his argument to the conclusion he wants them to draw. Both the NRSV and the NIV use *sensible* to translate the Greek word that they translated as *wise* in 1 Corinthians 4:10. Paul uses the same word to speak disparagingly of claims to wisdom in Romans 11:25; 12:16; and 2 Corinthians 11:19. Here he is challenging them to make good on their claim, to apply their wisdom to logical thought, and to follow his argument. By adding *as* (*I speak as to sensible people,* v. 15, emphasis added; NIV omits the word *as*), he continues to challenge their claim, much as he does when he writes *I do not want you to be unaware* (10:1) or *Do you not know?* (ch. 6 [six times]; 9:13, 24).

Verse 17 interrupts the easy flow of Paul's argument. The point he wants to make is that participating in the Lord's Supper unites one *with Christ*. But he cannot miss the opportunity to speak also of the unity *between participants* in the supper. To this he will return in chapter 11 and elaborate in chapter 12. But even when he writes about the "vertical" relationship of believers with Christ, he is compelled to note the "horizontal" relationships between believers. This, after all, is the issue that instigated the letter and is the thrust of his response to their dilemma about eating food offered to idols. He wants them to recognize that eating and drinking together creates a bond of unity, whether with fellow Christians or with idol worshipers. The underlying issue, as we saw in chapter 8, is sensitivity to the relationships between members. So he connects his argument also to that in this context.

The line of argument is quite simple.

1. In the Lord's Supper the participants are brought into "communal participation" (Thiselton's [2000: 750] translation of the Greek *koinōnia*; other translations use *sharing, partnership*, or *participation*) with Christ and with other believers (10:16-17).

2. This is like the partnership (*koinōnia*) that the people of Israel [lit. *Israel according to the flesh*] experience when they eat sacrifices (10:18; e.g., Deut 14:23, 26b).

3. Those who sacrifice to demons also become partners (*koinōnia*) with the demons (1 Cor 10:19-20).

4. God does not permit those who are partners with demons to be partners also with God (vv. 21-22).

And so Paul reinforces the warning already given: *Flee from idolatry* (v. 14 NIV).

Paul expects the Corinthians to agree with his first statement, so he writes *is it not . . . ?* when he states that the cup shared in the Lord's Supper is *a sharing* (or *participation*) *in the blood of Christ* (10:16). He calls it *the cup of blessing*, as named in the Passover service (the NIV translation, *the cup of thanksgiving*, reflects later Christian liturgy and is a less appropriate translation). Since he expects his readers to agree, and since this is neither a new teaching nor the point he is arguing, he does not elaborate. Likewise, he does not expect any disagreement with his point that in Jewish practice *those who eat the sacrifices* are *partners in the altar* (v. 18). Though the first readers of this letter were predominantly Gentiles, here as at other points Paul assumes that they know something of Jewish Scripture and practice, perhaps because Jews and Gentiles share parallel experiences of fellowship meals (see 11:17-34 on fellowship meals; Jamir: passim).

This is not the first time Paul has categorically forbidden idolatry. In chapters 5 and 6, three lists (5:9-10, 11; 6:9-10) identify behaviors that disqualify their doers from inheriting the kingdom of God. Christians are prohibited from associating with such people, including sharing meals with them. Idolatry is included in each list. Furthermore, Paul says that he has already written to the Corinthians in his previous letter that these behaviors are forbidden (5:9-10). They either did not accept his instruction (as chs. 5 and 6 intimate) or thought that they could eat food offered to idols in the temple without committing idolatry. Apparently they believed they could come into close contact with idolatry and those who practiced it without themselves being implicated in it. Paul says they should instead flee as far as they can from anything associated with idolatry.

Paul's argument is vulnerable at one point: he seems to be on the edge of saying that idols are real and like God. He addresses this potential misunderstanding directly in 10:19-20. First, he poses the possibility that those Corinthians whom he had quoted in 8:4 as saying *No idol in the world really exists* and *There is no God but one* (and Paul has agreed with them, 8:5-6) will accuse him of giving credence to idols. That accusation he rejects. Instead, he asserts that what *they* sacrifice they *sacrifice to demons*, and not to God. In other words, while the idols are not real, the demons behind the idols are real, and those who sacrifice to them intend to honor and do honor those demons.

Both the NIV and the NRSV attribute the sacrifice in 10:20 to *the pagans*. Although there are Greek manuscripts that include these two words, most scholars agree that they were probably not in the original text (Metzger: 494). Paul's words are a quotation from

Deuteronomy 32:17, where they are part of a longer accusation against the people of Israel, not of "pagans." Read in that light, Paul is suggesting that the Corinthian Christians who eat food offered to idols are in fact participants in sacrificing to demons. On the other hand, if Paul does intend to refer to *the pagans*, then he is saying that those who sacrifice in the pagan temples honor the demons, and those who participate with them by eating the food offerings are likewise partners with the demons. In either case, the result is the same, and Paul declares, *I do not want you to be partners with demons* (v. 20).

It is difficult to know what Paul thought about demons since these two verses are the only place in all the Pauline letters where he mentions them. He seems not to view them as personal beings, but rather as impersonal forces whose power has been destroyed by Christ and continues to crumble, though their residual influence must be avoided (Thiselton 2000: 775-76; cf. 233-39, 631-35).

The last words of this paragraph are a warning to the "strong" Christians in Corinth who were confident in their ability to enter the temples and eat food that had been offered to idols without compromising their relationship with God. Such practice, Paul warns, risks provoking the Lord to jealousy—again echoing Deuteronomy 32. Thiselton (2000: 750) translates verse 22 as *Surely it cannot be that we are "stronger" than he, can it?*

What to Do 10:23–11:1

After exploring the experiential (9:1-27), scriptural (10:1-14), and theological (10:15-22) arguments for avoiding food offered to idols, Paul now responds to two specific questions about food restrictions and offers a guiding moral principle for deciding about eating, drinking, and other actions. As in the opening statements, now at the close of this discussion his focus is on the effect of behavior on relationships between believers and on God's honor.

To introduce his conclusion, Paul again, as in 6:12-20, quotes the Corinthian slogan about freedom: *I have the right to do anything* (v. 23; as in 6:12, the NIV translation is preferable to the NRSV's *All things are lawful*). As he did in chapter 6, so here he quotes the saying twice and counters it twice. He accepts the premise, presumably an argument put forth by the "strong" Corinthian Christians, but he also upholds principles that mitigate the claim.

First, he says that the benefit of an action must be considered as well as whether it is permissible—exactly as he argued in 6:12. Then he says they should consider whether an action is *constructive* (NIV) or *builds up* (NRSV) as a criterion that limits what is permissible—a variation on *I will not be mastered* (NIV) or *dominated* (NRSV) in 6:12. As we have seen in chapter 9, Paul values freedom. Nevertheless, it is not an absolute value for him. More important than asking "Is this permitted?" is asking "Is this *beneficial*?" and "Does this *build up* myself or, more importantly, other people or the Christian assembly?" (10:23; cf. 14:26b).

Consistent with the principles stated earlier, Paul instructs his readers to weigh *advantage* (10:24 NRSV) or *good* (NIV) or *well-being* (NKJV) of others more than their own. The Greek text says simply, *Seek that of others*, and translators have inserted various nouns to make the point clearer.

The issue addressed in chapter 8 was whether Christians can eat *in the temple of an idol* (8:10). Up to this point, Paul has been responding to this question, and his answer is that Christians should not eat in the temples because of the clear association with idolatry.

Now Paul addresses two related but slightly different matters: (1) whether meat purchased in the marketplace can be eaten by Christians (v. 25), and (2) whether Christians should avoid eating food served by unbelievers (v. 27). The questions may have been raised in the letter from Corinth (see on 8:1), but it is impossible to know how the questions were framed. Throughout this letter the pattern has been that the Corinthian Christians were divided on these issues. We may assume that to have been true on these matters as well. Some believed that it was okay to eat meat from the marketplace; others thought not. Some felt free to eat whatever they were served as dinner guests; others thought it wrong to do so.

In each of these situations, the factor that determined whether food was suitable for Christians to eat was whether it had been sacrificed or offered to idols. In the meat market that was likely, because much, if not all, of the meat sold would have been portions dedicated but not eaten in the temples (Murphy-O'Connor 2002: 30, 106). In private homes, the meat would have been purchased in the marketplace and may additionally have been dedicated by the host who was serving it.

Among Jews, concerns over food purity were strong. Christians also carried those concerns (e.g., Acts 10:1-48; 15:20; Gal 2:11-16). Not only was there the risk of spiritual contamination; there were also additional risks that the food did not meet the laws of kosher (on the kosher meat market in Corinth, see Winter 2001: 287-301). Yet Paul, who in his former life as a Pharisee was preoccupied with such matters, dismisses any question about market purchases. His quotation of Psalm 24:1 suggests that all food is from God and can be eaten without moral qualm (1 Cor 10:26). In effect, he discards all food restrictions since he does not distinguish between clean and unclean meat or how it was slaughtered or even the possibility that the meat came originally from one of the temples! For a man who was once a dogmatic Pharisee, this is a shocking statement.

In the second case, where one may be invited to the home of a nonbeliever and offered food, Paul also dismisses any restrictions: *Eat whatever is set before you without raising any question on the ground of conscience* (v. 27).

There is, however, one circumstance that might cause Paul to change his counsel. That would be the hypothetical case (the Greek subjunctive case indicates this) where someone else would flag the issue by drawing attention to the fact that *this has been offered in sacrifice* (v. 28). The Greek word used here is *hierothyton*, which does not otherwise appear in the New Testament and is probably a word that a pagan might have used descriptively. Otherwise, in this passage the word is *eidōlothyton*, translated *idol food*, that a Christian or Jew might have used pejoratively (Thiselton 2000: 787).

Who might raise this concern? Many commentators understand it to be a believer whose conscience is weak and who would be offended by a fellow believer eating sacrificial food. Perhaps Paul envisions another believer who is also a guest (the Greek for *invites you* is plural), but one with a tender conscience would not likely have accepted an invitation in the first place. One might imagine a server at the meal who might be a believer, or perhaps even a believing onlooker who might see one on the way to such an event and guess what is about to follow. But Paul simply says *someone*, and since the food is described as *offered in sacrifice*, it seems most likely that it would be an unbeliever who is imagined to say this, perhaps even the host (Witherington: 227).

Is Paul imagining this as a friendly warning to protect the believer from inadvertent transgression of the believer's presumed moral standard? Or should we rather understand it as an adversarial warning that identifies, perhaps even contrives, the situation as a trap to test the believer's moral fiber? In either case, Paul's response is shaped by his assumption that the person who gives the warning presumes that Christians would avoid eating food *offered in sacrifice*. And out of consideration for that person's conscience or consciousness (v. 29a), Paul says, *Do not eat it* (v. 28). He is more concerned about the moral witness of a believer in the eyes of a nonbeliever than about the believer's freedom to eat.

The two questions posed in 10:29b-30 are difficult if they are read as a defense of Paul's freedom from subjection to other people's conscience. Witherington (228) and others (see Thiselton [2000: 788-89]) suggest that they are questions Paul imagines the Corinthians may raise in reaction to what he has just written. The grammatical clues—introducing the questions with *for* and the subsequent sentence with *so*—do not suggest that he is quoting, and the usual clue that Paul is quoting those who disagree with him is that he follows with a rebuttal, which he does not do here.

But if these are read as rhetorical questions posed by Paul in anticipation of objections that others might raise (Watson 1989: 312-13; Thiselton 2000: 791-92), then they are consistent with what he has already written in 8:13 and 9:22-23. He is willing to give up any right for the sake of the gospel. So although he has no conscience against eating food from the meat market or anything that he might be served in people's homes, his overriding concern is the effect of his actions on others, whether believers or nonbelievers. As in 6:12, "Truly Christian conduct is not predicated on whether I have the right to do something, i.e., whether it is to my own benefit or not, but whether my conduct is good, meaning ultimately helpful to those around me" (Fee: 279).

In closing the extended argument that he began at 8:1, Paul summarizes: everything a Christian does should be determined by whether it gives *glory* to *God*; God's glory is diminished if Jews or Greeks or Christians are offended by the believer's actions. This concern for God's glory has already been raised in 6:12-20, the passage where Paul first addressed the Corinthian slogan *All things are lawful for me* (6:12). The conclusion of that discussion is also a call to *glorify God in your body* (6:20). In both cases Paul reframes the issue from an anthropocentric (human-focused) to a theocentric (God-focused) perspective (Hays 1997: 179). What is most important is not human rights nor even obligations, but rather the greater glory of God.

Although the NRSV translation *Give no offense* (10:32) is possible, it may lead the reader to think that Paul is concerned with disrupting people's emotional comfort—especially when followed by a claim that he tries to please everybody (see on v. 33). The NIV translation, *Do not cause anyone to stumble*, is better at this point since Paul's concern is not to cause people to stumble in their faith or response to God (see Fee: 539; Thiselton 2000: 794).

We must not overstate Paul's desire to *please everyone in everything* (v. 33; cf. 9:19-23), though that is the literal translation of what he wrote. In the first place, it is impossible to please everyone on matters as contentious as what Paul is dealing with in this passage. Furthermore, an attempt to do so would be the polar opposite of *the glory of God* (v. 31). And *pleasing people* is something that Paul otherwise opposed (Gal 1:10; cf. 1 Thess 2:4). Thiselton's (2000: 795) translation, *I on my part strive to take account of all the interests of everyone*, retains the intention of the text without making Paul sound guilty of the very game playing that he rejected. Though others may have accused him of being a people pleaser, Paul makes it clear that his motive is not personal gain but winsome impact for the salvation of all.

This is how Paul lives, and he calls upon the Corinthian believers to do likewise. The conclusion of Paul's response to the questions of idol meat that occupies chapters 8–10 is found in the first verse of chapter 11 (chapter divisions were added in the thirteenth century and verse divisions in the fifteenth and sixteenth centuries). *Be imitators of me*, he writes, *as I am of Christ* (cf. NIV, *Follow my example, as I follow the example of Christ*; NJB, *Take me as your pattern, just as I take Christ for mine*).

Among his first readers, some rejected Paul's authority and were not interested in imitating his example. Many modern readers cringe at the seeming arrogance of his words. Paul too was opposed to boasting and arrogance (e.g., 3:21; 4:7; 5:6; 13:3-4).

Yet here, and in 4:16, and implicitly in chapter 9 (see also Eph 4:32–5:2; Phil 3:17; 1 Thess 1:6; 2:14; 2 Thess 3:7, 9), he invites his readers to follow his example. We can understand this practically because we know that morality is often better demonstrated than explained. Certainly if Paul's actions had not been consistent with his teaching, he would not have been a credible teacher of proper Christian behavior.

But there is a further rhetorical purpose behind the invitation or challenge to imitate him. Teachers of rhetoric wrote of imitation as an elementary level of learning. Paul's instruction implies that the Corinthians, whose claim to spiritual maturity to a large extent instigated this letter, are actually immature in their behavior and their understanding (see also 3:1-4).

Finally, Paul's instruction that the Corinthians should imitate him is not an end in itself. Rather, it is qualified by his own imitation of Christ. In the context of the argument he may be hinting at Jesus' reputation for eating with sinners and taking food laws lightly. More generally, and most relevant to his conclusion, Jesus subordinated his own freedom to the glory of God, even though it led to death (Phil 2:1-10).

THE TEXT IN BIBLICAL CONTEXT
Typology: "Examples for Us"

Paul wants his readers to learn from other people's mistakes—specifically, from the mistakes made by their spiritual ancestors and recorded in the Scriptures. He writes that their *experiences occurred as examples for us* (10:6) and *these things happened to them to serve as an example* (v. 11). As reported in the EN, the Greek word translated here as *example* is *typos*, from which come the English words *type* and *typology*. *Example* is a good translation, but a fuller sense of the meaning would be *paradigm* or perhaps *formative model* (Thiselton 2000: 732).

Scholars have identified typology as one of the ways by which writers in the New Testament applied the stories and characters of the Old Testament to their own context *[Scripture Quotations and Echoes, p. 367]*. They mean that later writers offered a theological interpretation of history by taking a historical figure or event (a "type") and interpreting it, in light of Christ, as corresponding with their own experience (an antitype). They did this as a way of acknowledging God's activity in the past and the present and highlighting the similarities between different eras. "The idea behind typology is that since God's character never changes, God acts in similar ways in different ages of history and, perhaps more important, provides persons and events that foreshadow other later persons and events in salvation history" (Witherington: 217).

Typological interpretation does not suggest that the earlier type was a prophecy of the later antitype. The type had its own meaning in its context. Nevertheless, the antitype gave a fuller meaning to the type even as it also had its separate meaning (Ellis: 126–35).

Several New Testament writers identified types that find their antitype in Jesus, including Jonah (Matt 12:40), Moses (Heb 3), Aaron (Heb 5), and Melchizedek (Heb 7). Sometimes typology is applied to other events, such as the flood of Noah as a type for baptism (1 Pet 3:18-21).

Paul uses typology several times when he juxtaposes Adam and Christ (Rom 5:12-21; 1 Cor 15:22, 45-49; see EN on 15:35-57). "Paul understood Adam to be a type of Christ because he prefigured Christ as one man who did one action that had consequences for all those who participated in his image" (VanMaaren: 281).

In the present chapter, Paul uses events of the exodus as types of the experiences of his readers. Passing through the Red Sea is a type for baptism, and the food and drink provided in the wilderness are a type for the bread and wine of the Lord's Supper. One effect of this typology is to remind the Corinthian believers that their rituals do not derive from similar pagan practices. Rather, they are fully anchored in Jewish history and Scripture (Witherington: 220).

But when he applies the lessons from the exodus, Paul does not use typology. Rather, he uses the stories of idolatry, sexual immorality, testing, and complaining as warnings to avoid repeating the behavior and suffering the consequences of the ancestors (Fee: 499–500). The rituals of baptism and communion reflect the types of the exodus experience, but repetition of the failures and resulting punishments are not inevitable.

THE TEXT IN THE LIFE OF THE CHURCH
Imitation of Christ

Paul ends this extended discussion by offering himself as a model of how to imitate Christ's example (11:1). The call to imitate Christ, or to follow his example, has captured the imagination of Jesus' followers ever since. It has, of course, been interpreted in many different ways. For Francis of Assisi (d. 1226), it meant living in poverty and humility. For Thomas à Kempis, author of the still-popular book *The Imitation of Christ* (ca. 1420), it meant withdrawal from the world and a focus on interior spiritual experience.

Charles Sheldon's book *In His Steps*, first published in 1896, inspired millions with its challenge in every decision to ask, "What would Jesus do?" In 1964 it was made into a movie, and in the 1990s the phrase was popularized through bracelets and other trinkets using simply the acronym WWJD. Though Sheldon's interest was in promoting a social gospel, others who picked up the term were interested in personal piety or even in improving business management skills. Sheldon's title is taken from part of a Scripture verse that speaks of Jesus "leaving you an example, so that you should follow in his steps" (1 Pet 2:21). The full verse and its context apply to one aspect of Jesus' life, which is his response to suffering.

> For to this you have been called, because Christ also suffered for you, leaving you an example, so that you should follow in his steps. "He committed no sin, and no deceit was found in his mouth." When he was abused, he did not return abuse; when he suffered, he did not threaten; but he entrusted himself to the one who judges justly. He himself bore our sins in his body on the cross, so that, free from sins, we might live for righteousness; by his wounds you have been healed. (1 Pet 2:21-24)

As the recipients of the letter were also experiencing suffering, this was offered as a word of encouragement to them.

All the New Testament texts that speak of imitation, except 2 Thessalonians 3:7, 9, are "linked to the conceptual field of love, forgiveness, servanthood, humility, and suffering" (Swartley 2006: 361). Since the sixteenth century, Anabaptist reflection on the imitation of Christ has focused on this. "There is but one realm in which the concept of imitation holds. . . . This is at the point of the concrete social meaning of the cross in its relation to enmity and power. . . . Thus—and only thus—are we bound by New Testament thought to 'be like Jesus'" (Yoder 1972: 131).

Most Anabaptist writers have used the language of "following" and "discipleship" more than "imitation," but whatever the vocabulary, the point is that the Christian calling is to live according to the ethic of love, servanthood, and suffering that Jesus demonstrated and taught. An oft-quoted statement of this by Hans Denck (1495-1527), in his treatise *Whether God Is the Cause of Evil* (1527), declares:

> But the Means is Christ, whom no one can truly know except he follow him with his life. And no one can follow him except insofar as one previously knows him. . . . Whoever knows him and does not demonstrate this by his manner of life, God will judge along with other perverted ones, regardless of the fact that he previously had been called and accepted in the fellowship of the Gospel. (quoted in Bauman: 113)

Jesus is presented in Scripture not as an object for worship, but as an example to imitate.

Individual Rights

In present times at the beginning of the twenty-first century, the Western world places a high value on personal freedom. Cultural commentator David Bentley Hart (21-22) describes it this way:

> We live in an age whose chief value has been determined, by overwhelming consensus, to be the inviolable liberty of personal volition, the right to decide for ourselves what we shall believe, want, need, own, or serve. The will, we habitually assume, is sovereign to the degree that it is obedient to nothing else and is free to the degree that it is truly spontaneous and constrained by nothing greater than itself. . . . For us, it is choice itself, and not what we choose, that is the first good, and this applies not only to such matters as what we shall purchase or how we shall live. In even our gravest political and ethical debates—regarding economic policy, abortion, euthanasia, assisted suicide, censorship, genetic engineering, and so on—"choice" is a

principle not only frequently invoked, by one side or by both, but often seeming to exercise an almost mystical supremacy over all other concerns.

Paul's long discussion about putting others ahead of one's own "rights," prompted by the question about eating food offered to idols, "strikes at the roots of a post-Kantian secular ethical liberalism which ranks 'autonomy' both as a *right* and as an absolute virtue" (Thiselton 2000: 781, emphasis original).

Freedom and joy come not from attaining and protecting one's rights, but from serving others. When freely offered—not when demanded—focusing on others' well-being rather than one's own can enhance marriages, friendships, work and business success, and politics. Of course, when the reason for putting others first is to achieve greater personal satisfaction, it is self-defeating. The right motivation is simply that it is the right thing to do.

Preaching and Worship

The Revised Common Lectionary assigns the reading of 1 Corinthians 10:1-13 (it should be extended to include v. 14) to the third Sunday of Lent in Year B. The Old Testament lesson for that day is taken from Isaiah 55:1-9, in which the theme of satisfying thirst could be tied to 1 Corinthians 10:3-4.

The rest of the chapter is not assigned in the lectionary, presumably because the drafters did not think it important for the Western church in the twentieth and twenty-first centuries, but these verses deserve the focus of preaching, either by themselves or as an extension of the reading of 10:1-13. Verses 16-17 should be incorporated into the Lord's Supper liturgy.

1 Corinthians 11:2–14:40

Worship Matters

1 Corinthians 11:2-14:40

OVERVIEW

In the next four chapters, Paul addresses several matters of proper decorum in worship. The first of these is a discussion that appears to have been initiated by the Corinthians about proper exposure or covering of the head when praying or prophesying in corporate worship (11:2-16). The second is a response to reports of drunkenness, gluttony, and class discrimination at the Lord's Supper (11:17-34). The issue that gets the longest treatment is a full discussion of the theological and practical matters raised by the Corinthians concerning manifestations of the Spirit, especially that of speaking in tongues in corporate worship (1 Cor 12–14). At the end of this discussion is a brief comment (in the NRSV, literally a parenthetical comment) about women's participation in public worship (14:34-36).

Even with this much attention to matters of worship, we do not catch a comprehensive overview of Paul's thinking about worship. As always in this correspondence, we listen in to a conversation in midstream. Paul taught and modeled proper worship when he was in Corinth. Subsequent variations, other influences, and new questions led to changes in practice and disputes about how things should be done. These contentious matters, not the core of good practice, receive attention in this letter.

Of the three issues that Paul addresses, only the last had been raised in the letter sent by the Corinthians to solicit Paul's counsel. The introductory words, *Now concerning*..., which are characteristic of Paul's acknowledgment of their questions, lead him into the discussion of spiritual manifestations in worship (12:1). The tone of this discussion, as of all his responses to the letter, is measured, reasoned, and logical, with careful rhetorical shape and style.

The second issue, the practice of the Lord's Supper (11:17-34), has a markedly contrasting tone: it is strident and critical. The introductory words, *I hear that there are divisions among you; and to some extent I believe it* (v. 18), echo the language and tone of 1:10-11, where Paul notifies his readers that Chloe's people have informed him of the divisions in the community. It is consistent with the tone we find in chapters 5-6, where he addresses the shameful things that happening in the faith community, about which the letter from Corinth apparently said nothing. We infer from this that 11:17-34 was also written in response to oral reports from Chloe's people.

What is the source of the information that lies behind 11:2-16? The tone is not aggressively confrontational, as we have seen in the sections identified with Chloe's people, and it is not introduced by *It has been reported* (1:11; see also 5:1) or *I hear* (11:18), but neither is it introduced by *Now concerning* (cf. 7:1, 25; 8:1; 12:1; 16:1, 12). The tone, though nuanced and balanced, seems less formal and logical than his responses to the Corinthians' letter. He tells the readers what he knows, as if to establish a starting point that would otherwise have been established by reference to their letter. He quotes and corrects without the scolding tone that he uses in addressing their shameful behaviors. Although there is much "shame" vocabulary in this part of the letter, it is used to discuss understandings about shameful behavior, not to instill shame.

It seems that the issue of headship and decorum in worship was raised neither in the letter nor by Chloe's people. The obvious conclusion (though not to all commentators: see Hurd [228-29]; Hays [1997: 182-83]) is that it was reported to Paul by Stephanas, Fortunatus, and Achaicus, who brought the Corinthians' letter to Paul and who *made up for [the] absence* of the rest of the congregations (16:17), no doubt by filling in details about the letter and matters not included in it.

OUTLINE

Headship and Decorum, 11:2-16
Sensitivity to "the Body" at the Lord's Supper, 11:17-34
Manifestations of the Holy Spirit, Part 1, 12:1-31
The "More Excellent Way" of Love, 13:1-13
Manifestations of the Holy Spirit, Part 2, 14:1-40

1 Corinthians 11:2-16
Headship and Decorum

PREVIEW

Although Paul writes *I want you to understand* (11:3), his argument in this passage is not easily understood from our vantage point. Indeed, this is the most difficult argument to follow in the letter—Hays (1997: 183) calls it "notoriously obscure"—and it leaves us with many unanswered questions. One study has identified at least forty-eight questions about the passage, some of which include a choice between several options (MacDonald: 72-80). Gordon Fee (543-44) summarizes the complexity of the passage in this way:

> This passage is full of notorious exegetical difficulties, including (1) the "logic" of the argument as a whole, which in turn is related to (2) our uncertainty about the meaning of some absolutely crucial terms and (3) our uncertainty about prevailing customs, both in the culture(s) in general and in the church(es) in particular (including the whole complex question of early Christian worship). Paul's response *assumes* understanding between them and him at several key points, and these matters are therefore not addressed. Thus the two crucial contextual questions, what was going on and why, are especially difficult to reconstruct. All of which has been further complicated by the resurgence in the 1960s (after being latent for nearly forty years) of the feminist concern for women's "rights," both within and outside the church, so that many of the more recent studies on this text . . . were specifically the result of that movement.

Distracted by the complex arguments and uncertainties, it is easy for readers to miss the most shockingly radical assumption underlying this whole issue. In the assemblies in Corinth, women were prophesying and praying in public worship! We will revisit the meaning of this when we come to consider 14:34-36, but in this passage there is no objection by Paul and none reported by the Corinthians to this practice. It is assumed that both women and men are praying and prophesying (in the sense of public proclamation of the gospel; see Thiselton 2000: 826) not only in private but also in public worship. At issue is their hairstyle and hair covering when they do so.

Many people dismiss this discussion lightly, assuming that hairstyles and exposure are trivial matters of personal preference. But anthropological and psychological studies of the meaning of hair, beards, and clothing demonstrate that these carried great significance as markers of gender, class, role, and occasion. In our own time, clashes over Sikh turbans and the Muslim hijab demonstrate that these are powerful symbols. Less controversial but still religiously significant are Jewish men wearing a kippah, North American Indigenous men with long, often braided hair, as well as Amish, Muslim, and Jewish men's beards, and various other styles of hair or hair coverings. The issues in Corinth were real, and the principles have continuing relevance.

OUTLINE

Introduction, 11:2
Honoring One's Head with One's Head, 11:3
Shame and Glory on One's Head, 11:4-7, 13-15
Counterbalancing Arguments, 11:8-9, 11-12
Power and Angels, 11:10
Closure, 11:16

OUTLINE AS CHIASM

Introduction, 11:2
Honoring One's Head with One's Head, 11:3
    Shame and Glory on One's Head, 11:4-7
        Counterbalancing Arguments, 11:8-9
            Power and Angels, 11:10
        Counterbalancing Arguments, 11:11-12
    Shame and Glory on One's Head, 11:13-15
Closure, 11:16

EXPLANATORY NOTES

Introduction 11:2

Having appealed to his readers to be imitators of himself, as he was of Christ (v. 1), Paul commends them for doing that *because you remember me in everything and maintain the traditions just as I handed them on to you* (v. 2). Many commentators think he does this ironically, but this passage does not have the tone of sarcasm or criticism that irony would imply. They have done what he requested. However, they do not have it quite right; hence, his corrective comments. This theme of commendation is picked up at the next section, where Paul says that they are doing other things for which he does not commend them and implies that it is because they imitate neither him nor Christ (11:17-34, esp. vv. 17, 22). There are points on which he cannot commend them, but when they do "get it right," he gives them credit.

Yet his commendation is tempered because he follows it immediately with *but*. He seems to suggest that their determination to follow the traditions unwaveringly has prevented them from adapting to the circumstances of their situation.

Honoring One's Head with One's Head 11:3

Paul starts his argument with a theological statement, namely, *that the head of every man is Christ, and the head of the woman is man, and the head of Christ is God* (v. 3 NIV). The Greek word *anēr*, used here, does not distinguish between "man" and "husband," and *gynē* can mean "woman" or "wife." The NRSV translates the middle clause with *husband* and *wife*, applying these instructions only to married persons (as in the NIV footnote). But throughout the rest of this passage—verses 3, 4, 6, 7, 8, 9, 11, 12, 13, 14—the translations in all versions are consistently *man* and *woman*. And so they should be here (NIV). In chapter 7, the same words are translated consistently and correctly as *husband* and *wife*.

As with the English word *head*, so also the Greek word *kephalē* has several meanings. It can refer to a person's literal head, as it does clearly in the NIV's verses 4 (*with his head covered*), 5 (*with her head uncovered; her head shaved*), and 7 (*cover his head*). (Although the Greek text of v. 13 simply says *uncovered*, English translations typically supply the words *her head*. The meaning is clearly of a hood or covering for the hair and not the face, as implied by NRSV's *unveiled*.)

But in verse 3 it is clear that a metaphorical, not literal, head is intended. So what is the metaphor? Is it like the head of a stream, its source? Or is it like the head of an organization, its ruler, chief, or commander? Although verse 12 does not use *kephalē*, it states that *man comes through* (NIV, *is born of*) *woman*, an event that makes her the source of man, rather than man as the source of woman. Despite some interpreters who wish otherwise, the apparent meaning of headship in verse 3 is hierarchical (see Thiselton's [2000: 812–22] extended discussion; he is unable to decide definitively between "hierarchy" and "source"; cf. Yoder Neufeld: 347–50; D. Martin 1995: 232–34).

Shame and Glory on One's Head 11:4-7, 13-15

Paul's interest here is not the exercise of authority by those higher in the ordered ranks. Instead, he draws attention to the implications that actions by those of lower rank create for the status of their *head*. Misbehavior by a man (who claims to be a follower of Christ) reflects badly on Christ. Misbehavior by a woman reflects badly on the men in her relationships. And in theory, misbehavior by Christ would reflect badly on God. This is understood without question in honor-based societies, including Corinth in the first century *[Shame and Honor, p. 368]*. Shame and honor reflect not only on the person who bears them, but also on his or her community. Above all, in first-century Mediterranean shame/honor culture, which was also thoroughly patriarchal, a woman's shameful behavior, especially sexual indiscretion or immodesty (which could include public exposure of her hair), diminished the honor of her husband, father, and brothers. Paul applied it not only in biological family relationships but also in faith-family relationships.

The language of shame and honor is prominent in this passage: hair and head covering in public worship, for both women and men, is a matter of glory and shame. In all, four sources of shame are noted and three sources of honor. All of them are gender-based.

The shameful, dishonorable, or disgraceful things are these (NIV):

1. *Every man who prays or prophesies with his head covered* (v. 4)

2. *Every woman who prays or prophesies with her head uncovered* (vv. 5, 13)

3. *For a woman to have her hair cut off or her head shaved* (v. 6)

4. *If a man has long hair* (v. 14)

The sources of honor or glory (Gk. *doxa*) are these (NIV):

1. *A man ... is the image and glory of God* (v. 7).
2. *Woman is the glory of man* (v. 7, with asymmetry, omitting *image*).
3. *If a woman has long hair, it is her glory* (v. 15).

(In verse 7 the NRSV translates *Man ... is the ... reflection; ... woman is the reflection*, offering a translation of the Greek word *doxa* that is used nowhere else and is inappropriate here.)

The assertion that having long hair is a shame for a man and glory for a woman is described as an observation of *nature* (vv. 14-15; or *the ordering of how things are*, Thiselton 2000: 844-46). Paul assumes that his readers will concur without further argument. He is trying to persuade the Corinthians that it is important for men to have their heads uncovered and for women to have their heads covered when leading in public worship. Length of hair is not at issue, though if it were, Paul may have argued for gender distinctions in hairstyle as he does for head coverings.

Only rarely does Paul appeal to the nature of things as an argument for behavior, though it was common for Stoic and Cynic philosophers to do so (Hays 1997: 189). Epictetus, for example, used nature to argue that gender differences should be marked by differences in facial hair.

> Is there anything less useful than the hair on the chin? What then, has not nature used this hair also in the most suitable manner possible? Has she not by it distinguished the male and the female? ... For this reason we ought to preserve the signs which God has given, we ought not to throw them away, nor to confound, as much as we can, the distinctions of the sexes. (*Discourses* 1.16 [Long])

Musonius Rufus, a Roman Stoic philosopher of the first century, argued that nature favors long hair on men. He derided the practice of shaving and cutting one's hair (unless the weight of it is burdensome) by appealing to nature and by scorning "men [who] have become slaves of luxurious living and are completely enervated, men who can endure being seen as womanish creatures, hermaphrodites, something which real men would avoid at all costs" (Lutz 128.5).

One of the many uncertainties about this text is whether Paul means to name one or two matters of shame. Is it shameful for a man to have either long hair or his head covered, or is the hair the covering, so that only one shameful act is named (i.e., for a man's head to be covered with long hair)? Verse 4 is ambiguous in Greek: it simply says, *Every man praying or prophesying having down from head shames his head*. To make grammatical sense of it in relation to what follows, English translations say *with something on his head* (NRSV) or *with his head covered* (NIV) or some such clarification. But what is *down from his head* could be long hair *or* some other covering. Verse 7 says his head should not be covered; verse 14 says he should not have long hair.

Likewise, for a woman, the text is clear that her hair is given as a covering (v. 15)—but is that the covering called for in verses 5 and 13? The Greek word translated *covering* in verse 15 is different from the word used in verses 5, 6, 7, and 13, but the meaning is parallel. It seems that references to hairstyles are asides and the concern addressed is only the covering or uncovering of the head.

Various people have explored whether common practice in first-century Corinth was for women to have their heads covered or uncovered in public, and for men to have their heads uncovered or covered. The evidence is mixed. Literature suggests that in both Judaism and Greek society, women were expected to have their heads covered in public. But archaeological evidence shows some women with heads uncovered and men with heads covered. In Roman society, men customarily worshiped with bare heads.

The account of creation of man and woman in Genesis 1:26-28 and 2:18-25 lies behind verse 7. Genesis 1:27 is especially relevant: "So God created humankind in his image, in the image of God he created them; male and female he created them." Although Paul applies to men the designation *image of God*, Genesis applies it to both men and women. Indeed, men and women separately are not complete images of God, but men and women together. Thus Genesis 1:26 says that God (plural) decided "Let *us* make humankind in *our* image, according to *our* likeness" (emphasis added). The complementarity of maleness and femaleness in relationship is needed to represent the image of the one-but-plural God.

Yet, drawing on the account in Genesis 2 of the sequential creation of man and woman—he was created first and she was created *from* him by way of his extracted rib (1 Cor 11:8)—Paul highlights the gender differences rather than the commonality in the creation of humankind. In this context, Paul is speaking not of the uniting of husband and wife in sexual union but of the uniting of male and female in worship as the attainment of the image of God.

The creation accounts in Genesis do not speak of *glory*. Paul's use of this term must be understood within the honor/shame value system. Both men and women bring honor, or *glory*, to their respective *heads* through appropriate behavior, and shame through inappropriate behavior.

Counterbalancing Arguments 11:8-9, 11-12

The hierarchical argument is supported by a sequential argument. The priority of men is explained by reference to the biblical account of creation in which man was created first and woman was created *for the sake of* man (11:9; see Gen 2:18, 20b-23). This argument, however, is not the last word on the relationship between women and men. Paul saw that the implications of Christian faith for gender relationships pointed toward equality and reciprocity. To the Galatians, Paul wrote, "There is no longer male and female; for all of you are one in Christ Jesus" (Gal 3:28). So to balance the argument that woman was created from man and for the sake of man, and not the other way around (vv. 8-9), he points out that men and women are not independent from each other *in the Lord* (v. 11). It is true that woman was (originally) created *from* man, but man (subsequently) comes *through* woman. The NIV translation of verse 12, *born of*, obscures the parallelism, though it accurately reflects the meaning. Furthermore, both women and men (indeed, *all things*) come from God, and that dependency is more important than any dependency they may have on each other.

Verse 11a (*woman is not independent of man*) refutes verse 9b (*woman [was created] for the sake of man*); 11b (*man [is not] independent of woman*) refutes 9a (*neither was man created for the sake of woman*), with the qualification that this is *in the Lord*. Verse 12a (*just as woman came from man*) repeats verse 8b (*woman [was made] from man*); 12b (*man comes through woman*) refutes 8a (*man was not made from woman*), with the qualifying reminder in verse 12c that *all things come from God*.

The format of this argument is a classic chiastic structure, so named because, like the Greek letter χ (*chi*), the second half mirrors the first half. It can be diagrammed as follows in the NIV translation:

A *For man did not come from woman,* (v. 8a)
   B *but woman [came from] from man;* (v. 8b)
      C *neither was man created for woman,* (v. 9a)
         D *but woman [was created] for man.* (v. 9b)
            E *It is for this reason that a woman ought to have authority over her own head, because of the angels.* (v. 10)
         D′ *Nevertheless, in the Lord woman is not independent of man* (v. 11a–b)
      C′ *nor is man independent of woman.* (v. 11c)
   B′ *For as woman came from man,* (v. 12a)
A′ *so also man is born of woman.* (v.12b)
      But everything comes from God. (v. 12c)

Set out in this way, we easily see that Paul presents a set of propositions that he then systematically qualifies, introducing his qualifications with *nevertheless, in the Lord* (v. 10) and concluding them with *but all things come from God* (v. 12c). Although he may have some degree of sympathy with the first set (some have suggested that those lines represent what he taught when he was first in Corinth—Hurd: 281-82), the second set is needed to provide a full appreciation of the interdependent relationship between women and men *in the Lord*.

The argument here for gender interdependence echoes the tone of similar arguments in chapter 7, especially 7:3-4. It seems that Paul had a fundamental understanding, unlike many of his contemporaries, that women and men equally need each other and complement one another, and their needs deserve equal consideration within marital (ch. 7) and worshiping-community (ch. 11) relationships.

Interdependence and complementarity do not eliminate the need for distinction between the sexes. Indeed, they require it. And Paul is arguing that distinction in dress—specifically head coverings for women and bare heads for men when leading in public worship—is important both to demonstrate that complementarity, as well as sensitivity to cultural expectations, and to honor the reputation of the Christian community.

Power and Angels 11:10

In the chiastic diagram above, the turning point—literally the pivot of the argument—is verse 10. For the first readers of this letter, it may have been decisive. For us, unfortunately, it is opaque on three points.

Our first difficulty in understanding is the ambiguous reference of *this reason*. It could refer to what has just been written, that woman was created for man, or to the longer argument of hierarchical order presented in verses 3-9. But the Greek text seems rather to refer to the following phrase, *because of the angels*. The statement stands by itself: *this reason* is *because of the angels*.

But what does this mean? Much speculation has been offered as explanation of this "pregnant ambiguity" (D. Martin 1995: 245). Apparently Paul shared with the Corinthians some understanding of the presence of angels (whether in general or specifically in public worship, we do not know) that gave moral significance to the exposure of women's hair. The meaning of it has been debated since the second century (Thiselton 2000: 839-40). The most likely meanings are either that the angels might lust after women (see Gen 6:1-4), and the covering of women's hair was a protection, or that the angels were seen as guardians of cosmic order (see, e.g., Acts 7:53; Gal 3:19) and would be disturbed by the exposure of a woman's hair. Perhaps both were intended. In any case, it was not necessary for him to explain the meaning to his intended readers. We do not know what it was.

Finally, what is the *power* or *authority* that a woman should have over her head? Although the Greek text says simply that *a woman should have authority over the head*, most English translators have offered *a symbol* [or *sign*] *of authority*. To their credit, the translators of the NIV omitted this in the 2011 edition and even drew attention to the change, noting,

> 1 Corinthians 11:10 now reads, "It is for this reason that a woman ought to have authority over her own head." The expression "a sign of" before "authority" in the 1984 NIV did not correspond to anything explicitly in the Greek and is increasingly recognized as an inadequate rendition of this verse. Whether Paul wanted the women in Corinth to wear an external head covering while praying or prophesying, or simply to have long hair, or maybe even to wear a partial face veil, the point is they should be able to control what they do or do not have on their heads. ("Notes from the Committee on Bible Translation" in the introduction to the 2011 edition)

The phrase *have authority over* never otherwise means having a symbol of being under authority. It is used when Jesus gives his disciples authority over demons (Luke 9:1) and over "all the power of the enemy" (Luke 10:19). In Revelation it is used of "authority over the nations" (2:26), "authority over waters to turn them into blood" (11:6), "authority over fire" (14:18), and "authority over these plagues" (16:9). The correct understanding in the present context must be that a woman does and should have authority, power, or control over her (physical, not metaphorical) head (D. Martin 1995: 245–46). What it cannot mean is that someone else has authority over a woman's praying or prophesying.

The implication, however, is that women ought to exercise their authority, not practice undirected liberty. For the Corinthians, it is like saying that parents should have authority over unruly children or masters should have authority over their slaves. That authority has limitations and is prescribed by social expectations that are enforced by commendation on one hand and shame on the other.

Unfortunately, this key verse does not have the information we need to understand it fully. We can only say for certain that Paul understood that there are spiritual (angelic) implications to human deportment in worship and that, in acknowledgment of this, women should exercise control over their heads by covering them when praying or prophesying.

Closure 11:16

Although there are significant gaps in our understanding of Paul's arguments, several points are clear. It is assumed that both women and men will lead and address the assembly at worship through praying and prophesying. Gender distinctions must be retained in comportment because the complementarity of male and female represents the image of God and honors God. When women and men pray and prophesy in a context where social expectations demand it, women should have their heads covered and men should have their heads uncovered, in conformity to the expectations, to avoid bringing shame on themselves, the assembly, and Christ. Instead, they should be concerned to bring glory to God (cf. 10:31). Considerations of unity and honor take priority over personal preference, personal freedom, or theological correctness.

The end of this section consists of a brief caution not to be contentious. This is once again a reference to the kinds of divisions, quarrels, and contention that Chloe's people had reported to Paul (1:10-11), though here presented as a hypothetical possibility rather than an actual situation that has been reported to him. Although the threat of contention lurks behind this discussion, there is no evidence of aggressive factionalism within the assembly nor of disagreement between Paul and the Corinthian Christians on the points that he argues. His dismissal of further argument—*We have no such custom, nor do the churches of God* (11:16)—implies that deviation from his teaching and the common practice of Christian communities should not be tolerated and reinforces the call at the transition to this discussion to imitate him as he imitates Christ (v. 1).

THE TEXT IN BIBLICAL CONTEXT

Hair

The Bible expresses little interest in hair, though there are occasional instructions about it. Priests, for example, must never shave their heads (Lev 21:5; Ezek 44:20). Such prohibitions seem to be intended to avoid the practices of other cultures and religions (e.g., Lev 19:27).

A man or woman who took a Nazirite vow was prohibited from cutting or grooming their hair, from consuming any product of a grapevine, and from touching a corpse (Num 6:1-21). Samson's legendary strength depended on keeping the Nazirite vow taken on his behalf by his parents, including never to cut his hair (Judg 16:17); when the vow was broken, he became as weak as a normal man. Luke makes special mention of Paul getting his hair cut in Cenchreae, "for he was under a vow" (Acts 18:18), presumably the vow of a Nazirite.

The attractiveness of abundant and well-groomed hair is recognized in the admiration of Absalom's long hair (2 Sam 14:25-26) and in the delight expressed in "hair . . . like a flock of goats, moving down the slopes of Gilead" (Song of Sol 4:1; 6:5). But excessive attention to one's hairstyle is discouraged in 1 Timothy 2:9 and 1 Peter 3:3 in preference for the inner beauty of character.

THE TEXT IN THE LIFE OF THE CHURCH

Clothing Matters

Paul counseled the Corinthians to accommodate their head coverings, or perhaps hairstyles, in ways that would not be seen as disgraceful or shameful. Since the definition of disgraceful or honorable ways of dressing or decorating the body is culturally defined, the implementation of this principle must necessarily vary from place to place and time to time.

The conversation in Christian circles almost always focuses on women's clothing—often explicitly because women are blamed for male sexual temptation and often because women's voices are excluded or muted in the discussion—and the language is about "modesty." Modesty has to do with shame. Modest people are not shameless, but rather unashamed. They have dignity or honor, and they confer that on the people with whom they are associated, such as their family, religious group, or ethnic group *[Shame and Honor, p. 368]*.

The Scripture most quoted about modesty is "that the women should dress themselves modestly and decently in suitable clothing, not with their hair braided, or with gold, pearls, or expensive clothes, but with good works, as is proper for women who profess reverence for God" (*1 Tim 2:9-10*). The word translated *modestly* occurs in the Bible only here and in *1 Timothy 3:2*, where it defines one of the requirements of bishops or overseers and is usually translated as *respectable*.

Although the first letter of Peter does not use the term *modesty*, it urges women to demonstrate "the purity and reverence of your lives" as a strategy for drawing unbelieving husbands to share their faith: "Do not adorn yourselves outwardly by braiding your hair, and by wearing gold ornaments or fine clothing; rather, let your adornment be the inner self with the lasting beauty of a gentle and quiet spirit, which is very precious in God's sight" (1 Pet 3:2-4).

Unrestrained sexuality, especially of women, is closely identified with shame, and in many cultures that is understood to be expressed by exposure of skin (which parts of the skin should not be exposed is culturally defined) or hair or by drawing attention to sexual characteristics through adornment or movement. The few biblical passages that are used in discussions about Christian modesty do not talk about exposure of skin, but they do talk about paying too much attention to outward impressions and too little attention to inner qualities of character and behavior. The consideration seems to be the amount of money and time spent on clothes, jewelry, and hair.

Some Christian groups (as also some Jewish, Muslim, and other religious groups) define appropriate clothing strictly and adhere to it uniformly. This is most noticeable in Hutterite, conservative Amish, and Old Order Mennonite groups, sometimes generically called "Plain people." In previous generations, many more Anabaptist groups legislated at least some aspects of both men's and women's clothing for several acknowledged and unacknowledged reasons, including patriarchal control.

> The elders and ministers may have such a strong sense of domination as shepherds over their flocks that they consciously or unconsciously seek for outward signs of submission which are most readily furnished by uniform, conservative, distinctive items of costume and drab and dark colors. The emphasis upon submission as one of the chief virtues desired in members may well be an index to the psychology of costume in such a patriarchal or near-patriarchal type of church life. (Wenger and Kreider)

The Bible prescribes that men should wear a fringe of tassels, including a blue cord, in order to "remember all the commandments of the LORD and do them, and not follow the lust of your own heart and your own eyes" (Num 15:37-40). Here men are instructed to dress in a way that helps them to take responsibility for their lusts, in contrast with the much more common insistence that women dress in a way that protects men from lust.

The discussion about comportment and dress in worship is a reminder that Christian faith does not eliminate gender differences, matters of sexuality or power, or the need to consider how our actions affect the reputation of the whole Christian community. The standard is that our actions should focus on honoring God and the faith community within the parameters of our cultural context.

Prayer Coverings of Conservative Amish, Brethren, Hutterite, and Mennonite Women

Among faith communities (Christian and other) that require women to cover their heads or hair (cf. the website of the Head Covering Movement) are many conservative Amish, Brethren, Hutterite, and Mennonite groups. Often these prescribe the size, material, style, and use of a standardized "head covering" or "prayer veiling." The style of the covering varies by local practice, but conformity to the local practice is usually not optional.

The symbolism of the head covering is more important than the functionality. Unlike faiths that are concerned to hide a woman's hair, the Amish, Hutterite, and Mennonite prayer coverings usually leave some hair exposed but insist that coverings should be worn as "symbols of divine order in the church" (the title of a book on this subject by Sanford Shetler and J. Ward Shank). Defenders of the ongoing practice of women covering their heads often emphasize the headship of a man over a woman (Brown: 149–52). Because of this, people who hold to the equality of women and men in the church as well as in society reject the continuing practice of wearing prayer coverings (Nyce: passim).

The argument for maintaining this practice is simple obedience to the face value of this scriptural instruction, which is understood to be universally binding (Shetler and Shank: 92). The desire to faithfully obey the teaching of Scripture is commendable, even by those who believe the veiling instructions in 1 Corinthians 11:2-16 are culture-bound and no longer applicable.

1 Corinthians 11:17-34

Sensitivity to "the Body" at the Lord's Supper

PREVIEW

Although the topic and tone shift abruptly from the previous section, the focus on behavior in worship continues. Here Paul addresses the matter of fractious behavior in the practice of the Lord's Supper.

Paul is aware of their behavior because it has been reported to him by Chloe's people. He does not name them as his source, but the discussion of divisions echoes the language and tone of what he wrote in 1:10-11. There, as here, he specified that the information had come to him orally and thus he needs to explain to them what he has learned.

Paul uses this opportunity to reteach proper practice of the Lord's Supper and the proper attitude for participation. Explicit liturgical instruction is rare in the New Testament, so this brief comment has been influential in shaping a communion liturgy in all Christian traditions.

Few details about the context of the Lord's Supper are given since it is not necessary for Paul to explain this to the letter's intended readers. It is evident, however, that the ritual of the bread and cup recalling Jesus' body and blood was conducted in the context of a fellowship meal. Fellowship meals were widely practiced in the ancient world, in both Jewish and Gentile settings, both religious and secular, with many functions and purposes (Jamir: 125-27). Identifying the exact paradigm for the Corinthian fellowship meal is challenging and has produced lots of controversy. In the end, it is not necessary to know what model(s) shaped their meal practices. The issue that Paul addresses is the division that was experienced in that setting, whatever the cultural and spiritual precedent.

OUTLINE

Factions in the Congregations, 11:17-19
Insensitive Behavior at the Lord's Supper, 11:20-22
The Lord's Supper, 11:23-26
Discerning "the Body," 11:27-32
Eating the Lord's Supper with Sensitivity to "the Body," 11:33-34

EXPLANATORY NOTES

Factions in the Congregations 11:17-19

In the previous discussion about head coverings, Paul commended the Corinthian Christians for imitating him and maintaining the traditions that he had handed to them. Now he turns to a matter that he cannot commend. This too has to do with traditions that he has handed on (v. 23). But in this case his concern is not with the tradition. Rather, it is relationships in the assembly. Paul cannot commend them because of the divisions among them.

Divisions in the faith community are the driving consideration of this entire letter (see on 1:10). Healing, correcting, and challenging division has been Paul's agenda in every topic that he has addressed. In this section the problem is highlighted by repeated references to the community *coming together* (vv. 17, 18, 20, 33-34). In both Greek and English this can and does refer both to gathering and to uniting. As Hays (1997: 194) puts it, "When they come together as a church they paradoxically do not 'come together' in unity and peace."

The divisions that Paul addresses in 11:17-34 are not, however, along the same lines as those in 1:11-12. In chapter 1 the divisions were aligned with respective loyalties toward Paul, Apollos, Cephas, and Christ. Here the divisions appear to be along social or economic lines, though there may also be some theological dimensions. The comment about the inevitability and perhaps even desirability of divisions or factions (v. 19) is not about sorting out *theological* differences in order to arrive at truth. Rather it is about identifying those whose *behavior* is appropriate *to show which of you have God's approval* (NIV).

Paul informs his readers of what he has heard about them, presumably from Chloe's people. From them he has heard the perspective of the community "from below." Paul gives credence to the rumor, though perhaps not fully, for he qualifies that he believes it *to some extent*.

Insensitive Behavior at the Lord's Supper 11:20-22

The behavior that has been reported to Paul and that elicited his censure is clearly described. His description of what happens when the assembly gathers for the Lord's Supper clearly indicates that they gathered in households for a common meal, in the context of which they remembered and proclaimed Jesus' death, as Paul describes in 11:23-26. He writes that when the assembly gathers in this way to celebrate the Lord's Supper, some eat and drink to excess while others receive nothing. This behavior offends Paul because it demonstrates contempt for relationships in the household of faith and humiliates some members, specifically those who *have nothing* (v. 22).

On this matter the community in Corinth is not divided on theological grounds or on allegiances. There is no evidence here of the party divisions named in 1:12—though the divisions were probably intensified by theological, cultural, and ethnic distinctions, perhaps even by the memories of various religions in which the members had previously been participants (Jamir: 136–39).

Gerd Theissen has argued that the divisions fall on socioeconomic lines. He notes that the early Hellenistic Christian congregations exhibited a much greater range of social class than in other associations in the ancient world. Some people *had nothing* (v. 22b) and went *hungry* (v. 21), while others owned their own *homes* (v. 22a) and could afford to bring their *own supper* (v. 20). Theissen has assembled illustrations from the writings of Eratosthenes, Plutarch, Hagias, and Plato to demonstrate the common practice of wealthy diners bringing their own provisions to public feasts, though it was also criticized by other ancient writers (149–50). Theissen believes that "the wealthy Christians not only ate separately that food which they themselves had provided, but it appears that they began doing so before the commencement of the congregational meal" (153). When the common meal did begin, some people were given more and better food than others, as was the common practice in meals hosted by wealthy patrons in other settings (153–63; Gooch: 7–46).

In this context, Paul does not address the general question of economic disparity, but only the impact of humiliating demonstrations of inequity. He does not suggest a more equitable sharing of food in general, only that those who are hungry should satisfy that need at home instead of humiliating others by their conspicuous consumption. Presumably those most hungry are those who do not have access to adequate food, and those who arrived late were probably slaves who did not have freedom to arrive at the gathering in time to eat with those who were free to come earlier (11:33). Paul addresses those who *do* have the resources to eat, pointedly describing them as being hungry rather than being wealthy. This has led some scholars to search for other explanations for the acknowledged tension in Corinth at the fellowship meals. Various theological tensions have been proposed, but no explanation is more satisfactory. Nevertheless, it seems likely that the theological disagreements and party factions reported by Chloe's people (1:12) accompanied economic disparity. The control that powerful people exercised in the fellowship meals, especially those who hosted the meals in their homes, surely contributed to the schisms experienced in the Christian community (Jamir: 134–35, 139).

The issue that concerns Paul is the disunity fostered by inequities in the common meal. The fellowship meal that they call the Lord's Supper should foster unity at a time when members of the assembly *come together*. The behavior that has been reported to him demonstrates that those who provided for themselves and their friends while others went without were eating their *own supper* (v. 21), *not really . . . the Lord's supper* (v. 20).

Paul's reaction to the situation is a series of rhetorical questions designed to shame those who have humiliated other members of the community (v. 22). The scolding tone is impossible to miss as he asks, *Should I commend you? In this matter I do not commend you!*

Having named the issue, Paul proceeds to address it first by reminding them of Jesus' example and teaching and then applying that to the assembly's fellowship meals.

The Lord's Supper 11:23-26

Although this is the only place in Paul's extant writings where the origin of the Lord's Supper is described, and here only briefly, it is apparent that Paul's initial teaching had included instruction on this rite. He had *handed on* this instruction in his first visit (v. 23). The reminder here does not explain the full "liturgy" that was practiced, but as the earliest written account of the supper, it does give insight into the way Paul and the congregations he established understood it. (Other accounts of the institution of the Lord's Supper have different nuances—see "Accounts of the Institution of the Lord's Supper" in TBC below.)

Paul says that he *received from the Lord* (v. 23) the instructions that he had *handed on* to them and of which he now reminds them. Of course, Paul did not meet Jesus "in the flesh," and when he met the risen Christ on the road to Damascus, they presumably did not talk about the Lord's Supper. Rather, Paul must have received these instructions as they were passed down from those who had been present when Jesus instituted these practices and explained them to his disciples the night before his crucifixion (Fee: 607).

What Paul writes now as a reminder may be an abbreviated version of what he had received and passed on. One obvious omission is a connection with the Passover, which the gospel writers highlight. We cannot know whether that link was important for Paul. However, the fact that he does not mention it suggests that already, at this early stage in the development of the practice of Lord's Supper, the connection had been broken. One reason for this was that the Lord's Supper was enacted frequently, perhaps at every worship service, while Passover was an annual event. As Paul presents it, the Lord's Supper takes its context more from fellowship meals commonly practiced in both Gentile and Jewish contexts (Jamir: 151; cf. "Fellowship Meals in the Bible" and "Accounts of the Institution of the Lord's Supper" in TBC below).

The meal that Christians call "the Lord's Supper" was instituted *on the night when he was betrayed* (v. 23). This is a historical reference to the night when Jesus was betrayed, or handed over, to the authorities who then instigated his crucifixion. It is also particularly apt in the Corinthian setting, where the Christians have "betrayed" Jesus in the way they commemorated this very event in Jesus' life (v. 27). On the other hand, the Greek word *paradidōmi* that is usually translated as *betrayed* is the same word that is translated *handed on* (of the teaching) earlier in this verse. If the second occurrence is also translated as *handed over*, then the focus shifts from Judas's betrayal (note that Judas is not named) to the understanding that Paul offers in Romans that Jesus "was handed over [*paradidōmi*] to death [by God] for our trespasses and was raised for our justification" (Rom 4:25). Again, Paul writes that God "did not withhold his own Son, but gave him up [*paradidōmi*] for all of us" (Rom 8:32). Paul is echoing the language of Isaiah, that "the LORD gave him [the suffering servant] up [*paradidōmi*] for our sins" (Isa 53:6 LXX) and "on account of their iniquities he was handed over [*paradidōmi*]" (Isa 53:12c LXX). This suggests that Paul's emphasis is not on Judas's betrayal of Jesus, but rather on the handing over of Jesus by God "for our sins" (Hays 1997: 198). Yet this offers no explanation of *how* Jesus' death deals with sin, simply *that* it does (see I. Friesen: 439-40).

The sayings over the bread and the cup are framed as reminders. In both cases Jesus says, *Do this in remembrance of me*. The bread is his *body that is for you* (v. 24), not literally but symbolically; and the cup is *the new covenant in [Jesus'] blood* (v. 25), again symbolically. The *body* language anticipates an extended discussion of participation in the body in 12:12-26, and the *covenant* is a further reminder of the relationship between all who drink the cup together.

For as often as you eat this bread and drink the cup, you proclaim the Lord's death (v. 26). The gospel accounts of the Last Supper do not include this statement. It is Paul's comment on the liturgy, and he specifically directs it to the Corinthians because of their behavior. The proclamation is in the actions of eating and drinking and in the words that are said over the bread and cup. That proclamation is the death of Jesus and especially the conviction that his death results in the salvation of those who follow him, which is the content of the gospel that Paul preached: *Christ crucified* (1:23; cf. 1:17).

Implicit in every reference to Jesus' death is the death of those who were baptized into his death. "Do you not know that all of us who have been baptized into Christ Jesus were baptized into his death?" Paul wrote to the Romans (Rom 6:3). Jesus himself had said, "If any want to become my followers, let them deny themselves and take up their cross and follow me" (Mark 8:34 parr.). The Corinthians, however, were not thinking about either Jesus' death or their own when they practiced their *own supper* (1 Cor 11:20-21).

The proclamation of Jesus' death continues *until he comes*, Paul writes (v. 26), reminding his readers of the eschatological context of their worship. They have not yet arrived at the culmination of God's work, as some of them thought (see esp. 4:8-10; also 1:7; 15:12). Yet what they do has implications for the final judgment, as the following paragraph elaborates.

When they came together, the Corinthians' behavior took no account of Jesus' death; it was all about their own status within the community. Moreover, it took no account of Jesus' coming again; it was all about their already-achieved spiritual maturity. There was no past (*the Lord's death*) nor future (*until he comes*). They had lost the vision of the grand scheme of God's salvation that was supposed to be remembered in the sharing of the bread and cup. They were occupied with themselves.

Paul clearly understands that the mispractice of the Lord's Supper in Corinth is an important aspect of the disunity in the assembly. Though serious enough in itself, it is not a separate error but part and parcel of the whole problem. The cause, Paul suggests, is that they have forgotten what they should have remembered every time they participated in this ritual: its historical and spiritual significance as a symbol of Jesus' death and of the unity of those who are saved by his death on the cross, the proclamation of which is Paul's entire mission.

Discerning "the Body" 11:27-32

The paragraph about judgment in the context of the Lord's Supper has often been misunderstood in the Western world because of the assumptions that are brought to it. Those assumptions include an individualistic understanding of sin and judgment, a sacramental view of the bread and cup in the Lord's Supper, and what Krister Stendahl (78-96) has named "the introspective conscience of the West." Because of these misunderstandings, individuals have barred themselves or have been barred from participation in the Lord's Supper and have suffered much anxiety of conscience. On the other hand, inappropriate participation has been condoned.

The warning is against those who participate *in an unworthy manner* (v. 27 NRSV, NIV), or *unworthily* (KJV, NJB). The former translation is preferable since it makes clearer that Paul's concern is not about the *who*, the worthiness of the participant, but the *how*, the worthiness of the manner of participation. The instruction to *examine yourselves* (v. 28) is not about searching one's heart and memory for evidence of sins committed or contemplated, but rather is an instruction to engage in sober assessment of how one's actions affect other members of the body of Christ.

Since the Lord's Supper is a proclamation of Jesus' death (v. 26), those who practice it *in an unworthy manner* are misproclaiming and thus are *answerable for the body and blood of the Lord* (v. 27). This is like the assertion in Hebrews that it is impossible to "restore again to repentance" those who "have fallen away, since on their own they are crucifying again the Son of God and are holding him up to contempt" (Heb 6:4-6).

The error that draws judgment, Paul says, is eating and drinking *without discerning the body* (v. 29). The NIV says *without discerning the body of Christ*, which points toward a correct understanding of Paul's point, though *of Christ* is not in the Greek. A reader may well be confused as to whether *the body* refers to Jesus' physical body, the bread as a representative of Jesus' physical body, or the body politic of the assembly. The translation *the body of Christ* rightly pushes the reader toward thinking about the Christian assembly—which is formed, of course, around the broken body of Jesus that is remembered in the Lord's Supper. *Discerning the body* is a matter of recognizing that the people gathered for the fellowship meal which is the Lord's Supper are indeed the body of Christ. Paul has already made this point in 10:16-17, especially in his statement that *we who are many are one body, for we all partake of the one bread.* The fuller meaning of this will be set out in the next chapter, specifically 12:12-26 *[Bodies in 1 Corinthians, p. 363].*

Fellowship meals of all kinds serve as boundary markers. The invitation to participate in a meal recognizes acceptance by the host, and the seating arrangements and food service demonstrate a person's ranking in the group. Conversely, ejection or expulsion (excommunication) from a fellowship meal is a form of judgment (Jamir: 179). The Corinthians were judging one another in the way they admitted people to the table and in the amount and kind of food and drink they received. Paul is challenging their right to judge, reminding them that it is the Lord who is the host, not the person who owns the house where the assembly meets. *If we judged ourselves, we would not be judged. But . . . we are judged by the Lord* (11:31-32). Those who fail to recognize whose supper it is and who fail to discern the right relationship of the participants *eat and drink judgment against themselves* (v. 29).

The judgment referred to is not the final judgment that is expected in the eschaton, but rather a present judgment, with the immediate consequence that *many of you are weak and ill, and some have died* (v. 30).

At least some of the Corinthian Christians had previously been involved in pagan religions. In Hellenistic cults, especially in the mystery religions, fellowship meals were associated with deities (Jamir: 97–102). They understood that honoring the deity in the meal would result in blessing, and offenses would result in sickness and death as punishment. We do not know exactly what illnesses and deaths had been experienced in the Corinthian congregations, but we do know that Paul associates those experiences with improper practice of the Lord's Supper. This would have been an apparent connection for the Corinthians because of their previous experiences.

Gerd Theissen (167) writes,

> Sacramental actions are dramatic representations of social processes, whatever else they may be. . . . The sacramental act of the Lord's Supper is a symbolic accomplishment of social integration. From many people emerges a single entity. Interpersonal tensions are

represented, and overcome, in the sacrifice. Sanctions are inculcated. This social dynamic is expressed in palpably perceptible actions. The fellowship here achieves embodiment.

This focus on the integrating power of the Lord's Supper is what Paul wants to accomplish, but Theissen errs in calling it "sacramental" in the sense that *sacrament* is used theologically. There is no suggestion in the text that Paul understands the bread and the cup to be anything other than a *remembrance* of Jesus' body and the covenant in his blood. They do not in themselves convey God's grace. The words said over them are words of gratitude and reminders, not incantations or mantras. The Lord's Supper is a symbolic act or a sign of remembrance; it is not a sacrament.

The point that Paul is making here has much in common with that made by the first-century Jewish historian Josephus, who wrote about Jewish sacrifices:

> When we offer sacrifices to him, we do it not in order to surfeit ourselves, or to be drunken; for such excesses are against the will of God, and would be an occasion of injuries and of luxury; but by keeping ourselves sober, orderly, and ready for our other occupations, and being more temperate than others. And for our duty at the sacrifices themselves, we ought, in the first place, to pray for the common welfare of all, and after that for our own; for we are made for fellowship one with another, and he who prefers the common good before what is peculiar to himself is above all acceptable to God. (*Against Apion* 2.24 [Whiston])

Eating the Lord's Supper with Sensitivity to "the Body" 11:33-34

So then, finally, Paul gives explicit instructions for correcting the problem of insensitivity in the practice of the Lord's Supper by the Corinthian assembly. The correct way to recognize or discern the unity of the body is to ensure that all members are fully included. Instead of going ahead with their own food, the wealthy, powerful, and well-connected members of the assembly should *wait for one another* (or *you should all eat together*, NIV). Likewise, those who hold allegiance to particular leaders (such as Apollos or Paul) or particular convictions (such as celibacy in marriage or freedom to eat food offered to idols) should include in table fellowship those with whom they disagree. This will both alleviate the humiliation of those who have been excluded and address the problem of gluttony and drunkenness that has been reported to Paul.

Some readers are disappointed that Paul does not address more strongly the inequities that underlie the problem with the Lord's Supper. They wish he had said that those who have enough resources to eat well should share with those who have less than enough. Instead, he allowed the inequities to continue, only directing that they should be practiced in private. Perhaps in Paul's mind this was another application of the principle *Let each of you remain in the condition in which you were called* (7:17-24, esp. v. 20). Like marriage, circumcision, and slavery, financial and social inequities are not worth the effort to correct *in view of the impending crisis* (7:26). But humiliation and exclusion of brothers and sisters on these grounds is intolerable and must be corrected immediately.

Significantly, even during this strong reprimand, Paul addresses his readers as *my brothers and sisters* (v. 33), as he does twenty-two times in this letter. In contrast to his instruction in chapter 5, here he is not recommending the expulsion of those who fail to discern the body, but their correction. In the context of urging inclusion, he could not advocate excluding even those who are behaving inappropriately.

The last sentence leaves us wondering what *other things* Paul would address in person. We cannot know whether they had to do with further corrections on the practice of the Lord's Supper or other matters on which he could not commend them. In introducing this section, he referred to matters in general, and *in the first place* (v. 18 NIV) he addresses the matter of behavior at the Lord's Supper. Perhaps other matters had been brought to his attention that he did not want to take up in a letter. We do not know to what he is referring, but the comment reminds us that this letter is part of an ongoing dialogue that Paul expected would continue in person as well as in writing.

THE TEXT IN BIBLICAL CONTEXT

Fellowship Meals in the Bible

The Lord's Supper builds on the power of shared meals, in every human culture throughout history, to establish and confirm relationships. The Bible includes many stories of shared meals that provide some of the context for this event.

The paradigmatic biblical story of table fellowship is found in Genesis 18:1-8, where Abraham hosted strangers later discovered to be messengers from God (perhaps with "the LORD" himself, v. 1), a story that later became a model for Jews and Christians to imitate

(Heb 13:2). The Old Testament features stories of meals shared to ratify covenants with God and people (Gen 26:27-31), to celebrate family events (24:54; 29:22-23; 43:24-34), and to extend hospitality to strangers (Exod 2:20).

The ultimate fellowship meal, at which abundant food is shared with the poor, the needy, and aliens, is anticipated in a vision described by Isaiah: "On this mountain the Lord of hosts will make for all peoples a feast of rich food, a feast of well-aged wines, of rich food filled with marrow, of well-aged wines strained clear" (Isa 25:6). It is not only the abundance of food that is the sign of God's salvation in this passage, but also and primarily the sharing of this blessing with "all peoples."

The Gospels include several stories of shared fellowship meals. The largest event is the feeding of the five thousand, reported in Mark 6:32-44 (cf. Matt 14:13-21; Luke 9:10-17; John 6:1-15), and the similar feeding of the four thousand in Mark 8:1-10 (cf. Matt 15:32-39). Luke's gospel highlights meal scenes where Jesus eats with "tax collectors and sinners" (5:27-32), Pharisees (7:36-50; 11:37-54; 14:1-24), and intimate groups of friends (10:38-42). Jesus' willingness to eat with the "wrong" people contributed to debates about his identity and the opposition toward him.

Prominent among the meals reported in the Gospels is Jesus' observance of the Passover, his last supper with his disciples (Matt 26:17-29; Mark 14:12-25; Luke 22:7-23; John 13:1-30). During this fellowship meal, Jesus spoke of the symbolic significance of the bread and the cup as reminders of his impending death and as a sign of eschatological hope. Shared meals were also the context for recognizing Jesus after his resurrection, both in Emmaus (Luke 24:30-31, 35, 41-43) and on the shore of Galilee (John 21:9-13).

The book of Acts says that after Pentecost the Christians met frequently to share in fellowship meals (2:42, 46; 20:7, 11). In one story, Paul shares a meal with non-Christian shipmates, which is reported with language that echoes Jesus' actions and words at the Last Supper and also the practice of the Lord's Supper: "He took bread; and giving thanks to God in the presence of all, he broke it and began to eat" (27:35). The boundaries of table fellowship are expanded as Peter receives a vision wherein he is instructed to eat nonkosher food, which he interprets as preparation for responding to an invitation to visit and to stay (and eat) with Cornelius, a Gentile (10:10-16). Other believers criticize Peter for eating with Gentiles (11:1-2), and Paul later criticizes Peter for failing to eat with Gentiles when certain people from Jerusalem are present (Gal 2:11-14).

Jude, like Paul in 1 Corinthians, recognizes what happens when the faith community fails to control these table gatherings. He writes about "intruders" who have attached themselves to the assembly, though they are sinful and unbelievers, and comments that they are "blemishes on your love-feasts" (Jude 4, 12; cf. 2 Pet 2:13). In writing this, he draws attention to both the continuing practice of table fellowship and the importance of boundaries to limit participation.

Finally, the vision of blessing and delight in God's presence is described as the ultimate fellowship meal, the messianic banquet or wedding feast of the Lamb (Rev 19:9), echoing the vision of Isaiah 25:6, noted above (cf. Matt 8:11; Luke 13:29).

Accounts of the Institution of the Lord's Supper

There are four accounts of the institution of the Lord's Supper in the New Testament. One is found in 1 Corinthians 11, which we have been considering. The others are in the first three (synoptic) gospels in the context of Jesus' last supper with his disciples on *the night when he was betrayed*, just before his arrest, trial(s), and crucifixion.

John's gospel includes an account of the Last Supper but does not report on the sharing of the bread and cup or any comments about their representative significance. Instead, there is an account of Jesus washing his disciples' feet that appears nowhere else (John 13:1-17).

John reports a long discourse by Jesus on bread (6:22-59) in the context of the story of feeding the five thousand (vv. 1-13), which is introduced as taking place when "the Passover, the festival of the Jews, was near" (v. 4). In this discourse Jesus declares, "I am the bread of life" (v. 35), and again, "I am the living bread that came down from heaven" (v. 51). John also reports that Jesus said, "Those who eat my flesh and drink my blood have eternal life, and I will raise them up on the last day" (v. 54). John may have intended this passage as an explanation of the Lord's Supper, but many scholars think he did not (Swartley 2013: 178-81, 186-88). Although it provides one theological perspective on the shared bread and cup, it does not institute a ritual for the Christian community to repeat, as do the other gospels and Paul in 1 Corinthians 11.

The four accounts represent two traditions, one of which is presented by Mark, closely followed by Matthew, and the other by Paul, closely followed by Luke. The following parallel columns taken, with adaptation, from Fee (605), show the comparisons. In the left column, the text from Mark is presented with Markan peculiarities in curly brackets { } and with Matthew's variations in square brackets [ ]. In the right column, Paul's text is presented with Pauline peculiarities in curly brackets { } and Luke's peculiarities in square brackets [ ]. Material common to all four accounts is in italics.

{Mark 14:22-24} [Matt 26:26-28]	{Paul: 1 Cor 11:23-25} [Luke 22:19-20]
While they were eating, {he} [Jesus] *took a loaf of bread,* and after blessing it he *broke it,* gave it to {them} [the disciples], and said, "Take [, eat], *this is my body."* Then he took a *cup,* and after giving thanks he gave it to them, {and all of them drank from it. He said to them,} [saying, "Drink from it all of you; for] *this is my blood* of *the covenant,* which is poured out for many [for the forgiveness of sins]."	{The Lord Jesus on the night when he was betrayed} [Then he] *took a loaf of bread,* and when he had given thanks, he *broke it* and {said,} [gave it to them, saying,] *"This is my body,* {that} [which] is [given] for you. Do this in remembrance of me." {In the same way he took} [And he did the same with] the *cup* {also,} after supper, saying, *"This* cup [that is poured out for you] *is* the new *covenant* in *my blood.* {Do this, as often as you drink it, in remembrance of me.}"

Luke uniquely reports a cup before the bread as well as the one after supper: "Then he took a cup, and after giving thanks he said, 'Take this and divide it among yourselves; for I tell you that from now on I will not drink of the fruit of the vine until the kingdom of God comes'" (22:17-18).

Matthew's account is unique in including the command to eat the bread and to drink the cup. Matthew is also the only account to specify that Jesus' blood was poured out "for the forgiveness of sins."

While Mark and Matthew say that Jesus blessed the bread, Paul and Luke say that he gave thanks for it. Giving thanks is implicit in Paul's and Luke's "in the same way / he did the same," and explicit in Mark's and Matthew's accounts of what Jesus did with the cup.

There are a few other variations, but the most significant difference between these accounts is that Paul, followed by Luke, states that the bread is shared *in remembrance of me*, and Paul alone says also that the cup is *in remembrance of me*. This emphasis addresses Paul's concern with the Corinthian congregations, which were not rightly remembering whose supper they were sharing or what it represents (Fee: 606).

THE TEXT IN THE LIFE OF THE CHURCH
Divisions at the Lord's Supper

The Lord's Supper continues to divide the Lord's body. In their desire to maintain the integrity of the "true church," many denominations and congregations welcome only their own members to the table. In general, Roman Catholics, Orthodox, and Protestant churches exclude each other. Many Protestant churches also exclude all or some other Protestants. Inclusion or exclusion from the Lord's Supper is the ultimate test of whether a person or denomination is recognized as legitimately "Christian." On rare occasions, denominations officially restore communion with each other, as the Anglican Church of Canada and the Evangelical Lutheran Church in Canada did in 2001. Occasionally in ecumenical settings or in a particular congregation, those who are officiating will invite to the table Christians who are not officially "in communion" with each other. When such demonstrations of unity and mutual respect occur, the witness of the church is enhanced and Christ is honored. Participants experience the *Lord's Supper*, not their *own supper*.

Other factors can also divide the church, even between those who in principle acknowledge each other as followers of Jesus. In South Africa during the apartheid era, different racial groups even in the same denomination would not share the Lord's Supper. In some churches in India (but not in many others), the members are separated by caste at the Lord's Supper. In the United States, some churches, at least in the past, have been racially segregated at communion.

On occasion, individuals or groups are excluded or feel excluded because of social status, wealth or poverty, theological differences, moral judgment, or other criteria. The failure of Christians to rightly discern the body is *not for the better but for the worse* (11:17) and continues to *show contempt for the church of God* (11:22; see also "Excommunication" in TLC for ch. 5).

Celebrating the Lord's Supper

Richard Hays (1997: 204) has an excellent summary of "what we are doing when we come together as a church around the table" to share the Lord's Supper. First, he writes, "the Lord's table must . . . express *the community's unity as the new covenant people of God*" (emphasis original). The Lord's Supper is "not just . . . a private act of piety focused on receiving individual forgiveness but . . . a coming together of the Lord's people at a common meal." In our era of globalization it is especially necessary, *when you come together* (vv. 17, 18, 20, 33, 34), to be aware not only of the people of a particular congregation but also of those "from every tribe and language and people and nation" (Rev 5:9). The proper approach to the Lord's Supper requires sensitivity to economic and other inequities and to any behavior that would *humiliate* (v. 22) other members of the body, whether present or far away. Properly *discerning the body* (v. 29) is not only necessary preparation, but also essential to the right practice of this event, which is highlighted by the recognition of its context as a fellowship meal. Terms like "communion" (2 Cor 13:13) or *the table* (1 Cor 10:21) for the Lord's Supper emphasize this communal dimension.

The Church of the Brethren and related groups emphasize this community aspect of the Lord's Supper by the extended service of the "love feast" (cf. Jude 12). Traditionally this was preceded by a community meal and a time of preparation by self-examination to assess one's relationship with fellow church members. The love feast itself includes washing each other's feet (John 13), the kiss of peace, and the sharing of the bread and cup—all accompanied with appropriate Scriptures, teaching, prayers, and hymns (Snyder 1983; fuller description in Brown: 126–32; broader perspectives in Stoffer). In some traditional Amish and Mennonite churches the communion service is always accompanied by footwashing (cf. John 13:1-17), or an "alms offering" for the poor of the congregation as further demonstrations of the community's unity and mutual support, or both (Neff, van der Zijpp, and Bender).

Hays continues, "The Lord's Supper also *focuses the church's memory on the death of Jesus*" (1997: 204, emphasis original). The term *eucharist* (from Gk. via Lat., meaning *thanksgiving*, as in 1 Cor 14:16; as verb in 11:24, *had given thanks*) is sometimes used for the Lord's Supper to emphasize gratitude for Jesus' sacrifice and the gift of salvation. Jesus' death is the focal point that draws attention also to his incarnation, life, and resurrection. The conviction that *Christ died for our sins* (15:3) is the essence of Christian faith. Christians who believe, as Paul did, that the proclamation of the cross is the crux of the gospel (e.g., 2:1-2) must agree that to *proclaim the Lord's death until he comes* (11:26) is vitally important, both as a *remembrance* (vv. 24, 25) for members of the faith community and as a witness to those outside.

Finally, Hays declares, "the Lord's Supper is an occasion for us to ponder *God's judgment*" (1997: 205, emphasis original). Judgment is often wrongly applied from the exhortation to *examine yourselves*

(v. 28; see EN). The emphasis that some traditions place on self-examination as searching one's memory for evidence of personal sin actually enables, perhaps even causes, people to avoid the real issue of division and failure to recognize the body (cf. Fee: 630). Hays (1997: 205) suggests that "the function of judgment language in this passage is very much like the parable of the sheep and the goats in Matthew 25:31-46: it summons the community to care for 'the least of these' in their midst." With that correction, it is important not to lose sight of the clear warning that self-judgment is necessary to avoid God's judgment and discipline (vv. 31-32).

How often should the Lord's Supper be shared? Christian traditions have a variety of customary practices: daily, weekly, monthly, quarterly, or annually. Some denominations prescribe frequency along with the liturgy. Others vary between congregations. Pragmatic factors influence this as well as theological issues. Theological traditions that understand the Lord's Supper to be a means of grace (or sacrament) want to receive it often. Those who understand it to be a symbol whose frequent practice diminishes its significance want to receive it less often. If the precedent for the Lord's Supper is the Passover, then an annual observance is appropriate. If it is a fellowship meal, as Lanuwabang Jamir and others argue, then it should be practiced frequently.

The example of the Corinthian congregations, understood in the context of biblical and fellowship meals, suggests that faith communities should practice frequent sharing of food, whether congregational meals or shared meals in homes. Those meals should include explicit reminders and proclamation of Jesus' life, his death *for our sins* (1 Cor 15:3), and his resurrection, plus explicit acknowledgment that the faith community is the body of Christ.

Perhaps the thorniest issue related to the Lord's Supper is "Who is invited?" (E. Kreider 1997: 169-88). This is not the question for the Corinthian congregations, so Paul does not directly address it in this letter. He does intimate, however, that it is members of the body of Christ who remember and proclaim his death and resurrection. This would preclude anyone who is not baptized or who is not demonstrating in life his or her commitment to follow Christ—anyone who has not "been buried with him by baptism into death" or who does not "walk in newness of life" (Rom 6:4). Paul's emphasis on discernment (1 Cor 11:29) and judgment (vv. 31-32) clearly implies the ability to do that, thus precluding children. Paul's depiction of the Lord's Supper as a fellowship meal, which both includes and excludes, points toward a more "closed" table. The analogy between the Lord's Supper and Passover that the writers of the synoptic (first three) gospels draw also suggests a table closed to people from outside the faith community, though in that case including children.

Preaching and Worship

The liturgical portion of this passage, 1 Corinthians 11:23-26, is often read, sometimes conflated with other Scriptures, as the "words of institution" in Lord's Supper liturgies in all Christian traditions (see, e.g., the "Words of Institution" entry on *Wikipedia*; esp. its discussions of denominational liturgical and worship orders). It is an appropriate text from which to preach on any occasion when the Lord's Supper is served. Churches that use the Revised Common Lectionary read this on the Thursday of Holy Week every year. However, the remainder of the chapter, which deals with the awkward context for the rehearsal of the liturgy and the teaching about judgment for failure to discern the body, is not included in the assigned readings. Because it is important for instruction in the understanding and practice of the Lord's Supper and proper discernment of the body of Christ, opportunities should be created to preach and teach the whole chapter. For preaching and teaching as well as for practicing the Lord's Supper, a good resource is Eleanor Kreider's 1997 book *Communion Shapes Character*.

1 Corinthians 12:1-31
Manifestations of the Holy Spirit, Part 1

PREVIEW

Chapter 12 introduces a new topic, spirituality, though Paul has alluded to it earlier. In the thanksgiving he refers to the Corinthians' *spiritual gifts* (1:4-9, esp. v. 7). He names their interest in spirituality and their claim of spiritual maturity in 2:1-3:4 (see EN), but here the matter of spirituality is focused by something that the Corinthians had written to Paul. It was surely an important issue: his response occupies chapters 12-14.

This new issue is not disconnected from either what has been discussed to this point or what will follow in chapter 15. It continues the general topic of appropriate behavior in worship. After his teaching on headship and decorum in worship (11:2-16) and sensitivity to others in the Lord's Supper (11:17-34), Paul now addresses manifestations of the Holy Spirit in public worship, especially speaking in tongues and prophecy. He does this in a way that is consistent with how he instructed them to accommodate "the weak" in chapters 8-10, and with the fundamentals that he set out in the first four chapters. In chapter 15 he will take their glorying in their present level of spiritual maturity and put it into the context of the eschatological hope of resurrection. The discussion of spiritual things is part and parcel of Paul's intent throughout this letter, *that all of you be in agreement and that there be no divisions among you, but that you be united in the same mind and the same purpose* (1:10).

Once again, Paul introduces the change in topic with the words *Now concerning* (see 7:1, 25; 8:1; 16:1, 12). We have recognized this as a sign that Paul is addressing a topic that was raised by the Corinthians in their letter to him (cf. preview to ch. 7). As usual, it is not easy to identify exactly what they might have written in their letter. From Paul's response, it seems likely that they wrote something about speaking in tongues in public worship. It may have been a question for clarification of his teaching or perhaps a statement of their practice. Fee (634-35) points out that there is no hint of division among the Corinthians on these matters and suggests that the tension was between their shared understanding and Paul's understanding of what it means to be spiritual. Because they were so confident in their view, it seems unlikely that they had posed a question in their letter and more likely that they had reported to Paul their satisfaction that so many of them could speak in tongues and did so in worship. They apparently thought this demonstrated the Holy Spirit's presence and blessing—at least on those who had this ability. Perhaps their letter said something like this: "We are delighted to report that many of us have the ability to speak in tongues. This evidence of our spiritual maturity has become a large part of our worship service, and our faith is built up through it" *[What the Corinthians Wrote, p. 372]*.

The structure of Paul's response is similar to the structure of his discussion of food offered to idols in chapters 8–10. He introduces the issues in the first chapter, broadens the context to general principles in the second, and returns to the presenting issue with his counsel in the third chapter.

OUTLINE

The Variety of Manifestations of the Holy Spirit, 12:1-11
The Christian Assembly as a Body, 12:12-26
The Variety of Manifestations of the Holy Spirit, 12:27-31a

EXPLANATORY NOTES

The Variety of Manifestations of the Holy Spirit
12:1-11, 27-31a

Most commentaries and Bible translations characterize chapters 12–14 as a discussion about "spiritual gifts." This commentary avoids that language. English translations commonly use *gift* half a dozen times in chapter 12 and twice in chapter 14. Several, but not all, of these are appropriate. In several cases, the text specifies that the giver of the gift is the Holy Spirit. However, the gifts themselves are not "spiritual," and because discussions of "spiritual gifts" have caused serious divisions in the history of the church (as they did in Corinth), it is better, and more faithful to the Greek, to avoid that language. This commentary uses the descriptor that Paul uses, *manifestation[s] of the Spirit* (v. 7).

Pneumatikos (from *pneuma*, spirit) occurs in the first verse of chapter 12, where it is commonly rendered as *spiritual gifts*. In its grammatical form it could be neuter, feminine, or masculine, and it should be translated as *spiritual things* or *spiritual persons* (perhaps specifically "women" or "men"), as it is in 2:13. Thus 1 Corinthians 12:1 begins, more literally, *Now concerning spiritual things* . . . or possibly, *Now concerning spiritual people* . . . When the discussion is resumed in 14:1, the same word is found in a distinctly neuter form, supporting the likelihood that *spiritual things* is what was intended in 12:1. On the other hand, in 14:37 (cf. 2:15; 3:1), Paul uses a different form of the same word. There he chastises those who think of themselves as spiritual persons. Since there is a definite article in 12:1, a good translation would be *Now concerning the spiritual*, leaving some ambiguity, but without introducing the word *gifts*. By introducing *gifts* in verse 1, translators obscure the allusion to earlier references to spiritual things (e.g., 2:10–3:1; esp. 2:13) or to people who claim spiritual superiority (e.g., 2:13, 15; 14:37). The first three verses of chapter 12 are a general introduction to "things of the Spirit" as practiced by "spiritual people." The discussion of manifestations of the Spirit grows out of that.

The second Greek word translated as *gift* is *charisma* (plural *charismata*), which is found in verses 4, 9, 28, 30, and 31. Three of those (vv. 9, 28, 30) specifically name *gifts of healing*. In verses 4 and 31, it is broadly *gifts*. Paul has used this word three times earlier in this letter. In 2:12 in a participial form it modifies the neuter pronoun and is appropriately translated as *what God has freely given us* (NIV). In 7:7, Paul uses it to recognize that each person has received a particular grace from God: his is the grace of celibacy, which he acknowledges not everyone has received. In 1:7, both NRSV and NIV translate it as *spiritual gift*, though there is no warrant for inserting *spiritual*; thus KJV, NKJ, and NJB say only *gift* (cf. Thiselton 2000: 97–98). In short, "the word *charisma* in Paul probably means no more than simply '(gracious) gift.' . . . It does not have the specific sense 'spiritual gifts,' even when it refers to such" (Turner: 267). When Paul wants to identify a spiritual gift, he uses two words: *pneumatikon* (spiritual) modifies *charisma* ("gift," Rom 1:11). In secular literature, *charisma* denotes an unearned gift or favor and has no particular spiritual connotation. Paul uses it to draw attention to unearned grace that is a gift from God.

As he did in 10:1, so here Paul chides the Corinthians for their claim to be experts in spiritual matters. *I do not want you to be uninformed*, he wrote. That was far from their self-perception. Some of them thought they had a high level of spiritual understanding and maturity.

Those who claimed spiritual maturity did not think all members had achieved that status. Their claims to spirituality pitted member against member, contributing to the schisms that prompted this letter. Paul is addressing that issue, and he begins by casting the most inclusive possible definition of those *speaking by the Spirit of God* (v. 3). Everyone who says *Jesus is Lord* is included. The affirmation of the lordship of Jesus is the evidence of Spirit's presence and activity. In a fractured community (1:10) where different expressions of spirituality added to divisions, they had at least this in common: they had all accepted Jesus as Lord. In a context where speaking in tongues or in prophecy was especially valued, he insists that the evidence of *speaking by the Spirit of God* is neither of those, but rather the confession that *Jesus is Lord*.

Paul writes that the Christians in Corinth used to be *ethnē*, which most English translations interpret as *pagans* (v. 2). The same translations otherwise consistently translate it as *Gentiles*, meaning any non-Jews, in all of Paul's letters (fifty-two times), with the exceptions of 1 Corinthians 5:1 and 10:20, where some translations say *pagans* and others say *Gentiles*. Outside of Paul's letters, the word is often translated as *nations* (e.g., Matt 28:19; Mark 13:10; Rev 21:24).

Sometimes Paul identifies the members of his congregations as Gentiles (e.g., Rom 16:4; Gal 2:12; Eph 3:1). Here, however, he writes, *when you were Gentiles* [or *pagans*, NRSV, NIV] (1 Cor 12:2 NKJV). The implication is double-sided: on one hand, it makes it clear that the Christians in Corinth were Gentiles. On the other hand, it affirms that they have been "grafted in" as Jews—a perspective that Paul elaborates in Romans 11:17-24 (Hays 1997: 209).

However it is translated, the point is that they have turned from idol worship, as practiced by most non-Jews and non-Christians, and have affirmed that *Jesus is Lord*. That proves that they are all "spiritual" in the sense of being led by the Holy Spirit. Perhaps Paul is also reminding them that ecstatic speech was practiced in some of the pagan cults: hence it could not be considered a distinctly Christian practice and certainly not the only or main evidence of the Holy Spirit's presence and activity (Fee: 640). Idols cannot speak. Their muteness is the characteristic most often used in the Old Testament to dismiss silent idols and turn to the God who speaks (Jer 10:5; Hab 2:18). The Holy Spirit, however, enables believers to speak the affirmation that *Jesus is Lord*. This earliest of Christian confessions (cf. Rom 10:9-10; Phil 2:11; Acts 2:36) is what distinguishes Christians from both pagans and Jews.

At least a dozen explanations have been offered for Paul's citing of *Let Jesus be cursed!* (v. 3), but there is no evidence that anyone in the Christian community at that time actually cursed Jesus (Thiselton 2000: 918-24). This is probably a hypothetical scenario that Paul projected as the opposite of declaring Jesus as Lord. He may have intended it exactly to demonstrate that no such people were in the congregations—a negative way of affirming their unity on this declaration of faith by the inspiration of the Spirit.

In their *gifts* (Gk. *charismata*), their *services* (Gk. *diakoniai*), and their *activities* (Gk. *energēmata*) there is variety (vv. 4-6). Yet the sources of these attributes—the Spirit who gives gifts, the Lord who is served, and God who activates—are one and the same for all believers. Although Paul nowhere develops a theology of the Trinity (nor does any other New Testament writer), he demonstrates here and elsewhere a functional trinitarian understanding of God.

Gifts, *services*, and *activities* in all their variety are *manifestation[s] of the Spirit*. Against anyone who thought that speaking in tongues is the only evidence of the Spirit's presence and activity, Paul asserts that all the various *gifts*, all the various *services*, and all the various *activities* are evidence of the Spirit's presence. Diversity, not uniformity, is the characteristic of the Spirit's activity, as is demonstrated by the very nature of the Trinity. Furthermore, the *gifts*, *services*, and *activities* are distributed to individuals *just as the Spirit chooses* (v. 11) *for the common good* of the community of faith (v. 7) and not for the glory of the recipient. The emphasis is on the giver, who is manifested in them, not on the manifestations themselves. This is the essence of Paul's teaching in chapters 12-14.

What follows is an illustrative list of what the Spirit distributes to members of the household of faith. It is not an exhaustive list; there are two different, though overlapping, lists in 12:28-30. Other lists appear in Romans 12:6-8 and Ephesians 4:11-13 (see chart below). Nevertheless, Paul offers this substantial list to expand the scope of recognized manifestations of the Spirit beyond the Corinthian preference for speaking in tongues and Paul's preference for prophecy.

Gordon Fee (655) has identified three clusters in this list of nine items (cf. Hays 1997: 211). The first two are separated by the Greek conjunction *allō*, meaning "to another of the same kind." The next five are likewise separated from each other, but the set is introduced by *heterō*, which means "to another of a different kind." The final set, consisting of two items, is also introduced by *heterō* and separated from each other by *allō*. Thus the list of 12:8-10 can be set out as Hays demonstrates:

> *To one is given through the Spirit the utterance of wisdom, and*
>
> *to another [allō] the utterance of knowledge according to the same Spirit,*
>
> *to another [heterō] faith by the same Spirit,*
>
> *to another [allō] gifts of healing by the one Spirit,*
>
> *to another [allō] the working of miracles,*
>
> *to another [allō] prophecy,*
>
> *to another [allō] the discernment of spirits,*
>
> *to another [heterō] various kinds of tongues,*
>
> *to another [allō] the interpretation of tongues.*

The first cluster consists of spiritual expressions (*utterance[s]*), of which the Corinthians were particularly proud. The last cluster includes two related items that are also important to the Corinthians and will be the focus of chapter 14. Between are five others that were perhaps less recognized or honored by the Corinthians, and they broaden the perspective of the readers as to what manifests the Spirit's activity.

Paul next turns to the metaphor of the body to drive home his point that all spiritual manifestations are important and that they are all given for the common good (vv. 12-27). After he elaborates the metaphor, he applies it to the matters raised by the letter from Corinth (vv. 27-31) and reiterates what he has written in the opening verses: God has distributed spiritual manifestations among members of the body; no one has them all, though all have been given to the community.

The following chart compares the three lists of spiritual manifestations in this chapter and the lists from Romans 12:6-8 and Ephesians 4:11.

1 Corinthians 12:1-31

1 Cor 12:8-10 (order number)	1 Cor 12:28	1 Cor 12:29-30	Rom 12:6-8	Eph 4:11
utterance of wisdom (1)	*apostles*	*apostles*	the exhorter (4)	apostles
prophecy (6)	*prophets*	*prophets*	prophecy	prophets
				evangelists
			ministry	pastors
utterance of knowledge (2)	*teachers*	*teachers*	the teacher	teachers
working of miracles (5)	*deeds of power*	*work miracles*		
gifts of healing (4)	*gifts of healing*	*gifts of healing*		
faith (3)				
discernment of spirits (7)				
			the giver	
	forms of assistance			
	forms of leadership		the leader	
			the compassionate	
various kinds of tongues (8)	*various kinds of tongues*	*speak in tongues*		
interpretation of tongues (9)		*interpret*		

The sequencing of the items listed in 1 Corinthians 12:28 (first, second, third, then others) may be just incidental or may represent the sequence of leaders needed to plant a congregation—apostles arrive first, followed by prophets, teachers, and then all the others (see also 3:6-10 and corresponding EN). The chart demonstrates that there is no consistent ordering or ranking of manifestations in Paul's thinking. However, verse 31 indicates that some manifestations are *greater* than others, and chapter 14 picks up that theme with prophecy ranked as *greater* than speaking in tongues (esp. 14:1, 5, 39). It will become clear in chapter 14 that Paul values most highly the spiritual manifestations that most directly build up the body of Christ, not those that build up the status of the one through whom they are demonstrated.

The questions listed in 12:29-30 are written in Greek in a way that implies a negative answer. The closest English equivalent would be *Surely not all are apostles, are they?* or *All are not apostles, are they? Surely not all are prophets*. Paul's concern here is not to teach about spirituality. He is certainly not giving a detailed ranking of different spiritual manifestations! Rather, he uses the variety of manifestations to teach appreciation for diversity and to call for unity within the body (Fee: 683).

Strive for (NIV, *eagerly desire*) *the greater gifts* (Gk. *charismata*), Paul writes in 12:31. With a significantly nuanced variation, he will pick that up in 14:1, *Strive for the spiritual gifts* (Gk. *pneumatika*). The translation *strive* presents a challenge because one does not normally strive for a gift, and Paul has been particularly careful to argue that the spiritual manifestations are unmerited gifts granted at the discretion of the Spirit. The Greek word translated as *strive for* is *zēloute*, from which we get the English word *zeal*. A better translation than *strive for* or *desire* would be Thiselton's (2000: 1024-25) proposal: *Continue to be zealously concerned about the "greatest" gifts*—with the proviso that the Corinthians accept his redefinition of which are the greatest. This he will pick up in chapter 14, but first he needs to show them *a still more excellent way* (12:31), the attitude and behavior that must provide the setting for spiritual practices.

The Christian Assembly as a Body 12:12-26

The image of the physical body as a metaphor for the social body or society was very common in ancient literature. Philosophers and politicians used it to argue that different gifts and abilities are essential to the whole, particularly in contexts where factionalism was a problem (M. Mitchell: 157-64). Its usual application was as an argument for lesser members of the body politic to defer to those in control. Paul, however, reverses this, using the image to argue that those who are stronger and more honored should give deference to those members who are weaker and less recognized.

He introduces the metaphor in a short paragraph (vv. 12-13). The human body is one, though it consists of many organs. Likewise, the social or political body is one, though it has many members. In both bodies the members perform different functions. In both, the purpose of each part is to contribute to the well-being of the whole. The same holds for the body of Christ.

Surprisingly, Paul did not write "the assembly," but rather *Christ* (v. 12). At the end of his discussion of this metaphor, he repeats the point, effectively bracketing the argument: *Now you are the body of Christ and individually members of it* (v. 27). It seems that he wanted to lift his readers' perspective beyond what was already becoming the institutional church to the organic union of those who are joined to Christ. They have been joined to this body in baptism by the Spirit, he reminds them. They *were made to drink of one Spirit*, he writes (v. 13), driving home the point that the Spirit entered them and filled them, and it is the Spirit, not their efforts or sociopolitical institutions, who creates their unity.

A passing reference to the criteria that formerly divided them into *Jews or Greeks, slaves or free* (v. 13) reminds them that the body of Christ is unlike other social bodies in that it encompasses people formerly separated from each other. (In Gal 3:28, Paul adds "male and female" along with "Jew or Greek, slave or free," but he has already dealt with gender issues in 1 Cor 7 and 11:2-16 and does not return to them here.)

Paul elaborates two aspects of the body metaphor. No member can say *I do not belong to the body* (12:15, 16), and no member can say *I have no need of you* (v. 21). For any physical or social body, including the body of Christ, to be healthy and to function, there is and must be diversity. Through a series of examples, Paul reminds his readers how bizarre it would be to have a "body" consisting of one organ. This eliminates the possibility of any member feeling unnecessary. On the contrary, each member is essential—as is easily demonstrated when any organ is in pain or not functioning properly.

In particular, those organs (members) whose social status and power are weakest and who are most humble do and must receive special care. The sexual organs are implied (Thiselton [2000: 1008] translates *unpresentable private parts*). On the one hand, they are shameful. At the same time, they are also treated with greater honor. Here he returns to a theme that he has already discussed, the relationship between the weak and the strong, the honorable and the dishonorable. *God chose what is foolish in the world to shame the wise; God chose what is weak in the world to shame the strong; God chose what is low and despised in the world, things that are not, to reduce to nothing things that are, so that no one might boast in the presence of God* (1:27-29; cf. 4:10 and 8:7-13). Those who are strong, who are "honorable members" of the body, who think of themselves as spiritually mature—they have a particular responsibility to include, care for, and honor those who are weak, the "dishonorable members."

This lesson, which applies at so many points to matters already discussed in this letter, is especially apt in its context just after the discussion of the Lord's Supper in 11:17-34. In the commentary on that passage, we noted that some members of means were humiliating others in the very ritual that should have unified the members. Paul has already used *body* language in that context; here he elaborates while the example is still fresh in their minds. He underscores the connection by reference to the *division* (12:25 NIV; Gk. *schisma*) in the body, using the same word that he had used in 11:18 to introduce his discussion of their abuses of the Lord's Supper.

Into the midst of this argument Paul drops two reminders that the arrangement of members in the body, whether the human body or the body of believers, is God's decision, not humans' (vv. 18, 24).

Both unity and diversity are essential to a healthy body, and the members are interdependent. What is not possible is uniformity (v. 14), and what is detrimental is dissension (v. 25). Paul's goal is for the congregations to recognize and celebrate all their members and the ways in which God's Spirit has gifted them. This clearly is the message permeating his letter. The divisions of 12:25 are rebuked in 11:17-34 and denounced in 1:10, the thesis statement for the entire letter.

THE TEXT IN BIBLICAL CONTEXT
Calling Jesus "Lord"

The affirmation around which the Christians in Corinth were united was that *Jesus is Lord* (1 Cor 12:3). In Paul's writings, Lord is the most common title given to Jesus. He uses it more than 180 times (in the undisputed Pauline letters). This basic confession is the ground of salvation (Rom 10:9, 13) and the "climactic expression of the universe's worship" (Dunn 1990: 50).

Most English translations of the Old Testament use LORD (with one large capital letter and three small capital letters) where the name of God (represented by YHWH in Heb.) appears in the Hebrew text. This follows the ancient and continuing practice in Judaism and in the LXX of avoiding the name of God as an expression of respect, substituting *Adonai* (Heb.), *Maryah* (Aram.), or *Kyrios* (Gk.) (Hurtado 2003: 109). However, the Hebrew Scriptures never use LORD for the Messiah (Lander: 288).

The Gospels report that Jesus was addressed as "Lord" during his lifetime, and in most cases it was simply a respectful address equivalent to "sir" or even "teacher" (cf. Mark 11:3 and 14:14). Only after Jesus' resurrection did believers begin to speak of him as Lord with an implication of divinity (Luke 24:34; John 20:28; Acts 2:36; Phil 2:9-11; cf. Dunn 1990: 51–53).

Within the Jewish context, the title Lord was probably not the most common or important way of talking about Jesus. Paul often quotes Old Testament passages where "the LORD" is God and then applies it to Jesus (e.g., 1 Cor 1:31 // Jer 9:23-24; 1 Cor 10:22 // Deut 32:21; 1 Cor 10:26 // Ps 24:1; cf. Hurtado 2003: 112–13).

When the faith spread into Hellenistic contexts, it took on a different significance. This was especially true because *kyrios* (Lord) was a key title used in emperor worship, with the claim that "Caesar is Lord" (Dunn 1990: 52). By using that title for Jesus, Christians rejected and challenged the cult of emperor worship and consequently attracted the wrath of Rome or leading local families that promoted emperor worship as a way of bringing honor and prestige to the locality.

Although the use of the title itself became the primary confession of Christian faith, the gospel writers insisted that speaking the title without following Jesus was meaningless for salvation; thus they attribute to Jesus the warning "Not everyone who says to me, 'Lord, Lord,' will enter the kingdom of heaven, but only the one who does the will of my Father in heaven" (Matt 7:21; cf. Luke 6:46; 13:25).

"Body" as a Metaphor of the Faith Community

The image of the body is one that Paul used several times to talk about relationships in the community of faith. The metaphor was not one that he created, but he found it useful as a way to understand the importance of each member [*Bodies in 1 Corinthians, p. 363*].

Earlier in this letter he alluded to the assembly as a body in the context of the Lord's Supper (10:17; 11:27-32), but here in chapter 12 he expands the metaphor to its greatest effect. What Paul elaborates in 1 Corinthians 12 he states more concisely in Romans 12: "For as in one body we have many members, and not all the members have the same function, so we, who are many, are one body in Christ, and individually we are members one of another" (vv. 4-5). His concern in Romans 12 is the same as in 1 Corinthians: members of the faith community should honor one another's place in the community while not denying their own role. He urges his readers "not to think of yourself more highly than you ought to think, but to think with sober judgment, each according to the measure of faith that God has assigned" (v. 3). He lists seven gifts (*charismata*) that should be exercised "according to the grace given to us" (v. 6) and follows that with appropriate attitudes and actions toward other members of the body. Prominent among those are the instructions to "let love be genuine" and to "love one another with mutual affection" (vv. 9-10), also featured in 1 Corinthians 13, which immediately follows and is explicitly tied to the discussion of body relationships in chapter 12.

There are also brief but significant uses of the image in Ephesians (1:22-23; 5:29-30) and Colossians (1:18, 24), where the emphasis is that the body belongs to Christ, its head.

THE TEXT IN THE LIFE OF THE CHURCH

"Jesus Is Lord"

When Paul wrote that *no one can say "Jesus is Lord" except by the Holy Spirit* (12:3), he was making both a theological and a political statement. The Roman imperial cult in the first century demanded the allegiance of all citizens. That allegiance included honoring symbols of the emperor, plus participation in public displays of loyalty and support for the military initiatives that defended and expanded the empire. The language that was used included the confession that "Caesar is Lord" (see "Calling Jesus 'Lord'" in TLC above).

The idols of nationalism in the twenty-first century continue to demand loyalty from citizens. That is expressed in many ways, including oaths of allegiance, willing sacrifice for "national interests," financial and verbal support, and participation in military initiatives. Nationalistic religion, sometimes co-opting a parody of Christian language and at other times rejecting that in favor of the language of secularism, demands the allegiance of citizens. The choice continues: Is the state (government, political party, or ideology) our Lord, or is Jesus our Lord? Will we serve an economic system or a cultural ethos, or will we serve Jesus? How should Christians avoid diluting their loyalty to God's global reign with loyalty to a particular nation?

John Toews, who has citizenship in both Canada and the United States, has described his journey with the question that led him to the point where

> I decided that I would not pledge allegiance in either country, and I would not sing the national anthem in either country.
> Some years later, I also decided that I would not vote in elections in either country. If Jesus is Lord, I reasoned, I should not compromise my allegiance to him by declaring allegiance to any national state. Whenever there is a call to the flag or to the singing of the national anthem in either country, I remain seated. I reject all national state claims to allegiance because I understand my confession that Jesus is Lord to be both a theological and a political statement. I will not compromise my confession that Jesus is Lord by declaring allegiance to Caesar in the form of the Canadian or U.S. national states. I, therefore, also reject both governments' claims that I must do the bidding of these nation states to kill people they define as enemies whether in times of war or peace. The theological-political call of Jesus to love my enemy takes priority over the political call to kill people in the name of any national state government.
> The confession that Jesus is Lord is more than a confession that Jesus is my personal savior. That confession calls for singular allegiance to Jesus over against all the other allegiances that make claims upon our lives. I have decided that these "other allegiances" include the claims of national states. . . . Our citizenship is in the kingdom of God and not in Rome or Canada or the United States. (Toews 2009: 14)

In a similar vein, Richard Hays (1997: 144) asks, "If we display national flags in our churches, are we leading the weak to lose sight of the distinctiveness of Christian discipleship and to confuse faith with patriotism?"

In affirming "Jesus is Lord," Christians reject the view that faith is personal and spiritual and unrelated to political or economic realities.

Spiritual Manifestations Today

A strong tradition in Christian theology called "cessationism" argues that the spiritual manifestations described in the New Testament came to an end as the New Testament era closed and there is no modern experience of them (Turner: 286–302). Although the view has a history dating to some of the early church fathers, it received more attention with the emergence of the Pentecostal movement in the early 1900s and the charismatic movement beginning in the 1960s. In reaction to these developments, some theologians, pastors, and laypersons developed a strong resistance to certain manifestations. But by 2011, Pentecostals and charismatics accounted for 26.7 percent of Christians worldwide, while evangelicals, some of whom also identify as Pentecostal or charismatic, accounted for 13.1 percent (Hackett et al.: 17). Their number continues to grow, and their presence cannot be dismissed by theological denial.

The manifestations of the Spirit given by God are not limited to those identified in 1 Corinthians 12 or any other scriptural compilation. While the experiences and ways of talking about them vary, God's Spirit continues to be active in the lives of people who are attentive to it. Sometimes that is experienced through speaking in tongues, sometimes through prophecy, sometimes through healing, sometimes through other experiences.

Body Image Issues

The Bible has no concept of a follower of Jesus who is not part of the body of Christ. Christ's body is not an invisible "spiritual" reality. It consists of relationships with other believers, all of whom are interdependent with each other and together dependent on Christ as their head.

Just as some people have body image issues in relation to their physical self, and feel anxious, ashamed, or self-conscious about how others perceive them, so also many Christians feel anxious, ashamed, and self-conscious about the body of Christ. This can be expressed in behavior and speech that distances themselves from the church in general, from particular parts of the church (e.g., charismatics, fundamentalists, liberals), or from particular people. Some people are so ashamed of the body of Christ that they deny any affiliation with it.

Counselors who work with people with negative body images try to help them achieve honest self-perception, a realistic expectation of the ideal body, and an acceptance of themselves. These are also appropriate goals for Christians in relation to the church, in both its local and its global configurations. Honest self-perception neither covers up nor overemphasizes the reality of disagreements, embarrassment with each other, and public shame. Realistic expectations depend on realizing that the church belongs to God, not to its members or just the people who agree with and act like us. Self-acceptance includes accepting the "less honorable" members (12:21-25) while also claiming our own place in the church (12:15-20). This applies to individuals, to congregations, and to denominations. The body includes parts that self-identify as Anabaptist, Protestant, evangelical, Catholic, Orthodox, charismatic, African Independent Churches—and some that do not accept any of those categories.

We may be tempted to write off others or to run away. We may fantasize about creating a "perfect body" or having a personal and private spirituality without the messiness of awkward relationships and embarrassing or offensive associations [Spirituality, p. 369]. But God has chosen to incorporate all believers into one body, and we are bound together with each other.

Preaching and Worship

The Revised Common Lectionary includes this whole chapter (1 Cor 12) in several parts. Verses 3b-13 are one of the alternatives to be read on Pentecost in Year A. This is a fitting opportunity to reflect on Paul's discussion of spiritual manifestations in relation to Acts 2:1-21 and other assigned readings for the day. The coming together of Jews and Greeks into one body (1 Cor 12:13); the manifestation of tongues in both passages; and the relationship between Acts 2:21, "Everyone who calls on the name of the Lord shall be saved," and 1 Corinthians 12:3b, *No one can say "Jesus is Lord" except by the Holy Spirit*—these are three of many profitable topics for consideration. The Old Testament lesson from Numbers 11 includes in verse 29 the exclamation "Would that all the LORD's people were prophets, and that the LORD would put his spirit on them!" This would be worth exploring alongside Paul's prioritizing of the manifestation of prophecy—though that is found in the verses after the prescribed reading for Pentecost, and most explicitly when he resumes the discussion about spiritual manifestations in chapter 14.

1 Corinthians 13:1-13

The "More Excellent Way" of Love

PREVIEW

Chapter 13 is commonly called "the love chapter," and rightly so, as the word *love* is used ten times in fourteen verses (including 14:1). Throughout this letter, Paul has written of his love for the Corinthian believers (4:14; 10:14; 15:58; 16:24). He has also written about love for God (2:9; 8:3). Once before he has commended love in contrast to knowledge (8:1), and in his summary injunctions at the end of the letter, he will remind them to *do everything in love* (16:14 NIV). There are several words for *love* in Greek, and Paul uses *phileō* (friendship love) in 16:22, where he points to those who do not have even the least affection for the Lord. Otherwise, throughout the letter he uses *agapē* to name God's love for people, human love for God, and human love between followers of Jesus. In this chapter he elaborates fully on the importance of love as the most important Christian characteristic, the sine qua non, the essential factor of all Christian actions.

This passage has often been used in the context of marriage, both in wedding services and in other reflections on the nature of marital love. Although it is profitable for such an application, we understand Paul's words better if we recall their context in the midst of a congregational debate where mutual respect was lacking and spiritual pride predominated.

The transition from chapter 12 to chapter 13 is found in 12:31b. Paul has discussed the matters of manifestations of the Spirit in worship that the Corinthians had raised and to which he will return in chapter 14. But first he "digresses" to a discussion of *a still more excellent way* (NRSV), or even *the most excellent way* (NIV). This pattern of inserting an argument into the middle of a longer argument is also found in chapter 9, in between chapters 8 and 10. In both places Paul uses this structure to locate a presenting issue within a larger perspective. He will return to answer the questions that were raised, but the broader principle elaborated in the insertion reorients the discussion and provides a rationale that applies even more broadly than the matter at hand.

OUTLINE

The Futility of Loveless Spirituality, 13:1-3
The Character of Love, 13:4-7
The Completeness of Love, 13:8-13

EXPLANATORY NOTES

The Futility of Loveless Spirituality 13:1-3

Love is not one of the manifestations of the Spirit in Paul's lists. Nor is it intended to supersede or replace the manifestations under discussion. Rather, it is the attitude with which all spirituality must be exercised *[Spirituality, p. 369]*. When Paul lists activities that are without value apart from love, he intends that the Corinthians should continue to practice these things, but to do them with an attitude of love that will reshape how these activities are done. Each of the activities listed in this chapter is also addressed elsewhere in the letter: each is a practice or characteristic that is valued by at least some of the Corinthian Christians.

The *tongues of mortals* are skills in oration, perhaps of rhetoric, that were valued in Corinth. In his thanksgiving at the beginning of the letter, Paul recognizes *speech . . . of every kind* (1:5) as part of the *grace* (1:4) or *gift* (1:7) that God has given to the Corinthian believers. He dismisses rhetorical flourishes and tries to make a virtue of his apparently ineloquent speaking style (2:1, 4-5). A frank further acknowledgment of his failure to measure up to their expectations is found in 2 Corinthians: "For they say, 'His letters are weighty and strong, but his bodily presence is weak, and his speech contemptible'" (2 Cor 10:10).

The gift of *speech . . . of every kind* (1:4) that God had granted (at least some of) the Corinthian believers included not only the *tongues of mortals*, but also *the tongues . . . of angels* (13:1). This is the ability to speak "in tongues" that was introduced in chapter 12 and will be discussed further in chapter 14. Paul does not dismiss that ability, but he insists that when practiced without love, it is worthless.

The analogy that he uses to dismiss loveless human or angelic speech had particular resonance in Corinth. The production of bronze ware was a significant part of the Corinthian economy, and the high quality of the workmanship was part of the city's reputation. English translations consistently use *gong* and *cymbal* for the bonze ware that Paul names (v. 1). *Cymbal* is a straight transliteration of the second Greek word (*kymbalon*), but *gong* misrepresents the first. *Chalkos* means copper, brass, or bronze, and it is sometimes used of money or other items made of those metals. But there is no record of it being used of a gong as a musical instrument. Paul may have been referring to the bronze acoustic vases used to amplify the voices of actors in the theater (Thiselton 2000: 1036; Murphy-O'Connor 2002: 75–77). Though that interpretation has been questioned, it is an interesting image and suggests that eloquent oration or speaking in tongues is a hollow echo if love is absent.

Prophecy as a manifestation of the Spirit is also discussed in chapter 12, and especially in chapter 14 (where the words *prophecy* and *prophet* occur fourteen times!). It is the manifestation that Paul favors (e.g., 14:1). Yet here he recognizes that prophecy can be practiced without love, and when that happens, he says, it is worthless.

Understanding mysteries and knowledge is another grace or gift that Paul identifies in the Corinthians in his thanksgiving, along with speech: *knowledge of every kind* (1:5). Though he is grateful for their knowledge, Paul has already discussed that at length as a problem in chapter 8, where he quotes the Corinthian slogan *All of us possess knowledge* and immediately challenges it with the comment *Knowledge puffs up, but love builds up* (8:1). That is much the same point that he is making here: knowledge without love is worthless. In chapter 8 he elaborates that *anyone who claims to know something does not yet have the necessary knowledge; but anyone who loves God is known by him* (8:2-3).

Mysteries are a particular class of knowledge that seems to have intrigued the Corinthians. Paul refers to them in this letter. In 2:1 he writes *I did not come proclaiming the mystery of God to you in lofty words or wisdom*. At that point it is not clear whether this is intended to mean he did not proclaim *the mystery of God*, or that he did not proclaim it in the way they wanted to hear it. Later he calls himself one of the *stewards of God's mysteries* (4:1) and describes as a *mystery* his proclamation that *we will not all die, but we will all be changed* (15:51).

The idea of mystery is associated with mystery cults in the ancient world, where those who were initiated gained secret knowledge. Some Corinthian Christians may previously have been members of mystery cults or may have understood Christianity in that framework. Jewish apocalyptic literature also features mystery, a secret divine plan that only a few insiders know (e.g., 2 Esd 14:5-6; cf. Yoder Neufeld: 49-50). In other letters, Paul writes about the mystery as a secret that in Christ is revealed to all (Eph 3:1-10; Col 1:25-27). Yet he declares that without love, knowledge of mystery is worthless (1 Cor 13:2).

In other letters Paul discusses faith more extensively, but he does not ignore it in 1 Corinthians. He names it as one of the manifestations of the Spirit (12:9)—indeed, as one in the culminating triad of faith, hope, and love in the present chapter (13:13). Elsewhere in the New Testament it is esteemed. For example, faith strong enough to move mountains is mentioned by Jesus in Mark 11:22-24 and Matthew 17:20. It is much valued, but without love even faith is worthless.

Finally, Paul names two extreme forms of self-denial. The first is easily understood, if not easily practiced: giving away all of one's possessions to the poor (1 Cor 13:3). Though Luke reports that Jesus demanded this (14:33; 18:22) and some of his disciples demonstrated it (Luke 5:11; 18:28; cf. Acts 4:32–5:11), it remained an extreme practice.

The most difficult expression in this paragraph is variously translated as *give over my body to the flames* (NIV footnote) or *give/hand over my body to hardship that I may boast* (NIV/NRSV). The difference arises from two manuscript traditions of one word, *kau_ēsōmai*, with one letter difference at the blank: with a *theta* (θ = th) it means *to be burned*, and with a *chi* (χ = ch) it means *that I may boast*. The oldest and best manuscripts have *boast*. The fact that martyrdom by fire was unknown at that time, together with the frequency with which Paul criticizes boasting in this letter (1:29, 31 [two times]; 3:21; 4:7; 9:15, 16; 15:31), tilts us toward thinking that Paul wrote *boast*. Even such a great personal sacrifice is meaningless if done in the absence of love.

Thus far, Paul has named six actions that might be claimed as evidence of advanced spiritual maturity:

speaking in tongues

having prophetic powers

having understanding

having faith

giving away possessions

giving over one's body

Each of these, however, amounts to nothing in the absence of love, "which is the *sine qua non* [there is nothing without it] of Christian behavior" (Fee: 704).

The Character of Love 13:4-7

This paragraph, with its heaped-up descriptors of love, has become a common reference point in weddings and music, secular as well as Christian, in which love is celebrated. It is often extrapolated from its context and used as a generic poem in praise of the attributes associated with selfless love. But when read within its context in this letter, the characteristics listed are specifically relevant to the conflicts between Christians in Corinth.

In almost all English translations, the characteristics of love in this list are in the form of adjectives: in Greek they are verbs. This means that Paul was not describing *qualities* but rather *actions* of love—not "how love looks," but "how love behaves" (Thiselton 2000: 1047). Among English translations, the best equivalent to the verbal structure is found in *The Message*, which says,

> *Love never gives up.*
>
> *Love cares more for others than for self.*
>
> *Love doesn't want what it doesn't have.*
>
> *Love doesn't strut,*
>
> *Doesn't have a swelled head,*
>
> *Doesn't force itself on others,*
>
> *Isn't always "me first,"*
>
> *Doesn't fly off the handle,*
>
> *Doesn't keep score of the sins of others,*
>
> *Doesn't revel when others grovel,*
>
> *Takes pleasure in the flowering of truth,*
>
> *Puts up with anything,*
>
> *Trusts God always,*
>
> *Always looks for the best,*
>
> *Never looks back,*
>
> *But keeps going to the end.*

Thiselton's (2000: 1026) translation also maintains the verb form and will be quoted below alongside the NRSV translation and variants in the NIV translation where they occur.

Paul first names two positive attributes: *Love is patient* and *kind* (v. 4; Thiselton, *waits patiently* and *shows kindness*). Patience is a characteristic of God (Rom 2:4; 9:22; 1 Pet 3:20; 2 Pet 3:9, 15) and of Jesus (*1 Tim 1:16*) and is often identified in the New Testament as a virtue that Christians should adopt. Thiselton (2000: 1046) coins the term *long-tempered* (in contrast to "short-tempered") as an appropriate translation. It is a quality that many people, including Christians, find difficult to exercise. Kindness is often listed together with patience as a characteristic of God (e.g., Rom 2:4; 11:22) and an expected characteristic of Christians (e.g., 2 Cor 6:6; Gal 5:22).

With these words, Paul's readers in Corinth may well have recognized his critique of their impatience in 4:8: *Already you have all you want! Already you have become rich! Quite apart from us you have become kings!* Their failure in kindness can be identified in his claim that he, unlike them, practiced kindness in the face of slander (4:13) or in his critique of their unkindly behavior toward the weak, or toward those they deemed socially or spiritually inferior (8:10-13; 11:17-22).

After two positive characteristics, eight negative statements follow that describe how love does *not* act. The Corinthian readers would quickly have recognized that this list is virtually a catalog of the behavior that Paul has criticized throughout the letter.

Envious (13:4; Thiselton, *burn with envy*) translates a Greek word that can have either positive or negative connotations. It is the word that Paul uses in this section (1 Cor 12–14) to encourage passion for spiritual manifestations (12:31; 14:1, 39). It is also the word that he used in 3:3 to criticize the Corinthians, pointing out that *there is jealousy . . . among you*. Common to both uses is the strength of passion, even of "burning" or "boiling" passion, as the word is used in the LXX. Clearly it is not the intensity of passion that Paul rejects, but rather the focus of it: desire for God's blessing is good; desire for what others have is wrong.

Boastful (13:4; Thiselton, *brag*) identifies another kind of behavior for which Paul has criticized the Corinthians often throughout this letter (e.g., 1:29, 31; 3:1; 4:7; 5:6).

Arrogant (v. 4; NIV, *proud*; Thiselton, *inflated with its own importance*) is closely related to *boastful*. Of the seven times the Greek term for *arrogant/puffed up* is used in the New Testament, six are in 1 Corinthians, where they name the attitude of some of the people to whom the letter is addressed: 4:6, 18, 19; 5:2; 8:1; and 13:4. The contrast between these poles is made explicit: *Knowledge puffs up, but love builds up* (8:1).

Rude (v. 5) is a weak translation of one of the strong Greek words for shame *[Shame and Honor, p. 368]*. A better translation would be *Love does not behave shamefully* (AT; Thiselton, *behave in ill-mannered impropriety*). In this letter the same word has been used to name the possibility that a man might behave shamefully toward his fiancée by refusing to marry her (see EN on 7:36). In 12:23 it identifies those parts of the body that are considered shameful and therefore receive special treatment. Many other behaviors have been identified in this letter as shameful—among them, having one's father's wife (5:1-13), taking a brother to court (6:1-11), consorting with prostitutes (6:12-20), inappropriate hairstyles or head coverings in worship (11:2-16), and ill treatment of fellow believers in the practice of the Lord's Supper (11:17-34). Perhaps most relevant here is the upcoming discussion of propriety in worship, in which Paul will conclude by directing, *All things should be done decently* [the antonym of *shamefully*] *and in order* (14:40).

Insist on its own way (v. 5; NIV, *self-seeking*; Thiselton, *preoccupied with the interests of the self*) is a characteristic of eros love, but not of agape love (Thiselton 2000: 1050–51). Throughout this letter, Paul has repeatedly addressed the Corinthians' preoccupation with self-interest. It pervades everything from subgroup rivalries (1:12-17) to marital relations (7:1-40) to eating food offered to idols (10:1–11:1, esp. 10:24 and 33, which use the same exact word). Followers of the crucified, self-giving Christ do not think first of defending their own rights and maintaining their own advantage.

Irritable (v. 5; NIV, *easily angered*; Thiselton 2000: 1026, *exasperated into pique*) is the result of lacking patience and being preoccupied with self-interest. Strong words, as in the NIV and especially in Thiselton's translation, are needed to convey the force of the Greek.

Resentful (v. 5; NIV, *keeps . . . record of wrongs*; Thiselton, *keep a reckoning up of evil*) suggests a long memory of wrongs suffered, perhaps with a desire for revenge. These last two characteristics are less clearly reflective of Corinthian behavior addressed in this letter. Many of the actions that Paul criticizes are done by those who have power and advantage (i.e., "the strong"). But he does also address "the weak," for whom pique and a record of wrongs might be especially tempting. That might include the one with a grievance in 6:1-11, or the abandoned marriage partners in chapter 7, or those who were humiliated and hungry at the Lord's Supper in 11:17-34.

Indeed, in every circumstance where one person acts unlovingly, the recipient of that action might respond with anger and resentment.

Does not rejoice in wrongdoing (NIV, *delight in evil*), *but rejoices in the truth* (v. 6) expresses two sides of one reality. Love sides with truth and against wrongdoing. In contrast, some of the Corinthians sided with the man who had his father's wife (5:2). They may even have thought that was the loving response to the situation (see EN on 5:2). The same attitude may have held for those who consorted with prostitutes (6:12-20) and those who exhibited various other behaviors.

The word translated here as *wrongdoing* or *evil* (v. 6; Gk. *adikia*) is elsewhere translated as *unrighteousness* or *injustice*. Perhaps Paul has in mind the injustice represented by the court case in 6:1-11 or the injustice that accompanied economic and status inequities (11:17-34).

Thiselton helpfully explores the meaning of *truth* (v. 6) here in the light of postmodern philosophy and critical thinking. "Postmodern philosophers and critical theorists perceive as clearly as Paul did that virtually every action and stance bears some relationship to the power interests of the self or to one's peer group." This leads Paul to understand truth as "disengaged from a power agenda" and reflecting "true disinterested integrity" (Thiselton 2000: 1055). This understanding returns us to *not preoccupied with the interests of self* (v. 5). In contrast to rejoicing in injustice, it describes a perspective free of considerations of power and advantage.

The final statement in this paragraph drives home the scope of love by repeating ... *all things* ... *all things* ... *all things* ... *all things* (v. 7). In Greek it is *panta*, which literally means *all things*, as in the NRSV, not *always* or *at all times*, as in the NIV and some other translations (but see below). What love does with all things is bear, believe, hope, and endure, according to the NRSV. Unfortunately, this translation leads the English reader to think that the person who loves is infinitely easygoing, credulous, optimistic, and tolerant of abuse. Indeed, victims of all kinds of abuse, mistreatment, and oppression have been counseled that this is how they should respond. On this basis, Christians have been taught that they should be passive, docile, and conformist.

But there is room in love for discrimination and correction, as Paul has demonstrated throughout this letter. Paul's intention here is to suggest the limitlessness of love; as he says next, *Love never ends*. The Revised English Bible translation conveys this sense: *There is nothing that love cannot face; there is no limit to its faith, its hope, its endurance*. This translation, unfortunately, loses the parallelism between the four statements and the rhythm of the repetition. But it has the advantage of translating the second word (*pisteuō*) as *faith*, thus preparing us for the triad of faith, hope, and love at the end of the chapter.

With this review we see that Paul is not quoting someone else's poetic description of love, nor is he developing his own universal definition. He is drawing together the objectionable behavior of the Corinthians and contrasting that with the behavior of people who love. While useful as a description of loving actions in other circumstances, it applies most directly to the Christians in Corinth and their conflicts. Paul is challenging them to change their behavior with the goal of overcoming the divisions between them.

The Completeness of Love 13:8-13

The statement *Love never ends* (v. 8a; NIV, *fails*; Thiselton 2000: 1026, *falls apart*) is transitional. It first seems to be part of the serial characteristics of love, but in fact it introduces a new thought: the permanence of love in contrast to the temporality of spiritual manifestations. *Love* is mentioned only at the beginning and end of this paragraph; the remainder is all about the contrasting impermanence of several actions that, in chapters 12 and 14, are identified as manifestations of the Spirit. In this way, Paul prepares the readers for the return to that discussion.

While the word *ends* may represent the point Paul is making, it does not capture the connotation of the Greek. Neither does *fails*. The Greek word means some variation of *fall*. It could be *falls away* (so Geneva Bible, 1599 ed.) or *falls down* (so Wycliffe), but Thiselton's proposal, *falls apart*, suggests the right sense of ending and disappearing that Paul says will come for the spiritual manifestations and will not come to love (Thiselton 2000: 1060-61).

Love, Paul writes, is an eternal reality. In contrast, he pointedly names the manifestations of the Spirit most valued by at least some of the Corinthians: prophecy, speaking in tongues, and knowledge (see vv. 1, 2). He does not say that these are bad, but that they are temporary and incomplete; they are contingent (Thiselton 2000: 1061). Eventually they will fall away. In the end—*the complete* (NRSV) or *completeness* (NIV); *the completed whole* (Thiselton 2000: 1027)— they will not be needed. Though of some value in the present, they are only *partial* (vv. 9-10).

Paul drives his point home with two analogies. A child's understanding is appropriate for a child but inadequate for an adult

(v. 11). Thought processes and vocabulary may be age appropriate, but are only partial. An adult's thoughts and speech are more complete than a child's, but they are still not perfected. The comparison of children to adults is an image that Paul has already used in this letter. He scolds them *not . . . to make you ashamed, but to admonish you as my beloved children* (4:14), and describes himself as their spiritual *father* (4:15). He says they are *infants in Christ*, able only to drink milk and not eat solid food (3:1-2). Shortly he will urge them to *stop thinking like children. In regard to evil be infants, but in your thinking be adults* (14:20 NIV). In each case he is dismissing their claim to spiritual maturity.

The other analogy Paul uses here is that of seeing an image *in a mirror* (v. 12; not *through a glass*, as in KJV) *enigmatically* (AT; Gk. *en ainigmati*). First-century mirrors were made of polished metal, and one of the industries in Corinth was the production of the best bronze mirrors available. Again, Paul was not criticizing the quality of mirrors but making the point that their use is temporary and will come to an end when superseded by face-to-face interaction. Perhaps when he writes of images perceived dimly or poorly, Paul is alluding to Plato's "Allegory of the Cave" (*Republic*). Plato had suggested that unenlightened people are like those who live in a cave and think that the shadows they see reflected on the wall are reality. Those who study philosophy are like those who climb out of the cave and see things in the full light of the sun. But that philosophical discussion of the nature of knowledge is not necessary to support the point he is making.

In contrast to face-to-face interaction, Paul is thinking of using a mirror to see other people or objects. The idea that in the eschaton we will be able to see ourselves fully, in contrast to our current distorted self-perceptions, also serves Paul's argument well, both in this section (chs. 12–14) and in the letter as a whole. Indeed, one might characterize the point of the letter as helping the Corinthians to see themselves *face-to-face*.

Here Paul is echoing the point he made in 8:1-3: *Knowledge puffs up, but love builds up. Anyone who claims to know something does not yet have the necessary knowledge; but anyone who loves God is known by him*. Knowing, even when it will be complete, is less important than being known (by God; 13:12; cf. Gal 4:9), and even that is wrapped up in love.

In the present, Paul writes, faith, hope, and love are active. This triad is named repeatedly (sometimes with other elements) in Paul's letters (Rom 5:1-5; Gal 5:5-6; Eph 4:2-5; Col 1:4-5; 1 Thess 1:3; 5:8) and elsewhere in the New Testament (*Titus 2:2*; Heb 6:10-12; 10:22-24;

1 Pet 1:3-8). Yet in the eschaton, when hope is fulfilled and disappears (for "hope that is seen is not hope," Rom 8:24) and faith is replaced by the full knowledge and presence of God, only love will remain. Love alone persists eternally. All else is temporary and partial. And love is *the greatest* (v. 13).

THE TEXT IN BIBLICAL CONTEXT

Love

The Bible is saturated with love. It spans God's love for humanity (John 3:16), especially for his chosen people (Deut 4:31-37), human sexual love (Song of Sol 8:6-7), close friendship (1 Sam 18:1-3), parental love for children (Luke 15:11-32), and even love for foreigners (Lev 19:34 NIV) and enemies (Luke 6:27-36).

The Hebrew word used for the love of God (and sometimes of humans for God or other humans) is *ḥesed*. English translations use *loving-kindness*, *steadfast love*, or *mercy*. The sense of affection, commitment, forgiveness, and loyalty is represented in this declaration:

> The LORD, the LORD, a God merciful and gracious, slow to anger, and abounding in steadfast love and faithfulness, keeping steadfast love for the thousandth generation, forgiving iniquity and transgression and sin, yet by no means clearing the guilty, but visiting the iniquity of the parents upon the children and the children's children, to the third and the fourth generation. (Exod 34:6-7)

The prophet Hosea used the imagery of marital longing and infidelity to depict Israel's unfaithfulness to Yahweh. His personal marital experience reflected the story of Yahweh's passion and Israel's wanton pursuit of other gods. The pain of God's unrequited love is especially poignant in chapter 11.

> When Israel was a child, I loved him. . . . I was to them like those who lift infants to their cheeks. I bent down to them and fed them. . . . My people are bent on turning away from me. . . . How can I give you up, Ephraim? How can I hand you over, O Israel? . . . My heart recoils within me; my compassion grows warm and tender. (Hos 11:1-8; see Guenther: 182–86)

The New Testament continues to affirm God's love and to call on people in return to love God and those whom God loves. When asked which is the most important commandment, Jesus quoted Deuteronomy 6:4-5 and Leviticus 19:18:

The first is, "Hear, O Israel: The Lord our God, the Lord is one; you shall love the Lord your God with all your heart, and with all your soul, and with all your mind, and with all your strength." The second is this, "You shall love your neighbor as yourself." There is no other commandment greater than these. (Mark 12:29-31)

While every part of the New Testament speaks of God's love and calls on people to respond with love (Acts is the only book that does not include the word *love*), it is especially prominent in the writings of John. God's love for "the world" is declared (John 3:16), and followers of Jesus are instructed to love one another: "I give you a new commandment, that you love one another. Just as I have loved you, you also should love one another. By this everyone will know that you are my disciples, if you have love for one another" (John 13:34-35). This instruction carries forward into the Johannine letters, especially 1 John 4: "Beloved, let us love one another, because love is from God; everyone who loves is born of God and knows God. Whoever does not love does not know God, for God is love. . . . Beloved, since God loved us so much, we also ought to love one another" (1 John 4:7-11).

Paul writes about love in all his letters, not least in 1 Corinthians. Chapter 13 provides concrete instructions for demonstrating love for fellow believers. Paul declares that *anyone who loves God is known by him* (8:2-3). The letter concludes with a declaration of Paul's love for the people to whom he is writing (see "Love the Church" in TLC for 16:1-24).

THE TEXT IN THE LIFE OF THE CHURCH
Failure to Love

Why does the Bible keep repeating the command to love God and to love the people whom God loves? Because people repeatedly fail to do it. Excuses for that abound. The other person is blamed for being unlovable. The meaning of love is distorted to justify unloving actions "in the person's best interest." Love is spiritualized to warrant a claim to love but not to like someone, or to love them but not who they are or what they do. Certain people are excluded from those-we-must-love, as Jesus' questioner did in asking "Who is my neighbor?" in order to narrow the responsibility to "love your neighbor" (Luke 10:25-37). Some forms of Calvinist theology and much folk theology understand that there are people whom God does not embrace, so God's people need not and should not love them.

The inability to act lovingly is reinforced by, if not caused by, a failure to love ourselves. The commandment "Love your neighbor as yourself" (Matt 22:39; Lev 19:18) assumes self-love. But how can you love your neighbor if you hate yourself? People who do not love themselves may think they are unlovable because they have not experienced love. The possibility of loving depends on being loved, and ultimately on being loved by God: "We love because he first loved us" (1 John 4:19; cf. all of 1 John 3–4). How do we know that God loves us? "God's love was revealed among us in this way: God sent his only Son into the world so that we might live through him. In this is love, not that we loved God but that he loved us and sent his Son to be the atoning sacrifice for our sins" (1 John 4:9-10). The incarnation demonstrates God's love, as do Jesus' actions and words as reported in the Gospels. But it is especially Jesus' death on the cross that is, for Christians, the ground of our experience of love and our ability to love others. Paul's focus on the cross as the core of the gospel (1 Cor 1:18-25; 2:1-5) is essential not only to right theology but also to Christians' ability to love and to live in right relationships—which is what ties this whole letter together.

Miroslav Volf upholds the centrality of the cross in his book *Exclusion and Embrace*. He writes, "A genuinely Christian reflection on social issues must be rooted in the self-giving love of the divine Trinity as manifested on the cross of Christ; all the central themes of such reflection will have to be thought through from the perspective of the self-giving love of God" (25). Volf addresses cultural clashes, national or "tribal" animosity, interreligious conflict, and gender identity. The principles he identifies apply equally to relationships in families and in faith communities.

The dynamic of exclusion that Volf addresses is the human inclination to define "us" and "them" and, when pressed, to dehumanize "them." He explains that sometimes we do this because of "a projection of our own individual or collective hatred of ourselves; we persecute others because we are uncomfortable with strangeness within ourselves" (Volf: 77–78). At other times "we are uncomfortable with anything that blurs accepted boundaries, disturbs our identities, and disarranges our symbolic cultural maps." Furthermore, "we exclude because we want to be at the center and be there alone, single-handedly controlling 'the land'" (78). And at the root of all these is sin: "'Exclusion' names what permeates a good many of sins we commit against our neighbors [though it is] not what lies at the bottom of all sins" (72).

The opposite of exclusion is what Volf calls "embrace"—that is, in essence, redefining "them" as "us." "God's reception of hostile humanity into divine communion is a model for how human beings should relate to the other" (100). Surely this is what Paul was attempting in his discussion of the body (12:12-26) and the need to embrace both the weak and the strong in the faith community (8:7-13). Volf uses this model, illustrated by the story of the prodigal son, as a backdrop for detailed discussion of repentance, forgiveness, making space in oneself for the other, and healing memories. In all of this he is informed, among many factors, by his experience as a Croat reflecting on the violent civil war in the former Yugoslavia.

Volf offers specific applications of exclusion and embrace to issues of oppression and justice, deception and truth, and violence and peace. Oppression, deception, and violence—sometimes overtly and sometimes subtly—are present in faith communities and families. The goal of reconciliation and the reign of God demand that they be overcome with justice, truth, and peace. Therefore it is essential that we pay careful attention to the forces that prevent us from embracing and loving our relatives, our friends, our fellow Christians, our neighbors, and our enemies. Embrace is, in effect, a way of talking about love, and exclusion is a failure to love.

Preaching and Worship

Particular care must be taken to avoid sentimental or emotional reflection on this text that is easily absorbed into romanticized ideas of either erotic or pious affection. Although Paul wrote this passage for a situation of conflict in the Corinthian congregations, it is not inappropriate to use it to discuss love in marriage and other relationships.

1 Corinthians 14:1-40
Manifestations of the Holy Spirit, Part 2

PREVIEW

Back now to the questions about particular manifestations of the Spirit. Having established that love is *the most excellent way* (12:31 NIV) to practice the gifts that God gives, Paul now returns to the discussion that he had interrupted at the end of chapter 12. The two particular manifestations that he discusses are speaking in tongues and prophecy. Some of the Corinthians favored the first. Paul's favorite, in the context of congregational worship, was the second.

The criterion that Paul offers for valuing spiritual manifestations was what contribution they make *for building up the church*, the body of believers (vv. 4, 12, 26). Intelligible speech, especially prophecy, has the potential to build up the community, he argues. Unintelligible speech cannot do so unless someone interprets and thus makes it intelligible to the listeners. This is what he means by *the greater gifts* (12:31).

Paul uses building imagery in 1 Corinthians more frequently than in any other letter (and more than any other New Testament author). In 3:9-15 he uses building-related words twelve times, talking of the faith community as God's building. Earlier he framed his response to the questions about eating idol food by reference to love that builds up the family of faith (8:1; 10:23). Now he writes another six times about building up the body, culminating with *Let all things be done for building up* (vv. 4 [two times], 5, 12, 17, 26). The theme is picked up again in 2 Corinthians 10:8; 12:19; 13:10. Clearly this is an image of considerable importance for his counsel to the Corinthian assembly.

His conclusion to the discussion of exercising spiritual manifestations in worship is also the conclusion to the longer section, where he addresses several issues related to worship, including headship and decorum (11:2-16) and sensitivity to the body in the Lord's Supper (11:17-34). So his instructions for orderly worship (14:26-40) apply to all aspects of worship, not only to speaking in tongues or prophesying.

Within those concluding comments is a brief discussion of the silencing of women in worship (14:34-36). We will consider that separately from the rest of the passage.

OUTLINE

Body Building through Exercising Manifestations of the Spirit,
    14:1-25
Orderly Worship, 14:26-33
Side Note: Rebuking Those Who Silence Women in Worship,
    14:34-36
Concluding Instructions about Worship, 14:37-40

EXPLANATORY NOTES

Body Building through Exercising Manifestations of the Spirit 14:1-25

Verse 1 is transitional: it restates the point of chapter 13, *Pursue love*; it recalls the end of chapter 12, *Strive for the [greater* in 12:31] *spiritual gifts*; and it introduces what follows, *especially that you may prophesy* (14:1).

There is a difference, however, between 12:31 and 14:1: the former speaks of *charismata*, and the later of *pneumatika*. This is the word that Paul used to introduce the topic in 12:1. In returning to the subject of *pneumatika*, he reminds the readers of his starting point for this discussion. Here, unlike in 12:1, the form of the word is clearly neuter. A more appropriate translation would be simply *the spiritual*, or *spiritual things*, rather than *spiritual gifts* (see EN on 12:1).

We recall that Paul is responding to something that the Corinthians wrote to him in their letter, perhaps a statement about their worship practices (see preview to ch. 12) *[What the Corinthians Wrote, p. 372]*. While we cannot know with certainty what they had written, it seems clear that at least some of them were proud of their ability to speak in tongues and enthusiastic about practicing that in worship.

But Paul advances several arguments to support his view that prophecy is better than speaking in tongues in public worship.

1. What is spoken *in tongues* is addressed to God, not to people. People cannot understand what is said. Paul describes it as *speaking mysteries in the Spirit* (v. 2). Prophecy, on the other hand, can be understood by people who hear it *for their upbuilding and encouragement and consolation* (v. 3).

2. *Those who speak in a tongue build up themselves* (v. 4a). Paul recognizes the value of speaking in tongues for the speaker's spiritual encouragement, but not for the community, and thus its place is in private devotion rather than in corporate worship. In contrast, *those who prophesy build up the church* (v. 4b), so prophecy is to be preferred in corporate worship over speaking in tongues.

3. Paul, in agreement with the Corinthians, values speaking in tongues, and he wishes everyone to experience that manifestation of the Spirit. Even more, he wishes everyone to exercise the manifestation of prophecy (v. 5).

4. Prophecy is better, although if *someone interprets*, then speaking in tongues can also build up the body (v. 5). So Paul says that someone should interpret. Later he says that *one who speaks in a tongue should pray for the power to interpret* (v. 13; see discussion below).

Paul broadens the categories of intelligible speech to include *some revelation or knowledge or prophecy or teaching* (v. 6). He considers prophecy to be the greatest manifestation of the Spirit, but his criterion is that intelligibility of speech determines whether the listeners will be built up. Thus, all forms of intelligible speech in public worship are preferable to unintelligible speaking in tongues without interpretation.

Paul uses three analogies to drive home his point. In the first, he compares speaking in tongues to playing a *lifeless* musical instrument, *such as the flute or the harp*. It will not be understood *if they do not give distinct notes* (v. 7). He seems to have in mind a player whose melody is unrecognizable and thus does not communicate to the listener. In that case, the hearer would not be moved by the music.

Next, he compares speaking in tongues to an *indistinct* military *bugle* call: if not properly understood, it will not communicate the urgency of going into battle (v. 8).

Finally, he says, *Undoubtedly there are all sorts of languages in the world, yet none of them is without meaning* (v. 10 NIV; cf. NRSV, *many different kinds of sounds . . . without sound*). If someone speaks a language we do not understand and no one translates for us, we are foreigners to each other, we are "estranged" (Hays 1997: 236). This also applies when someone speaks in tongues and does not interpret the message.

Once again Paul mentions the Corinthians' zeal—not commending them for being *eager for spiritual gifts* (NRSV; see discussion on *pneumatika* above and at 12:1), but rather asserting that they are *zealous for things of the Spirit*, or perhaps simply *spiritual zealots* (v. 12 AT). He does not discourage this but urges them to focus their zeal toward those manifestations of the Spirit that build up the body. Here he does not name prophecy specifically, though he has argued that prophecy is one activity that builds up the body. Prophecy itself is not his goal, but rather the building up of the body.

Speaking in tongues does not engage the mind of either the speaker or the listener (v. 14). It is not created in the mind of the speaker, but is exercised by the Spirit, so the speaker does not understand what is being said (it has spiritual value for the speaker that does not depend on intellectual understanding, explains Fee [728]), and certainly the listener does not. Thus the listener cannot *say the "Amen"* or confirm what is spoken (v. 16), nor is the listener *built up* by it (v. 17). The solution is not to disallow speaking in tongues, but to insist that such speaking be interpreted. Paul says he will *pray* and *sing praise with the spirit* (or *with the Spirit*, i.e., in tongues) and also *with the mind* (i.e., intelligibly, v. 15).

After all his arguments in favor of prophecy and other intelligible speech, Paul shocks his readers by proclaiming, *I speak in tongues more than all of you* (v. 18). It is not because of his lack, but rather because of his frequent speaking in tongues that he could call others to restrain themselves. Once again, as in chapters 8–10, and especially chapter 9, Paul holds himself up as a model of restraint. Even if it is his right to do so, he will do nothing that might hinder another believer. This principle, which has come out several times in this letter, also applies to speaking in tongues.

While he may practice speaking in tongues in private, he implies that in the assembly of believers he would choose to speak a few *(five) words* intelligibly than many *(ten thousand) words in a tongue* that cannot be understood (v. 19).

Brothers and sisters, Paul writes, *do not be children in your thinking* (v. 20; NIV, *stop thinking like children*). Perhaps they would hear echoes of his similar language in 3:1-4. Certainly they would recognize that he was shaming those who thought themselves to be spiritually mature.

The appeal to Scripture in 14:21 seems to be from Isaiah 28:11-12, though that is part of the Prophets, not of the Torah (*the law*) in the Hebrew Scriptures, and the quotation is not quite the same as either the Hebrew Bible or the Septuagint translation. It appears that Paul intentionally modified the quotation. His point seems to be that when people are addressed in a language they cannot understand, they do not listen. If even God were to address people of faith in an unknown language, as in the case of speaking in tongues, they would not listen.

Verse 22 is difficult as a straight statement because it is immediately contradicted in the following comments and is inconsistent with what precedes it. It is possible that this jarring statement was actually made by some of the Corinthians who argued that unbelievers would be impressed by the spiritual manifestation of speaking in tongues, while only insiders would understand prophecy. Perhaps they supported their claim by the (awkwardly quoted) reference to *the law* in verse 21 (Janzen: 64–65). Alternatively, it may be a sarcastic comment by Paul that could be paraphrased this way: "You think speaking in tongues is a sign for unbelievers? Sure: a sign that you are all out of your minds. You think that prophecy is a sign for believers? Sure: it convicts people of sin and they become believers."

Up to this point, Paul's arguments in favor of prophecy and other intelligible speech have been entirely focused on what would build up those who are members of the faith community. Now he turns briefly to the impact on *outsiders or unbelievers* (v. 23). He suggests that if uninitiated persons attend a gathering where *everyone* (NIV; probably overstated, certainly hypothetical) is speaking in tongues, surely they will say, "*You are out of your mind*." This does not mean insane but rather that "they have temporarily been caught up in a fit of religious ecstasy, a common phenomenon in that culture" (Hays 1997: 238; see v. 15, contrasting *mind* and *spirit*).

On the other hand, if *everyone* (NIV; again, probably overstated, certainly hypothetical) in the assembly is prophesying, a visitor will be *reproved* (NIV, *convicted of sin*) *by all and called to account by all* (v. 24). Clearly the word of prophecy is a pronouncement of the gospel that touches the heart of the hearer as unintelligible speech cannot. *The secrets of the unbeliever's heart are disclosed* (v. 25), not by fortune-telling, for that is not what prophecy is, but by the exhortation of inspired proclamation. That person will recognize God's presence in the assembly, in contrast to the one who sees people *out of their mind* (v. 23) in ecstasy, and will be moved to worship. The worshipful response to the witness of God's people echoes Isaiah 45:14 and Zechariah 8:20-23 (Hays 2005: 1-4).

Orderly Worship 14:26-33

We have now reached the end of four chapters in which Paul has been addressing issues of proper decorum in worship. They began with a discussion about proper exposure or covering of the head when praying or prophesying in corporate worship (11:2-16). Then there was a response to reports of drunkenness, gluttony, and class discrimination at the Lord's Supper (11:17-34). The longest discussion has concerned the manifestations of the Spirit in public worship, especially speaking in tongues and prophecy (12:1-14:25).

We noted in the preview to chapters 11-14 that even with this much attention to matters of worship, we do not have a comprehensive introduction to Paul's thoughts about the significance or practice of worship. Several implications for such a statement can be drawn, but as always in this correspondence, we listen to one side of a conversation in midstream. Paul taught and modeled proper worship when he was in Corinth. Subsequent variations, other influences, and new questions led to changes in practice and disputes about how things should be done. These matters are contentious, not the core of good practice, and receive attention in this letter.

Having dealt with several divisive issues, Paul now wonders: *What then shall we say* (14:26a NIV; NRSV, *what should be done*) about how worship ought to be conducted? He says two things. First, *each one has a hymn, a lesson, a revelation, a tongue, or an interpretation* (v. 26b). We can understand that these were elements of worship in the congregations that Paul established, though not a complete listing since there is no mention of reading Scripture or of preaching (the *lesson* and *revelation* do not seem to cover the kind of preaching represented in Acts) or of the Lord's Supper. Nothing is said about the sequence of these events, and nothing is said about leadership. Everyone is expected to contribute to the worship experience. The impression is that the assembly participates according to the prompting of the Holy Spirit, without formal liturgy (except for the simple liturgical forms around the Lord's Supper, described in 11:23-26; possibly also the "Amen" response to a thanksgiving in 14:16), and without formal leadership. Yet it is not undisciplined or unfocused, as we shall see below.

Second, *Let all things be done for building up* (14:26c). This is the twentieth and final time in this letter that Paul uses building language to talk about the faith community. It summarizes his concern not only for worship (cf. 14:4, 5, 12, 17) but also for other behavior (8:1; 10:23) and for his own and others' roles in establishing the assembly in Corinth (3:9-15). The importance of this language for the Corinthian situation is underscored by the fact that Paul rarely uses it in other letters. Building up the community is the goal toward which he is calling them throughout the whole letter, the implementation of his desire set out in his thesis statement, *that all of you be in agreement and that there be no divisions among you, but that you be united in the same mind and the same purpose* (1:10).

The general directive is followed by several specific instructions. Speaking in tongues is acceptable, but only two or at the most three should do so; and only one at a time. Given the Corinthians' fondness for speaking in tongues, this was probably a constraint on their practice. And if one or more people speak in tongues, each should be followed by interpretation, as Paul has argued earlier (12:10, 30; 14:5, 13). *But if there is no one to interpret, let them be silent in church and speak to themselves and to God* (v. 28; i.e., in private devotion).

Two or three people *may* speak in tongues, provided interpretation is given, and two or three *should* prophesy (v. 29 NIV). Again we see Paul's preference for this gift. Even words of prophecy must be weighed by *the others*—apparently by the whole congregation, since each one has received a *manifestation of the Spirit for the common good* (12:7). The purpose of prophecy is building up the body, *so that all may learn and all be encouraged* (14:31). Furthermore, one who is prophesying cannot dominate, and must be silent if another receives *a revelation* (v. 30). Prophecy is not uncontrolled speech, but rather is controllable by the speaker (v. 32).

All of these instructions shape worship to build up the faith community, and it should be done with control and dignity, for *God is a God not of disorder but of peace* (v. 33a). As Fee (772) states, "The character of one's deity is reflected in the character of one's worship." The God who made order out of chaos in creation, whose mission is to establish peace in the world, must not be worshiped in disorder and unrestraint.

Side Note: Rebuking Those Who Silence Women in Worship 14:34-36

Just before the end of this discussion of worship regulations, there is a brief statement that the NRSV editors have placed in parentheses. The NRSV and some other translations include verse 33b with 34-36, but NIV 2011, along with some other translations and commentators, includes 33b with 33a (Fee: 772–73). Some ancient manuscripts include this paragraph after verse 33; others place it after verse 40. It may well be considered an aside or even an interjection or a marginal gloss, probably from some other source (Fee: 780–81; cf. Hays 1997: 245–49; Thiselton 2000: 1147–50). Many arguments have been offered, but the flow of the argument from verse 33a to verse 37 is smoothest without verses 34-36, and thus we understand the decision of the NRSV editors to bracket the three and a half verses.

If Paul did write this paragraph, this "aside" can only be understood as a genuine argument between Paul and the Christians at Corinth about right worship practices (M. Mitchell: 281–82n536).

Because the instruction for women to keep silent in the assembly (vv. 34-35) contradicts the assumption in 11:2-16 that women will be praying and prophesying in public worship, many commentators find it hard to believe that Paul wrote this. Furthermore, the evidence in Romans 16 and Philippians 4:2-3 of women in leadership in the congregations that Paul established and Paul's declaration in Galatians 3:28 that "there is no longer male and female . . . in Christ Jesus" raise doubts about whether he would have argued for women to be *silent* and *subordinate* in worship. Would he have argued that on the basis that it is *as the law . . . says* and that *it is shameful*?

A clue to the correct reading of this interjection is found in the relationship of verse 36 to what precedes it. The sarcastic questions *Or did the word of God originate with you? Or are you the only ones it has reached?* are clearly dismissive of those who disagree with Paul. This is a rhetorical device that we have seen often in this letter, always where it contradicts what has just been quoted (6:12-13; 7:1; 8:1). Indeed, the statements that are (almost) universally agreed to be quotations from Corinthian opponents are identified exactly by the contradiction that immediately follows them: for example, the statement that *all things are lawful* is contradicted by Paul's *but not all things are beneficial*, and further, *but not all things build up* (10:23). This pattern suggests that verses 34-35, justified by 33b (though some take 33b to be the conclusion of 33a, we take it to be the beginning of the following verses; cf. Thiselton 2000: 1148), are in fact a statement made by some of the Corinthian Christians and that Paul disagrees with it (Nighswander: 185–92; Janzen: 55–70).

Some commentators argue that "there is no precedent for such a long quotation and countering argument that is also full of argumentation" (Fee: 705). But as we have noted throughout this commentary, the other quotations are taken from the letter that Paul had received, or they are slogans easily recognized, so a brief reference would suffice to identify them. In this case, however, it was necessary to state in full what Paul understood his opponents to be saying. We do not know who presented this argument, but there is no hint that it came from the letter the Corinthians sent to Paul. Without his quotation of their statement, or at least their views, they would not have known that this matter was "on the table." Yet it is consistent with the resistance to marriage (7:1) and the insistence on women having their heads covered in worship (11:2-16) that we have identified as views held rigidly by some in the Corinthian assembly, and only in a modulated form by Paul.

Paul did not agree with the silencing of women, as his dismissive reply in verse 36 demonstrates. As with the anti-marriage statement of 7:1 and other examples throughout this letter, subsequent interpretation has missed Paul's intention by taking the words of his opponents as his own.

Concluding Instructions about Worship 14:37-40

We have seen that some members of the Corinthian assembly were critical of Paul and questioned his authority. Several times he asserts his right to give instructions (see esp. EN on ch. 4). Here too, after giving directions for proper worship, he declares his authority to do so. His instructions, he says, are *a command of the Lord* (v. 37). To any self-styled prophets or persons who take pride in their spiritual maturity, he throws out the challenge to acknowledge this. *Anyone who does not recognize this*, he says, *is not to be recognized* (v. 38). The naming of *anyone who claims to be* (NIV, *thinks they are*) *a prophet, or to have spiritual powers* (v. 37) recalls those who think they *are wise* (3:18) and those who think they *know something* (8:2). Together these three characteristics represent "the self-understanding of the 'strong' Corinthians: wisdom, knowledge, and spirituality" (Hays 1997: 245; cf. Fee: 777). Paul consistently calls these people to humility and to recognition of his authority.

After this stern warning to anyone who would disagree with him, the concluding words are a summary of this chapter and of the longer section on worship that begins at 11:1. It reiterates Paul's dominant concern that *all things should be done decently and in order* (v. 40; NIV, *in a fitting and orderly way*; AT, *with due propriety*; cf. v. 33a). That includes prophecy, which he encourages the Corinthians to pursue zealously (cf. 12:31; 14:1, 12), and speaking in tongues, which he says should be permitted (14:39): notice the difference in emphasis. It also includes the vocal participation of women (11:5; 14:34-36) and other activities of worship (14:26), as well as the Lord's Supper (11:17-34) and decorum while praying and prophesying (11:2-16).

THE TEXT IN BIBLICAL CONTEXT
Worship in the Bible

The Bible includes many stories about worship, including informal and spontaneous outbursts of praise (e.g., Jacob, in Gen 28:16-20), simple rituals performed in families (e.g., Noah, in Gen 8:20), or by appointed priests (e.g., Samuel, in 1 Sam 7), and massive gatherings of people around elaborate liturgies (e.g., the rededication of the temple, in Ezra 6:16-22). It includes instructions for proper worship and rebuke for improper worship. These include warnings against idolatry (e.g., Deut 32) and denunciation of hypocrisy (e.g., Hos 6:6).

There are elaborate instructions for every detail of the construction of the tabernacle and its furnishings (Exod 25-27, 30), the liturgical vestments (Exod 28), and the liturgy of investiture (Exod 29), followed by reports on how the instructions were implemented. Likewise, the building of the temple in Jerusalem by King Solomon is described in detail (2 Chron 1-7). The rituals for various festivals are described, as are the instructions for performing appropriate sacrifices (e.g., Lev 1-7; the first story of sacrifice is told of Cain and Abel, Gen 4).

The largest book in the Bible (Psalms) is a collection of psalms, or hymns, for use in personal and corporate worship. Many additional hymns are recorded in the Old Testament, such as Moses's and Miriam's songs of praise after the crossing of the Red Sea (Exod 15), and the victory song of Deborah and Barak (Judg 5).

At some point after the destruction of the first temple, a new venue for worship was created: the synagogue. Whereas temple worship focused on sacrifice, synagogue worship focused on the written Scriptures and consisted mostly of reading a prescribed text and elaborating on it in a sermon (see Luke 4:16-27). The first followers of Jesus participated in temple worship (Acts 2:46), as had Jesus (Luke 2:41-52; 21:1, 38). Outside of Jerusalem, and especially as the faith spread in Hellenistic contexts, the structure of synagogue worship influenced early Christian worship.

The pattern of worship described in 1 Corinthians 11-14, especially in 14:26-40, is informal and spontaneous, with many people contributing. It includes readings, prayers, hymns, and manifestations of the Spirit, such as prophecy and speaking in tongues. Baptism and the Lord's Supper were practiced with limited ritual formality. In other early Christian communities, worship was more controlled, with only authorized leaders reading and teaching (e.g., 1 Tim 4:13; Titus 1:9-11). John's gospel represents a community where the spirit of worship is valued above institutions and rituals (John 4:23).

As Christianity became increasingly differentiated from Judaism, temple worship, sacrifice, the priesthood, and the religious festivals of Judaism were repudiated or reinterpreted (John 2:19-22; Rom 12:1; Heb 10:1-14; 1 Pet 2:4-9; Col 2:16-17; 1 Cor 5:7-8).

Common to all the teaching about and examples of worship in the New Testament is the focus on Christ (see Hurtado 1999: 63–97). Scriptures were interpreted in light of his life, death, and resurrection (e.g., Acts 2:14-26), and hymns declared his praise (e.g., Col 1:15-20; Phil 2:6-11). Prayer was offered in his name (e.g., Rom 1:8; John 16:23-24), and the rituals of baptism (e.g., Acts 2:38; 8:16; 10:48; Rom 6:3-4; Gal 3:27) and the Lord's Supper (1 Cor 10:14-21; 11:17-34) both imitated and interpreted his life. The culminating vision of the New Testament is the gathering of all people to worship God and the Lamb of God (Rev 19:6-8 et passim).

Speaking in Tongues in the First Century

The phenomenon of "speaking in tongues" is named only in 1 Corinthians 12–14, in four instances in the book of Acts, and in the appendix to Mark (16:17). In each case, except perhaps Mark, it is recognized by believers as a manifestation of the Holy Spirit. Some of the incidents in Acts depict speaking in human languages unknown to the speaker. The experiences discussed in 1 Corinthians are speaking in human or nonhuman languages (*tongues of mortals and of angels*, 13:1) that need interpretation to be intelligible to the speaker or to bystanders.

In Acts 2:1-13, the apostles were given the ability to speak in languages they had not learned. This oral phenomenon accompanied a visual phenomenon of "divided tongues, as of fire" that "appeared among them, and a tongue rested on each of them" (v. 3). The vision was apparently visible only to the 120 disciples (1:15)—or perhaps only the twelve apostles—who were gathered in one room, but the speaking was audible to all, presumably in a larger setting (Faw: 42), and it attracted the attention of the "devout Jews from every nation under heaven living in Jerusalem" during the Passover festival (v. 5). Some of these hearers attributed the ability of uneducated Galileans to speak many languages to drunkenness (v. 13). Others were "amazed and perplexed" (v. 12), giving opportunity for Peter to address them (in what language?) with the message about Jesus.

Later, Peter was convinced through a dream to share the message of Jesus with Cornelius, a Gentile. As he did so, "the Holy Spirit fell upon all who heard the word," and they began "speaking in tongues and extolling God" (Acts 10:44-46). Peter observed that "these people . . . have received the Holy Spirit just as we have" (10:47), but it is not clear whether the tongues in which they spoke were human or "angelic" languages. Peter and his companions baptized these Gentile believers after the Holy Spirit fell on them.

Two similar incidents are reported in Acts when the Holy Spirit came upon people. The first was when Peter and John were sent by the believers in Jerusalem to the new believers in Samaria (8:15-17). Although they had been baptized in the name of Jesus, they had not received the Holy Spirit. When Peter and John laid hands on them and prayed, these too received the Holy Spirit. Although it is not specified that they spoke in other languages, that seems to be implied (v. 18).

The parallel event occurred when Paul learned that the believers in Ephesus had been baptized "into John's baptism" and had not received the Holy Spirit (19:1-7). Paul rebaptized them "in the name of the Lord Jesus" and laid his hands on them (apparently in prayer), and they received the Holy Spirit. This was manifested by speaking in tongues, presumably in nonhuman languages, and prophesying.

The Holy Spirit's activity is often mentioned in Acts (the Spirit is named fifty-eight times), but only in these instances is speaking in tongues mentioned.

THE TEXT IN THE LIFE OF THE CHURCH

The Practice of Worship

Paul was concerned that the Corinthians were being disorderly in their worship. That is not a problem in most Christian churches in the twenty-first century. The process of institutionalization has imposed order in the form of liturgy and fixed traditions, even in "free" and "charismatic" churches, so that worship in most churches is predictable and constrained—done *decently and in order* (1 Cor 14:40).

Have we overlearned the principle of orderliness? If he were writing a letter to our congregations, would Paul advise us to be more free in worship? In reading "other people's mail," as we do when we study this letter addressed to *the church of God that is in Corinth*, it is important to discern which instructions pertain only to those specific circumstances and which pertain also to life in our congregations that are removed by two millennia of history and vastly different cultural settings.

Several principles about worship practice that Paul wrote to the Corinthian congregations are relevant twenty centuries later. Here are several that are offered as a starting point for testing and refinement in particular settings.

First, worship is for building community, not just for the individual believer (14:3). Worshipers are in relationship with each other, not only with God. The criterion for right worship is not what it does for me as a worshiper, but how it contributes to building up the whole body. That sometimes means giving up what I think would be right for "me" in favor of what is right for "us." This applies not only to speaking in tongues, but also to musical styles, meeting space architecture and furnishings, and use of technology—indeed, every aspect of corporate worship.

Second, although the primary purpose of worship is not "marketing" faith to nonbelievers, worship should be open to visitors (14:16, *an outsider*; NIV, *an inquirer*). Indeed, their presence should be expected, and worship should be sensitive to their ability to understand and participate (vv. 16, 23-24). This does not mean that the language or format of worship needs to be "dumbed down," but it must be in a language that visitors can understand, and the actions of worship must be explained. The problem of being foreigners to each other in worship (v. 11) is overcome when there is interpretation of words and actions.

Third, right worship should engage worshipers emotionally and intellectually (14:14-15). Considering what we now know about different learning styles, right worship must engage people who are imaginative learners (through reflecting on their life experiences), others who are analytic learners (valuing rationality and linear thinking), those who are commonsense learners (learning through actions), and some who are dynamic learners (looking for creative applications of what they receive) (Lefevre: 178–92; see also, e.g., "Overview of Learning Styles" on the website Learning Styles Online). Virtually all personality-type classifications have been applied to worship styles. We might think of this as engaging our brains and our hearts, or as finding ways to "love the Lord your God with all your heart, and with all your soul, and with all your mind, and with all your strength" (Mark 12:30).

Fourth, proclamation of the gospel (*prophecy*) is important in worship (see "The Importance of Proclaiming the Gospel" in TLC for 1:18-25; and "Sharing the Gospel" in TLC for 9:1-27). Throughout its history, Christian worship has highlighted the ministry of the word in the reading of Scripture and preaching. In the Protestant Reformation, the Reformed and Anabaptist streams especially elevated this. In the Roman Catholic and Anglican Mass, the Eucharist continued to hold the center, and in Lutheran worship the Word and Sacrament held equal emphasis. The form and style of preaching have varied over time, influenced by changing communication patterns and the abilities of the preacher. In the twenty-first century, some preachers are moving toward extended sermons with an emphasis on preaching, while others are shortening sermons and embellishing them with visual images and other formats to accommodate the expectations of listeners and ideas about effective communication.

Though the style should vary by local expectations and circumstances, some form of proclamation of the gospel is essential to right worship. It is important for building up, encouraging, and consoling those who are already part of the faith community (14:3-4), and for convicting "outsiders" (vv. 24-25). The Corinthians preferred speaking in tongues over prophecy, perhaps because the prophetic word might challenge, convict, and correct them. They would rather practice their private worship (in a public setting) that revealed nothing. In the same way, "praise and worship" can be used to avoid the theological and moral challenge of the proclamation of the gospel.

At the same time, proclamation needs to be tested, as Paul writes (v. 29). This obligation to *weigh what is said* is every worshiper's responsibility, and it extends beyond silent listening and personal reflection. It should not happen only through criticism muttered in the parking lot, at home after the service, or through anonymous messages via social media. Worship should include ways for people to say "Amen" or "Yes, but" or even "That's wrong" to the preacher and the congregation. In some traditions, designated persons, often other clergy, state an "Amen" or a further comment after the preacher finishes. In other traditions there is ongoing response from people in the congregation as they call out during the service. Some preachers use interactive technology to gather responses from their listeners in real time. Others have discussion groups before or after the sermon for further elaboration and testing. Each congregation and preacher must find suitable ways in their setting to *weigh* the proclamation in the manner of the people in Berea, who "welcomed the message very eagerly and examined the scriptures every day to see whether these things were so" (Acts 17:11). Anabaptists valued this principle so highly that they dubbed it the "rule of Paul," which is that Scripture is best interpreted in and by the community of believers as a whole (Swartley 1989; Brown: 86, 101, 210; Murray: 125-57).

Fifth, many voices should be heard in worship (1 Cor 14:26; see Williams and Williams). Worship is not "going to church" and observing passively what one or a few people present. Several people should contribute prayers, music, preaching, and other components of worship, both within each service and over time. This should not be limited to "professional" or highly competent voices. Participation is more important than polish. Women and men, including children and adults of all ages, should contribute. Special attention should be paid to how people with physical and cognitive disabilities can play a significant part in corporate worship.

Multivoiced worship requires sensitive management of time and restraint of those who might be inclined to dominate or to contribute inappropriately (vv. 27, 29-30; Williams and Williams: 71-72), but those considerations should not excuse complete silencing of any voice.

Sixth, there should be room in corporate worship for spontaneous irruptions of the Holy Spirit. This may take the form of speaking in tongues and interpretation; it could also be unscripted testimonies, prayers, and songs.

Scripted liturgy has many advantages. It reduces the possibility of omitting important acts or words, it can help an inexperienced leader and congregation to worship with more grace and dignity, and it can connect one worship experience with the long history of worship over time and with other congregations that use the same liturgy around the world. A prescribed form of worship with prepared prayers, songs, responses, confessions, Scripture readings, sermon, and rituals—whether planned for a specific service or prescribed by tradition and denominational regulation—can ensure that worship is done *decently and in order* (v. 40).

But worship without room for unscripted prompting of the Spirit can suppress the prophetic voices that institutions may not welcome and the contributions of less eloquent voices. It can also become boring, routine, and irresponsive to the needs of the worshipers as well as the "new things" that God wants to do and say (cf. Isa 48:6).

Speaking in Tongues in the Twentieth and Twenty-First Centuries

When Pentecostalism emerged in the United States early in the twentieth century, the spiritual manifestation of speaking in tongues was the focus of much debate. Pentecostal revivalists emphasized it as evidence of Holy Spirit's presence. Opponents insisted that the practice or "gift" had ended with the early church (even though it has been practiced by individuals and marginal Christian groups at various times throughout history), and that the movement to reintroduce it was heretical, even demonic. Established denominations rejected the practice, and new denominations emerged that accepted and expected speaking in tongues and other manifestations.

By the late 1960s, however, the charismatic movement was affecting Catholic and Protestant churches of all denominations. Some new denominations emerged that were sympathetic to the practices of speaking in tongues, healing, prophecy, and uninhibited worship, but many people who were attracted to and touched by these trends, including some clergy, remained in their denominations and introduced changes in them.

Charismatic understandings and expressions of Christian faith have found enthusiastic welcome in many parts of the world. The number and size of charismatic churches globally is growing both through missionary activity and through new religious movements.

Despite continuing resistance in some circles, it is now widely recognized that speaking in tongues and other "spiritual gifts" or manifestations can be exercised by some Christians, but they are not experienced by all Christians and are not a necessary demonstration of the Holy Spirit's presence and blessing (cf. Faw: 55–56, 319–20).

Prophecy in the Twentieth and Twenty-First Centuries

Thiselton (2000: 956–65, 1087–94) has reviewed the scholarly discussion on prophecy in Paul's writing, especially in 1 Corinthians, and has summarized it in eighteen pages. He concludes,

> In summary, prophesying in Paul's theology and in his argument in this chapter [14] *is the performing of intelligible, articulate, communicative speech-acts, the operative currency of which depends on the active agency of the Holy Spirit mediated through human minds and lives to build up, to encourage, to judge, to exhort, and to comfort others in the context of interpersonal relations.* (1094, emphasis original)

"Such a definition," Thiselton adds, "is not comprehensive." Clearly, this is a controversial topic.

What is noticeably missing from this definition is any hint of prophecy as prediction of future events. "In Paul's view the primary focus of a prophetic utterance is not the future, but the present situations of the people of God" (Fee: 729). In contrast, much of the discussion about prophecy in the last century has focused on interpreting Bible passages in relation to current events, in order to forecast the future.

The Corinthians would have been familiar with the prophetic activities of various oracles (Witherington: 277). Those who were familiar with the Hebrew Scriptures would also have known that although the prophetic tradition included some prediction, prediction was not primary. "Forthtelling" was more common than "foretelling" in both Jewish and Hellenistic prophecy. Prophecy was more about *upbuilding and encouragement and consolation* (14:3) than it was about omens. It belongs in the same classification as *revelation, knowledge*, and *teaching*, but is distinct from them (14:6).

Many Christian traditions do not recognize prophecy as a continuing manifestation of the Holy Spirit. Pentecostal and charismatic churches are the exception. John Penney, a scholar in the Pentecostal tradition, recognizes that the risks of unaccountable prophecy today parallel the hazards faced in the early church.

The Pentecostal tradition rejects prophecy characterized by the following:

- a triumphalism which uncritically applied promises from the biblical traditions to excite the unstable masses with what they wanted to hear.

- the proud aspirations and spiritual self-recommendation of prophets who placed themselves above critical judgment.

- a popular following of those who were weak and insecure in their faith, looking for easy solutions and solace to answer difficult problems and avoid repentance.

- the extravagant lifestyle and sometimes immorality of the prophet, financed by his personal popularity in the circles of the wealthy and powerful.

- a claimed ability to prophesy on request and in private and to impart prophetic inspiration to others, with apparent disregard for the sovereignty of God. (Penney: 82)

To avoid such perils, Penney writes, Paul insists that prophecy is to be tested; and the advice is as relevant now as it was in the first century (Penney: 83–84).

Intelligible Communication

Many people like to quote a statement attributed (wrongly) to Francis of Assisi, "Preach the gospel at all times; if necessary use words." It seems to reflect 1 John 3:18: "Little children, let us love, not in word or speech, but in truth and action," or Jesus' denouncement of those whose words ("Lord, Lord") are not consistent with their actions, of whom he asserted instead, "You will know them by their fruits" (Matt 7:15-27). It is a welcome relief to those who are uncomfortable with verbalizing their convictions.

Inconsistency between one's "talk" and one's "walk" invites scorn and criticism. Actions, "fruits," are more reliable indicators of beliefs and values than words. But actions are notoriously ambivalent. Like words spoken in an unknown tongue, acts of piety, rituals, and jargon must be accompanied by interpretation in order to be understood, especially by those who do not share the same culture, values, and assumptions. In worship and in witness, faith must be both demonstrated and articulated.

Silencing Women in the Twenty-First Century

The brief paragraph in 14:34-36 has been quite controversial in the history of the church. Together with *1 Timothy 2:11-15*, these few verses have been used to restrict women's participation and especially leadership in worship and other church activities. As Western cultures have become more receptive to women participating and leading other institutions, this restriction has come under increasing criticism.

It is argued above that the desire to silence women's voices came from the Corinthians, not from Paul. His recognition of women leaders and his teaching on gender relationships were inconsistent with this demand. In any case, the argument that *it is shameful for a woman to speak in church* (v. 35) is clearly at odds with contemporary Western culture. It does not have continuing relevance where women and men have equal access to education, manifestations of the Spirit, and social status. In contexts where women's voices are silenced in the twenty-first century, the church's responsibility is to demonstrate acceptance, respect, and freedom. In addition to honoring the full participation of women in worship, teaching, leadership, and service in the church, Christians should also promote the full exercise of women's voices in other social institutions, including families.

Preaching and Worship

Churches that use the Revised Common Lectionary exclusively will never hear a reading from this chapter. Yet it is an important resource for preaching on manifestations of the Spirit (perhaps together with portions of chs. 12–13), on building up the community of faith (perhaps together with other portions of 1 Corinthians), and on proper worship. Pastors will want to find opportunities to preach this part of the letter.

1 Corinthians 15:1-58

Christ's Resurrection and Ours

1 Corinthians 15:1-58
The "Sure and Certain Hope" of Resurrection

PREVIEW

The body of this letter is almost complete. The contentious issues have been addressed, and a couple of questions that the Corinthians had raised will be dealt with briefly before the closing words. There remains one important topic to be addressed: what the traditional Anglican/Episcopalian funeral service aptly calls the "sure and certain hope of the resurrection to eternal life, through our Lord Jesus Christ" (BCP).

Although there is no hint here that the Corinthians had written a question to Paul about resurrection, he knew something of the views that they held. He states, *some of you say there is no resurrection of the dead* (15:12), and in typical diatribe fashion he names questions that *someone will ask* (v. 35), likely reflecting questions he knew some Corinthians were asking. He may also have heard that some Corinthians were being baptized on behalf of the dead (v. 29). Despite the fundamental importance of the subject matter (v. 3), the tone of this chapter does not have the emotional intensity of Paul's discussion of matters raised by Chloe's people (1:11), which characteristically includes reference to what has been *reported* (1:11; 5:1) or what Paul has heard (11:18). Most likely, therefore, Paul's source of information about the Corinthian views on resurrection was the letter carriers, Stephanas, Fortunatus, and Achaicus (16:17).

From the beginning of chapter 5 to the end of chapter 14, Paul has addressed behavioral matters. Now he turns to an issue of doctrine, of faith rightly understood. Throughout his arguments to this point, Paul has identified doctrinal bases for the behaviors and attitudes that he promotes. This is the first time in the letter that he presents a sustained discussion of a theological matter. Yet even here he points to the ethical implications of the theology (15:33-34, 58). Getting the ideas right is not the end, but a means toward the end of living rightly in relationship with God and with people.

The divisions that caused tension in Corinth (1:11-13 and throughout) are not at the forefront in this chapter. Although Paul suggests that some—not all—of the members hold false understandings, there is no evidence that these questions are contentious in the assembly. Nevertheless, Paul is still addressing the fundamental issue of disunity. His point is that the death and resurrection of Jesus and the anticipated resurrection of Jesus' followers are fundamental convictions (*of first importance*, v. 3) that they *all* share (vv. 28, 51) and that are the ground for their faithful work (v. 58).

This discussion of the resurrection concludes the body of this letter. Chapter 16 is essentially a series of closing remarks. Because of its prominent placement, we must understand this section (ch. 15) to be Paul's crowning argument for the thesis stated in 1:10, *Now I appeal to you, brothers and sisters, by the name of our Lord Jesus Christ, that all of you be in agreement and that there be no divisions among you, but that you be united in the same mind and the same purpose.* From the resurrection of Jesus and the hope of resurrection of his followers flow all the arguments for unity and ethics in the intervening chapters.

The arguments of chapter 15 are complex, with many subclauses and side comments, all of which are important, but which may obscure the main line of reasoning. The outline of Paul's statement is this: The core of the gospel is the resurrection, after the crucifixion, of Jesus: *Now I would remind you, brothers and sisters, of the good news. . . . For I handed on to you as of first importance what I in turn had received: that Christ died for our sins, . . . and that he was buried, and that he was raised on the third day, . . . and that he appeared* (15:1-8). Jesus' resurrection ensures the resurrection of his followers: *Now if Christ is proclaimed as raised from the dead, how can some of you say there is no resurrection of the dead? . . . In fact Christ has been raised from the dead, the first fruits of those who have died* (vv. 12, 20). The resurrection body will be different from our current bodies but no less real: *But someone will ask, "How are the dead raised? With what kind of body do they come?" . . . Flesh and blood cannot inherit the kingdom of God, nor does the perishable inherit the imperishable. Listen, I will tell you a mystery! We will not all die, but we will all be changed* (vv. 35, 50). So hold fast: *Therefore, my beloved, be steadfast... because you know that in the Lord your labor is not in vain* (v. 58).

OUTLINE

The Core of the Gospel is Embodied in Jesus' Crucifixion and Resurrection, 15:1-11
Jesus' Resurrection Ensures the Resurrection of His Followers, 15:12-34
The Resurrection Body: Different from Our Current Bodies Yet No Less Real, 15:35-57
So Hold Fast, 15:58

EXPLANATORY NOTES

The Core of the Gospel is Embodied in Jesus' Crucifixion and Resurrection 15:1-11

Paul introduces this topic by anchoring it in the message he had first proclaimed at Corinth. He calls it a reminder (lit. *make known*—yet another instance where knowledge is an issue between Paul and the Corinthians) and points out the following:

1. He had preached the *good news*, or *gospel* (NIV).
2. They accepted it.
3. They continue to stand in it.
4. They are being saved through it.

The *gospel*, as Paul uses it, encompasses the message about the cross (see 1:17) and the resurrection—indeed, the whole message of salvation (4:15; 9:12-23; see Thiselton 2000: 1184 and works cited there). Salvation through the gospel is conditional on continuing to hold firmly to the message that he has proclaimed, he cautions, perhaps anticipating the ethical counsel of 15:33-34, 58. If they are not being saved by this message, then their faith is in vain—a point that he will pick up in verses 14-19.

As Paul has done previously (1:18), so too he writes here of salvation in the present tense, *you are being saved* (15:2). This is not a past event already completed, as some of the Corinthians held, nor is it only a future event (though Fee [800n33] sees "a futuristic nuance"), but one that is ongoing, being played out in the present. Furthermore,

Paul reminds them that salvation is at God's initiative, named in the passive and not the active voice.

At this point it is not Paul's intention to teach new understandings to the Corinthians but to remind them of the beliefs they had already accepted and held in common with him. He reminds them of this in verse 1 and again in verse 11.

The good news that Paul preached was a message he had himself received from others. The language here echoes the language of 11:23, although here he does not specify that he received this *from the Lord*. It is generally understood that he is quoting from an early confessional formula, on the bases summarized by Fee (798n22) as "(1) The fact that he says it is something he both 'received' and 'passed along' to them; (2) the stylized form of four statements in two balanced sets; (3) the repeated *hoti* [= that] before each clause, which implies a kind of quotation; and (4) the appearance of several non-Pauline words in such a short compass."

The message is described in four actions:

Christ died

>   *for our sins,*
>
>   *in accordance with the scriptures;* . . .

he was buried, . . .

he was raised

>   *on the third day,*
>
>   *in accordance with the scriptures,*

and he appeared. . . .

The first and third of these are most important; each is highlighted by the addition of an adverbial phrase and by noting that it happened *in accordance with the scriptures*. It is not clear to what specific Scriptures, if any, the confession refers in either case.

In the first case, the phrase *in accordance with the scriptures* does not modify *died*, as no Old Testament Scripture anticipates that the Messiah would die. If it modifies *for our sins*, the closest parallel may be the servant song in Isaiah 53, which several New Testament writers understood to be fulfilled in Jesus' passion (cf. Matt 8:17; Luke 22:37, though not exact parallels).

The reference to the resurrection on the third day is similar. Since no Old Testament Scriptures anticipate the death of Messiah, none explicitly anticipate his resurrection either. Several passages, such as Psalm 16:9-10, may be interpreted as anticipating a resurrection.

Hosea 6:2 and Jonah 1:17 have been suggested as anticipations of resurrection after three days. But none of these is specific enough to be the source for the claim that Paul seems to be making.

Since specific scriptural references cannot be found as proof texts for the confessional claims, it is likely that the allusion is to the general thrust of the (Old Testament) Scripture, which Christians reinterpreted in light of their encounter with Christ and their knowledge of his death and resurrection. Thus, we should understand "the resurrection of Christ as the witness to a climactic fulfillment of a cumulative tradition of God's promised eschatological act of sovereignty and vindication in grace" (Thiselton 2000: 1195).

In this chapter Paul uses the word *raised* eight times (and once more in 6:14) in reference to the resurrection of Christ (vv. 4, 12, 13, 14, 15, 16, 17, 20). In each case he uses the perfect passive indicative form of the verb. The indicative mood is used for a simple statement of fact. The perfect tense indicates that it happened in the past and has continuing effect into the present. And the passive voice serves to remind the reader that Christ did not raise himself. Rather, God acted to bring this about. In comparison, each time Paul refers to the resurrection of people (vv. 15, 16, 29, 32, 35, 42, 43 [twice], 44) he uses the present passive indicative. The present tense implies that the action is currently happening. Only once, in his climactic statement in verse 52, does Paul use the future tense to indicate his confidence that *the dead will be raised* (emphasis added).

While the affirmations *that Christ died . . . and that he was raised* are the most important of these four statements, the other two are significant in their support of these. *That he was buried* underscores the physicality of his death, an important emphasis in this context where the discussion turns on the expectation of a bodily resurrection. And the reminder *that he appeared* testifies to the physicality of the resurrection. Some of the Corinthians had reacted to the anticipation of a bodily resurrection, as the rest of this chapter shows, so the additional reminders of Christ's bodily burial and bodily appearances prepare the reader for this argument.

The list that Paul provides of witnesses to the resurrection is intended to remove any doubt about it. Cephas (Paul's usual name for Peter—see 1:12; 3:22; 9:5; also Gal 1:18; 2:9, 11, 14) is listed first. Matthew's gospel (28:1-10) and John's gospel (20:11-18) report that Mary Magdalene (and Matthew adds "the other Mary") was the first to meet the resurrected Jesus, but these stories were written long after Paul wrote this letter, and he apparently did not have access to the traditions that remembered this event.

After mentioning Christ's appearance to Cephas, Paul lists an appearance to *the twelve* (v. 5; he ignores the absence of Judas, probably using the traditional designation for the group without consideration of the literal number), then to *more than five hundred brothers and sisters at one time* (v. 6). There is no other account of a resurrection appearance to such a crowd, but Paul names it and underscores the reliability of his witnesses by noting that *most* of them, not all, *are still alive* (v. 6), implying that his claim can be verified by asking the witnesses directly. After this he lists another appearance to James (most commentators understand this to be the brother of Jesus [Matt 13:55; cf. Gal 1:19], not the disciple who was a son of Zebedee [Mark 1:19]), and another to *all the apostles* (v. 7), which, especially given Paul's inclusive use of the term, could have included more than *the twelve*.

While the Gospels recount several resurrection appearance stories (see "Postresurrection Appearances of Jesus" in TBC below), each one reports different events. Paul's list of appearances is not the same as those reported in the Gospels, though there is some overlap. This is not a significant problem. It simply demonstrates that each of the writers who reported resurrection appearances either selected or had access to only part of the story. Even a combination of all of these accounts probably does not represent all the resurrection appearances.

If the amount of elaboration indicates the importance of his points, Paul is clearly concerned to claim his own place among the witnesses to the resurrection. This is a challenge, because he was not one of the twelve nor even one of the five hundred. Indeed, he acknowledges that the appearance to him was untimely and unique. Nevertheless, he does claim that the risen Christ appeared to him, no doubt referring to his experience on the road to Damascus (Acts 9:1-6). He did not understand this to be a mystical vision, but a bodily appearance of the resurrected Jesus equivalent to that experienced by the other witnesses (cf. 1 Cor 9:1).

The word that Paul uses as a metaphor of his inclusion in this list is peculiar. It means miscarriage, abortion, or stillbirth. Translators have chosen euphemisms like *one untimely born* or *one abnormally born* (NIV). It is an awkward expression for this context, and many commentators have suggested that Paul used it because his opponents in Corinth had used it of him (e.g., Fee [813]). So Paul takes their derogatory term and uses it to acknowledge his late (not literally premature) coming to faith and call to apostleship.

Paul's self-effacing posture in 15:8-10 is consistent with the humility that he has demonstrated earlier in the letter, especially in 2:1-5; 4:9-13; and 9:1-27. Although he uses the opportunity to restate his claim to recognition as an apostle, he describes himself as least among the apostles (15:9), taking responsibility for his persecution of believers, and giving credit entirely and exclusively to God's *grace* for the claim he makes, named three times in verse 10 (cf. 3:10).

In the end, however, Paul's qualifications do not matter, nor do those of the other apostles. He makes and defends these claims only to substantiate the reliability of the message he has first proclaimed in Corinth and continues to proclaim (the verb is in the present tense), the basis of the Christians' first belief: that *Christ died* and *was raised*, resurrected.

This opening to the argument is not intended to prove that Christ has been resurrected but to remind the Corinthian Christians of what they and Paul have already affirmed in common. They have already *come to believe* this to be true (15:11). Where they differed was in how they understood what this belief implied for the anticipated resurrection of Christ's followers. It is to this that Paul now turns.

Jesus' Resurrection Ensures the Resurrection of His Followers 15:12-34

The summary of the first eleven verses is given in verse 12. The literal translation of the Greek text is *Christ is preached, that he was raised from the dead*. The NRSV is closer than the NIV to the Greek text here, making the point that Christ is the content and focus of Paul's and others' preaching, and that proclamation includes his resurrection.

What Paul has heard (see preview to ch. 15) is that *some of* [the Corinthians, not all] *say there is no resurrection of the dead* (v. 12). They did not deny the resurrection of Christ; they have come to believe through Paul's proclamation (v. 11). What they have denied is the resurrection of others, the physical resurrection of Christians who have died. Paul has chosen to respond with words that emphasize the physicality of death and of resurrection. He does not write about resurrection from death (Gk. *thanatos*; only in vv. 21a, 22, *death came . . . all die*, and in vv. 54-56, *death has been swallowed up in victory*), but from or of *the dead*, or literally *of the corpse* (Gk. *nekros*—many English words referring to a corpse use the prefix *necro-*).

Since only some of the Corinthians denied the resurrection of corpses, we might speculate about which faction in the assembly would resist that doctrine. The most likely candidates are those who adhered to Greek philosophy as their standard. Various Greek philosophers, in particular Plato (see his *Phaedo*), taught a dualism of body and soul. It is likely that those Christians in Corinth who had been exposed to or educated in philosophy held such views and were repulsed by the physicality of Paul's teaching about resurrected corpses. Most likely they would have been among those few who were *wise, powerful,* and wellborn (1:26).

In reply, Paul identifies the implications for Christian faith and experience of denying the resurrection. He declares that you cannot have it both ways: *If there is no resurrection* [or *If the dead are not raised*], *then Christ has not been raised* (15:13, 16). Later he states the same point in reverse: [*Christ*] *whom* [*God*] *did not raise if it is true that the dead are not raised* (v. 15b).

If Christ has not been raised, then Paul's proclamation, which is founded on the death (15:3; cf. 1:17, 23) and resurrection (15:4) of Jesus, obviously has been in vain and indeed has misrepresented God. Furthermore, the Corinthians' *faith has been in vain* (15:14) and *futile* (v. 17): they have not been forgiven or freed from their sins, the forgiveness that Paul declares in verse 3. In addition, their brothers and sisters in Christ who have died have not experienced that for which they had hoped. That is, they have died in their *sins*, with no hope of a future, because an unresurrected Christ could not have saved them from their sins (vv. 17-18; Fee: 825). Indeed, if Christ has not been raised, then Christians are most pitiable *of all people* (v. 19). Hays (1997: 262) summarizes it nicely: "There is no authentic Christian faith without fervent eschatological hope, and there is no authentic eschatological hope without the resurrection of the dead."

Paul does not think that Christian faith is only about "pie in the sky by and by." That would overstate the meaning of verse 19. He recognizes the value of Christians' hope in Christ for living this life, but he insists that is not the whole of it. The salvation that Paul preaches is for this life and beyond.

Thus far, Paul has been describing the implications of hypothetical possibilities: *if* the dead are not raised and *if* Christ has not been raised, all these things follow. But all of that argument he now casts aside. Finished with speculation, he turns to certainty, from "what if" to *in fact*.

In fact Christ has been raised from the dead (v. 20). And because Christ has been raised as *first fruits*, then *in fact* Christians will also be raised from the dead. *First fruits* is a common expression for the earliest products of the harvest, which assure the subsequent fullness of harvest. Here it is a metaphor of the promise of resurrection (repeated in v. 23; cf. 2 Thess 2:13, where the Thessalonian believers are called "first fruits for salvation"; Deut 26:1-11). The expression triggers a longer discourse on the inevitability of the subsequent harvest and the sequence of events by which the harvest will unfold (1 Cor 15:21-28).

Resurrection is as inevitable as death, Paul writes. Both were initiated by one person's experience, which led the way for followers: Adam led the way for all people to die, and Christ led the way for all to be made alive. This point is so important that Paul states it in verse 21 and then restates it other words in verse 22.

The sequence of events, Paul writes, is very orderly.

First was Christ's resurrection. Second, and only at the time when Christ appears, is the resurrection of those who *belong to Christ* (v. 23). The faith community in Paul's day and until now lives between phase one and phase two of the resurrection sequence. After the resurrection of believers will be the end, the highlight of which is Christ handing over the kingdom to God the Father, with every enemy, including death, having been defeated. Finally, *the Son himself* will submit to the Father, and God will be *all in all* (vv. 24-28).

Paul says that *all* will die (though in v. 51 he modifies this to exclude those who are alive at the last day—cf. 1 Thess 4:15-17), *all* will be raised (v. 22), and that finally *all* will be subject to God (v. 27), who will be *all in all* (v. 28—not meaning the merging of all things into a metaphysical unity, but the full exercise of God's sovereignty; see Fee: 841). However, the only people whose resurrection Paul includes in this sequence are *those who belong to Christ* (v. 23). Silence about those who do not belong to Christ does not necessarily mean they are excluded from resurrection, but Paul does not address that. His intention is only to convince his readers that Christians will be resurrected as Christ was resurrected. In this instance, the fate of unbelievers was not addressed. It is characteristic of Jewish apocalyptic literature that it is interested only in the resurrection of "the righteous," not the resurrection of all people (Thiselton 2000: 1231).

In listing the enemies of God who will be defeated at the end, Paul names *all dominion, authority and power* (v. 24 NIV). These refer to cosmic forces and also to the political forces of the empire (see Eph 3:10; Rom 8:38; Col 1:16; 2:10-15; Eph 1:21; 6:12). Witherington (295-98, 305-6) points out that one of the titles of the emperor was "father of the fatherland," a title and honor that Paul attributes to God. The assertion that all things, including the empire and its rulers, will be subjected to God through Christ is thus a rejection of the claims of Rome and any other human who attempts to usurp God's authority.

Paul alludes to Psalm 110:1 and Psalm 8:6 (1 Cor 15:25, 27), drawing from those texts support for his understanding of Christ's role. These texts, which originally referred to the king (Ps 110:1) or to human beings (8:6), take on added significance when read through the early Christians' experience of Christ.

Verse 29 (of 1 Cor 15) is an enigma. Although a great deal of speculation has been offered about who might have received baptism on behalf of the dead and why, we do not know to whom or to what practice Paul was referring (see, e.g., Fee: 845–49; Thiselton 2000: 1240–49). This practice is mentioned nowhere else in early Christian literature. (Second Macc 12:42-44 speaks of prayers on behalf of the dead, but not of baptism.) Apparently some people in Corinth were practicing vicarious baptism, though Thiselton (2000: 1248–49) and several others suggest that they were baptized not *on behalf of* but *for the sake of* the dead, that is, in the hope of joining those who have gone before. In any case, we note with interest that Paul neither condemned nor condoned the practice. He simply points out that there is no point in being baptized on behalf of the dead if there will be no resurrection.

Furthermore, Paul argues (1 Cor 15:30-32), his own (*we* in v. 30 is immediately focused to *I*) voluntary submission to danger on behalf of the gospel is pointless if there is no resurrection because that would render his gospel *vain* (see v. 14). Fighting with wild beasts is a metaphor for the struggles to which he has exposed himself. Dying *every day* (v. 31) is a hyperbole, though in 16:9 he mentions the many adversaries he faces in Ephesus, and 2 Corinthians 1:8-11 elaborates on the life-threatening dangers he experienced there. The reality of putting his life on the line (Thiselton [2000: 1250] translates *I court fatality*) is real, and Paul points out that it is pointless if there is no resurrection hope.

Finally, Paul says there is no incentive for moral living if there is no resurrection (vv. 32b-34a). The quotation *Let us eat and drink, for tomorrow we die* echoes Isaiah 22:13, a passage that scolds the people of Jerusalem who, surrounded by the Assyrian army and threatened with death *tomorrow*, decided to party the night away. They should rather, Isaiah had written, have repented with "weeping and mourning, . . . baldness and putting on sackcloth" (22:12). So too those Corinthians who denied the hope of a bodily resurrection were given, Paul suggests, to dissipation and self-indulgence. Perhaps he is alluding to the earlier discussions about eating in temples (1 Cor 10) and drunkenness at the Lord's Supper (11:17-22). This judgment is not unlike his earlier quotation of Exodus 32:4, 6: *The people sat down to eat and drink, and they rose up to play* (1 Cor 10:7).

Bad company ruins good morals is a quotation from a play by Menander that had become a common proverb. Framed by *Do not be deceived* and *Come to a sober and right mind*, it suggests that Paul understands the Corinthian Christians to have come under the influence of outsiders who have led them astray, both in their understanding of resurrection and in their behavior (15:33-34). These two are related, and Paul's correction of their thinking will, he believes, straighten out the errant behavior that he has addressed throughout this letter.

It seems likely that the *some* of verse 12 are the same as the *some* who *have no knowledge of God* in verse 34. Paul pokes at their propensity to boast about their superior knowledge in this twelfth and last reference to *knowledge* in this letter. *Knowledge puffs up*, he wrote in 8:1 (see corresponding EN). Here, as in 8:2 (and more subtly in 3:2; 6:2, 3, 9, 15, 16, 19; 9:13, 24), he deflates their claim to knowledge. Indeed, their lack of knowledge, he says, is a matter of *shame* (cf. 4:14; 6:5) *[Shame and Honor, p. 368]*.

In sum, Paul offers five arguments to support his contention that Christians do and should anticipate that they will be resurrected from the dead:

- Without resurrection, preaching the gospel or believing it is pointless.
- Christ was raised from the dead, so those who belong to Christ will also be raised.
- The practice of vicarious baptism is pointless if there is no resurrection.
- Paul's exposure to danger makes sense only if there is hope of a resurrection.
- Nonbelief in resurrection has negative moral implications.

The Resurrection Body: Different from Our Current Bodies Yet No Less Real 15:35-57

Paul now turns to address questions that he thinks some of the Corinthians are asking: *How are the dead raised? With what kind of body will they come?* (v. 35). There is no suggestion that these questions had been posed in their letter. It is likely that those who carried the letter explained that this was an issue.

The shift from the previous argument is represented by a change in language. In verses 12-34, when writing about the possibility of resurrection of the dead, Paul uses *nekros* (see EN on v. 12). In verses 35-57 the discussion is about bodies, and he uses *sōma* [Bodies in 1 Corinthians, p. 363].

The questions that Paul poses are a rhetorical device, characteristic of a diatribe, to introduce the topic that he wants to address. He raises hypothetical questions to give himself an opening to answer them. However the questions were raised, Paul clearly understood that some of the Corinthians recoiled from the idea of a literal, physical resurrection of dead believers, as we have already noted in the discussion above.

To Greeks, the dualistic worldview that separated the physical realm from the spiritual created an impossible barrier to a bodily resurrection. They did not deny the reality of the spiritual realm, but the idea that a physical body could enter that realm was impossible. So while they could embrace the possibility of an immortal soul continuing beyond the death of the body, they could not imagine a bodily resurrection (Wright: 35-36). No doubt their respect for Paul was diminished, in part, by this "crude" concept that he taught.

Paul responded to their objection by addressing the nature of the resurrection body. The two hypothetical questions he poses are the same. *How are the dead raised?* means *With what kind of body do they come?* (v. 35). Although that question doesn't encompass their whole objection, it is crucial to their failure to understand.

Paul's first response is a dismissive interjection: *Fool!*, or *How foolish!* (NIV), or perhaps *You nonsense person!* (Thiselton 2000: 1257). Their question and their objection are not to be taken seriously. They have stumbled over too literal an understanding of the resurrection of the body, when their imagination should have opened their minds. It was the Corinthians, not Paul, who had conceived the vision that repulsed them.

An adequate understanding of resurrection bodies can be gained from the natural world, Paul says. Seeds die to produce life (v. 36; cf. John 12:24). By looking at a seed, one cannot imagine the plant that will grow from it (v. 37). God has given each plant its shape and form, and likewise to its seed (v. 38). It is foolishness to look at seeds and ask, *With what kind of body do they come?* Through experience one can look at a grain of wheat or rice, or the seed of a radish or marigold, and imagine the plant that will grow from it. But when presented with an unfamiliar seed, whose mature plant we have never seen, our imagination does not serve.

Just as varieties of plants differ from each other, so also do varieties of animals (v. 39). If he had cared to do so, Paul could again have made the point that he made with plants, that an egg does not show us the form of the turtle or emu that will hatch from it, and a tadpole is not a frog.

In all of these examples we must remember that Paul was using the understanding of botany and astronomy that was available to him. There was widespread agreement among ancient philosophers and laypeople alike that human souls become heavenly bodies after death, a view that was shared by some Jews, as Daniel 12:3 demonstrates: "Those who are wise shall shine like the brightness of the sky, and those who lead many to righteousness, like the stars forever and ever" (D. Martin 1995: 117-20; this view is still held by many in the twenty-first century). We should not make too much of the (un)scientific value of his metaphors.

Paul's point in 1 Corinthians 15:35-41 is simply that nature is replete with varieties of bodies, and bodies develop from seed to their mature forms. We should not expect anything different from the human experience in being transformed from our present bodies to our resurrection bodies.

Furthermore, he argues in the next paragraph (vv. 42-49), the nature of the resurrection body is not only different from but also far superior to our present bodies. Continuing with the metaphor of planting seed, he says that our current bodies (the seed) are perishable, dishonorable (or humiliated), weak, and physical (but see discussion below on this translation), while resurrection bodies are imperishable, glorious, powerful, and spiritual (vv. 42-44). Thiselton (2000: 1272) argues that *imperishable* is an inadequate translation because the Greek word does not mean "permanent," but rather "flourishing." He suggests the pairing of *decay* and *decay's reversal*. As Hays (1997: 272) puts it, "[Paul] is seeking to make the resurrection of the dead seem appealing rather than appalling to the Corinthians." This much is obvious.

Less obvious is Paul's argument in the rest of this paragraph (vv. 44-49). The point that he wants to make is apparent: our present bodies are not the bodies of the resurrection (which point he has already made). The differences are represented by the contrasts between Adam, *the first . . . Adam*, and Christ, *the last Adam*. How he makes this point requires some explanation, especially since it is difficult to express in English translation. To understand it we must resort to Greek vocabulary.

Verse 44 speaks twice of a *sōma psychikon*, which is translated into English as *natural body* (NIV and most others; NRSV's *physical body* is an unfortunate translation because it supports the physical/spiritual dualism that Paul was rejecting [Thiselton 2000: 1275]). *Sōma* is the common Greek word for body, and it is used twenty-four times in 1 Corinthians to mean physical (see, e.g., 6:13-20) and sociological (see 12:12-27) bodies *[Bodies in 1 Corinthians, p. 363]*. But *psychikon* means "pertaining to the *psychē*," which is usually translated as *soul*, or as *life* itself. Paul's reason for using *psychikon* is probably to connect with the Scripture that he quotes, that Adam became *a living being* (v. 45; see Gen 2:7; LXX, *psychēn zōsan*). It also echoes and recalls the earlier discussion of the *physical person* (*psychikos anthrōpos*, 1 Cor 2:14-15), which is translated as *the person without the Spirit* (NIV) or *those who are unspiritual* (NRSV).

The contrasting reality he speaks of is consistently and correctly translated as *spiritual body* (Gk. *sōma pneumatikon*) twice in verse 44. What exactly a *spiritual body* might be is difficult to imagine. Furthermore, the person is elsewhere said to be composed of "spirit" (*pneuma*), "soul" (*psychē*), and "body" (*sōma*) (1 Thess 5:23), distinguishing between these aspects of a person that in 1 Corinthians 15 are combined quite differently (though here Paul is "not . . . addressing the question of the composition of the body" [Thiselton 2000: 1276]).

The less literal translation of the (original, 1966) Jerusalem Bible conveys what Paul surely meant: *When it is sown it embodies the soul, when it is raised it embodies the spirit. If the soul has its own embodiment, so does the spirit have its own embodiment* (NJB reverts to *natural* and *spiritual* bodies). Thiselton (2000: 1258) offers this translation: *If there is a body for the human realm, there is also a body for the realm of the Spirit*. Hays (1997: 272) comments, "That is Paul's point: our mortal bodies embody the *psychē* ('soul'), the animating force of our present existence, but the resurrection body will embody the divinely given *pneuma* ('spirit')."

Paul uses a typology of Adam and Christ (*the last Adam*), a favorite of his, to depict the relationship between the human and the spiritual. He has already referred to this typology in verses 21-22. He expands it in Romans 5:12-19. Here, in a series of paired statements (1 Cor 15:45-47), he elaborates the differences between these two representatives:

first Adam (the first person of creation represents all humanity)	last Adam (Christ initiates the new creation and represents those who will be raised)
living being (Heb. *nephesh*, meaning "that which breathes," Gen 2:7; *nephesh* is also used of animals, as in Gen 2:19)	life-giving spirit (the contrast is between natural and spiritual, and also a contrast of agency—Adam receives life; Christ gives life)
first the *physical* (Gk. *psychikon*) (in contrast to Philo, who understood that the spiritual ideal comes before the physical "earthly copy")	then the *spiritual* (Gk. *pneumatikon*) (not from the human spirit, but by the activity of the Holy Spirit)
from the earth or dust (the Heb. word *adamah* means "ground"; this calls to mind "dust . . . to dust," Gen 3:19)	from heaven (i.e., the realm of God, not a location; points both to the incarnation and to the eschatological role of Christ)

Christians, Paul says, combine both lists. As human beings, Christians participate fully in the reality of the *first Adam*. And enlivened by *the life-giving spirit*, Christians also participate in the reality of the *last Adam*. So, Paul concludes, *Just as we have borne the image of the man of dust, let us also bear the image of the man of heaven* (v. 49 NET; cf. NRSV footnote, NIV footnote).

Instead of *let us*, most translations read *we shall* or *we will bear the image of the man from heaven*. Both the NRSV and the NIV have footnotes indicating that "other ancient authorities read *let us*. In fact, *let us* is the reading in many more manuscripts, including those that are most reliable. The difference between the two is one letter, a short *o* (Gk. o) for the future indicative *we will*, or a long *o* (Gk. ō) for the aorist subjunctive *let us*. As the NET footnote explains, "If the original reading is the future tense, then 'we will bear' would be a guarantee that believers would be like Jesus (and unlike Adam) in the resurrection. If the aorist subjunctive is original, then 'let us bear' would be a command to show forth the image of Jesus, i.e., to live as citizens of the kingdom that believers will one day inherit." Commentators do not agree on what Paul most likely wrote (Fee: 879–80; Hays 1997: 273; Thiselton 2000: 1288–89; Metzger: 502). One's predisposition to emphasize the grace of salvation or the obligation that arises from it affects one's reading of this. The NET footnote continues:

In light of the extremely weighty evidence for the aorist subjunctive, it is probably best to regard the aorist subjunctive as original. This connects well with v. 50, for there Paul makes a pronouncement that seems to presuppose some sort of exhortation. . . . The subjunctive makes a great deal of sense in view of the occasion of 1 Corinthians. Paul wrote to combat an over-realized eschatology in which some of the Corinthians evidently believed they were experiencing all the benefits of the resurrection body in the present, and thus that their behavior did not matter. If the subjunctive is the correct reading, it seems Paul makes two points: (1) that the resurrection is a bodily one, as distinct from an out-of-body experience, and (2) that one's behavior in the interim does make a difference (see 15:32-34, 58).

Paul now tries to summarize and clarify what he has written about resurrection bodies: *What I am saying, brothers and sisters, is this: flesh and blood cannot inherit the kingdom of God, nor does the perishable inherit the imperishable* (v. 50). *Flesh and blood* does not mean the physical body, but rather the unspiritual person (Thiselton 2000: 1275, 1291-92). He is not reversing his proclamation that flesh-and-blood believers will be resurrected, but simply restating that the nature of the resurrection body will be different from the body inhabited in the present life. It is the same point he has made in a variety of ways, beginning at verse 35. He makes it again, more succinctly, in his later letter to the Philippians: "The Lord Jesus Christ . . . will transform the body of our humiliation that it may be conformed to the body of his glory, by the power that also enables him to make all things subject to himself" (Phil 3:20-21; cf. Zerbe: 220-21).

Yet there remains a further question: If Paul's analogies explain the transformation at the resurrection of those who have died, what about the bodies of those who remain alive? Paul expects to be included among the latter, as indicated by the use of *we* in 1 Corinthians 15:51-52 (cf. 1 Thess 4:15-17). They too, he explains, *will be changed*. Those who have died, whose bodies have decayed or have otherwise been destroyed (perished), and those who are alive and still embodied, will *all* be reembodied in imperishable, immortal bodies (cf. 1 Cor 15:42). This will happen instantaneously, *in a moment, in the twinkling* [or *blinking*, Thiselton 2000: 1258] *of an eye* (v. 52). It will be announced by the blast of *the last trumpet*, a common way to summon people in the Old Testament (Exod 19:13; Lev 25:9), and an image of the eschaton in Jewish apocalyptic literature (e.g., Joel 2:1; Zeph 1:14-16; 2 Esd 6:23; Matt 24:31). That those who are alive will be transformed along with those who have died, Paul says, is a *mystery*—probably in the sense of a mystery that he has now revealed to them (1 Cor 15:51; as in 2:1), but possibly one that is beyond humanity's present ability to understand.

Only after both those who have died and those who are alive have been *changed* will victory over death be achieved. This will fulfill *the saying that is written* in Isaiah 25:8, which with some variation Paul quotes from the Septuagint: *Death has been swallowed up in victory* (v. 54). The longer context of that quotation is a vision of God's ultimate victory over death and grief and disgrace (or *shame*, NJB).

> On this mountain the LORD of hosts will make for all peoples a feast of rich food, a feast of well-aged wines, of rich food filled with marrow, of well-aged wines strained clear. And he will destroy on this mountain the shroud that is cast over all peoples, the sheet that is spread over all nations; he will swallow up death forever. Then the Lord GOD will wipe away the tears from all faces, and the disgrace of his people he will take away from all the earth, for the LORD has spoken. (Isa 25:6-8)

This passage is also echoed in the language of Revelation: "God himself . . . will wipe every tear from their eyes. Death will be no more; mourning and crying and pain will be no more, for the first things have passed away" (Rev 21:3-4). Note that Isaiah, like Paul, declares that this will apply to all people.

The quotation from Isaiah is followed by another: *Where, O death, is your victory? Where, O death, is your sting?* (1 Cor 15:55). The quotation is usually attributed to Hosea 13:14, though here it has the opposite message of either the Hebrew original or English translations of that passage (Guenther: 203–4). If Paul had this verse in mind as he wrote, it was only the language and not the context he was referencing. The language he uses seems to be drawn from a Greek translation, though it is different from the Septuagint and may have been adapted by Paul to echo the language of the Isaiah quotation and to fit with Paul's intention (Hays 1997: 276).

Having mentioned the *sting* of death, Paul feels compelled to explain that *the sting of death is sin, and the power of sin is the law* (1 Cor 15:56). God's victory over death is also a victory over sin and the law (cf. Rom 5:12-14; 7:7-13). Although sin gets little attention and *the law* is not often mentioned in 1 Corinthians (only in 9:8-9, 20-21; 14:21, 34; 15:56), 15:34 also suggests a connection between *sin* and *death*.

Paul is building toward a crescendo of celebration of God's victory over death by the resurrection, not only of Jesus, but also of Jesus' followers (i.e., *us*). For not only does God defeat death: what is more, God *gives us the victory through our Lord Jesus Christ* (v. 57, emphasis added; cf. Rom 7:25).

So Hold Fast 15:58

Finally, Paul draws the behavioral implication of the "sure and certain hope of the resurrection to eternal life, through our Lord Jesus Christ" (BCP). *Therefore, my beloved, be steadfast, immovable, always excelling in the work of the Lord, because you know that in the Lord your labor is not in vain.*

To what does *therefore* refer? Clearly, assurance of *victory through our Lord Jesus Christ* (v. 57) is a ground for confidence and fidelity. But *therefore* applies to more than the immediately preceding sentence or paragraph. The vocabulary of this conclusion reminds the reader of references to laboring *in vain* earlier in this chapter (esp. v. 2; also vv. 10, 14). Likewise, Paul has already introduced the ideas of standing and holding firm (vv. 1-2). So the encouragement of the final sentence wraps up the whole discussion of resurrection. Let those who deny the resurrection take note: it is only because Jesus was raised and because his followers will be raised—indeed, they already participate in the resurrection—that it is possible to do *the work of the Lord* with confidence and energy. *Excelling* suggests a high level of success with an implication of moral judgment, as does *give yourselves fully* (NIV). On the basis of word analysis and under the influence of David Ford (44, 112), Thiselton (2000: 1305) argues that a better translation is *abounding more and more without measure in the work of the Lord always*. The message is not to work ever harder, but to let the work of the Lord flow from the abundance of gratitude generated by the victory that God has given us through Jesus Christ.

The exhortation at the end of this discussion of resurrection hope is echoed in the exhortation in the conclusion to the letter: *Keep alert, stand firm in your faith, be courageous, be strong. Let all that you do be done in love* (16:13-14).

This is the climactic end of the letter body. Only the closing comments remain.

THE TEXT IN BIBLICAL CONTEXT

Postresurrection Appearances of Jesus

The conviction that Jesus was raised from the dead is pervasive in the New Testament. Often it shows up in variations of the formula that names God as the one who has raised Jesus (or Christ) from the dead, or that names Jesus as the one whom God has raised from the dead (Acts 3:15, 26; 10:40; 13:33; Rom 4:24, 25; 6:4; 8:11 (two times), 34; 10:9; 1 Cor 6:14; 15:3-4, 15; 2 Cor 4:14; Gal 1:1; Eph 1:20; Col 2:12; 1 Thess 1:10; 1 Pet 1:21; 1 Thess 4:14 uniquely says "Jesus . . . rose again" rather than "was raised"). In most cases, the affirmation is stated without details.

A summary statement that Jesus "presented himself alive to them by many convincing proofs, appearing to them during forty days" appears at the beginning of Acts (1:3) as an introduction to the account of Jesus' ascension. Fuller accounts of appearances of the resurrected Christ are found in five places. The common structure of those accounts is easily charted.

	Matthew	Mark	Luke	John	1 Corinthians
death	27:45-54	15:33-39	23:44-48	19:28-30	15:3
burial	27:56-61	15:42-47	23:50-55	19:38-42	15:4a
raised on third day	28:1-8	16:1-8	24:1-8	20:1-10	15:4b
appears to one	28:9-10	16:7 (?)	24:13-35	20:11-18	15:5a, 7a, 8
appears to eleven or twelve disciples/ apostles	28:16-20	16:7	24:36-51	20:19-22	15:5b, 7b

The consistency between these accounts is strong. There is diversity, but the pattern is common to all, including the sequential similarities. Paul's account is more like than unlike the gospel stories, which themselves have differences. The variations upon a common pattern, however, are worth noting:

1. A separate appearance to Cephas/Peter is reported in 1 Corinthians 15:5, of which the Gospels do not have an account, though Luke 24:34 indicates that it happened and Mark 16:7 hints at it.

2. The Gospels report appearances to groups, but none as large as five hundred (1 Cor 15:6).

3. Paul reports a separate appearance to James that is not otherwise reported (15:7).

4. Paul does not report any appearances to women, which the Gospels attest for Mary Magdalene, sometimes in company with other women (Matt 28:1, 8-10; Mark 16:9-11; Luke 24:1-11 [angels in the empty tomb, not Christ]; John 20:11-18).

5. John reports an extra appearance to the disciples to alleviate Thomas's doubts (20:24-29) that is not reported elsewhere, though

all sources have an appearance to the whole group of disciples—not including Judas, of course (Matt 28:16-20; Mark 16:7; Luke 24:36-49; John 20:19-23; 1 Cor 15:5).

6. Luke has an extended account of an appearance on the road to Emmaus that is not otherwise recorded (24:13-35).

7. Several sources mention that Jesus appeared to his disciples in Galilee, but the narrative reported in John 21:1-22 is unique in its details.

8. The gospel writers, of course, do not report an appearance to Paul: that is beyond the scope of their time frame. Luke seems to close off the resurrection appearances with the ascension, both in his gospel (24:51) and in Acts (1:1-9). But Luke also confirms Paul's claim that the risen and ascended Christ appeared to him. In fact, Acts tells this story in detail three times (9:1-8; 22:6-10; 26:12-18). Paul refers to this in Galatians (1:15-16) and in 1 Corinthians (9:1; 15:8), but without elaboration. This event is similar to other sending appearances where Jesus commissioned his disciples (Matt 28:16-20; John 20:19-23; 21:1-19). It was this experience on which Paul based his claim to be an apostle (Gk. *apostolos*, one who was sent).

Resurrection of the Dead

At several points the Old Testament hints that death may not be the final end of a person, but the only passage that speaks clearly of a resurrection of the dead is in Daniel 12:1-3:

> At that time Michael, the great prince, the protector of your people, shall arise. There shall be a time of anguish, such as has never occurred since nations first came into existence. But at that time your people shall be delivered, everyone who is found written in the book. Many of those who sleep in the dust of the earth shall awake, some to everlasting life, and some to shame and everlasting contempt. Those who are wise shall shine like the brightness of the sky, and those who lead many to righteousness, like the stars forever and ever.

Even here, the anticipation is that "many [not all] of those who sleep shall awake" to receive their reward. The expectation of individual resurrection is blended with the anticipation of the deliverance of the collective people. Other Old Testament texts that are sometimes interpreted in light of a belief in resurrection, such as the vision of the revival of dry bones in Ezekiel 37, are clearly expectations of the postexilic renewal of Israel (Lederach: 254, 262–66).

Daniel 12 is one of the last portions of the Old Testament to have been written. Its literary style and worldview are apocalyptic. Both apocalyptic writing and anticipation of the resurrection of the dead continued to develop during the late Second Temple period. In the first century CE this was still debated by the Jews. Pharisees believed in a general resurrection, but Sadducees did not (Acts 23:6-8). Jesus and his followers sided with the Pharisees (Mark 12:18-27 parr.). John's gospel even reports that Jesus claimed, "I am the resurrection and the life. Those who believe in me, even though they die, will live, and everyone who lives and believes in me will never die" (11:25-26).

Paul, who had been trained by Pharisees and was one himself (Phil 3:5; Acts 23:6; 26:5), believed in the resurrection of the dead. As a follower of Jesus who had personally encountered the risen Christ, his understanding of resurrection was profoundly shaped by what had happened to Jesus. Besides the discussion in 1 Corinthians 15, Paul elaborates his understanding of resurrection in five other passages.

In 1 Thessalonians 4:13-18 he offers a message of pastoral comfort and encouragement (v. 18) to those who are grieving the death of loved ones, assuring them that they will be reunited in the resurrection (Elias 1995: 188–89).

In Romans 6:1-14 he discusses baptism, using the imagery of death and resurrection to signify the transfer from the "dominion" of "sin" to life in God. "What is clear is that a real death to a past world occurs and Christians are transferred to a new world order" (Toews 2004: 187–89).

In Romans 8:18-25, Paul anticipates release from suffering for all of creation, including believers who have received the Holy Spirit as the firstfruits, or first installment, of salvation. Resurrection is not named in this passage, but it is implicit in the eschatological hope that outweighs the present suffering.

Likewise, in 2 Corinthians 5:1-10 Paul presents resurrection hope as the antidote to the groaning (v. 2) of the present suffering and links that to the renewal of creation (v. 17). Confidence in the resurrection, not yet fully experienced, but "guarantee[d]" by the Holy Spirit (v. 5), affects how a believer lives in the present (vv. 9-10).

In Philippians 3:20-21 Paul briefly states the hope that "a Savior, the Lord Jesus Christ," will come from heaven and "transform the body of our humiliation that it may be conformed to the body of his glory." This is a goal that Paul eagerly anticipates: though it is effected by Christ, Paul strives toward it (vv. 10-14).

The anticipation of resurrection is also mentioned in sermons and testimonies recorded in Acts (4:2; 17:32; 24:21). In Hebrews it is listed as one of the core teachings of faith (6:1-2). And resurrection is clearly one dimension of God's restored creation described in Revelation (20:1-15), as it is in other apocalyptic literature.

THE TEXT IN THE LIFE OF THE CHURCH

The Absence of Resurrection Hope among Christians

"I believe in Jesus Christ, God's only Son, our Lord. . . . On the third day he rose again. . . . I believe in . . . the resurrection of the body" (Apostles' Creed).

Though they may recite the words occasionally or often in worship, many Christians no longer believe these affirmations. For some, the possibility exceeds rational explanation or imagination, and the hope of resurrection is reduced to "a symbol for human potential or enlightened self-understanding" (Hays 1997: 278). For others, the pious dream of "going to heaven when I die" is the extent of their hope and understanding. In a misguided effort to comfort the bereaved, even pastors often resort to trite bromides about the deceased person having gone to heaven or more vaguely to their reward. This is *not* the Christian hope of the resurrection.

Many Christians find the Corinthian misunderstandings more congenial than Paul's corrective teaching. Some of the Corinthians thought that *there is no resurrection of the dead* (15:12). Their concern was only for the present life (15:19, 32c). Because they could not understand the biology of resurrection, they dismissed it (15:35). They were satisfied with the general hope of some ongoing dimension of an immortal disembodied soul (see EN above). In short, they thought the resurrection of believers was at best optional and at worst an embarrassment for Christian faith.

N. T. Wright's *Surprised by Hope* is a call for Christians to rethink heaven, the resurrection, and the mission of the church. Wright makes the case that resurrection is the transition to life *after* life after death (148–49). It is not what happens to individuals at the time of their death; rather, it is what Christians anticipate will happen to all people in the eschaton, when God will come to dwell on the earth (as opposed to the common misperception that people will be taken up into heaven: see Rev 21:1-3). This hope has implications for our attitude toward and our treatment of our bodies and the earth (189–230).

The Christian hope of bodily resurrection brings together the realities of creation and redemption and shapes an ethic that values our bodies as well as our souls. It enables us—indeed, forces us—to face the reality of death with real grief and real hope. It roots our faith in history (Jesus' resurrection) and in the future (our resurrection; Hays 1997: 278-81). Belief in the bodily resurrection results in concern about "preparing for heaven" and also concern about the present life. It implies paying attention to the realities of the spiritual realm and taking part in ethical care for the realities of the physical world. It gives purpose to participation in *the work of the Lord* (1 Cor 15:58) in the present and the assurance that *God ... gives us the victory through our Lord Jesus Christ* (v. 57).

Preaching and Worship

Many Christians and non-Christians alike are puzzled by the possibility of resurrection. Preachers often occupy themselves and their congregations with arguments about the historic and rational possibility of Jesus' resurrection and ours. This rarely inspires, comforts, or challenges people. Preachers do well to proclaim the resurrection, rather than argue it.

Most of 1 Corinthians 15 is assigned by the Revised Common Lectionary to be read over three Sundays after Epiphany in Year C, and portions are offered as alternative texts at other times. Unfortunately, verses 35-50 are not assigned to be read at all. They could profitably be used in a funeral service but should also be preached separately from that emotionally laden setting.

1 Corinthians 16:1-24

The Letter Closing

1 Corinthians 16:1-24
The Letter Closing

PREVIEW

After the resounding conclusion of chapter 15 and the end of the letter body, Paul writes one more chapter to conclude this letter. He has a few dangling questions from their letter to answer, and he needs to report on his travel plans and give final instructions.

The letter-closing form is standard. It includes formulaic benedictions and final greetings, sometimes also a reference to the writing process (see "Paul's Letter" in the introduction). Although some of the content is defined by the letter he has received, Paul never loses sight of the issue that drives this entire letter: the unity of the community of believers. He addresses that concern by reminding the Corinthians how they are part of a larger Christian movement that includes congregations in Galatia (v. 1), Jerusalem (v. 3), Macedonia (v. 5), Ephesus (v. 8), and Asia [Minor] (v. 19). He also names key people, with commendations that identify them as links between himself and the Corinthians. His travel plans (recall his warning in 4:19-21) add force to his authority.

OUTLINE

Instructions about the Collection, 16:1-4
Plans to Visit, 16:5-12
Letter Closing, 16:13-24

EXPLANATORY NOTES

Instructions about the Collection 16:1-4

Twice in these closing remarks (vv. 1, 12) Paul introduces a new topic with *Now concerning*. As we have noted above ("The Body of the Letter," overview to 1:10–15:58), this phrase probably refers to a question raised in the letter that the Corinthians had sent to Paul (7:1). We do not know exactly what they asked, but we presume that in the first case they asked for clarification of the procedures to be followed with gathering up and forwarding a monetary collection that had been discussed previously *[What the Corinthians Wrote, p. 372]*. The idea of the collection may have been introduced when Paul was in Corinth, but in that case the procedures probably would have been clarified on the spot. It seems more likely that Paul presented the matter without many specific instructions in his previous letter to them (5:9). Paul's answer assumes they have some information, and here he answers the questions they have posed in their letter.

The collection is not a local matter. Paul mentions that he has also given instructions to the congregations in Galatia, and he writes that the money is to be delivered to Jerusalem (see "The Collection for the Poor" in TBC below). Although elsewhere he writes about sending money to Jerusalem, this is the only place where he uses the word *collection* (16:1-2). Otherwise he uses euphemisms like fellowship, service, grace, blessing, or divine service (see Fee: 898). Most of his discussion is about the relationship between the givers and receivers.

Paul's instructions for the collection are brief and deal only with the logistics: *On the first day of every week, each of you is to put aside and save whatever extra you earn, so that collections need not be taken when I come* (v. 2). In contrast, 2 Corinthians has an extended exhortation to give generously that occupies two chapters of that letter (chs. 8–9). In both letters it is clear that all members of the congregations are to participate in this offering, not only those who are wealthy. They are to set money aside systematically and regularly so that it will be ready when he arrives. The specific instruction to do this *on the first day of the week* is often understood to imply that this was the day on which Christians met for worship, though nothing is said of bringing the money together on that day, only of setting it aside. The intention seems to be that each would set aside the funds in their own home.

As for the delivery of their gifts to Jerusalem, Paul writes that he is undecided whether he will personally accompany those who will deliver it. Although the collection is important to him, and from 2 Corinthians and Romans we see his concern that it should be of a generous amount, he avoids any possible impression that he will personally benefit from it (see also 2 Cor 8:20-21). The Corinthians themselves will choose and approve the carriers (v. 3). Besides ensuring the integrity of the funds, these accompaniers would in their persons represent the fellowship and service of the gift (Fee: 901).

Plans to Visit 16:5-12

Having mentioned his intention to come again to Corinth (v. 2; cf. 4:19 and 11:34), Paul naturally proceeds to clarify his own travel plans (vv. 5-9). That leads to discussion of Timothy's intention to come to Corinth (vv. 10-11) and Apollos's plan not to come at this time (v. 12).

Paul intends to come to Corinth soon, but for the present he is fully engaged in Ephesus with *effective work* that is resisted by *many adversaries* (v. 9). Who these adversaries are he does not explain, though he has hinted at the intensity of the opposition by reporting that he *fought with wild animals at Ephesus* (15:32). Nevertheless, he expects to leave Ephesus *after Pentecost* (v. 8), the concluding festival of the grain harvest, which the Jewish calendar puts in early summer. He plans to travel by way of Macedonia to Corinth, where he expects to stay for some time, perhaps even through the winter, since travel, especially by sea, would not be possible during the winter.

When the time comes for him to leave Corinth, either to accompany the offering to Jerusalem or to further missionary travels, he will accept financial help from them (*You may send me on my way*, v. 6). When he was in Corinth, he did not accept financial patronage from the believers (9:12, 15-18). His policy seems to have been not to accept support from the congregations where he was working, but to do so for the furtherance of his work elsewhere (cf. 2 Cor 11:7-9; Phil 4:10-20; see Zerbe: 250-59).

Before Paul himself comes to Corinth, however, he is sending Timothy as his envoy (v. 10; cf. Zerbe: 177-78). Although this plan, introduced as *if Timothy comes*, seems tentative, it had already been introduced as a completed act: *For this reason I sent you Timothy, who is my beloved and faithful child in the Lord, to remind you of my ways in Christ Jesus, as I teach them everywhere in every church* (4:17). When Paul was writing to reestablish his authority and was preparing the Corinthians for his own visit, it was important to state the reason for Timothy's visit (4:18-21). Here the issue is the manner in which

Timothy will be received and sent back to Paul. Timothy's visit was intended to coincide with the delivery of this letter. As Paul wrote, he expected Timothy to accompany Stephanas, Fortunatus, and Achaicus in carrying his response to the letter that the latter three had brought from Corinth (16:17).

It was standard practice in the first century to write letters of recommendation (Acts 15:22-29; Rom 16:1-2; 2 Cor 3:1-3; 8:16-24) for someone who was unknown or who was acting on behalf of another. In this situation, Timothy was already known to the Corinthians, but Paul needed to endorse him for a challenging task. As we have seen throughout this letter, there was tension between Paul and the assembly in Corinth. This letter, though intended to bring unity, might well add to the tension as Paul forthrightly addressed various issues in the congregations. Timothy, already known to be a supporter of Paul, might well face those who *despise him* (1 Cor 16:11) or *treat him with contempt* (NIV), those who do not respect Paul and may be offended by Paul's letter. That was Timothy's unenviable position.

Paul has decided to send Timothy to Corinth at this time. The Corinthians, on the other hand, had requested that he send Apollos. We understand *Now concerning* (v. 12) to refer to the letter they had sent, which had apparently included a request that Paul encourage Apollos to return to Corinth *[What the Corinthians Wrote, p. 372]*. The Corinthians perceived competition between Paul and Apollos—or more likely had created a competitive situation through their own allegiances (see EN on 1:12). Paul, on the other hand, claimed that he and Apollos were colaborers in God's field (3:5-9). If Apollos had arrived in Corinth at the same time as Paul's letter, there may well have been some awkwardness between the very factions that Paul was trying to reconcile. Or perhaps Apollos's presence could have diffused the tension. In any case, Paul does not resist Apollos's visit, which is strong evidence that he really does see Apollos, whom he here calls *our brother*, as a colleague, not a threat. He states that he had encouraged Apollos to accompany the letter carriers back to Corinth, but Apollos had refused. Perhaps sensitivity to potential interference with Paul's relationship with the Christian community in Corinth motivated Apollos to postpone his visit.

Letter Closing 16:13-24

The letter is now drawing to a close. It remains only to add some standard letter-closing greetings, including a few personal notes, and then to sign off with a final blessing.

In two verses, four injunctions charge the readers to be resolute in faithfulness. A fifth imperative commands that everything be done in love (vv. 13-14). These two verses have been called "an emotive recapitulation of the basic thesis . . . of the letter, which was stated in 1:10" (Witherington: 318). Although not explicitly a call to unity, they do echo some of the themes of the letter and, rightly practiced, would overcome the divisiveness that prompted Paul's writing.

Keep alert (sometimes translated *keep awake* or *watch*, v. 13) is an injunction often used in the New Testament where eschatological attentiveness is demanded. It is used this way in 1 Thessalonians 5:6 and in Mark 13 (esp. vv. 35, 37). Romans 13:11-14 makes a similar point, though a different Greek word translated *wake up* is used there. Throughout this letter we have noticed Paul's emphasis on eschatological awareness (e.g., 1:7-8; 2:9; 3:13-15; 15).

The second injunction is to *stand firm in the faith* (16:13 NIV)—not *your* faith (NRSV), but *the* faith that has been passed on. The exhortation to courage (lit. *act like a man*) is not found elsewhere in the New Testament, though it does occur in the Septuagint and in other Greek literature. As well as a call to courage, the injunction to manliness is a contrast to the immaturity that the Corinthians have demonstrated and that Paul has already challenged in 3:1; 13:10-11; and 14:20 (Thiselton 2000: 1336).

Courage and strength are named together in Psalm 31:24: "Be strong, and let your heart take courage." *Be strong* is not the same as the strong who are named in 1:27 and 4:10, or those who are implied in 8:7-13. Rather, it is used here with a similar meaning to that elaborated in Ephesians, "I pray that out of his glorious riches he may strengthen you with power through his Spirit in your inner being" (3:16 NIV).

The instruction to act in love (1 Cor 16:14) is a reminder of the theme that is introduced in 8:1-3 and elaborated in chapter 13: the behavior to make possible the unity that Paul was trying to restore with this letter.

After these instructions, Paul commends the household of Stephanas to the recipients (16:15-18; cf. 1 Thess 5:12-14). Early in the letter, Paul states that he had personally baptized the members of this household, along with Crispus and Gaius—the *only* people he remembers having baptized in Corinth (1 Cor 1:16). Here he says they were his first converts and exemplary members of the assembly. Now Stephanas, together with Fortunatus and Achaicus (of whom we know nothing else; it has been suggested that they were servants, either slaves or freedmen, of Stephanas [Fee: 919]), has come to visit Paul in Ephesus on behalf of the assembly in Corinth. We presume that they carried the Corinthian letter to Paul and in return took the present letter back to Corinth.

In addition to acknowledging the delegation from Corinth, Paul's comments reflect his personal respect for these men and his joy in their visit. In commending them back to the Corinthians, he once again reminds them of his relationship with the whole assembly. As in chapter 3, he gently points out his role in planting the Christian community in Corinth and his strong personal connection with the prominent members whom they had selected as their representatives in this delegation.

Further greetings are sent from *the churches of Asia*, that is, the Roman province of Asia, including Ephesus, and also from *Aquila and Prisca* (or *Priscilla*, NIV), from *the church that meets at their house* (NIV), and finally from *all the brothers and sisters* (16:19-20). Aquila and Priscilla are apparently living in Ephesus at this time. In Luke's account of Paul's first visit to Corinth, they figure prominently as Paul's colleagues in tentmaking (Acts 18:3) and in proclaiming the gospel. They accompanied Paul when he left Corinth and traveled to Ephesus (v. 18). While there, it was they who taught Apollos "the Way of God" (v. 26). In his letter to the Romans, Paul sends greetings to Priscilla and Aquila, "who risked their necks for my life" (16:3-4), and also to "the church that meets at their house" (16:5a NIV; see a similar greeting in *2 Tim 4:19*). They were prominent and respected leaders in the Christian community in several cities and were close associates of Paul.

The greetings from Aquila and Priscilla were no doubt personal, since they knew and were known by the Christians in Corinth. The other greetings are appropriate greetings between Christian assemblies in different cities. They also serve as a reminder that the larger context of the factionalism in Corinth includes witnesses in other cities. The letter opened with a similar reminder when Paul addressed his readers as those who were *called to be saints, together with all those who in every place call on the name of our Lord Jesus Christ, both their Lord and ours* (1:2). Now at the end of the letter, Paul again reminds them that their behavior is being observed by acquaintances and strangers who are *brothers and sisters* in faith.

The command *Greet one another with a holy kiss* is a further reminder of the importance of love and respect between factions. The same injunction is found elsewhere (Rom 16:16; 2 Cor 13:12; 1 Thess 5:26; 1 Pet 5:14). In the New Testament, "the kiss of love . . .

gives public evidence that holy people experience the love of God in their interaction in the body of Christ" (Klassen: 135). The practice continues formally in some liturgies, including among some Anabaptists and in other streams of Christianity. "The kiss of peace survives among those who wish to express publicly their reconciliation to each other through the power of the cross" (ibid.; cf. E. Kreider 1987; Brown: 148-49; Shuman: 698-99).

Paul signed the original copy of this letter in his own hand (1 Cor 16:21). In 2 Thessalonians he claims that he did this habitually: "This is the mark in every letter of mine; it is the way I write" (3:17; cf. Col 4:18; Gal 6:11; Philem 19). Up to this point, the writing had been done by Sosthenes, following the usual practice of dictating a letter to a professional scribe (1:1; see EN; cf. Rom 16:22).

The curse (Gk. *anathema*, 1 Cor 16:22) is not common in Paul's writing, though it is found also in Galatians 1:8-9. Here it serves as a final warning, in Paul's own handwriting, not only to those who oppose his teaching, but especially to those who fail to *love the Lord* (NIV). In every other reference to love in this letter, Paul uses the word *agapē*. This is the only place where he uses the verb *phileō*, which refers to friendship love. He is condemning those who do not have even the least affection for the Lord.

The eschatological invocation, *Come, Lord!* (1 Cor 16:22b NIV), is an Aramaic phrase (*maranatha* in manuscripts that included no spaces between words), perhaps one that came into the Christian vocabulary through liturgical use. It could be a statement, "Our Lord has come" (*maran atha*), or an invitation, "Our Lord, come!" (*marana tha*). The latter is more likely what is intended here. At the close of the letter, Paul is placing all his advice and all the issues of the Christian community in Corinth in the context of eschatological hope. The expected return of the Lord is both the standard and the motivation for the behavioral changes that he has proclaimed. The unity on which he has insisted throughout is essential for believers to stand shoulder to shoulder and look toward that ultimate hope.

The benediction of *grace* (v. 23) is standard in all of Paul's letters. It echoes the greeting in 1:3 so that God's initiative of grace toward Paul and the Corinthians encompasses all their complex relationships and all the content of the letter.

Finally, with a declaration of love for *all of you* (16:24), as a last expression of Paul's desire to maintain his relationship with the congregations and their relationships with each other and as a reminder of the most important virtue of all (13:13), the letter comes to an end.

THE TEXT IN BIBLICAL CONTEXT
The Collection for the Poor

The collection that Paul discusses here is a substantial initiative also named in Romans, Galatians, and 2 Corinthians. In each case, he refers to what other congregations are doing. It is clearly a coordinated effort to provide financial assistance to needy Christians in Jerusalem.

The letter to the Galatians does not include the instructions to which Paul here refers (1 Cor 16:1, but he writes that James, Cephas, and John, leaders of the assembly in Jerusalem, "asked only one thing, that we remember the poor, which was actually what I was eager to do" [Gal 2:10]). The context of this was Paul's report on his trip to Jerusalem in which his mandate to preach to the Gentiles was endorsed by the "acknowledged pillars" of the faith community (Gal 2:1-10). This story seems to be Paul's version of an incident reported quite differently in Acts 15:1-29. The account in Acts does not include a request for financial assistance. Instead, it reports that the leaders in Jerusalem directed Gentile believers "to abstain only from things polluted by idols and from fornication and from whatever has been strangled and from blood" (15:20; cf. v. 29). However, Acts does report that Paul brought the collected funds to Jerusalem "after some years" (24:17). Acts also reports an earlier relief mission to Jerusalem, which Paul and Barnabas delivered on behalf of the Antioch congregation (11:27-30; 12:25). This experience undoubtedly shaped Paul's subsequent understanding of financial aid, especially for the poor in Jerusalem.

In his letter to the Romans, Paul elaborates on this project:

> Now, however, I am on my way to Jerusalem in the service of the Lord's people there. For Macedonia and Achaia were pleased to make a contribution for the poor among the Lord's people in Jerusalem. They were pleased to do it, and indeed they owe it to them. For if the Gentiles have shared in the Jews' spiritual blessings, they owe it to the Jews to share with them their material blessings. (Rom 15:25-27 NIV; cf. vv. 15-16, 31)

The longest discussion and fullest explanation of the reasons for this collection are found in 2 Corinthians 8–9. Here Paul argues that the example of Christ's generous gift of grace demands a corresponding generosity from Christ's followers (8:8-9; 9:14-15). Furthermore, there ought to be a "fair balance" of resources between believers that will fluctuate depending on who has need and who has abundance (8:13-15).

This offering was important for practical reasons and as a sign both to Gentiles and to Jews that the prophecies of Isaiah 66:18 and Haggai 2:6-9 were being fulfilled, that "the Lord would shake the nations and gather the Gentiles to meet in Zion to witness his glory and rejoice in his deliverance" (Shillington 1998a: 262).

The collection that Paul was gathering represents a well-established Jewish tradition of sharing with the poor, or almsgiving. Asking for alms was a way for disabled people to support themselves (Acts 3:2-3). Tabitha, or Dorcas, was renowned for her "acts of charity" (lit., *almsgiving*, 9:36). Cornelius, though a Gentile, was honored by God for his almsgiving and prayers (10:2, 4, 31). Jesus spoke of almsgiving as one of three acts of piety, along with prayer and fasting, that should be practiced without public fanfare (Matt 6:1-18). He encouraged his followers to sell their possessions and give alms (Luke 12:33). The deuterocanonical book of Tobit is a study in the merit of giving alms. The title character is the primary model, and he advises his son, Tobias, to do likewise.

> To all those who practice righteousness give alms from your possessions, and do not let your eye begrudge the gift when you make it. Do not turn your face away from anyone who is poor, and the face of God will not be turned away from you. If you have many possessions, make your gift from them in proportion; if few, do not be afraid to give according to the little you have. So you will be laying up a good treasure for yourself against the day of necessity. For almsgiving delivers from death and keeps you from going into the Darkness. Indeed, almsgiving, for all who practice it, is an excellent offering in the presence of the Most High. (Tob 4:6-11; cf. 1:3, 16; 2:14; 12:8-9)

The principle of generosity in giving to those in need is set out in Deuteronomy 15:7-11, culminating with "Open your hand to the poor and needy neighbor in your land" (v. 11). The context for this is the instruction to remit all debts owed by "a neighbor who is a member of the community" (v. 2) every seven years. This is accompanied by the assurance that in the Promised Land will be such abundance that there will be no needy people (v. 4) and hence no need to hoard resources. Further specific instructions for sharing with the needy include leaving a portion of the harvest for the poor and foreigners (Lev 19:9-10; 23:22). The fallow year was instituted "so that the poor of your people may eat" (Exod 23:11).

This generosity toward the poor, which is encouraged throughout the whole of the Bible, is in addition to tithes that were prescribed for Jews to support the temple and the priesthood (Num

18:21-32), the various sacrifices that were prescribed, and the taxes that were levied by governments on all people. Almsgiving was an act of righteousness in response to the grace of God.

THE TEXT IN THE LIFE OF THE CHURCH
Systematic Giving and Responsible Management of Charitable Gifts

Sharing financial and other resources for the support of the poor has been a teaching and requirement in many faiths. Christianity, Judaism, and Islam have similar values and practices of "almsgiving." Hinduism and Buddhism have differences, but they also value sharing with others.

The most extreme practice of sharing resources is the "community of goods," where all assets are held by the community rather than by individuals. The first Christians practiced this, at least for a time: "All who believed were together and had all things in common; they would sell their possessions and goods and distribute the proceeds to all, as any had need" (Acts 2:44-45; cf. 4:32–5:11). The practice continues in many religious orders where members take a vow of poverty and implement it by giving away all personal possessions.

In the sixteenth century, Anabaptists were accused of practicing this, though most of them did not do so and even argued against it. The notable exception to this was and continues to be the Hutterites. Since the second half of the twentieth century, some additional small intentional Christian communities were formed that practice various degrees and forms of community of goods.

Under the influence of cultural expectations, most Christians practice private ownership of property. Yet the commitment to share resources is also strong. Spontaneous responses to need are common. Many churches also have established systems of care to meet needs of their members and others. Many church and parachurch organizations are dedicated to the distribution of wealth, assistance of those in need, economic development, and justice, which have institutionalized these values. Paul's instruction to set aside funds systematically (1 Cor 16:2) is a good beginning point for practicing planned giving, not only impulsive giving. The more detailed instructions in 2 Corinthians 8 include the principles that such giving should be voluntary, proportional to one's ability, and equitable between groups (Shillington 1998a: 188-89).

There is increasing awareness that money is not the only resource worth giving and receiving (see Tshimika and Lind) and that sharing of resources should be understood and experienced reciprocally.

Where there is a commitment to sharing resources, there is also concern that those resources are distributed efficiently, effectively, and appropriately. Some people are challenging the approach that the Western church has traditionally taken to charity (e.g., Lupton). In North America, where governments shape charitable giving through tax incentives, regulating agencies as well as public demand are forcing churches and other charitable agencies to raise their standards of transparency and accountability for the funds they manage. Faith-based institutions need to know their legal obligations and limitations and adhere to policies that conform to these.

Paul's intention that (several) authorized representatives from the congregations should handle *the collection for the Lord's people* (1 Cor 16:1 NIV; cf. 2 Cor 8:18-21) is a good beginning point for developing policies and procedures that minimize the risk of misuse or the impression of misuse of resources given to support others.

Part of a Bigger Whole

In his closing words to the small faith community in Corinth, Paul finds several opportunities to remind them that they are in relationship with congregations in other cities, just as he had done at the beginning of the letter. He mentions the regions of Galatia, Macedonia, and Asia and the cities of Jerusalem and Ephesus. From the very beginning of the letter he has been locating *the church of God that is in Corinth* in the context of *all those who in every place call on the name of our Lord Jesus Christ* (1:2; cf. 4:17; 7:17; 11:16; 14:33, 36).

Though from a twenty-first-century perspective communication in the first century was limited, scattered assemblies of Christians did get information about each other from itinerant preachers (e.g., Paul, Apollos, Timothy), those who traveled for business or on behalf of the congregations (e.g., Chloe's people; Priscilla and Aquila; Stephanas, Fortunatus, and Achaicus), and occasional letters. However, it is easy to forget about those who are absent when dealing with issues in the immediate community.

With instant access to news and social media, the bombardment of stories and images and the ease of travel makes it possible for people to know others around the world. Nevertheless, local congregations sometimes forget that they are part of a community of faith that transcends time and space.

Elaborate institutional systems make it possible for individual believers and local congregations to relate to a denomination and to multiple networks for mutual support, shared mission, common interests, and other purposes. Yet it is possible for a congregation to live as if independent of others. Some have vital connections with others in their own denomination or theological tradition, even in far corners of the globe, but have no awareness of or interest in what their neighboring congregations of other traditions are doing or thinking. And some congregations have little knowledge of or interest in what is going on in their local communities. Many have distanced themselves from other churches because of different theology, ethics, or ways of worshiping. Historical animosities originating in the split between the Eastern and Western churches in the eleventh century or between the Catholic and many varieties of Protestant churches in the sixteenth century or in subsequent fragmentation have fostered competition and mutual rejection. Despite some successful acts of reconciliation, divisions continue to multiply.

The church in the twenty-first century needs to pay attention to Paul's insistence that the Corinthians recognize their relationship with *all those who in every place call on the name of our Lord Jesus Christ* (1:2). The need for unity is not limited to one assembly. One congregation does not exhaust the metaphor of the body. Churches need to pay attention to congregations of all denominations in their own communities and to their own and other denominations in their geographical region and around the world. Churches in the Global North must especially pay attention to the majority church in the Global South. Congregations and individual Christians need to pay respectful attention to fellow believers of other languages, cultures, and traditions, whether in near proximity or in the "global village."

Awareness of the vast diversity of the church—remembering that we all affect each other and that *together* (1:2) we represent the purposes of God—provides essential perspective when dealing with local issues, tensions, and challenges.

Cooperation and Respect between Leaders

First Corinthians ends, as it begins, with an appeal to the Christians in Corinth not to be divided over allegiances to different leaders. It opens by responding to a report that some of them were loyal to Paul, some to Apollos, some to Cephas, and some to Christ (1:11-17). While this extended appeal for unity addresses many issues, the undercurrent of leadership tensions is always present.

In his closing words, Paul once again addresses this by honoring his apparent rival, Apollos, treating him as a peer (cf. 3:4-23). He recognizes the important roles played by Fortunatus, Achaicus, and especially Stephanas (cf. 1:16), who were apparently well respected in Corinth. He also names Priscilla and Aquila, who were formerly with him in Corinth and are at present with him in Ephesus (Acts 18:2-26). He commends Timothy, a younger leader, to the believers, asking them to respect and support him.

Throughout the sorry history of division and contention between followers of Jesus, rivalry between leaders or those who want leadership power has caused and exacerbated most of the conflict. From congregational conflict to denominational splits, from intrareligious persecution to excommunication, competition for power and influence drives people apart from each other. Tensions are expressed as theological (e.g., what is the right way and age to baptize people: see 1 Cor 1:17), moral (e.g., what action is appropriate when business relationships fall apart: see 6:7), or aesthetic (e.g., what music is appropriate in worship: see 14:26). Their roots, however, are often found in subtle (or not-so-subtle) quests for power through questions about who gets to make decisions, whose voice is heard, and whose honor will be raised by the outcome.

For the sake of the church's health and reputation, it is essential that leaders respect and honor each other, as Paul did Apollos, Timothy, Stephanas, Fortunatus, Achaicus, and others. That requires appropriate humility, self-awareness, a proper perspective on leadership (see 1 Cor 3:5-23), and learning the skills of conflict resolution. Collaboration, public support and affirmation, and honest working out of differences in private, perhaps with the assistance of gifted mediators (see Matt 18:15-20), are essential practices for those called to plant or water in the field where God is giving growth, who are called to lay a foundation or build upon it in God's temple.

Love the Church

Paul's final word, in his own handwriting, is a declaration of love. Despite their conflicts, theological weaknesses, and bad behavior, he loves the believers in Corinth. Throughout his scolding, his teaching, his nuanced negotiation of sensitive issues, his affirmation, and his self-defense, he loves them. The lofty (and challenging) things he wrote about love in chapter 13 he exercises toward them. Paul loves the church. He loves them as individuals, and he loves them as a group.

Because he loves them, he also wants them to love each other. That is why he charges them to *let all that you do be done in love*

(16:14). While they *keep alert, stand firm in their faith*, are *courageous*, are *strong* (v. 13), they are to do it *in love* (v. 14), growing out of their *love for the Lord* (v. 22).

Let this be the confession of the church: we have failed to live up to this charge. May our meditation on Paul's letter to our spiritual sisters and brothers in Corinth teach, inspire, and enable us to apply "the text in the life of the church" to better effect, to the glory of God.

Outline of 1 Corinthians

GREETINGS AND THANKSGIVING	1:1-9
The Letter Opening	1:1-3
The Letter Writers	1:1
The Letter Readers	1:2
Greeting	1:3
Thanksgiving	1:4-9
Gratitude to God for Gifts	1:4-7a
Eschatological and Ethical Value of Gifts	1:7b-9a
The Community Context of Gifts	1:9b
THE BODY OF THE LETTER	1:10–15:58
The Purpose of the Letter	1:10
Divisions between Believers	1:11-17
The Source of Paul's Information	1:11
Divisions in the Corinthian Assembly	1:12
Redefining the Center	1:13-17
Fundamental Convictions and Values	1:18–4:21
The Gospel of the Crucified Christ	1:18-25
Values of Shame and Honor in God's Realm	1:26-31
Spiritual Discernment	2:1–3:4
It's God's Congregation	3:5-23
Paul's Credibility	4:1-21

Issues Reported from Corinth — 5:1–15:58

Protection of Boundaries against Immorality — 5:1-13
- The Scandal — 5:1-2
- The Prescribed Resolution — 5:3-5
- The Principle behind the Prescription — 5:6-8
- The Implication for Understanding Community Boundaries — 5:9-13

Lawsuits and Judgment — 6:1-11
- Shame on the Assembly — 6:1-6
- Shame on the Litigants — 6:7-8
- Boundary Markers of God's Kingdom — 6:9-11

The Principle of Sexual Purity — 6:12-20
- Corinthian Slogans and Christian Critiques — 6:12-14
- Why It Is Wrong to Consort with Prostitutes — 6:15-17
- General Principles for Sexual Ethics — 6:18-20

Marriage and Singleness — 7:1-40
- To the Married: Enjoy Sexual Union — 7:1-7
- To the Formerly Married: Be Celibate or Marry — 7:8-9
- To the Married: Do Not Initiate Divorce — 7:10-16
- To the Engaged: Marriage Is Good, but Not the Highest Good — 7:17-38
- To the Widows: Summary — 7:39-40

Idol Food and Divisions in the Community, Part 1 — 8:1-13
- Love for the Family of Faith, Not Knowledge, Is the Basis for Ethical Discernment — 8:1-6
- Applying the Principle to the Issue of Eating Idol Food — 8:7-13

Subordinating Freedom to Love: A Personal Example — 9:1-27
- Paul's Claim to Be an Apostle — 9:1-2
- The Rights of an Apostle — 9:3-14
- Why Paul Has Forfeited His "Rights" — 9:15-27

Idol Food and Divisions in the Community, Part 2 — 10:1–11:1
- Biblical Arguments — 10:1-14
- Theological Arguments — 10:15-22
- What to Do — 10:23–11:1

Outline of 1 Corinthians

Worship Matters — 11:2–14:40

Headship and Decorum — 11:2-16
- Introduction — 11:2
- Honoring One's Head with One's Head — 11:3
  - Shame and Glory on One's Head — 11:4-7
    - Counterbalancing Arguments — 11:8-9
      - Power and Angels — 11:10
    - Counterbalancing Arguments — 11:11-12
  - Shame and Glory on One's Head — 11:13-15
- Closure — 11:16

Sensitivity to "the Body" at the Lord's Supper — 11:17-34
- Factions in the Congregations — 11:17-19
- Insensitive Behavior at the Lord's Supper — 11:20-22
- The Lord's Supper — 11:23-26
- Discerning "the Body" — 11:27-32
- Eating the Lord's Supper with Sensitivity to "the Body" — 11:33-34

Manifestations of the Holy Spirit, Part 1 — 12:1-31
- The Variety of Manifestations of the Holy Spirit — 12:1-11
- The Christian Assembly as a Body — 12:12-26
- The Variety of Manifestations of the Holy Spirit — 12:27-31

The "More Excellent Way" of Love — 13:1-13
- The Futility of Loveless Spirituality — 13:1-3
- The Character of Love — 13:4-7
- The Completeness of Love — 13:8-13

Manifestations of the Holy Spirit, Part 2 — 14:1-40
- Body Building through Exercising Manifestations of the Spirit — 14:1-25
- Orderly Worship — 14:26-33
- Side Note: Rebuking Those Who Silence Women in Worship — 14:34-36
- Concluding Instructions about Worship — 14:37-40

The "Sure and Certain Hope" of Resurrection — 15:1-58
- The Core of the Gospel is Embodied in Jesus' Crucifixion and Resurrection — 15:1-11
- Jesus' Resurrection Ensures the Resurrection of His Followers — 15:12-34

The Resurrection Body: Different from Our Current Bodies Yet No Less Real	15:35-57
So Hold Fast	15:58

THE LETTER CLOSING — **16:1-24**

Instructions about the Collection	16:1-4
Plans to Visit	16:5-12
Letter Closing	16:13-24

Essays

BODIES IN 1 CORINTHIANS First Corinthians is full of bodies; forty-six of them, to be precise, in thirty-five verses. They all have the same Greek name, *sōma*, but they mean different things.

Sometimes the body is a physical person, such as these: *The body is meant not for fornication* (6:13), or *The husband does not have authority over his own body, but the wife does* (7:4), or *I punish my body and enslave it* (9:27). Paul also writes about different kinds of bodies in his discussion of the resurrection: *heavenly bodies and earthly bodies* (15:40), *physical* and *spiritual* bodies (15:44).

Other times, the body is a corporate unit, such as the Christian community. For example, *You [plural] are the body of Christ and individually members of it* (12:27), or *Because there is one bread, we who are many are one body, for we all partake of the one bread* (10:17).

As we have seen throughout, the concern of this letter is to unify the corporate body. To do that, it is necessary to control the individual bodies. Many of the issues addressed in this letter are about matters of body control, especially sex, eating, and speaking. A sharp distinction between the physical body of a person and the corporate body of society was not imaginable in Paul's mind nor in the Corinthians' minds. "In the ancient world, the human body was not *like* a microcosm; it *was* a microcosm—a small version of the universe at large" (D. Martin 1995: 16).

According to Dale Martin's (1995) study *The Corinthian Body*, all the issues that Paul addresses in 1 Corinthians have to do with bodies, and the division in the assembly (body) that Paul is addressing had to do with two opposing views of the body. These, Martin argues, are characteristic of two socioeconomic "classes": the "strong" and the "weak." The strong, the wealthy and educated minority (the *not many* of 1:26), shared an ideological construction of the body that held that it was necessary to maintain balance in all the body's constituents. They were not much concerned about boundaries or pollution, since everything was an important aspect of bodily balance. They saw the ethical issues of eating meat sacrificed to idols, prostitution, and sexual desire not as moral absolutes but as a matter of maintaining a healthy balance. They considered hierarchical relationships within the communal body to be natural and necessary for balance (D. Martin 1995: 143, 159–62).

The weak, on the other hand, constituted the majority in Corinth and came primarily from the socially disadvantaged class. In their ideological construction, they saw the body as "a dangerously permeable entity threatened by polluting agents" (D. Martin 1995: xv). These people viewed disease and pollution not as imbalance but as an invasion from the outside by potentially demonic forces. Any deviation from what they deemed natural relationships within the communal body (e.g., in terms of sexuality, spiritual manifestations, or a woman's self-presentation while prophesying) reflected the presence of evil supernatural powers within the community.

According to Martin (1995), these two competing ideologies of the body lie behind most of the conflicts at Corinth. Martin argues that Paul's positions on the various subjects addressed in this letter represent conflicts between Paul's views of the body—both the individual body and the church as the body of Christ—and the view of "the strong." That does not mean that Paul always takes the side of "the weak"; wherever possible he supports "the strong," though with some corrective instruction. However, Paul's understanding of the body does not fit either group's assumptions. He repeatedly calls them to understand both their physical bodies and their corporate body in the context of what God has done in Christ and the eschatological hope of resurrection.

CHURCH First Corinthians is all about the church. It is addressed to the church of God that is in Corinth (1:2). In English translations, the word church occurs some twenty-two times in this letter, where it represents the Greek word *ekklēsia*. In this commentary, however, church is rarely used. It would be misleading for readers. Over a century ago, Fenton J. A. Hort (1) identified the problem: The English term church "carries with it associations derived from institutions and doctrines of later times, and thus cannot at present, without a constant mental effort, be made to convey the full and exact force which originally belonged to *ekklēsia*." There were no dedicated Christian buildings in the first century, and there were no religious institutions with constitutions, creeds, property, and leadership hierarchies. These are assumed in most people's understanding of church, and if we bring that perspective to our reading of 1 Corinthians, we will misunderstand it.

Ekklēsia is used often in Greek literature to denote a political gathering, an assembly of citizens or political officials (e.g., Acts 19:32, 39, 40). Other gatherings could also be called *ekklēsia*. The word always referred to the assembled group, not the meeting place. In Jewish literature, the Septuagint uses *ekklēsia* to refer to assemblies. Moses talks about gathering at the foot of Mount Sinai as "the day of the assembly" (Deut 4:10; 9:10; 18:16), and subsequent gatherings of the people are called assemblies (*ekklēsia*) (e.g., Deut 31:30; 1 Kings 8:14). Both the Jewish and the Greek uses of this familiar term influenced Christians to adopt it for their assemblies.

There is no concept of a universal church in 1 Corinthians, and certainly not of an invisible, idealized, heavenly mystery. There are only local assemblies of believers who gather in household groups for worship, fellowship, and mutual support. They recognize that they are connected with similar assemblies of Jesus-followers wherever they are located. The *ekklēsia* is primarily the household group, but with hints of the larger affiliations.

In the hope of reducing confusion and challenging misperceptions, this commentary avoids the use of *church* to refer to the Christians in Corinth. Instead, we have used words like *saints, body, household, brothers and sisters, congregation, community of faith, believers,* and *assembly*. *Church* is used in quotations from the text or from other commentators.

In the sections titled "The Text in the Life of the Church," which are prescribed by the commentary series, the word *church* is appropriate because the discussion is about the institutions that have developed over the intervening twenty centuries and that continue to represent the Christian movement.

FIRST CORINTHIANS IN THE REVISED COMMON LECTIONARY Along with those in traditionally liturgical churches, many pastors and worship planners in the free church traditions have begun to use a lectionary of prescribed Scripture readings for at least part of the liturgical cycle. Of the several options, the most commonly used is the Revised Common Lectionary. In the three-year cycle of this reading system, much of 1 Corinthians is read. The following passages, however, are never assigned for Sunday reading. They are offered here with suggestions for possible preaching themes.

4:6-21	Humility and suffering, not "success," are the marks of discipleship.
5:1-5	Confront immorality; do not boast about it.
5:9-13	Christian morality exceeds "worldly" expectations.
6:1-10	Mediate disputes within the church.
7:1-16	Keep mutual sexual intimacy within marriage; honor celibacy; avoid divorce.
7:24-30	Be content within your life situation.
7:36-40	Honor both marriage and celibacy.
9:1-15	Provide remuneration for ministry.
10:18-30	Have sensitivity to the consciences of others.
11:2-22, 33-34	Keep decorum and sensitivity to others in worship.

14:1-11	Recognize the Holy Spirit in worship.
14:21-40	Have multivoiced worship.
15:29-34	Belief in the resurrection affects behavior.
16:1-24	Practice financial sharing and accountability, mutual respect, and support in the global family of faith.

Pastors who use the Revised Common Lectionary should consider using these unassigned portions of the letter when they speak to the needs of their congregation.

An abundance of resources has been and continues to be developed for preaching and worship using texts that are used in the Revised Common Lectionary. Many of these are accessible through the links provided at the website The Text This Week (available at http://www.textweek.com). Worship planners and preachers who do not use the Revised Common Lectionary will find access to many good resources through the scripture index at The Text This Week.

PATRONS AND CLIENTS *Patronage* is a disreputable word in many people's minds. It suggests political leaders bestowing favors as rewards for financial and electoral support. It smacks of corruption and nepotism, and sometimes it is exposed as a scandal. Likewise, to patronize someone is to condescend and disrespect them. On the other hand, to patronize a store means to give it your business. Patrons of the arts provide the funding that many artists depend on for their livelihood.

These examples demonstrate the characteristics of relationships between patrons and clients. Typically, such a relationship occurs between people with unequal access to resources who exchange what they have for what they need. For example, a wealthy philanthropist (the patron) may make a large donation to the symphony orchestra (the client) in exchange for the prestige of a prominent seat at the concert and recognition in the concert program.

In the ancient Roman world, patron-client relations played a key role in public and private life (Elliott: 153). In brief, patrons used their power and privilege to protect and support their clients. In return, clients enhance the prestige and honor of their benefactors at every opportunity.

> Very often, the favors granted by the patron are immediately tangible items: . . . farming land for tenants, economic aid, a job or promotion, and/or protection against the encroachment of hostile forces, legal or illegal. The clients usually pay back more intangible goods. They may, for example, publicize the good name of the patron to the people in the community. . . . They may also serve as informants to the patron. . . . The relationship is often long-term and binding on both parties. (Chow: 31–32)

Patron-client relations affected the Christian community at Corinth in many ways. Paul recognizes the differences in access to power and wealth when he observes that *not many of you were wise by human standards, not many were powerful, not many were of noble birth* (1:26). Those who were wealthy enough to host assemblies in their homes were patrons to the congregation. The loyalty of people to particular leaders (1:11-17) may represent the support of clients for their patrons. We have speculated how patronage may have influenced the congregation's response to the man who *is living with his father's wife* (5:1-13). It may also have influenced perceptions on eating food offered to idols (8:1-13) and the expectations around fellowship meals (11:20-34). Paul's refusal to accept financial support, which offended some who wanted to support him, was a way to avoid getting caught in the obligations incumbent upon a client (9:15-18).

SCRIPTURE QUOTATIONS AND ECHOES IN 1 CORINTHIANS Paul's arguments in 1 Corinthians, as in other letters, especially Romans, include many references to the Hebrew Scriptures. His education and religious practice had immersed him in the Law, the Prophets, and the Writings, which were the Scriptures of the Judaism of Jesus' day. In the Christian assemblies that he established, "the Old Testament remains definitive for a mixed congregation from a predominantly Gentile background, but . . . a distinctively Christ-related lens enables scripture to speak and to be heard with a fresh voice" (Thiselton 2000: 719).

Isaiah is quoted most often, followed by the Psalms. Paul also quotes or alludes to Genesis, Deuteronomy, Exodus, Job, Jeremiah, Hosea, and the deuterocanonical book of Sirach. He introduces many of the quotations formally: "It is written . . ." Usually he quotes from a Greek translation similar to the Septuagint rather than from Hebrew versions that we know, though in some cases he quotes from other Greek versions or from Septuagintal variations. Some of his quotations are not from any version available to us (Collins: 95; Longenecker 1999: 97).

First Corinthians includes some sixteen explicit quotations from the Hebrew Scriptures, mostly in a Greek version. In addition, there are many allusions to and echoes of scriptural stories and themes, such as Israel's disobedience in the wilderness in 1 Corinthians 10:1-15. When Paul cites a text, it is often the whole textual context that is relevant, not just the words quoted (Collins: 96; cf. Hays 1997: 29). These are not proof text quotations or legalistic propositions. Rather, Paul is inviting his readers into an understanding of experience, theology, and ethics that is immersed in the Hebrew Scriptures. The cumulative impact of these uses of Scripture is a letter that is saturated with the stories, worldview, and language of Judaism.

Like other Jewish interpreters of his time, Paul applied the Scriptures to his situation (Collins: 95). In addition, like other early Jewish Christians, he understood that the "real" meaning of the Scriptures is to be found in their Christological application (Longenecker 1999: 89). In particular, he quoted texts where God was addressed as Lord and applied them to Christ (see "Calling Jesus 'Lord'" in TBC on 12:1-31).

Richard Hays (2005: xv–xvi) has identified key themes of Paul's use of Scripture in this and other letters:

First, Paul's interpretation of Scripture is always a pastoral, community-forming activity. . . . Second, Paul's readings of Scripture are *poetic* in character, . . . a rich source of image and metaphor. . . . Third, . . . Paul reads Scripture *narratively* . . . [as] the saga of God's election, judgment, and redemption of a people through time. . . . Fourth, the fulfillment of those promises has taken an entirely unexpected turn because of the world-shattering apocalyptic event of the crucifixion and resurrection of the Messiah, Jesus. . . . Paul seeks to teach his readers to read Scripture eschatologically. . . . Finally, Paul reads Scripture *trustingly*. He believes that Scripture discloses a God who loves us and can be trusted, in his righteousness, to keep his promises and to save us.

Paul's brief quotations often require knowledge of longer texts or a recognition of allusions or echoes, yet he provides no elaboration. In short, Paul expects his readers to have a substantial familiarity with the Hebrew Scriptures. Since most of if not all the Corinthian Christians were (previously: see 12:2) Gentiles, we must assume that Paul's initial teaching included a lot of instruction in that literature.

SHAME AND HONOR In the cultures represented in the Bible, honor was the greatest social value. One's reputation in the eyes of one's social group was the most important dimension of life (Moxnes: 20; deSilva: 2). Honor could be gained by achievement in craftsmanship, athletic competition, military heroism, political leadership, or generosity. More than that, however, honor helped to build up the reputation of one's people—one's family, occupation, place of origin, race, religion, and social status (deSilva: 9–11). Cultures where honor is highly valued expend a lot of energy enhancing and especially protecting the honor of oneself and one's people.

The opposite of honor is shame, dishonor, and disgrace. For a long time, Western cultures ignored the power of shame. Although significant in children's development and in non-Western cultures, the general understanding was that shame is an influence that people and cultures leave behind as they grow up and evolve. More recently, social scholars have acknowledged the power of shame to shape behavior, to censure people, and to affect psychological and spiritual health (see, e.g., publications and videos by Brené Brown). The use of social media to shame people has especially drawn attention to this. Those who experience shame have always known its power.

Aristotle defined shame as "misdeeds, past, present, or future, which seem to tend to bring dishonor" (*Rhetoric* 2.6.2). If you are shamed by athletic or military defeat, you lose valued honor. If someone of your people—your guild, your race, or your family—does something disgraceful, the whole group is shamed. In many such cultures, the greatest shame comes from sexual indiscretion by yourself, if you are a woman, or by any of the women in your family or other circle (Moxnes: 21–22, 30–33; deSilva: 13–14). Male sexual indiscretion is often not considered shameful.

Western theology has not paid much attention to the problem of shame because it has focused on the problem of guilt (Nighswander:

220-21). It assumes that people carry a burden of guilt, from which they need to be freed. However, in non-Western cultures, people have been more attuned to the problem of shame than the problem of guilt. Increasingly, this is also the case in Europe and North America.

David Augsburger (1986: 117) has listed many forms of shame that people experience: innocent shame ("when one's character is slandered without justification"); guilty shame ("when one violates an ethical norm"); social shame ("when one makes a social blunder or error"); familial shame ("disgrace from the behavior of another family member"); handicap shame ("embarrassment over some bodily defect or physical imperfection"); discrimination shame ("downgrading of persons treated as socially, racially, ethically, religiously, or vocationally inferior"); modesty shame ("related to sexual, social, or dress norms and proscribed behavior"); inadequacy shame ("feelings of inadequacy and inferiority from passivity, repeated failure, or abuse"); public shame ("open ridicule as punishment or group pathology"); and anticipated shame ("fear of exposure for any planned or desired behavior").

People long to be unashamed before God and each other, as Eve and Adam were in Eden (Gen 2:25). To respond to these needs requires a reconsideration of the language and the constructs that people use to talk about salvation (Kraus; Baker and Green: 192-209).

Shame and honor were important to the Corinthian Christians. It shaped their rivalries, separated the "weak" from the "strong," and affected their social values (deSilva: 118-43). Every issue that Paul addresses in 1 Corinthians is related to the honor and shame of his readers and of himself.

Paul used this sensitivity to shame and honor to influence his readers' self-understanding and thus to affect their behavior (deSilva: 137-39; Nighswander: 211-21). Several times he states that their actions are shameful (e.g., 6:5), and at other times he scolds them for their shamelessness (e.g., 5:2). His self-defense in 4:8-13 is a shaming speech, even if he claims that this is not his chief goal (4:14). He is critical of their shameless boasting and concerned for the reputation of the faith community (e.g., 5:1). He scolds them for showing contempt and humiliating each other (e.g., 11:22). He tries to reorient their understanding of what is shameful and what is honorable: *God chose what is foolish in the world to shame the wise; God chose what is weak in the world to shame the strong; God chose what is low and despised in the world, things that are not, to reduce to nothing things that are, so that no one might boast in the presence of God* (1:27-29).

SPIRITUALITY Spirituality is "both one of our fuzziest concepts and one of the most appealing. . . . In popular usage it now refers to a privatized, individualized, nonrelational reverence for one's 'unique humanness,' 'universal core,' or 'essential humanity'" (Augsburger 2006: 9). When we read Paul's words about spiritual things and spiritual people in this letter while influenced by all the fuzziness of contemporary ideas, we misunderstand the significance of his argument and miss the challenge that his words pose to twenty-first-century Christians.

The Bible does not use the word *spirituality*. Even *spiritual* is rare. Except for three occurrences in 1 Peter, it is found only in the Pauline letters, most often in 1 Corinthians. On the other hand, the reality of the spirit world is unquestioned. The active presence of God (or gods) and lesser spirits, both benevolent and malicious, is an axiom of the universe to the biblical writers and the people they represent. In the religiously cosmopolitan city of Corinth, everyone had access to many ways of understanding and engaging with the spiritual world.

When Paul wrote about spirituality he used various forms of the word *pneumatikos*, from *pneuma*, which means "spirit" (see above, esp. EN on 12:1-11). For Paul, it was always about the Holy Spirit. He could imagine *many gods and many lords*, yet he proclaimed, *For us there is one God, the Father, from whom are all things and for whom we exist, and one Lord, Jesus Christ, through whom are all things and through whom we exist* (1 Cor 8:5-6).

David Augsburger (2006) has identified three kinds of spirituality. The first, which he calls "monopolar spirituality," focuses on "one's own inner universal self" (11). The second, "bipolar spirituality," is about the individual person's relationship with God. This is the typical Christian view of what it means to be spiritual (12). The third kind is "tripolar spirituality," that is, "inwardly directed, upwardly compliant, and outwardly committed" (13). By this he means that "we come to know Christ through participation in the practices of discipleship that express love of others and result in practices of inner depth" (21). While Augsburger identifies models of this in many parts of the Christian tradition, he says that it is most typical of the Anabaptist understanding of following Jesus (19-22).

Similarly, Philip Sheldrake (60) writes that spirituality is about "the whole of human life in depth" and defines it as "a conscious relationship with God, in Jesus Christ, through the indwelling of the Spirit and in the context of the community of believers."

This captures Paul's discussion in 1 Corinthians, not only in chapters 12-14, but also throughout the letter. While the people to whom he was writing were satisfied with monopolar (e.g., 11:20-21) or bipolar (e.g., 14:1) spirituality, Paul called them to tripolar spirituality (e.g., 11:29; 12:31b-13:13). It would not be an overstatement to say that Paul's purpose in writing this letter is to reorient the Christian believers to understand and practice every aspect of their life with awareness that they are known by God, they are "in Christ," they are gifted by the Holy Spirit, and they together are the body of Christ (cf. "Two Kinds of People" in TLC on 2:1-3:4).

VICE AND VIRTUE LISTS In both Greek and Jewish cultures, one of the standard forms of ethical exhortation was the compilation of lists of undesirable characteristics (vices) and/or of desirable characteristics (virtues; Thompson: 88-90; cf. extensive listing in Longenecker 1990: 248-51). In Paul's letters, we also find examples of this form. The three such lists in 1 Corinthians are found in 5:10; 5:11; and 6:9-11. Other lists—more of vices than of virtues—in the Pauline literature are found in Romans 1:29-32; 13:11-14; 2 Corinthians 12:19-21; Galatians 5:16-26; Ephesians 4:17-24,

25-32; 5:3-14; Colossians 3:5-11. They are also present in the pastoral epistles (*1 Tim 1:9-10; 6:4-5; 2 Tim 3:2-3; Titus 3:3*) and in 1 Peter 4:3.

Because both the form and the contents of these lists are prevalent in nonbiblical materials, many scholars have denied that there is any significance in them. Hans Conzelmann (101), for example, writes that "the recognition of the fact that we have here a traditional form forbids an assessment in terms of the contemporary scene, as if, for example, we had to do with a realistic description of conditions in Corinth." Likewise, in dismissing Paul's inclusion of homosexual activities in such lists, Robin Scroggs (101-9) presumes that Paul exercised no particular selectivity in compiling these lists. But a closer reading shows that Paul's lists omit the virtues and vices that were commonly named by Greek philosophers and included some that were rooted in Judaism (Thompson: 108-9).

Although Paul was using a common rhetorical form, the issues in the community that he was addressing shaped the content of the lists. The context in which he used them was teaching, or catechism, and "this transforms the significance of such a 'list' into guidelines explicit for teaching on the nature of the Christian life." In contrast with Greek philosophers, Paul's interest was "not harmony with the universe, but harmony with the likeness of God in Christ (1 Cor 2:13-16)" (Thiselton 2000: 442–43).

Unique in Paul's use of vice and virtue lists is his focus on community relationships. Whereas Greco-Roman lists are intended for "life in the polis or the individual's place in the cosmos," and Hellenistic Jewish lists "depict an ethic for an ancient people with ancestral ties," Paul's lists "focus on relationships of community members with each other" (Thompson: 109).

Paul did not intend that the vices and virtues he identified for believers should be imposed on those outside the faith community. He remarks on this explicitly in 1 Corinthians 5:9-13 and implicitly in 6:1-11. Through the era of Christendom, the church attempted to enforce its understanding of right and wrong, virtues and vices, on the whole of society. Even as the era of Christendom fades, many Christians continue to long for and sometimes demand that the values that rightly apply to those who *were washed, . . . sanctified, . . . justified in the name of the Lord Jesus Christ and in the Spirit of our God* (6:11) should also be imposed on "unbelievers," "outsiders," or "the world."

WHO TOLD PAUL WHAT? With his own experience in Corinth and the ongoing correspondence and visits after he left (see "Paul and the Corinthians" in the introduction), Paul had a good understanding of what was happening there. The letter that we know as 1 Corinthians draws on all this information, but it was prompted by three new reports that shaped the agenda for Paul to write. We can reconstruct parts of each of those reports.

What Chloe's People Said A large part of 1 Corinthians is written in response to information that Paul received from Chloe's people (1:11; see corresponding EN). This report reached him at about the same time as the letter from Corinth (see below), but its content was different. As unofficial messengers without leadership responsibility, Chloe's people were free to make independent observations. It is likely that they lived in Ephesus and traveled to Corinth on business, but they knew and were known by the Christians in Corinth, so they had access to stories. It is possible that because of their status as employees or slaves and perhaps even because they represented a woman, they had access to the views and stories of their peers, so they had a different perspective on relationships than the leaders had. In addition, they seem to have had an allegiance to Paul.

Their report to Paul was given orally by several people and perhaps over time. We do not know everything they reported, only what Paul told the Corinthians that he knew in order to respond to it. We can deduce certain reports that they told Paul:

- The assembly is divided, and the factions coalesce around three leaders—Paul, Apollos, and Cephas, while others claim to be loyal only to Christ (1:11-15; 3:4-6, 21).
- Those who do not support Paul question his authority and criticize his style as well as his wisdom (2:1-16; 4:1-21).
- There is a lot of arrogance and boasting (1:29-31; 3:21; 4:7), and much diminishing, silencing, and ignoring of others.
- One of the members "has his father's wife," and others approve of the arrangement (5:1-13).
- Two (or more?) members have a disagreement that they have taken to court (6:1-11).
- Some of the men are visiting prostitutes, who may have been affiliated with the worship of pagan deities—and this despite talk of sexual abstinence (6:12-20; cf. ch. 7).
- When the assembly comes together to share the Lord's Supper, the wealthy and powerful members get all the food and the good wine, while less prominent members (probably including Chloe's people and their friends) get crumbs and have to sit on the margins (11:17-34).
- Women are being silenced (14:34-36).
- Besides these specific items, they surely reported other things about people and events that influenced Paul's reading of the letter that the assembly wrote, his second source of information.

What the Corinthians Wrote We know that the Corinthians had written to Paul (7:1) and that their letter, together with the report from Chloe's people, formed the occasion and agenda for what we know as 1 Corinthians. We also know that Paul had written an earlier letter that, perhaps with other causes, prompted their letter to him (5:9).

It is impossible for us to know what the Corinthians wrote to Paul. This commentary accepts the view of many scholars that the passages introduced by *Now concerning...* refer to items raised in their letter. It is quite possible that the letter contained matters on which Paul did not comment, and there is no reason to assume that Paul dealt with the items in the order that they appeared in their letter. His responses follow his own rhetorical structure and his agenda, while topics from Chloe's people and from the letter carriers, Stephanas, Fortunatus, and Achaicus, are interspersed.

Any reconstruction of the Corinthian side of the conversation is speculative, but assumptions about what they wrote shape our understanding of Paul's response. It makes a significant difference if one assumes that they wrote statements of their convictions and practices or that they asked questions, whether out of insolence, puzzlement, or a desire for further teaching.

Here are some suppositions about what may have been in that letter that shape this commentary.

1. Concerning marriage: "We are trying to live pure lives, abstaining from sexual intimacy. It is well for a man not to touch a woman. This has caused hardship for some, especially those who are married to nonbelievers. Should they seek a divorce rather than give in to their spouse's demands?" (7:1-24).

2. Concerning virgins: "Your example of not marrying has been an inspiration to us. We want everyone to follow your example in this. Some of our people, however, are not willing to forego marriage. What should we do with them?" (7:25-40).

3. Concerning food offered to idols: "You taught us that we do not have to follow the food laws of the Jews, but some people are trying to impose those laws on us. We do not think there is anything wrong with participating in meals in temples. As you taught us, the gods and goddesses that others worship are powerless idols: 'The LORD is our God, the LORD alone.' All of us possess knowledge about this: we know that no idol in the world really exists and that there is no God but one. Therefore, we enjoy the fellowship and the good food at temple feasts with a clear conscience, knowing that all things are lawful to followers of Jesus and that food will not bring us closer to God. As for those who object, we will not allow their views to hold us back" (8:1–11:1). (In his time in Corinth, Paul preached that salvation through Jesus does not require circumcision, observance of Jewish festivals, or adherence to Jewish food laws. Other itinerant teachers, perhaps the "Cephas party," may have taught otherwise. Alternatively, perhaps in his previous letter, Paul had instructed them not to eat food offered to idols—maybe in deference to the decision of the Jerusalem Council reported in Acts 15—thus creating some confusion and resistance among the believers.)

4. Concerning spiritual manifestations: "We are delighted to report that many of us have been gifted by the Holy Spirit to speak in tongues. This has become a large part of our worship service, and it builds up our faith. We think this demonstrates our spiritual maturity, and we want everyone in the assembly to speak in tongues" (12:1–14:40).

5. Concerning the collection: "How shall we manage the collection that you asked us to gather?" (16:1). [Perhaps Paul had introduced the

request in his previous letter or in some other message after leaving Corinth, yet without specific instructions on the process.]

6. Concerning Apollos: "Please send Apollos to visit us again, for we benefit from his teaching" (16:12; cf. 3:4–4:6).

An official delegation from the assembly delivered the letter and provided oral interpretation and supplementary comments, thus Paul's third source of information.

What the Delegation Reported The letter from Corinth was carried by three delegates: Stephanas, Fortunatus, and Achaicus (16:17). We know nothing else about Fortunatus and Achaicus, but Stephanas's household was the first to become believers in Corinth—among the few whom Paul baptized (1:16), and he was devoted to the service of the congregations (16:15). We presume that he was given this responsibility because he was trusted by both the assembly and Paul. The others may have been members of his household, traveling with him on business and carrying the letter as a matter of convenience. Or they may have been representatives of other factions chosen to ensure balanced representation.

It is impossible to know how much Paul's understanding of the questions, challenges, and views of the Corinthians was shaped by conversation with the delegates and how much was written in the letter. Even if we assume that the letter named the issues that Paul addresses, as above, it is possible that the apparent quotations came from the delegates. At least, we would assume that they clarified the nuances. Moreover, it seems likely that Paul would have asked the delegates for their perspective on issues raised by Chloe's people.

Two matters addressed in 1 Corinthians do not appear to be attributable to either the letter or Chloe's people, so it can be presumed to have come to Paul's attention through conversation with Stephanas, Fortunatus, and Achaicus. They are the matter of head coverings in worship (11:2-16) and the confusion about the hope of resurrection for believers (15:1-58).

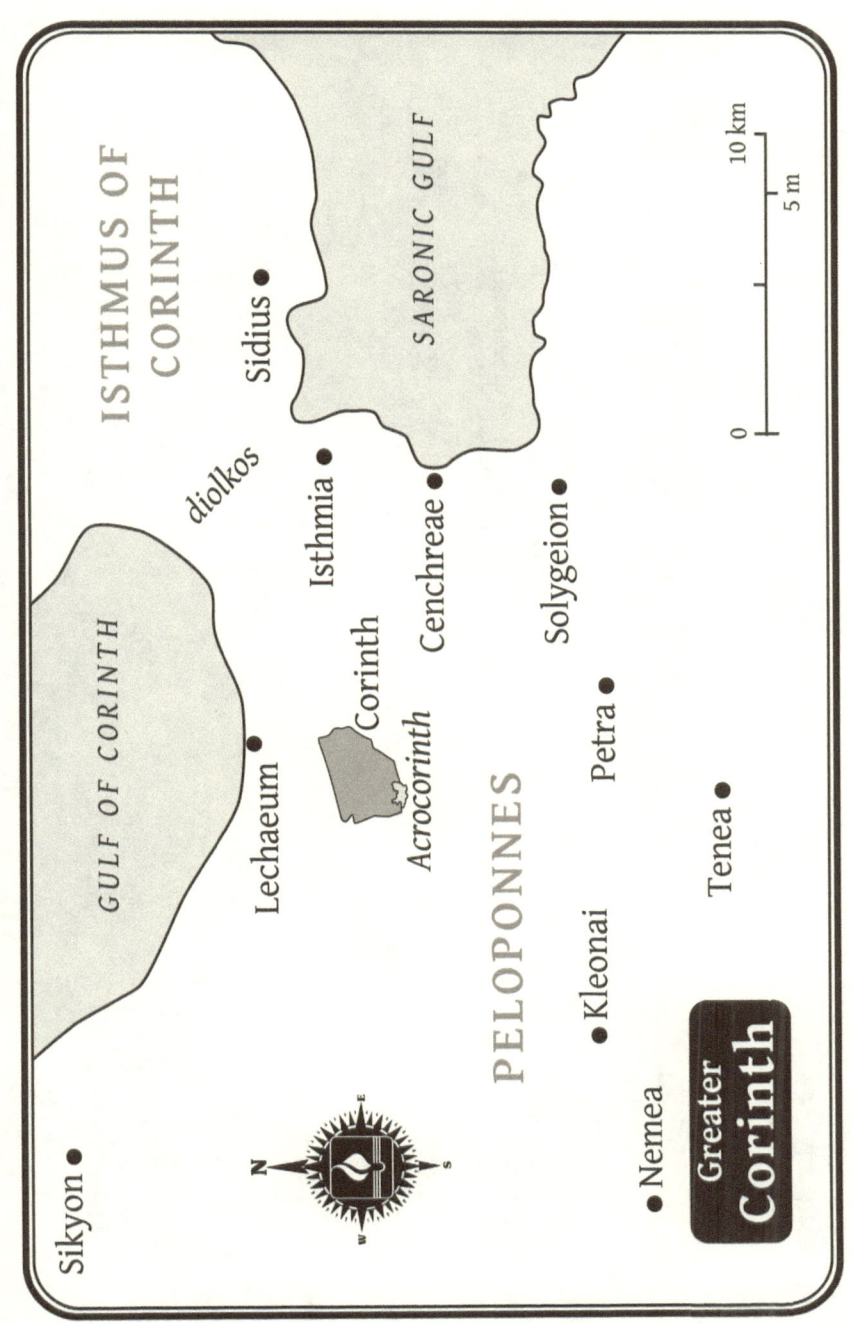

Bibliography

Ancient Writers
Aristotle
    Rhetoric. Translated and edited by John Henry Freese. Loeb Classical Library. Cambridge: Harvard University Press, 1968.
Cicero
    De finibus. Translated by C. D. Yonge. London: G. Bell & Sons, 1875. Reissued as ebook, http://www.gutenberg.org/ebooks/29247.
    "In Defense of Aulus Cluentius Habitus." Pages 208–441 in *Cicero: The Speeches*. Translated by H. Grose Hodge. Loeb Classical Library. Cambridge: Harvard University Press, 1927.
Epictetus
    Discourses. Translated by George Long. London: G. Bell & Sons, 1908. Reissued as ebook, 1994–2009. http://classics.mit.edu/Epictetus/discourses.mb.txt.
Gaius (d. ca. 180)
    Institutes of Gaius. Translated by Francis De Zulueta. Vol. 1. Oxford: Clarendon, 1991.
Josephus, Flavius
    Against Apion. Translated by William Whiston. 1737. Reissued as ebook, 2008. http://www.gutenberg.org/ebooks/2849.
Musonius Rufus, Gaius (d. ca. 101)
    Musonius Rufus: The Roman Socrates. Translated and edited by Cora E. Lutz. Yale Classical Studies 10. New Haven: Yale University Press, 1947.
Plato
    "Allegory of the Cave." In *Republic* 7. Translated by Benjamin Jowett. 1901. Reissued as ebook, 2013. http://www.gutenberg.org/ebooks/1658.
    Gorgias. Translated by Benjamin Jowett. 1892. Reissued as ebook, 2008. http://www.gutenberg.org/files/1672/1672-h/1672-h.htm.

    Phaedo. Translated by Henry Cary. Reissued as ebook, 2004. http://www.gutenberg.org/files/13726/13726-h/13726-h.htm.
Seneca
    De beneficiis. Edited by Aubrey Stewart. London: G. Bell & Sons, 1887. Reissued as ebook, 2013. http://www.gutenberg.org/ebooks/3794.

Modern Writers

Achtemeier, Paul J.
    1996   *1 Peter: A Commentary on First Peter*, ed. Eldon Jay Epp. Hermeneia—a Critical and Historical Commentary on the Bible. Minneapolis, MN: Fortress Press.

Augsburger, David W.
    1986   *Pastoral Counseling across Cultures*. Philadelphia: Westminster.
    2006   *Dissident Discipleship: A Spirituality of Self-Surrender, Love of God, and Love of Neighbor*. Grand Rapids: Brazos.

Baker, Mark D., and Joel B. Green
    2011   *Recovering the Scandal of the Cross: Atonement in the New Testament and Contemporary Contexts*. 2nd ed. Downers Grove: IVP Academic.

Barrett, C. K.
    1982   "Cephas and Corinth." Pages 28–39 in *Essays on Paul*. London: SPCK.

Bauman, Clarence
    1991   *The Spiritual Legacy of Hans Denck: Interpretation and Translation of Key Texts*. Leiden: Brill.

Bender, Harold S.
    1962   *These Are My People: The Nature of the Church and Its Discipleship according to the New Testament*. Scottdale, PA: Herald Press.

Bender, Harold S., and Owen H. Alderfer
    1989   "Sanctification." *GAMEO*. Revised, 2013. http://gameo.org/index.php?title=Sanctification&oldid=93449.

Bennett, David
    1993   *Metaphors of Ministry: Biblical Images for Leaders and Followers*. Grand Rapids: Baker.

Berger, Peter, and Anton Zijderveld
    2009   *In Praise of Doubt: How to Have Convictions without Becoming a Fanatic*. New York: Harper Collins.

Blomberg, Craig
    2005   *Contagious Holiness: Jesus' Meals with Sinners*. New Studies in Biblical Theology 19. Downers Grove, IL: InterVarsity.

Boers, Arthur Paul
    1999   *Never Call Them Jerks: Healthy Responses to Difficult Behavior*. Durham, NC: Alban Institute.

Bonhoeffer, Dietrich
    1954   *Life Together*. Translated by John W. Doberstein. New York: Harper & Row.

Bossert, Gustav, Jr., Harold S. Bender, and C. Arnold Snyder

Bibliography

    1989   "Sattler, Michael (d. 1527)." *GAMEO*. Revised by Richard Thiessen, 2014. http://gameo.org/index.php?title=Sattler,_Michael_(d._1527)&oldid=121298.

Braght, Thieleman J. van
    1938   *Martyrs Mirror*. Translated by Joseph F. Sohm. First published in Dutch, 1660. 1685. 3rd English ed., 1886. Scottdale, PA: Herald Press. http://www.homecomers.org/mirror/index.htm.

Branick, Vincent P.
    1989   *The House Church in the Writings of Paul*. Zacchaeus Studies: New Testament. Wilmington: Glazier.

Brenneman, Laura L.
    2005   "Corporate Discipline and the People of God: A Study of 1 Corinthians 5:3-5." PhD diss., Durham University. http://etheses.dur.ac.uk/1767/.

Brown, Dale W.
    2005   *Another Way of Believing: A Brethren Theology*. Elgin: Brethren Press.

Brownson, James V.
    2013   *Bible, Gender, and Sexuality: Reframing the Church's Debate on Same-Sex Relationships*. Grand Rapids: Eerdmans.

Budin, Stephanie Lynn
    2008   *The Myth of Sacred Prostitution in Antiquity*. New York: Cambridge University Press.

Castelli, Elizabeth A.
    1991   *Imitating Paul: A Discussion of Power*. Louisville: Westminster/Knox.

Charlesworth, James H.
    2003   "Lady Wisdom and Johannine Christology." Pages 92–133 in *Light in a Spotless Mirror: Reflections on Wisdom Traditions in Judaism and Early Christianity*. Edited by James H. Charlesworth and Michael A. Daise. Harrisburg: Trinity.

Chow, John K.
    1992   *Patronage and Power: A Study of Social Networks in Corinth*. JSNTSup 75. Sheffield: JSOT Press.

Church, Richard P.
    2008   *First Be Reconciled: Challenging Christians in the Courts*. Scottdale, PA: Herald Press.

Clarke, Andrew D.
    1993   *Secular and Christian Leadership in Corinth: A Socio-Historical and Exegetical Study of 1 Corinthians 1-6*. AGJU 18. Leiden: Brill.

Collins, Raymond F.
    1999   *First Corinthians*. Sacra Pagina. Collegeville: Liturgical Press.

Colón, Christine A., and Bonnie E. Field
    2009   *Singled Out: Why Celibacy Must Be Reinvented in Today's Church*. Grand Rapids: Brazos.

Conzelmann, Hans
    1975   *1 Corinthians: A Commentary on the First Epistle to the Corinthians*. Hermeneia. Philadelphia: Fortress.

Daube, David
    1971   "Pauline Contributions to a Pluralistic Culture: Re-creation and Beyond." Pages 223–45 in vol. 2 of *Jesus and Man's Hope*, edited by D. G. Miller and D. K. Hadidian. Pittsburgh Theological Seminary.

deSilva, David A.
    1999   *The Hope of Glory: Honor Discourse and New Testament Interpretation*. Collegeville: Liturgical Press.

Dunn, James D. G.
    1990   *Unity and Diversity in the New Testament: An Inquiry into the Character of Earliest Christianity*. 2nd ed. Valley Forge, PA: Trinity Press International.
    1998   *The Theology of Paul the Apostle*. Grand Rapids: Eerdmans.

Ehrman, Bart D.
    1990   "Cephas and Peter." *JBL* 109:464–74.

Elias, Jacob W.
    1995   *1 and 2 Thessalonians*. BCBC. Scottdale, PA: Herald Press.
    2006   *Remember the Future: The Pastoral Theology of Paul the Apostle*. Scottdale, PA: Herald Press.

Elliott, John H.
    1996   "Patronage and Clientage." Pages 144–56 in *The Social Sciences and New Testament Interpretation*, edited by Richard L. Rohrbaugh. Peabody: Hendrickson.

Ellis, E. Earle
    1957   *Paul's Use of the Old Testament*. Repr., 1981. Grand Rapids: Baker.

Enns, Peter
    2016   *The Sin of Certainty: Why God Desires Our Trust More Than Our "Correct" Beliefs*. New York: HarperCollins.

Faw, Chalmer Ernest
    1993   *Acts*. BCBC. Scottdale, PA: Herald Press.

Fee, Gordon D.
    2014   *The First Epistle to the Corinthians*. Rev. ed. New International Commentary on the New Testament. Grand Rapids: Eerdmans.

Fellows, Richard
    2005   "Renaming in Paul's Churches: The Case of Crispus-Sosthenes Revisited." *Tyndale Bulletin* 56.2:111–30.

Finger, Reta Halteman, and George D. McClain
    2013   *Creating a Scene in Corinth: A Simulation*. Harrisonburg, VA: Herald Press, 2013.

Ford, David F.
    1999   *Self and Salvation: Being Transformed*. Cambridge: Cambridge University Press.

Francis I
    2013   *Evangelii Gaudium*. Apostolic Exhortation on the Proclamation of the Gospel in Today's World. http://w2.vatican.va/content/francesco/en/apost_exhortations/documents/papa-francesco_esortazione-ap_20131124_evangelii-gaudium.html.

Bibliography

Friesen, Ivan
    2009   *Isaiah*. BCBC. Scottdale, PA: Herald Press.
Friesen, Patrick
    1980   *The Shunning*. Winnipeg: Turnstone Press.
Gardner, Richard B.
    1991   *Matthew*. BCBC. Scottdale, PA: Herald Press.
Geddert, Timothy J.
    2001   *Mark*. BCBC. Scottdale, PA: Herald Press.
Gehring, Roger W.
    2004   *House Church and Mission: The Importance of Household Structures in Early Christianity*. Peabody: Hendrickson.
Gooch, Peter
    1993   *Dangerous Food: 1 Corinthians 8–10 in Its Context*. Waterloo, ON: Wilfrid Laurier University Press.
Guenther, Allen R.
    1998   *Hosea, Amos*. BCBC. Scottdale, PA: Herald Press.
Hackett, Conrad, Brian J. Grimm, Vegard Skirbekk, Marcin Stonawski, and Anne Goujon
    2011   *Global Christianity: A Report on the Size and Distribution of the World's Christian Population*. Pew Forum on Religion and Public Life. Washington, DC: Pew Research Center. http://www.pewforum.org/files/2011/12/Christianity-fullreport-web.pdf.
Hart, David Bentley
    2009   *Atheist Delusions: The Christian Revolution and Its Fashionable Enemies*. New Haven: Yale University Press.
Hays, Richard B.
    1997   *First Corinthians*. Interpretation. Louisville: John Knox.
    2005   *The Conversion of the Imagination: Paul as Interpreter of Israel's Scripture*. Grand Rapids: Eerdmans.
Hege, Christian, and Harold S. Bender
    1957   "Martyrs' Synod." Revised by Richard Thiessen, 2014. *GAMEO*. http://gameo.org/index.php?title=Martyrs%27_Synod&oldid=128581.
Hershberger, Anne Krabill, ed.
    2010   *Sexuality: God's Gift*. 2nd ed. Scottdale, PA: Herald Press.
Hershberger, Anne Krabill, and Willard S. Krabill
    2010   "The Gift." In *Sexuality: God's Gift*, edited by Anne Krabill Hershberger, 17–34. 2nd ed. Scottdale, PA: Herald Press.
Hiebert, Paul G.
    1978   "Conversion, Culture and Cognitive Categories." *Gospel in Context* 1.4:24–29.
Hock, Ronald F.
    1980   *The Social Context of Paul's Ministry*. Philadelphia: Fortress.
Hort, Fenton J. A.
    1897   *The Christian Ecclesia*. London: Macmillan. Reprinted, Eugene, OR: Wipf & Stock, 2001.
Hurd, John C.
    1983   *The Origin of 1 Corinthians*. Macon, GA: Mercer University Press.

Hurtado, Larry W.
    1999   *At the Origins of Christian Worship: The Context and Character of Earliest Christian Devotion.* Grand Rapids: Eerdmans.
    2003   *Lord Jesus Christ: Devotion to Jesus in Earliest Christianity.* Grand Rapids: Eerdmans.

Instone-Brewer, David
    2006   *Divorce and Remarriage in the Church: Biblical Solutions for Pastoral Realities.* Downers Grove, IL: InterVarsity.
    2007   "What God Has Joined: What Does the Bible Really Teach about Divorce?" *Christianity Today* 51.10:26.

Jamir, Lanuwabang
    2016   *Exclusion and Judgment in Fellowship Meals: The Socio-historical Background of 1 Corinthians 11:17-34.* PhD diss., Middlesex University, 2012. Eugene, OR: Pickwick.

Janzen, Marshall
    2013   "Orderly Participation or Silenced Women? Clashing Views on Decent Worship in 1 Corinthians 14." *Direction* 42:55–70.

Klassen, William
    1993   "The Sacred Kiss in the NT: An Example of Social Boundary Lines." *NTS* 39:122–35.

Kraus, C. Norman
    1990   *Jesus Christ Our Lord: Christology from a Disciple's Perspective.* Scottdale, PA: Herald Press.

Kreider, Alan
    1987   *Journey toward Holiness: A Way of Living for God's Nation.* Scottdale, PA: Herald Press.

Kreider, Eleanor
    1987   "Let the Faithful Greet Each Other: The Kiss of Peace." *Conrad Grebel Review* 5.1:29–49.
    1997   *Communion Shapes Character.* Scottdale, PA: Herald Press, 1997.

Kruse, Colin G.
    1988   "The Offender and the Offence in 2 Corinthians 2:5 and 7:12." *Evangelical Quarterly* 88:129–39.

Kuepfer, Tim
    2007   "Matthew 18 Revisited." *Vision,* 8:33–41.

Lander, Shira
    2012   "1 Corinthians Introduction and Annotations." Pages 287–314 in *The Jewish Annotated New Testament.* Oxford: Oxford University Press.

Lebold, Ralph
    1990   "Decision-Making." *GAMEO.* Revised by Richard Thiessen, 2013. http://gameo.org/index.php?title=Decision-making&oldid=103756.

Lederach, Paul M.
    1994   *Daniel.* BCBC. Scottdale, PA: Herald Press.

Lefevre, Marlene
    2004   *Learning Styles: Reaching Everyone God Gave You.* Colorado Springs, CO: David C. Cook.

Longenecker, Richard N.
    1990   *Galatians*. Word Biblical Commentary. Dallas: Word Books.
    1999   *Biblical Exegesis in the Apostolic Period*. 2nd ed. Grand Rapids: Eerdmans.

Lupton, Robert
    2011   *Toxic Charity: How Churches and Charities Hurt Those They Help (and How to Reverse It)*. New York: HarperCollins.

MacDonald, Dennis R.
    1987   *There Is No Male and Female: The Fate of a Dominical Saying in Paul and Gnosticism*. Philadelphia: Fortress.

Malherbe, Abraham J.
    1989   *Moral Exhortation*. Library of Early Christianity 4. Philadelphia: Westminster.

Martens, Elmer
    1986   *Jeremiah*. BCBC. Scottdale, PA: Herald Press.

Martin, Dale B.
    1990   *Slavery as Salvation*. New Haven: Yale University Press.
    1995   *The Corinthian Body*. New Haven: Yale University Press.

Martin, Ernest D.
    1993   *Colossians, Philemon*. BCBC. Scottdale, PA: Herald Press.

Messer, Donald
    1989   *Contemporary Images of Christian Ministry*. Nashville: Abingdon.

Metzger, Bruce M.
    1994   *A Textual Commentary on the Greek New Testament*. 2nd ed. Stuttgart: German Bible Society.

Miller, John W.
    2004   *Proverbs*. BCBC. Scottdale, PA: Herald Press.

Minear, Paul
    1960   *Images of the Church in the New Testament*. Philadelphia: Westminster.

Mitchell, Alan C.
    1993   "Rich and Poor in the Courts of Corinth: Litigiousness and Status in 1 Corinthians 6:1-11." *NTS* 39:562–86.

Mitchell, Margaret M.
    1991   *Paul and the Rhetoric of Reconciliation: An Exegetical Investigation of the Language and Composition of 1 Corinthians*. Tübingen: Mohr Siebeck.

Moxnes, Halvor
    1996   "Honor and Shame." Pages 19–40 in *The Social Sciences and New Testament Interpretation*, edited by Richard L. Rohrbaugh. Peabody: Hendrickson.

Murphy-O'Connor, Jerome
    1977   "1 Corinthians V, 3-5." *Revue biblique* 84:239–41, 245.
    1978   "Corinthian Slogans in 1 Cor 6:12-20." *Catholic Biblical Quarterly* 40:391–96.
    1979   "Food and Spiritual Gifts in 1 Cor 8:8." *Catholic Biblical Quarterly* 41:292–98.

> 1993 "Co-authorship in the Corinthian Correspondence." *Revue biblique* 100:562–79.
> 1996 *Paul: A Critical Life.* Oxford: Clarendon.
> 2002 *St. Paul's Corinth: Texts and Archaeology.* 3rd ed. Collegeville, MN: Liturgical Press.

Murray, Stuart
> 2000 *Biblical Interpretation in the Anabaptist Tradition.* Studies in the Believers Church Tradition 3. Kitchener, ON: Pandora Press.

Myrou, Augustine
> 1999 "Sosthenes: The Former Crispus (?)." *Greek Orthodox Theological Review* 44:207–13.

Neff, Christian, Nanne van der Zijpp, and Harold S. Bender.
> 1953 "Alms." *GAMEO.* http://gameo.org/index.php?title=Alms&oldid=132622.

Nighswander, Daniel
> 1994 "Paul's Use of Shame as a Sanction in 1 Corinthians." ThD diss., Toronto: Victoria University.

Nouwen, Henri J. M.
> 1972 *The Wounded Healer: Ministry in Contemporary Society.* New York: Doubleday.

Nyce, Dorothy Yoder
> 1989 "Headcovering." *GAMEO.* Revised by Richard Thiessen, 2014. http://gameo.org/index.php?title=Headcovering&oldid=113405.

O'Brien, Peter Thomas
> 1977 *Introductory Thanksgivings in the Letters of Paul.* NovTSup 49. Leiden: Brill.

Oswalt, John
> 1999 *Called to Be Holy.* Nappanee, IN: Evangel.

Peace, Richard V.
> 1999 *Conversion in the New Testament: Paul and the Twelve.* Grand Rapids: Eerdmans.

Penney, John
> 1997 "The Testing of New Testament Prophecy." *Journal of Pentecostal Theology* 10:35–84.

Plank, Karl A.
> 1989 *Paul and the Irony of Affliction.* Atlanta: Scholars Press.

Redekop, Calvin W.
> 1984 "Anabaptism and the Ethnic Ghost." *Mennonite Quarterly Review* 58.2:133–46.

Richardson, Peter
> 1983 "Judgment in Sexual Matters in 1 Corinthians 6:1-11." *NovT* 25:37–58.

Roop, Eugene
> 1987 *Genesis.* BCBC. Scottdale, PA: Herald Press.

Rosser, B. S.
> 1998 "Temple Prostitution in 1 Corinthians 6:12-20." *NovT* 40.4:336–51.

Schellenberg, Ryan S.
  2013   *Rethinking Paul's Rhetorical Education: Comparative Rhetoric and 2 Corinthians 10-13*. Early Christianity and Its Literature 10. Atlanta: Society of Biblical Literature.
Schlabach, Gerald W.
  2014   "What Is Marriage Now? A Pauline Case for Same-Sex Marriage." *Christian Century* 131.22:22-27.
Schmithals, Walter.
  1971   *Gnosticism in Corinth: An Investigation of the Letters to the Corinthians*. Translated by John E. Steely. New York: Abingdon.
Schütz, John H.
  1975   *Paul and the Anatomy of Apostolic Authority*. Cambridge: Cambridge University Press.
Scroggs, Robin
  1983   *The New Testament and Homosexuality: Contextual Background for Contemporary Debate*. Philadelphia: Fortress.
Segal, Alan F.
  1989   *Paul the Convert: The Apostolate and Apostasy of Saul the Pharisee*. New Haven: Yale University Press.
Sheldrake, Philip
  1995   *Spirituality and History: Questions of Interpretation and Method*. Rev. ed. New York: Orbis Books.
Shetler, Sanford G., and J. Ward Shank
  1983   *Symbols of Divine Order in the Church*. Harrisonburg, VA: Sword and Trumpet.
Shillington, V. George
  1998a *2 Corinthians*. BCBC. Scottdale, PA: Herald Press.
  1998b "Atonement Texture in 1 Corinthians 5.5." *JSNT* 71:29-50.
  2011   *Jesus and Paul before Christianity: Their World and Work in Retrospect*. Eugene: Cascade Books.
Shuman, L. Herman
  1983   "Kiss, Holy." *BE* 2:698-99.
Snyder, Graydon F.
  1983   "Love Feast." *BE* 2:762-65.
  1992   *First Corinthians: A Faith Community Commentary*. Macon, GA: Mercer University Press.
Stamps, Dennis
  2002   "The Christological Premise in Pauline Theological Rhetoric: 1 Corinthians 1.4-2.5 as an Example." Pages 441-57 in *Rhetorical Criticism and the Bible*, edited by Stanley E. Porter and Dennis L. Stamps. London: Sheffield Academic.
Stendahl, Krister
  1976   *Paul among Jews and Gentiles: And Other Essays*. Philadelphia: Fortress.
Stoffer, Dale R.
  1997   *The Lord's Supper: Believers Church Perspectives*. Scottdale, PA: Herald Press.

Swartley, Willard M.
   1983   *Slavery, Sabbath, War, and Women.* Scottdale, PA: Herald Press.
   1989   "Biblical Interpretation." *GAMEO.* Revised by Sam Steiner, 2013. http://gameo.org/index.php?title=Biblical_Interpretation&oldid=104210.
   2006   *Covenant of Peace: The Missing Peace in New Testament Theology and Ethics.* Grand Rapids: Eerdmans.
   2013   *John.* BCBC. Harrisonburg, VA: Herald Press.

Theissen, Gerd
   1982   *The Social Setting of Pauline Christianity: Essays on Corinth.* Philadelphia: Fortress.

Thiselton, Anthony C.
   2000   *The First Epistle to the Corinthians: A Commentary on the Greek Text.* New International Greek Testament Commentary. Grand Rapids: Eerdmans.
   2006   *1 Corinthians: A Shorter Exegetical and Pastoral Commentary.* Grand Rapids: Eerdmans.

Thompson, James W.
   2011   *Moral Formation according to Paul: The Context and Coherence of Pauline Ethics.* Grand Rapids: Baker Academic.

Toews, John E.
   2004   *Romans.* BCBC. Scottdale, PA: Herald Press.
   2009   "The Politics of Confession." *Direction* 38.1:5–16.

Tshimika, Pakisa, and Tim Lind
   2003   *Sharing Gifts in the Global Family of Faith: One Church's Experiment.* Intercourse, PA: Good Books.

Turner, Max
   1996   *The Holy Spirit and Spiritual Gifts: Then and Now.* Carlisle: Paternoster.

VanMaaren, John
   2013   "The Adam-Christ Typology in Paul and Its Development in the Early Church Fathers." *Tyndale Bulletin* 64.2:275–97.

Volf, Miroslav
   1996   *Exclusion and Embrace: A Theological Exploration of Identity, Otherness, and Reconciliation.* Nashville: Abingdon.

Watson, D. F.
   1989   "1 Corinthians 10:23–11:1 in the Light of Greco-Roman Rhetoric: The Role of Rhetorical Questions." *JBL* 108.2:301–18.
   1994   *Rhetorical Criticism of the Bible: A Comprehensive Bibliography with Notes on History and Method.* Leiden: Brill.

Welborn, L. L.
   1987   "On the Discord in Corinth: 1 Corinthians 1–4 and Ancient Politics." *JBL* 106:85–111.

Wenger, John C., and Robert S. Kreider
   1989   "Dress." *GAMEO.* Revised by Richard Thiessen, 2014. http://gameo.org/index.php?title=Dress&oldid=118119.

White, John Lee
   1972   *The Form and Function of the Body of the Greek Letter: A Study in the*

        Letter-Body in the Non-Literary Papyri and in Paul the Apostle. 2nd ed. SBL Dissertation Series 2. Missoula, MN: Scholars Press for the Society of Biblical Literature.

Williams, Sian Murray, and Stuart Murray Williams
    2012   *The Power of All: Building a Multivoiced Church.* Harrisonburg, VA: Herald Press.

Winter, Bruce W.
    1994   *Seek the Welfare of the City: Christians as Benefactors and Citizens.* Grand Rapids: Eerdmans.
    1997   *Philo and Paul among the Sophists.* Society for New Testament Studies Monograph Series 96. Cambridge: Cambridge University Press.
    2001   *After Paul Left Corinth: The Influence of Secular Ethics and Social Change.* Grand Rapids: Eerdmans.

Witherington, Ben
    1995   *Conflict and Community in Corinth: A Socio-Rhetorical Commentary on 1 and 2 Corinthians.* Grand Rapids: Eerdmans.

Woodberry, Robert D.
    2012   "The Missionary Roots of Liberal Democracy." *American Political Science Review* 106.2:244–74.

Wright, N. T.
    2008   *Surprised by Hope: Rethinking Heaven, the Resurrection, and the Mission of the Church.* New York: HarperOne.

Yarborough, O. Larry.
    1985   *Not like the Gentiles: Marriage Rules in the Letters of Paul.* SBL Dissertation Series 80. Atlanta: Scholars Press.

Yoder, John Howard
    1972   *The Politics of Jesus: Vicit Agnus Noster.* 2nd ed. Grand Rapids: Eerdmans.
    1982   "The Hermeneutics of Peoplehood: A Protestant Perspective on Practical Moral Reasoning." *Journal of Religious Ethics* 10.1:40–67.

Yoder Neufeld, Thomas R.
    2002   *Ephesians.* BCBC. Waterloo, ON: Herald Press.

Zerbe, Gordon
    2016   *Philippians.* BCBC. Harrisonburg, VA: Herald Press.

Selected Resources

Commentaries

There are many good commentaries on 1 Corinthians, and their number continues to grow. Four of the best have been used extensively in this commentary:

Fee, Gordon D. *The First Epistle to the Corinthians*. New International Commentary on the New Testament. Grand Rapids: Eerdmans, 2014. Fee provides a valuable, comprehensive commentary for the serious scholar. On some passages, such as the discussion of manifestations of the Holy Spirit, Fee's perspective as a Pentecostal scholar sheds a fresh light. The 2014 edition, a revision of his 1987 work, is based on the newer edition of the NIV (2011) and scholarship of the intervening decades.

Hays, Richard B. *First Corinthians*. Interpretation. Louisville: John Knox, 1997. This work is also quite readable and includes some excellent "Reflections for Teachers and Preachers."

Thiselton, Anthony C. *1 Corinthians: A Shorter Exegetical and Pastoral Commentary*. Grand Rapids: Eerdmans, 2006. For those who want to benefit from Thiselton's scholarship without all the details and with more attention to contemporary application. This is accessible to readers without knowledge of Greek.

———. *The First Epistle to the Corinthians: A Commentary on the Greek Text*. New International Greek Testament Commentary. Grand Rapids: Eerdmans, 2000. This comprehensive, scholarly reference work is indispensable for serious study for those who are able to use Greek and want to know all the interpretive possibilities, including the patristic commentaries.

Other Resources

"Excavations in Ancient Corinth." American School of Classical Studies at Athens. http://www.ascsa.edu.gr/index.php/excavationcorinth. This website contains an extensive collection of images and the archaeological reports of the American School of Classical Studies at Athens.

Finger, Reta Halteman and George D. McClain. *Creating a Scene in Corinth: A Simulation.* Harrisonburg, VA: Herald Press, 2013. A simulation guide with instructions to give a study group insight into the experience of a household congregation in Corinth.

Mitchell, Margaret M. *Paul and the Rhetoric of Reconciliation: An Exegetical Investigation of the Language and Composition of 1 Corinthians.* Tübingen: Mohr Siebeck, 1991. An excellent resource for anyone wanting to understand the rhetorical strategies that Paul uses in this letter and the background of Greek rhetorical teaching.

Murphy-O'Connor, Jerome. *St. Paul's Corinth: Texts and Archaeology.* 3rd ed. Collegeville, MN: Liturgical Press, 2002. Murphy-O'Connor has published several books and articles about 1 Corinthians, including this excellent source for understanding the physical and cultural background to this letter.

Nighswander, Dan. *Community and Conflict: Realities of Church in Corinth and Our Congregation* is available as a free download from the Herald Press website. One of Nighswander's two study guides on 1 Corinthians, this one is designed for use with this commentary.

———. *Praying Over the Broken Body of Christ.* Winnipeg: Mennonite Church Canada Formation, 2004. This second is a guide for five sessions of small-group study and prayer on selected themes addressed in 1 Corinthians. It is available as a free download from the CommonWord Bookstore and Resource Centre at http://www.commonword.ca/ResourceView/16/6461.

Witherington, Ben, III. *A Week in the Life of Corinth.* Downers Grove, IL: InterVarsity, 2012. In addition to Witherington's other writings on 1 Corinthians, this unique book, in accessible and engaging form, presents the social and cultural life of first-century Corinth, narrated from the perspective of a fictional person, Nicanor. The story is supplemented by sidebars of "A Closer Look," along with pictures and diagrams of objects found at Corinth.

Index of Ancient Sources

OLD TESTAMENT
.... 193, 224, 368

Genesis
.... 367
1:2 97
1:26-28 244
2:7 332–33
2:18 245
2:18-25 244
2:19 333
2:20b-23 245
2:24 .... 162, 167, 187
2:25 369
3:19 333
4 307
6:1-4 246
8:20 307
9:24-27 186
12:1-3 .... 43, 108
17:9-14 179
18:1-8 261
19:8 187
19:30-38 139
20:12 139
24:35 186
24:54 262
25:27-34 69
26:27-31 262
27 69
28:16-20 307
29:22-23 262
30:43 186
32–33 69
35:22 .... 133, 139
37 69
39:7-10 164
43:24-34 262
49:3-4 133
49:4 139–40

Exodus
.... 367
2:20 262
3:4-10 43
10:5 187
12:14-20 137
12:15 140
13–15 218
13:21-22 219
14:19-31 219
14:22 219
15 307
15–17 220
16 219
17:1-6 219
19 140
19:3-6 44
19:13 334
20:3-4 201
20:17 221
21:10-11 187–88
21:20-21 186
21:26-27 186
23:11 353
25–30 307
32 .... 201, 203
32:3-6 220
32:4 329
32:6 .... 220, 329
34:6-7 .... 50, 294
34:12-15 201

Leviticus
1–7 307
17:4 140
17:9 140
18:6-18 131

Index of Ancient Sources

18:7-18 139
18:9 139
18:24 139
19:9-10 353
19:18 .... 294, 296
19:27 248
19:34 294
20:11-12 131
20:11-21 139
20:23 139
21:1-16 211
21:5 248
23:4-8 137
23:22 353
25:9 334

Numbers
6:1-21 249
11 219
11:4 221
11:13 221
11:24-30 97
11:31-34 221
11:34 221
12 69
14–17 220
15:37-40 250
18:21-32 353–54
19:20 140
21:4-9 220
22:30 139
25:1-9 220
27:20 139
27:22 139
27:22-23 139

Deuteronomy
.... 367
4:10 364
4:31-37 294
6:4-5 294
7:1-4 201

7:9-10 50
9:10 364
14:23 223
14:26b 223
15:2 353
15:4 353
15:7-11 353
18:1-8 211
18:16 364
24:1-4 186
25 211
26:1-11 327
26:5-10 87
31:20 201
31:30 365
32 .... 225, 307
32:17 225
32:21 279

Joshua
2 140
6 140
7 140

Judges
3:10 97
5 307
6:34 97
11:29 97
14:6 97
16:17 249

Ruth
4:13-17 140

1 Samuel
2:1-10 91
2:10 88
3 43
7 307
10:6 97
10:10 97

11:6 97
16:7 87
16:21-22 140
18:1-3 294

2 Samuel
5:2 122
13 140
14:25-26 249

1 Kings
8:14 365
11:1-6 201
18:12 97

2 Chronicles
1–7 307

Ezra
6:16-22 307
9–10 188
9:14–10:19 201
10 140–41

Nehemiah
13:23-27 201

Job
.... 80, 367
5:12-13 116
5:13a 104
28:28 80
33:4 97

Psalms
.... 307, 367
6:10 88
8:6 328
16:9-10 322
24:1 .... 227, 279
25 91
25:3 88

31:17 88	**Isaiah**	12:1-3 338
31:24 349	 367	12:3 331
35:4a 88–89	6 43	
35:26 88–89	22:12-13 328	**Hosea**
40:1-11 53	25:6 262–63	.... 121, 367
51:11 97	25:6-8 335	6:2 323
71 84	29:13-14 76	6:6 307
71:1-14 84	29:14 116	9:7 97
78:18 220	40:13 116	11:1-8 294
80:1-7 53	42:1-4 .... 108, 121	13:14 335
80:17-19 53	44:17 201	
94:11 .... 104, 116	45:14 303	**Joel**
104:30 97	48:6 312	2:1 334
110:1 328	49:1-6 .... 108, 121	
111:10 80	49:1-7 .... 53, 84	**Amos**
139:1-6 169	50:4-9 .... 108, 121	7:14-15 43
139:13-18 169	52:13–53:12 ... 108, 121	
	53:6 256	**Jonah**
Proverbs	53:12c 256	1:17 323
.... 80	55:1-9 233	
1:7 80	63:10-11 97	**Micah**
3:11-12 119	64:1-9 53	3:8 97
3:13-18 81	64:4 93–94	
6:25-33 164	66:18 353	**Habakkuk**
8 220		2:18 273
9:10 80	**Jeremiah**	
13:24 119	 367	**Zephaniah**
15:33 80	1 43	1:14-16 334
19:18 119	7:23 108	
22:15 119	9:23-24 ...... 88, 91, 116,	**Haggai**
23:13-14 119	279	2:6-9 353
	10:5 273	
Ecclesiastes	23:1-4 122	**Zechariah**
.... 80		8:20-23 303
22:10-11 140	**Ezekiel**	11:1-17 122
	2:2 97	
Song of Solomon	37 338	**Malachi**
4:1 249	44:20 248	2:13-16 187
6:5 249		3:2 102
8:6-7 294	**Daniel**	
	4:8-9 97	
	4:18 97	

Index of Ancient Sources

NEW TESTAMENT

Matthew

Reference	Page
1:5-6	140
1:18	97
1:20	97
3:10	102
3:12	102
4:18-22	43, 108
4:21	61
5:25	154
5:27-32	187
5:28	221
5:31-32	176
5:38-42	154
6:1-18	353
7:1-5	116
7:15-27	315
7:21	45, 279
8:11	263
8:17	322
9:9-13	87
10:1	43
10:10	211
10:24-25	186
10:38	99
11:8	151
11:25	87
12:32	92
12:40	230
13:24-30	186
13:33	137, 178
13:40-42	102
13:55	324
14:13-21	262
15:32-39	262
16:6	178
16:11-12	178
17:20	287
18:4	107
18:8	154–55
18:15-17	141, 154
18:15-20	357
18:15-35	70
18:23-35	186
19:3-12	176, 186
19:4-6	187
19:5	167
19:5-6	162
19:6	167
19:8	188
19:9-12	187
19:13-15	87
19:23-26	87
19:28	156
20:25-28	107
21:33-44	186
21:33-46	120
22:1-10	87
22:2-10	186
22:37	169
22:39	169, 296
24:31	334
24:45-51	186
25:2-3	78
25:8	78
25:14-30	186
25:31-46	267
25:40	90
25:45	90
26:17-29	262
26:26-28	263–64
27:6	166
27:9	166
27:45-54	337
27:56-61	337
28:1-8	337
28:1-10	323
28:9-10	337
28:16-20	337–38
28:19	272
28:19-20	215

Mark

Reference	Page
1:10	97
1:12	97
1:19	61, 324
2:15-17	87
6:7	43
6:32-44	262
8:1-10	262
8:15	137, 178
8:34	257
9:35	107
10:2-12	176, 186
10:5	188
10:6-8	167, 186
10:7-8	162
10:13-16	87
10:23-27	87
10:42-44	107
11:3	279
11:22-24	287
12:1-12	120
12:18-27	339
12:29-31	295
12:30	310
13	349
13:10	272
13:24-37	53
14:12-25	262
14:14	279
14:22-24	263–64
14:43–15:37	121
15:33-39	337
15:42-47	337
16:1-8	337
16:7	337–38
16:9-11	337
16:17	308

Luke

Reference	Page
	38
1:1-4	24
1:45-55	91

1:46-55 87	20:9-16 186	15:6 102
2:41-52 307	20:9-19 120	15:26 97
4:16-27 307	21:1 307	16:12-13 97
5:11 287	21:38 307	16:23-24 308
5:27-32 262	22:1 137	17 71
5:29-32 87	22:7-23 262	19:28-30 337
6:13 38	22:17-20 263–64	19:38-42 337
6:27-36 294	22:25-27 107	20:1-10 337
6:46 279	22:28-30 156	20:2-9 69
7:25 151	22:37 322	20:11-18 .... 323, 337
7:36-50 262	23:44-48 337	20:22 97
9:1 247	23:50-55 337	20:28 279
9:1-2 43	24:1-8 337	20:19-22 337
9:10-17 262	24:1-11 337	20:19-23 338
9:23 99	24:13-35 337–38	20:24-29 337
10:7 211	24:30-31 262	21:1-19 338
10:19 247	24:34 279	21:1-22 338
10:21 87	24:35 262	21:7 69
10:25-37 295	24:36-49 338	21:9-13 262
10:30-37 87	24:36-51 337	21:20-22 69
10:38-42 262	24:41-43 262	
11:37-54 262		**Acts**
12:1 178	**John**	....38, 67, 166, 303, 308
12:13-14 154	1:1-18 81	1:1-9 338
12:15-21 154	1:29-42 53	1:8 97
12:33 353	1:42 67	2:1-4 97
13:20-21 137	2:19-22 308	2:1-10 108
13:21 178	3:16 294–95	2:1-13 308
13:25 279	4:23 308	2:1-21 283
13:29 263	6:1-13 263	2:14-26 308
14:1-24 262	6:1-15 262	2:36 .... 273, 279
14:16-24 87	6:22-59 263	2:38 308
15:11-32 294	10:1-16 122	2:42 262
16:18 .... 176, 187	11:25-26 339	2:44-45 354
17:7-10 186	12:20-36 84	2:44-47 108
18:8 40	12:24 330	2:46 .... 262, 307
18:9-14 87	13:1-17 ... 108, 263, 266	3:2-3 353
18:15-17 87	13:1-30 262	3:15 336
18:17 40	13:23-24 69	3:26 336
18:24-27 87	13:34-35 .... 70, 295	4:2 339
18:28 287	14:12-14 97	4:32–5:11 .... 287, 354
18:30 92	14:17 97	5:17-42 121

Index of Ancient Sources

6:2-4 82	15:36-41 69	22:6-10 338
6:9 .... 24, 186	16:37 24	22:6-16 25
7:53 247	17:1 25	22:19-20 121
7:58 24	17:10 25	22:20 25
7:58–8:1 186	17:11 312	22:27-28 24
7:58–8:3 121	17:17 25	23:6 339
8:1 24–25	17:22-31 75	23:6-8 339
8:3 25	17:32 339	23:7 61
8:15-18 309	18:1 26	23:27 24
8:16 308	18:1-18 25	24:17 352
8:34 108	18:2 29	24:21 339
9 44	18:2-26 357	25:4 210
9:1-2 .... 25, 121	18:3 350	26 44
9:1-6 324	18:4 25	26:5 339
9:1-8 338	18:7 .... 26, 29	26:9-12 25
9:1-20 25	18:8 .... 28, 68	26:12-18 .... 25, 338
9:10-19 25	18:11 26	26:20-23 75
9:36 353	18:17 28	27:35 262
10:1-48 226	18:18 .... 29, 249, 350	
10:2 353	18:18-23 26	**Romans**
10:4 353	18:19 25	.... 38, 41
10:10-16 262	18:24-26 66	1:1 .... 107, 186
10:31 353	18:26 .... 29, 350	1:7 42
10:40 336	19:1 .... 26, 66	1:8 308
10:44-47 309	19:1-7 309	1:8-15 30
10:48 308	19:8 25	1:23 202
11:1-2 262	19:8-10 26	1:26-27 190
11:25-26 25	19:32 364	1:28-31 202
11:27-30 352	19:39-40 364	1:29-32 .... 150, 370
12:1-5 121	20:1 27	2:4 289
12:25 352	20:2-3 27	2:7 166
13:1-5 25	20:3–21:15 27	4:24-25 336
13:14 25	20:7 262	4:25 256
13:16-41 75	20:11 262	5:1-5 293
13:33 336	20:21 75	5:3-5 125
14:1 25	20:28 122	5:12-14 335
14:4 61	21:25 195	5:12-19 332
15 .... 69, 195, 373	21:39 24	5:12-21 230
15:1-29 352	22 44	6:1-14 339
15:20 .... 195, 226	22:3 24	6:3 .... 148, 257
15:22-29 348	22:4 25	6:3-4 .... 69, 308
15:29 ...... 193, 195, 221	22:4-5 25	6:4 .... 267, 336

6:16 148	16:16 350	8:18-21 355
7:1 148	16:21 29	8:20-21 347
7:7 221	16:22 .... 29, 39, 351	10:8 298
7:7-13 335	16:23 .... 27–29, 68	10:10 .... 31, 79, 121,
7:25 .... 186, 335	16:25-26 92	147, 285
8:11 336		10–13 .... 27, 208
8:18-25 339	**1 Corinthians**	11:7-9 .... 210, 347
8:19 51	Not indexed; see	11:19 223
8:24 294	contents	11:23-30 .... 118, 121
8:32 256		11:28 182
8:34 336	**2 Corinthians**	12:1 51
8:35-36 .... 118, 121	.... 38, 41, 208	12:7 51
8:38 327	1–9 27	12:10 .... 118, 121
9:22 289	1:1 .... 39, 41	12:19 298
10:9 .... 278, 336	1:2 42	12:19-21 370
10:9-10 273	1:3-7 30	13:1-2 27
10:13 278	1:8-11 328	13:2 26
11:2 148	1:12 115	13:10 298
11:17-24 272	1:19 39	13:11 61
11:22 289	1:23–2:1 26	13:12 350
11:25 223	2:1-11 26	13:13 266
12 280	2:4 26	
12:1 308	2:5-11 141	**Galatians**
12:4-5 .... 61, 108	2:12 27	.... 38, 161, 208
12:6-8 273–75	2:13 27	1:1 .... 38, 336
12:16 223	3:1b-2 208	1:3 42
13:11-14 .... 349, 370	3:1-3 348	1:4 92
14:1-3 200	4:8-12 .... 118, 121	1:8-9 351
14:3 147	4:14 336	1:10 .... 107, 229
14:10 147	5:1-10 339	1:11-12 51
14:17 198	5:17 339	1:13 25
14:19 70	5:18-19 70	1:13-17 44
14:20 198	6:4 107	1:15-16 .... 25, 338
15:15-16 352	6:4-10 .... 118, 121	1:16 .... 25, 51
15:19 27	6:6 289	1:17b-19 25
15:22-29 347	6:14–7:1 177–78	1:18 .... 67, 323
15:25-27 352	7:5 27	1:19 324
15:31 .... 27, 352	7:6-16 26	1:23 25
16 305	7:8 26	2:2 51
16:1-2 348	8 354	2:9 .... 67, 323
16:1-3 29	8–9 .... 346, 352	2:10 352
16:4 272	8:16-24 348	2:11 323

Index of Ancient Sources

2:11-13 198
2:11-14 .... 67, 69, 262
2:11-16 226
2:12 272
2:14 323
3:19 247
3:27 308
3:27-28 179
3:28 .... 28, 185, 245, 277, 305
4:9 .... 196, 293
4:14 147
4:19 27
5:5-6 293
5:6 179
5:9 137
5:16-26 370
5:22 289
5:22-23 97
6:1 .... 61, 141
6:11 351
6:11-17 39
6:15 179

Ephesians

.... 38
1:2 42
1:3-23 30
1:9 92
1:17 51
1:20 336
1:21 .... 92, 327
1:22-23 .... 108, 280
3:1 272
3:1-10 287
3:3 51
3:3-5 92
3:7 107
3:9 92
3:10 327
3:16 349
4:2-5 293

4:3-6 70
4:11 .... 210, 274–75
4:11-13 273
4:17-24 370
4:25-32 371
4:32–5:2 229
5:1 119
5:3-14 371
5:4 78
5:21–6:9 27
5:29-30 .... 108, 280
5:31-33 167
5:32 92
6:5-9 185
6:12 .... 93, 327
6:19 92

Philippians

.... 40
1:1 107
1:2 42
1:3-11 30
2:1-10 229
2:2 70
2:5-8 .... 95, 98
2:5-11 70
2:6-11 308
2:9-11 279
2:11 273
2:22 123
2:25 210
3:5 339
3:5-6 24
3:5-7 12
3:6 .... 25, 115
3:10-14 339
3:17 229
3:20-21 .... 334, 339
4:1-3 60
4:2-3 305
4:8 204
4:10-20 .... 210, 347

Colossians

.... 38
1:1 39
1:2 42
1:3-14 30
1:4-5 293
1:7 107
1:15-20 308
1:16 327
1:18 .... 61, 108, 280
1:23 107
1:24 .... 108, 280
1:25 107
1:26-27 .... 92, 287
2:1 41
2:2 92
2:10-15 327
2:12 336
2:16-17 308
2:18 196
3:5-11 371
3:11 185
3:18–4:1 27
3:22–4:1 185
4:3 92
4:7 107
4:12 107
4:13 41
4:14 211
4:15 41
4:16 .... 29, 41
4:16-18a 39
4:18 351

1 Thessalonians

1:1 .... 39, 42
1:2-10 30
1:3 293
1:5 148
1:6 .... 119, 229
1:10 336
2:1-2 148

2:4 229	1:20 141	5 230
2:5 148	2:9 249	7 230
2:9 210	2:9-10 249	6:1-2 339–40
2:10-11 123	2:11-15 315	6:4-6 258
2:11 .... 27, 148	3:2 249	6:10-12 293
2:14 .... 119, 229	4:6 107	10:1-14 308
3:3-4 148	4:13 308	10:22-24 293
3:10 61	5:18 211	13:2 262
4:2 148	6:1-6 185	13:21 61
4:13-18 339	6:3-5 70	
4:14 336	6:4-5 371	**James**
4:15-17 ... 176, 327, 334		1:1 107
5:2 148	**2 Timothy**	5:10-11 121
5:6 349	.... 38, 42	5:19-20 141
5:8 293	2:3 210	
5:12-14 349	2:23 78	**1 Peter**
5:20 147	2:24 107	1:3-82 294
5:23 332	3:2-3 371	1:21 336
5:26 350	4:11 211	2:2 370
5:26-27 29	4:19 350	2:4-9 308
		2:5 370
2 Thessalonians	**Titus**	2:9-10 108
1:1 39	 38	2:13 263
1:2 42	1:1 107	2:13-3:7 27
1:3-12 30	1:9-11 308	2:18-20 185
1:6-8 51	2:2 293	2:21-24 231
1:8 102	2:9-10 185	3:2-4 249–50
2:3-8 51	3:3 371	3:3 249
2:6 148	3:9 78–79	3:18-21 230
2:13 327		3:20 289
3:6 60	**Philemon**	4:3 371
3:7 .... 148, 229, 232	 40	4:13 51
3:7-12 210	2 210	5:1-4 122
3:9 .... 229, 232	3 42	5:10 61
3:14-15 141	4-7 30	5:14 350
3:17 .... 39, 351	10 123	
	16 185	**2 Peter**
1 Timothy	19 .... 39, 351	 196
.... 38, 42	24 211	1:1 107
1:9-10 .... 186, 371		3:9 289
1:10 152	**Hebrews**	3:15 289
1:16 289	3 230	

Index of Ancient Sources

1 John
3-4 296
3:10-18 70
3:18 315
4:7-11 295
4:9-10 296
4:19 296
5:16 141

Jude
1 107
4 263
12 .... 263, 266

Revelation
1:1 107
2:14 221
2:20 221
2:26 247
2:26-28 155
3:21 155
5:9 266
11:6 247
14:18 247
15:3 107
16:9 247
19:6-8 308
19:9 263
19:10 107
20:1-15 340
20:4 155
21:1-3 340
21:3-4 335
21:24 272
21:26 166
22:9 107

OT APOCRYPHA

Tobit
1:3 353
1:16 353
2:14 353
4:6-11 353
12:8-9 353

Wisdom of Solomon
.... 80
3:1 155
3:8 155
6:22 81
7:26-27 81
8:2 81
10:15-11:4 219
11:4 81
14:23-27 202

Sirach (Ecclesiasticus)
.... 80, 367
1:14 80
1:16 80
1:18 80
1:20 80
1:27 80
4:18 81
14:21 81
19:20 80
21:11 80

Baruch 80
3 81

1 Maccabees
1:15 179

2 Maccabees
12:42-44 328

2 Esdras
2:41 44
6:23 334
14:5-6 287

OT PSEUDEPIGRAPHA

Apocalypse of Elijah
.... 94

1 Enoch
1.3 155
1.9 155

Testament of Reuben
.... 133

DEAD SEA SCROLLS

Community Rule
1QS 5.25-6.1 . 142, 155

Essenes 173

RABBINIC TEXTS

Mishnah Pesach
1.1 137

Laws/tradition
.... 161, 219

OTHER JEWISH TEXTS

Jewish literature
.... 244

Josephus
Against Apion
2.24 260

Therapeutae 173

NT APOCRYPHA

Acts of Paul and Thecla
.... 189

Gospel of Thomas
17 93–94

EARLY CHURCH

Irenaeus
Against Heresies
1.6.3 134

Ambrose 190

Apostles' Creed .. 340

Augustine 190

Jerome 190

Origen 94

Tertullian 190

GRECO-ROMAN

archaeology 244

Aristotle
Rhetoric
1.3.1–6 31
2.6.2 368
2.6.4 133
2.6.11 117

Cicero 31
De finibus 3.22.75 ... 104
In Defense of Cluentius
5.12–6.16 133

Cynic and Stoic philosophers 118, 122, 128, 160–61, 173, 209, 243

Epictetus
Discourses 1.16 243

Eratosthenes 254

Gaius
Institutes 1.63 133

Greek literature
.... 244

Greek philosophers
.... 371

Hagias 254

Isocrates
To Demonicus
9 119–20

Musonius Rufus
.... 149, 243
Lecture 12 133

mystery cults 287

Plato 254
Gorgias 149
Phaedo 326

Plutarch 254

Quintilian 31

Seneca
De beneficiis
7.3–7.4 104

The Author

Dan Nighswander has been engaged in the life of the church throughout his whole life. He has been a pastor in three congregations—Cassel Mennonite and Waterloo North Mennonite in Ontario, and Jubilee Mennonite in Winnipeg, Manitoba. He was the denominational minister for the Conference of Mennonites in Canada for two years, and was for six years the general secretary for Mennonite Church Canada. He and his wife were mission workers for three years in South Africa and served a short-term assignment at Union Biblical Seminary in India. Nighswander has taught part time at Conrad Grebel University College. He has also worked in camping ministry and as a district youth minister.

Nighswander has academic degrees from McMaster University (Hamilton, Ont.), Anabaptist Mennonite Biblical Seminary (Elkhart, Ind.), Wilfrid Laurier University (Waterloo, Ont.), and a ThD in New Testament from Toronto School of Theology (Toronto, Ont.). His doctoral dissertation was a study of Paul's use of shame as a sanction in 1 Corinthians.

While rooted in the Mennonite church, Nighswander has also had involvements in Mennonite Brethren, Brethren in Christ, and conservative Mennonite churches, and in a range of other Christian denominations. The blending of academic study and deep involvement in the life of the church, a strong commitment to the global church, and appreciative engagement with many Christian denominations shapes his perspective on the issues that Paul addressed to the Christian assemblies in Corinth.

After spending much of his life in southern Ontario, Nighswander currently lives in Winnipeg, Manitoba, with his wife, Yvonne Snider-Nighswander. They have two daughters, two sons-in-law, and four grandchildren. Nighswander is recently retired and continues to be actively involved in Home Street Mennonite Church and several other ministries.

"Dan Nighswander's commentary on Paul's letter of correction and counsel to the Christian communities of first-century Corinth gives readers a front-row seat to the contested issues of that time—power, sex, and money. More than that, Nighswander helps twenty-first-century Jesus communities construct analogies to the similarly contested issues of today." —*Jon Isaak, director, Centre for Mennonite Brethren Studies*

"The issues that divide the church today seem pronounced and, to some, overwhelming. Dan Nighswander's commentary is a never-to-be-ignored resource as he unveils the wisdom of Paul, who gracefully handled divisive issues of his time. Our Christian educators and all church leaders will find the commentary relevant, practical, and useful." —*Danisa Ndlovu, global director, FaithWalk Ministries International, and former president, Mennonite World Conference*

"A thoughtful commentary by a scholar and church leader who has spent many years poring over the puzzles of 1 Corinthians. This commentary, and its companion online study guide, will help those interested in navigating the choppy waters of this ancient letter with contemporary resonance to a Christian community in conflict." —*Laura L. Brenneman, New Testament editor, Studies of Peace and Scripture series, Institute of Mennonite Studies*

"How does one navigate Paul's pastoral letter to the contentious congregation in ancient Corinth? Dan Nighswander explores 1 Corinthians in a way that will richly reward motivated ordinary readers. Scholars will also benefit from his careful exegesis and informed theological reflection." —*Jacob Elias, professor emeritus of New Testament, Anabaptist Mennonite Biblical Seminary*

"Dan Nighswander provides the mature voice of a churchman well versed in finding paths to unity, holiness, and healthy discipleship in the church amid cultural pressures to conform to worldly values. His wisdom is evident as he relates to today the highly relevant issues of 1 Corinthians." —*David Wiebe, executive director, International Community of Mennonite Brethren*

"Having also labored over 1 Corinthians, I read Dan Nighswander's commentary with a critical eye. It is both detailed and accessible to interested readers. The author analyzes Paul's theology and rhetorical skill in persuading the divided believers to work towards unity. He also highlights their social and cultural realities in a busy city in the ancient Roman Empire." —*Reta Halteman Finger, coauthor, Creating a Scene in Corinth*

www.ingramcontent.com/pod-product-compliance
Lightning Source LLC
Chambersburg PA
CBHW030516230426
43665CB00010B/641